History of Vardan
and the Armenian War

Harvard Armenian Texts and Studies, 5

EŁISHĒ

History of Vardan and the Armenian War

Translation and Commentary by

Robert W. Thomson

Harvard University Press
Cambridge, Massachusetts
London, England   1982

Library of Congress Cataloging in Publication Data

Eliseus, Saint, Vardapet, d. 480.
    History of Vardan and the Armenian War.

    (Harvard Armenian texts and studies ; 5)
    Translation of: Vasn Vardanay ew Hayots'
Paterazmin.
    Bibliography: p.
    Includes indexes.
    1. Armenia—History—Persian and Greek rule,
429-640. 2. Vardan Mami Konian, Saint, d. 451.
I. Thomson, Robert W., 1934-   . II. Title.
III. Series.
DS186.E3413   1982   939'.55   81-7117
ISBN 0-674-40335-5   AACR2

To Judith

The preparation of this translation was made possible by a grant from the Translations Program of the National Endowment for the Humanities, an independent federal agency. This assistance is most gratefully acknowledged.

R. W. T.

Preface

THE importance of Elishē's *History*, both as a document in its own right and as a text that lives on in Armenian tradition, is explained in the Introduction that follows. Here I would like to acknowledge the help I have received from numerous friends and colleagues who over the past few years have endured my spoken or written words and in turn have made useful comments. I am grateful to Frank Cross for carefully documented criticisms, and to many others for verbal remarks. But I cannot hold anyone else responsible for my interpretations, or misinterpretations.

It also seems appropriate to state in this preface my general objective, for this study of Elishē follows closely on studies of two other early Armenian Histories, those of Agathangelos and Moses Khorenats'i. In the first place, these great works of Armenian literature are of sufficient interest outside the small circle of readers of classical Armenian to merit translation. They contain information of relevance for the study of Armenian political and social history, Armenian literature, theology, and art history, as well as information of interest for the study of numerous other peoples and cultures with whom Armenians came into contact over the ages. Second, these histories are literary documents of some complexity, intriguing to unravel. In the Introduction that follows the problems of Elishē are spelled out in detail. Here it will suffice to say in more general terms that the classical Armenian histories are not untutored recollections of events seen by their authors or told them by witnesses.

They are learned works that impose a certain form on the historical matter and seek to interpret events. Their authors had some basic assumptions (such as a Christian outlook) that colored their view of things, and sometimes they had more specific motivations (for instance, the need to flatter a patron and his family).

Unfortunately, a critical investigation of these works which may cast doubt on the veracity of their narratives or hint at bias in their authors has sometimes been received with animosity. The ire of some modern readers is particularly aroused by the suggestion that these ancient authors may have surreptitiously altered their sources, and indeed may have claimed to be eyewitnesses of the events they describe, when in fact their histories were composed at a later period. In this regard, it must be stressed that Armenian writers of the fifth century are not being singled out as especially culpable of tendentiousness. A modern scholar looks at texts that have come down through manuscripts—themselves often copied a thousand years after the original text was written—with the same critical eye, be they copies of Homer's *Iliad,* the book of Genesis, a Syriac chronicle, or Moses Khorenats'i's *History of the Armenians.* If the critic discerns (or thinks he discerns) anomalies and difficulties in the text as it has survived, it is his duty to say so. If he thinks that the text does not date to the period it describes, but is the work of a later author who has treated his material in order to state a certain case, he must try to identify the sources, isolate the succeeding revisions, and elucidate the author's motivation. Of course, the critic may be wrong in his interpretations, but he is not wrong in applying such methods of historical and literary analysis to any given text.

Adverse public reaction to the study of texts some fifteen hundred years old does point to one very significant feature that makes such work so timely. These are not dead but living histories with a message for the present day and an interpretation of the past that is relevant for contemporary situations. That is why they are classics, and that is why there are "orthodox" and "unorthodox" ways of reading them. Some of these points are discussed in the Introduction. But we are now only at the beginning of an understanding of the development of the Armenian tradition. So my commentary is more concerned with how Ełishē put together his narrative and with the models he used than with the later life of his *History* as an authoritative text.

viii

Contents

Introduction   I

Vardan and the Armenian War   57

Appendix: The Armenian War According
    to Łazar P'arpets'i   251
Bibliography   329
Index of Scriptural Quotations
    and Allusions   338
Index   346
Map: The Armenia of Ełishē   356

Transcription

ա	բ	գ	դ	ե	զ	է	ը	թ	ժ	ի	լ	խ	ծ	կ	հ	ձ	ղ
a	b	g	d	e	z	ē	ĕ	tʻ	zh	i	l	kh	ts	k	h	dz	ḷ

ճ	մ	յ	ն	շ	ո	չ	պ	ջ	ռ	ս	վ	տ	ր	ց	ւ
ch	m	y	n	sh	o	chʻ	p	j	ṙ	s	v	t	r	tsʻ	w

փ	ք	ու	օ
pʻ	kʻ	u	ō

Note on Texts

All references to the texts of Ełishē and Łazar are to the pages of the critical Armenian editions. For details of these see the Bibliography under Armenian Texts. The pages of the Armenian texts have been noted in the texts of the translations.

All references to the Bible are to the Armenian version, which follows the numbering of the Septuagint for the Old Testament. Where an allusion to the Bible is noted, the parallel is a verbal one in Armenian; this may not be apparent if the English translation of Ełishē is compared with the text of the English Bible.

Introduction

CLASSICAL Armenian literature, which begins with an astonishing efflorescence in the fifth century of the Christian era, is rich in historical writing. The majority of these works were composed by learned clerics familiar with a wide range of literary sources in Greek and Syriac, but also conscious of the non-Hellenistic, Iranian cultural background of Armenia. For the conversion of King Trdat (Tiridates) to Christianity in the early fourth century and the work of Saint Gregory the Illuminator in founding an organized church did not bring about an immediate and total rejection of pre-Christian Armenian traditions. Thus, early Armenian historiography presents us with a fascinating picture of the interplay of cultures pagan and Christian, Iranian and Hellenistic. But the Armenian historians themselves, being Christians, impose upon that complicated amalgam interpretations based upon their own beliefs and ideals, using imagery drawn from the Judaeo-Christian world. The unraveling of the numerous strands of cultural tradition that have gone into the making both of the historical situation in Armenia and then of its interpretation in the early Armenian writers is thus a very complex task. The present work deals with only one history, that of Eḷishē, and with one of those strands, his literary models in Christian literature. Therefore, in what follows I shall primarily be concerned with this history as a conscious and sophisticated interpretation of events that took place in the fifth century in an Iranian setting as viewed through the eyes of a Christian. I trust that other scholars will in turn take up other strands, so that in time a fuller understanding of Ełishē's cultural milieu and the interaction of rival ideologies will emerge.

Early Armenian historians are of interest for what they tell us about events in Armenia, or which affected Armenia, and also for their interpretations of those events—in other words, for both the form and the matter of their literary compositions. But there is a third reason why these histories are significant. They are part of a living Armenian tradition that has persisted to the present day. For the image of the Armenian past as expounded by these classical authors has had a profound impact in the last two centuries on the way in which Armenians look upon themselves, their history, and their nation.

In this respect, three works stand out as being of very special importance. The *History* of Agathangelos, which describes the conversion of Armenia to Christianity; the *History* of Moses Khorenats'i, which describes the origins of the Armenian nation and its early history down to the time of Mashtots, inventor of the Armenian script; and the *History* of Ełishē, which describes the resistance of Christian Armenians to religious persecution in the fifth century. Other histories may be of greater interest to modern scholars as sources for understanding Armenian culture in certain periods of change—that of Faustos Buzand, for example, which describes fourth-century Armenia and the conflicts between church and traditional pagan society. But Agathangelos, Moses Khorenats'i, and Ełishē have a particular place in Armenian tradition as enshrining the received account of Armenian history: Armenia, a small country but of great antiquity where many manly deeds have been performed (Moses); a nation converted to Christianity before others, where God's grace has been manifested (Agathangelos); a people steadfast in their faith, true to their ancestral traditions, and ready for martyrdom should larger and stronger empires attempt to suppress Armenian liberties (Ełishē).

This Introduction is therefore divided into two sections. In the first part the sources used by Ełishē are discussed and an attempt made to elucidate his motivation and to date the text. The second part deals with the role of this *History* in later Armenian literature, the development of legends about the author, and the continuing influence of the figure of Vardan as an Armenian hero and patriot. For it is that continuous life of Ełishē's *History* that has made it a classic in Armenian literature, a work of perennial significance for Armenians, a book that must be read and appreciated by all who would try to understand the Armenian spirit.

The Armenian revolt of 450/1 against Sasanian rule and the subsequent fate of the Armenian prisoners in Iran are described in two Armenian sources: the Histories of Ełišē and of Łazar P'arpets'i. There is, however, no mention of these events in any non-Armenian source. The present work is devoted to a study of Ełišē, but it will be helpful to begin by comparing the two accounts, for the differences may shed some light on the attitude of both writers to this episode in particular and to historical writing in general.[1]

The original cause of the persecution that eventually led to rebellion is differently described by Ełišē and Łazar. For the former the matter was simply the malicious plotting of King Yazkert, abetted by his evil counselors, who see in the Christians potential enemies of state. But for Łazar the problem began in Armenia as a personal quarrel between the prince of Siunik' (Vasak), the *marzpan* (governor) of Armenia, and his son-in-law Varazvałan. For an unspecified insult to his daughter, Vasak had expelled Varazvałan from Armenia. The latter renounced Christianity, and in concert with the Iranian *hazarapet* (vizier), Mihrnerseh, persuaded King Yazkert to force the Armenians to apostatize. Whatever the Armenian reaction, Varazvałan saw revenge for himself: great honor from the Iranians should the Armenians in fact apostatize; the sweet sight of their destruction should they resist the king of kings.

Ełišē does not mention Varazvałan or his rancor against Vasak; unlike Łazar he does not see the ultimatum of Yazkert to the Armenians as a sudden decision. Łazar says that the Aryan nobility and magi "were astonished" when they were informed of the king's plan to force a confrontation. But for Ełišē the persecution came as no surprise, since Yazkert for most of his reign had been ill-disposed to the Christians. His first chapter therefore sets the scene. Military success against the Roman Empire encouraged the shah's megalomania. His magi advised him that if only he brings to one faith (that is, Zoroastrianism) all the peoples of his empire, then the Greeks will also submit. Although Yazkert did persecute the Christians

---

1. For details of the Armenian texts and translations of Ełišē and Łazar see the Bibliography.

in Persia proper, for a while he hid his intentions from the Armenians and other Christians in the Caucasus who were serving in his army on a campaign against the Kushans. But a warning of things to come was given by the fate of Garegin, who dared remind the king of Christ's Second Coming and the Last Judgment.[2]

The undaunted spirit of the Armenians led Yazkert to try and break their unity; according to Ełishē this policy lasted from the fourth to the eleventh year of his reign (441/2–448/9) and the king was urged on by the advice of his magi. Finally an oppressive tax burden was laid on Armenia, which for Ełishē is particularly obnoxious in that the churches and monasteries, the bishops, priests, and monks, were for the first time included in the census. Furthermore, a Persian, a chief-magus, was appointed governor of Armenia in place of a native Armenian.

For Łazar, however, the shah was persuaded to force the Armenians to apostatize simply by Mihrnerseh's arguments; there is no suggestion of a long-standing plot. Mihrnerseh's arguments were: (1) that the gods reward those who save souls from error. (The responsibility of the shah for his subjects in that he has to give a reckoning to the gods is also a theme in Ełishē);[3] (2) that Armenia, Georgia, and Caucasian Albania are valuable lands; (3) that their religion is that of the Roman Empire, and therefore their friendship and loyalty can only be secured by their acceptance of the Aryan religion; and (4) that the honor and glory given to Varazvałan (who had apostatized) will encourage the other Armenians to accept Zoroastrianism. Yazkert applauded the reasoning; he had the tenets of the Mazdaean religion written down and sent to Armenia, and also addressed an edict to the Armenians.

For both Łazar and Ełishē the final ultimatum came in the form of a letter or edict. But they differ in describing both the author and the form of the missive. Łazar says that Yazkert himself composed the edict, in which he indicated that as shah he was responsible to the gods for the salvation of his subjects' souls, and so the Armenians should accept his infallible and just religion. He also requested a statement from the Armenians about their erroneous religion. But Ełishē does not have the king write the ultimatum. Rather, he claims that it was the vizier, Mihrnerseh, who composed it, ordered to do so by the

2. This ends the first chapter in Ełishē; cf. Łazar, pp. 39–41.
3. See references at p. 15, n. 3.

4

Persians (unspecified), who saw that their policies in Armenia up to then had not brought the desired results. And although the basic purpose of the letter, like Ḷazar's, is to persuade the Armenians to abandon Christianity for Mazdaeism, it is three times longer than Ḷazar's and contains both an explicit account of the myth of Zrvan's begetting of Ormizd and Haraman and various sarcastic comments about the errors of Christianity.[4]

For Ḷazar the Armenian response is brief and to the point: the Persian religion is false and ridiculous; the Armenians do not worship the elements and many gods, but the one only true God who made heaven and earth. But Eḷishē pens a twelve-page epistle. It begins with a short treatise on the nature of God, goes on to discuss the nature of the material world and the interaction of the four elements, discusses free will and the nature of evil, presents a reasoned account of the divine and human natures of Christ, and ends with the defiant statement that the Armenians will die rather than forsake Jesus Christ—although they are loyal subjects of the shah in every other respect.[5]

The Persian king's reaction was to summon some of the leading Armenian nobles to court in person. They attempted to persuade Yazkert that they were indeed loyal in all respects save that of religious faith. But they realized that their only chance to escape with their lives lay in deception. (The basic theme here is common to both writers, though Eḷishē's account is more elaborate.) So the Armenian princes feigned submission to Mazdaeism and performed the cult as demanded by Yazkert. Ḷazar, however, goes to great lengths to show how unwilling was Vardan Mamikonean, the uncle of his own patron, Vahan Mamikonean. On the other hand, Eḷishē does not single out any one of the Armenian apostates as being less culpable or more unwilling.[6]

Following this (supposedly feigned) submission, Yazkert sent the nobles back home in great honor, but also in the company of a host of teachers of magism, who were to convert the mass of the Armenian people. When the Armenians who had weakened returned home, they met with contempt from their fellow-countrymen. According to Ḷazar, this reception, plus the zeal of the magi who had come to Armenia in propagating the

4. The letters in Eḷishē run from p. 24 to p. 47.
5. The letters in Ḷazar run from p. 43 to p. 47.
6. Eḷishē, pp. 48–50; Ḷazar, pp. 47–54.

cult of fire, led Vardan Mamikonean to choose exile as a Christian over life under Persian rule as an apostate. But Ełishē says nothing of Vardan's scruples. Rather, the clergy of Armenia were horrified at the nobles' weakness, and in concert with the common people of the country they began forcible resistance to the magi.

According to Łazar, the departing Vardan was persuaded to return and lead the Armenians in revolt by the insistent supplications of the Armenian nobility, led by Vasak. Ełishē does not mention Vardan's departure, but both authors agree that armed rebellion was the next step, and that Vasak was from the beginning a traitor to the cause. Ełishē says that Vasak had sincerely accepted the Persian religion, but for Łazar the fact that Vasak's sons were hostages at the Persian court was not insignificant.

The Armenian princes then took a common oath, the covenant (*ukht*), which plays a very significant role in the narratives of both Łazar and Ełishē.[7] According to the latter, the Armenians made a general attack on the Persians in Armenia, destroying fire-temples and penetrating as far as Atrpatakan. Łazar gives a briefer version of these events. Both agree that the Albanians sent word to Armenia of Persians there, and that the Armenians wrote to the Greek emperor asking for help. Ełishē expands the account to indicate that after receipt of this request Theodosius died, Marcian came to the throne, but influenced by his evil counselors thought it better to preserve peace with the heathen than to go to war for the Christian covenant. So no help was forthcoming. (The Armenian request seems to be unknown to Byzantine sources. Certainly there were no Armenian representatives at the Council of Chalcedon held the following year [451], a circumstance explained by Armenians as due to the revolt. But it is unknown whether invitations to Chalcedon were in fact sent to Armenia under Iranian control. On the other hand, Armenian sources say nothing of the threat to Constantinople posed by Attila at this time.)[8]

Nevertheless, under the leadership of Vardan the Armenians scored great military successes in Albania. This is one of the few episodes described in greater detail by Łazar, for as the uncle of his patron, Vardan's prowess was especially appropriate to record. Following these victories the Armenians made an

7. For the *ukht* see the full discussion below.
8. Ełishē, pp. 51–73; Łazar, pp. 54–63.

6

alliance with the Huns. That season's campaigns ended with news of Vasak's treachery and depredations; and the Armenians returned home for the winter.[9]

On the arrival of spring in 451 Łazar passes immediately to the Persian advance into Armenia and the decisive battle at Avarayr. But Ełishē's account is far more circumstantial. First, he claims that the Armenian bishops wrote to their brethren in Constantinople asking for their prayers. Then he expands on Yazkert's equivocal policy following the Armenian success in Albania, his feigned kindness to the Christians, and his deceptive amnesty. These were delaying tactics while he secretly probed the intentions of the Greek emperor. When Yazkert was sure that the emperor would not help the Armenians, he dispatched Mihrnerseh with an army to Armenia. Ełishē then gives details of Vasak's treacherous behavior, of his efforts to encourage apostasy through false priests, and of his role as informer to the Persians.[10]

The preliminaries to the confrontation at Avarayr are differently described by Łazar and Ełishē. According to the former, the Armenians came across the Persians at Avarayr while the latter were quite unprepared, but the Armenians held off, as they were more anxious for martyrdom than victory.[11] That evening the priest Łevond and the general Vardan addressed the troops, reminding them of the glorious fate of earlier Christian martyrs, including Saint Gregory the Illuminator, and urging them to hasten to share in their inheritance. The two speeches are summarized in a paragraph each. On the other hand, Ełishē lays great stress on the content of these speeches. Vardan speaks first, when the troops originally mustered, long before the arrival of the Persians. Picking up the theme of heavenly valor that runs through his entire *History,* Ełishē has Vardan urge the troops on to a holy death on behalf of their ancestral and divinely bestowed religion—a theme basic to the books of the Maccabees, whose very examples, says Ełishē, Vardan read aloud to the army.[12] Later, the day before Avarayr, Łevond addressed the troops, and Ełishē devotes eight pages to this exhortation. It is remarkable for the absence of Christian

9. Ełishē, pp. 74–80; Łazar, pp. 64–67.

10. Ełishē, pp. 81–97 (the end of ch. 4); Łazar, p. 68.

11. Łazar, p. 69. The Armenian enthusiasm for martyrdom is a constant theme in Ełishē.

12. For the role of the Maccabees in Ełishē see the full discussion below.

parallels and the emphasis on the warrior heroes of ancient Israel.[13] Ełishē adds a third speech—that of the Persian general warning his soldiers against desertion.

Of the fateful battle itself Łazar gives no details, whereas Ełishē's account is fairly circumstantial. Both report the final death-toll, but differ again in their accounts of the aftermath. According to Łazar, the Persian general Mushkan was recalled after reporting the Persian losses and was replaced by Atrormizd, who declared freedom of worship. Vardan's brother Hmayeak, who had led the Armenian embassy to Constantinople to request aid, returned empty-handed, too late to fight at Avarayr; he was killed in guerilla warfare in the province of Taykʻ. The Armenian nobles and clergy were summoned to the Persian court. At a tribunal there the Armenians defended their actions and revealed Vasak's duplicity. So the latter was kept at court in disgrace until his death, while his principality of Siunikʻ was given to his foe, the apostate Varazvałan. Łazar then names the nobles and clergy who were kept in captivity in Iran.[14]

Ełishē's account is somewhat different. Mushkan, greatly distressed at the Persian losses, was persuaded to let Vasak have a free hand in Armenia. Vasak deceitfully pretended that a pardon had been granted, so that he could seize surviving Armenians in their strongholds. But the Armenians continued to resist in the deserts and mountains, in which guerilla warfare Hmayeak was killed. (Ełishē does not say that he had joined the embassy to Constantinople.) But the continued disorder in Armenia so angered the shah that Vasak was summoned to court. Atrormizd was appointed governor; he calmed the country and granted freedom of life and worship. At the Persian court Vasak's duplicity was revealed. Condemned to prison, he died of horrible diseases (patterned in Ełishē's account on the deaths of Herod in Eusebius and of Antiochus in Maccabees). Ełishē ends this section with the statement: "These things have been written concerning him in order to reprove his sins, so that everyone who hears and knows them may cast curses on him and not envy his deeds."[15]

Both Łazar and Ełishē immediately proceed to the fate of

13. See the discussion below.
14. The preliminary exhortations and the battle of Avarayr are described in Ełishē, pp. 98–120; Łazar, pp. 70–73.
15. Events after the battle of Avarayr down to Vasak's death are described in Ełishē, pp. 121–140 (end of ch. 6); Łazar, pp. 73–86 (end of §47).

the prisoners in Iran, beginning in 453/4. In this section their accounts are much closer, though Ełishē's is again longer. He adds the story of the Hun Bēl as a spy sympathetic to the persecuted Christians. He also adds the long account of the conversion of the chief-magus to whose care the imprisoned Armenians had been entrusted. This gives Ełishē an opportunity to introduce Vardan and the martyred Armenian soldiers as angelic beings who had already attained their heavenly rewards. He makes the interchanges between the saints Sahak, Yoseph, Łevond, and their companions, and the Persians far more elaborate than those reported by Łazar. He also deals at greater length with the life and work of Abraham who, following his own release, spent many years collecting contributions to alleviate the lot of those prisoners still left in Iran. The circumstances of the nobles' final release are also more elaborately set out by Ełishē than by Łazar. But his most significant expansion is the exordium on the virtues of the Armenian women—the wives of the prisoners and widows of the fallen—who remained at home for so many years. Łazar's brief and rather sarcastic paragraph is expanded into several pages of complicated prose in which their praises are systematically extolled. Ełishē ends this section, and thus his whole book, with the same basic theme with which he had begun: heavenly virtue and the devotion of the Armenians to it, be they warriors and martyrs or the women who suffered at home.[16]

Ełishē's *History* is clearly a carefully constructed piece of literary work. We should now turn to the major themes which recur throughout. An analysis of these themes will help us understand Ełishē's motivation and purpose.

In the very first paragraph Ełishē states his purpose: to describe the Armenian war in which "more than a few showed virtue." Here the verb "showed virtue" (*arak'inets'an*) is significant, for virtue (*arak'inut'iwn*) in the sense of spiritual virtue is one of Ełishē's main themes, picked up on the last page: "they did not lose heart or slacken in heavenly virtue" (*och inch' kaseal t'ulats'an yerknawor arak'inut'enēn*).

Ełishē's second paragraph gives the themes for each of the seven sections to follow. Here two terms should be noted: the "covenant" (*ukht*) and the "secession" (*erkpařakut'iwn*) of those

16. Ełishē, ch. 7 (pp. 141–203); Łazar, pp. 86–110 (the release of the nobles in Łazar comes at the beginning of his Book III). For the theme of heavenly virtue and its importance in Ełishē see below.

who abandoned the convenant. For Eḷishē the covenant is a
"covenant of the church"; he emphasizes not merely that the
pact to which Armenians swore allegiance was one of loyalty to
God and country, but that in that pact the church played the
leading role. His hero, Vardan Mamikonean, cannot raise the
flag of revolt and lead the Armenian resistance until the clergy
had prayed over him and received him back into the fold "of
virtue."[17] And Eḷishē makes it abundantly clear that he who
cleaves to the covenant is pious and virtuous, while he who
abandons the covenant is impious and base. Patriotism and
Christian faith are inextricably intertwined. There is no middle
way.

Therefore those who abandoned the convenant were
"apostates" (*uratsʻeal*) and not merely "cowards" (*vattʻar*). This
is brought out in the third paragraph of the Preface, where
Eḷishē contrasts the valor of the virtuous (*arakʻineatsʻn kʻajutʻiwn*)
with the cowardice (*vattʻarutʻiwn*) of those who fell behind. He
emphasizes that there were many who seceded; and where secession (or "discord," *erkparakʻutiwn*) enters, there heavenly virtue (*erknawor aṙakinutʻiwn*) departs.[18]

But even more significant than the covenant was the cause
for which Armenians made the convenant and in which they
displayed heavenly virtue: namely, the preservation of their
ancestral and divinely-bestowed *awrēnkʻ*, a term which em-
braces more than religion to include customs, laws, and traditions, a whole way of life that characterized Armenians as Armenians. It was because the shah attempted to impose Iranian
awrēnkʻ on the Armenians that they were forced to resist, despite their previous loyalty to the shah as individual princes
and soldiers and the many services that they had rendered.[19]

We should now turn to these basic themes and examine
them in greater detail.

Although the convenant is such a basic theme in Eḷishē,
the Armenian word *ukht* is one of even wider meaning. At the
beginning of the first chapter Eḷishē describes how the Persian
king, Yazkert, caused many to fall away from the "holy covenant of the Christians," where *ukht* refers to the Christian
church in general and not to a specific pact made by Arme-

17. P. 64.
18. The theme is picked up again at the beginning of p. 89.
19. P. 9. For Armenian services to the shah see p. 45.

nians. In a narrower sense *ukht* can refer to the clergy as a group or class: either the Armenians who gather as a synod, or the Greek clergy to whom they write a letter.[20] In this restricted sense the Armenian term renders the Greek word *klēros*. Then *ukht* can refer to the specific pact made by a group of people— as when the nobility and clergy swear together to resist the Persians.[21] In this pact the apostate Vasak later joined, swearing on the Gospel and sealing the written compact with his ring.[22] But most generally, *ukht* refers to the Armenians who have sworn as a body (laity and clergy alike) to uphold Christianity, or rather to support the Armenian religious tradition. Hence the frequency of the expression "the covenant of the church" applied to all loyal Armenians.

The concept of the "holy covenant" as the body of the faithful does not occur in the New Testament. There the new covenant (*diathēkē*) is contrasted with the old covenant, but both are covenants between God and man, going back to Noah and Abraham.[23] However, Ełishē's concept of the convenant as the community of faithful who have united to preserve their religion and way of life from destruction has a very definite precursor in the Judaism of the second century B.C. In 1 Macc. 1:15–16, for example, the renegade Jews who introduced non-Jewish customs, intermarried with gentiles, and took up evil ways are described as repudiating the holy covenant (*diathēkē hagia* in the Greek, *ukht ktakaranats'n srbut'ean* in the Armenian). Similarly in Dan. 11:18–30, the animosity of the Seleucid Antiochus toward the Jews is described: his heart was against the holy covenant (*berit qōdesh* in Hebrew, *diathēkē tou hagiou* in Greek, *ukht surb* in Armenian). This holy covenant is not the pact between God and the Jews, but the community of Jews who have united to preserve the purity of their religion and customs from contamination.[24]

This parallel with the situation of the Jews in opposing persecution is brought out even more clearly by Ełishē's use of *awrēnk'*, which he explicitly links to the Maccabees. Despite this

20. P. 81, n. 1.
21. P. 65.
22. P. 66.
23. E.g., Heb., ch. 8, 9, where the roles of Moses and Jesus as mediators are stressed.
24. But this use in Daniel and Maccabees is an extension of the concept of the divine covenant to the covenanted community.

indebtedness to the books of the Maccabees throughout his *History*,[25] Ełishē only once refers to them by name. In Vardan's exhortation to the Armenian troops as they prepare for the battle at Avarayr, he mentions them as exemplifying themes relevant to the Armenian struggle: they fought against the Seleucid king in defense of their religion; even though they died in battle, their fame survived both on earth and in heaven; and some of them had split away from the union, had offered impure sacrifices and abandoned God, only to be killed by the holy covenanters.[26]

"The Maccabees fought for their God-given religion" (*astuatsatur awrēnk'*). This immediately recalls to mind an earlier phrase in Vardan's speech: "Let us struggle against the impious prince for our ancestral and God-given religion," where the Armenian is a direct borrowing from 3 Macc. 1:12: *i veray kargats'n nakhneats' ew hayreni awrinats'n.* Ełishē had previously used a similar phrase when one of the Persian captives was given a list of Armenian complaints to bring before the shah: "he had constrained them to abandon their ancestral religion."[27] However, the rendering "religion" for *awrēnk'* is misleading. Obviously, Armenia had not been a Christian country from time immemorial. Koriun's biography of Mashtots' makes it clear that even in the early fifth century there were many in Armenia still unconverted. Nor is it likely that by saying "ancestral" Ełishē was optimistically moving back to the time of Gregory the Illuminator the conversion of the whole country, which would allow several generations to elapse before the revolt of 450. More important, the term *awrēnk'* includes the sense of "customary way of life." So it is relevant to note that Ełishē also speaks of the Armenians being deprived of their ancestral liberty (*hayreni azatut'iwn*), and being forced to abandon their ancestral land (*hayreni erkir*) for foreign slavery.[28]

It is therefore interesting that Ełishē does not compare the Armenians who are being persecuted to the early Christian martyrs who died for their faith—though the theme of personal

25. Ełishē is not the only Armenian historian to have used the books of the Maccabees; see Thomson, "Maccabees." However, other writers quote from those books to illustrate certain specific *episodes,* whereas Ełishē patterns his whole *interpretation* of the Armenian revolt on the general situation there described as well as making specific comparisons (for example, between Yazkert and Antiochus; see further below).

26. P. 105.

27. P. 82.

28. Pp. 22, 98, 115.

salvation does play a large role in his *History*. Nor does he draw attention to Armenia as a Christian land in order to compare it with other Christian lands. Although Ełishē refers to those other Christian nations in the Caucasus that were under the control of the Iranian shah,[29] he does not write of Armenia as being but one small part of a larger Christian world. Rather, he emphasizes that the Armenians are alone, that they are fighting for their individuality as Armenians. The phrase *hayreni awrēnkʻ*, therefore, means not only the practice of Christianity—which was relatively new in Armenia—but also a traditional way of life.[30]

Ełishē then has Vardan go on to say that the Maccabees died for their faith (*kataretsʻan*). Now the verb *katarel* in this sense is a calque on the Greek *teleiousthai* or the Syriac *eshtamli*, which carries the connotation of martyrdom.[31] Much of the terminology in Ełishē is reminiscent of the vocabulary applied to Christian martyrs, as will be explained in greater detail below. But the main point here is that the dead heroes—that is, the Armenians who are about to be killed—will not merely be remembered for their valor as were the Maccabees; Vardan and his companions will immediately attain bliss in heaven. So there is a significant difference between the Maccabees and the Armenians, for the only passage in Maccabees that definitely associates eternal life with loyalty to the convenant is 2 Macc. 7:36; where the youngest of the seven brothers to be martyred says to Antiochus: "My brothers have now fallen in loyalty to God's covenant, after brief pain leading to eternal life." But for Ełishē, as for Łazar, the goal of a martyr's death in battle provides strong motivation for armed resistance.

As a foil to those Maccabees who died for their cause, Vardan refers to the relatives of Mattathias who had split away from the union, abandoned God, and received the punishment of death. Here too Ełishē's terminology is paralleled in the books of the Maccabees. But more especially he draws attention to one of his main concerns throughout the *History:* the disunity of the Armenians. The noun *erkpaṙakutʻiwn* and the cognate verb and adjective occur frequently in Ełishē and recall 1 Macc. 3:19, which refers to the discord that Antiochus had brought about by abolishing traditional laws and customs. On

29. Pp. 10, 51.
30. For a different meaning of *awrēnkʻ*, the "elements" of communion, see p. 114, n. 3.
31. See references on p. 78, n. 4.

the other hand, Mattathias himself and his companions had not weakened or slackened but became even firmer—all terms used elsewhere in Ełishē and reminiscent of numerous passages in the books of the Maccabees.[32]

There were, naturally, heroes other than the Maccabees whose examples might inspire the Armenians. So on the eve of the fateful battle, claims Ełishē, the priest Łevond also addressed the assembled troops and reminded them of various Old Testament figures who vanquished the enemies of truth.[33] It is not insignificant that these are the heroes of Israel, not the Christian martyrs of previous centuries who had died for their *faith,* but men who fought for their *country* and their *people.*

But of more direct relevance to our theme than the individual heroes mentioned by Łevond is the fact that his speech as a whole is modeled on that of Mattathias himself in 1 Macc., ch. 2. This is his dying speech, and in his final moments he recalls the earlier heroes of Israel. Mattathias's list of famous men has parallels with that in Eccles., ch. 44–45, which in turn is echoed by Paul in Heb., ch. 11. And it is perhaps worth noting that this passage from Paul forms part of the readings for the Christian festival of the Maccabees as celebrated in Armenia.[34] Interestingly enough, the heroes enumerated by Łevond in Ełishē's *History* are derived from all three lists, without following any one of them exclusively. Again, the contrast with the speech put into Łevond's mouth by Łazar is noteworthy. Łazar speaks of the advantages of a martyr's death and holds up Gregory the Illuminator as an example.[35] But Ełishē has no reference anywhere in his *History* to this Christian Armenian hero.

Another passage from the books of the Maccabees should be considered here. In Book II, ch. 6, the example of Eleazar, who preferred an honorable death to an unclean life, is described and his final speech reported: "So if I now die bravely, I shall show that I have deserved my long life and leave the young a fine example, to teach them how to die a good death, gladly and nobly, for our revered and holy laws." This rendering from the New English Bible does not bring out the close parallels between Ełishē and the Armenian text of the Macca-

32. See references on p. 14, n. 1.
33. Pp. 106–113.
34. See P. 109, n. 3.
35. P. 70. Łazar refers very frequently to Saint Gregory the Illuminator throughout his *History.*

bees. In the latter we read: *awrinak bareats'n ew aṙak'inut'ean* ("an example of good behavior and *virtue*")—so that they may be able to strive even unto death gladly and bravely (*k'ajut'eamb*) for the holy *awrēnk'*. Even though virtue is a theme in the Pauline epistles, and the adjective "virtuous" (*aṙak'ini*) is a standard expression for Christian martyrs,[36] Eḷishē's emphasis on virtue (as noted above) in defense of traditional values shows the profound influence of the Maccabees on his interpretation of events.

The books of the Maccabees have also provided Eḷishē with some very specific imagery. It is not necessary here to recapitulate all the parallels and borrowings that are noted in the commentary to the translation.[37] But it may be helpful to pick out a few examples to serve as an introduction to a more general discussion of Eḷishē's literary sources.

In view of the direct parallel between the situation of the Armenians vis-à-vis Sasanian Iran and that of the Jews, led by the Maccabees, vis-à-vis the Greek Seleucids, it is hardly surprising that the Shah Yazkert is sometimes described in terms reminiscent of King Antiochus. Yazkert to Eḷishē is a "murderous" tyrant as is Antiochus in 2 Macc. 9:28 (*mardakhoshosh*).[38] Likewise Yazkert returns "humiliated" from his war in the East just as Antiochus had returned from Persia in 2 Macc. 9:1 (*kamakor*).[39] And just as Antiochus had died a horrid death, worms crawling from his eyes and the stench of his decay offending his escort, in 2 Macc. 9:9, so did the apostate Vasak perish most horribly. Eḷishē has here added some sordid details taken from the description of Herod's death in Eusebius's *Ecclesiastical History*, I, 8.[40]

Several Armenian historians borrow imagery from the books of the Maccabees to enhance their descriptions of battle scenes. Many examples are found in Faustos Buzand and Moses Khorenats'i.[41] So it is hardly surprising that Eḷishē's account of Avarayr shows similar imagery: the wild attack, the glittering of swords and lances, the tremendous commotion, the

36. As in the *Vkayk'*, passim.
37. See the Index of Scriptural Quotations and Allusions.
38. P. 22.
39. P. 82.
40. P. 139. Eusebius is quoting Josephus' *Jewish Antiquities* (which was never translated into Armenian).
41. See above, n. 25.

anguish of the soldiers as they collided in battle, the rolling of the mortally wounded.[42] These are rather vague terms used for rhetorical effect. More interesting, perhaps, is the psalm of victory sung by the Armenian troops in their first campaign of the war in the Caucasus. Ełishē quotes from Psalm 135—the same psalm that was sung by the Maccabees following Judas's victory over Gorgias.[43] Other parallels of a more or less military nature include the Armenian readiness to die for their cause,[44] expressed in the same Armenian words as 2 Macc. 7:2; the fact that they did not weaken or slacken but rather were steadfast,[45] where the verbs *lk'anel, pndel, chgnel,* and cognates have many parallels in Maccabees; and the Armenians being goaded into fury,[46] which is an exact verbal parallel to the zeal of Mattathias in 1 Macc. 2:24. Finally, the purification of Armenia from the impurity of fire-worship[47] is directly reminiscent of 1 Macc. 13:48, where Simon purifies Gadara from idolatry. But these examples give only an inkling of the extensive verbal parallels between Ełishē's *History* and the Armenian books of the Maccabees.

Ełishē's debt to biblical imagery is more obvious, since he frequently quotes explicitly from Scripture. As with many other Armenian writers, however, Ełishē's debt to the Bible goes far beyond the use of direct quotation, for he was deeply imbued with scriptural imagery and uses it more or less unconsciously in many situations that do not necessarily have any particular theological overtones. Therefore it is difficult to draw up a precise list of quotations and allusions, since it is not always clear whether a biblical phrase was intended to be an allusion to Scripture or was simply a well-known expression that happened to fit the context. For example, the simile of bears in their dying pangs, applied to Yazkert,[48] is from Isa. 59:10–11, but the direct comparison between bears and wicked rulers is from Prov. 28:15. Later we read that the true believers in Christ were not all "irresolute or doubtful";[49] the Armenian words recall Matth. 14:31, where Peter, walking on the water,

42. See notes to p. 117.
43. P. 80; cf. 1 Macc., ch. 4.
44. See references on p. 73, n. 10.
45. E.g., pp. 14, 43, 105.
46. P. 127.
47. P. 77.
48. P. 8.
49. P. 48.

sinks because his faith is too weak. The Persian magi about to set out for Armenia are described as "rising up from each one's gloomy lair,"[50] which recalls the wicked Abimelech in Judg. 9:35. Describing the tribulations inflicted upon defenseless women and children, Ełishē says: "many children fell and hit the rocks along the paths."[51] This obscure phrase is from Nah. 3:10, which describes the fate of the captives from Nineveh. Likewise Vasak's separation from the church[52] is described in the same words as is Paul's account of James separating himself in Gal. 2:12. On the same page Vasak is also described as a "vessel of evil," reminiscent of Jer. 51:34. However, that epithet is used of Diocletian by Agathangelos, where the theme of the snake is also elaborated upon as in the same paragraph in Ełishē.[53] But as the dating of both Ełishē and Agathangelos is a matter of dispute, this parallel between them can hardly be used as evidence for the priority of one over the other.

Clearly enough, Ełishē uses biblical imagery to enhance the effect of his narrative without always so acknowledging, or indeed even wishing, to make a theological point. Similarly he is greatly indebted to the imagery of hagiographical texts, notably descriptions of martyrdom. Given the subject matter of his narrative, this is not surprising. So again only a few general examples are given here; a cursory glance through the commentary will reveal the full extent of this hagiographical imagery.

It is not always possible to say whether Ełishē had a particular text in mind on every occasion when parallels may be discerned. As with biblical imagery, many of the figures of speech, epithets and stock phrases, and even narrative descriptions were so commonplace as to be in the public domain. It is not, then, so much to prove that Ełishē was dependent on, or borrowing from, another text that these parallels are cited. It is rather to show that they were in fact *common* themes and therefore cannot be taken in every case as a *literal* description of a very *specific* occasion.

In the first place, it is worth noting that Ełishē refers to the Armenians as heroes or champions, *nahatak*—a term basic to hagiography, rendering the Greek *agonistēs*.[54] And the usual verb that is used of their dying is *katarel*, a calque on the Greek

50. P. 51.
51. P. 81.
52. P. 91.
53. Agathangelos, §141.
54. See references on p. 5, n. 2.

and Syriac, as noted above, which means not merely to "be perfected" but to "be martyred." So throughout his *History* Eḷishē uses terms that have connotations of martyrdom whenever the Armenians face the Persians in battle.

With respect to specific accounts of martyrdom we may note here the charge against Christians of sorcery, a very common theme attested in Agathangelos and the Armenian version of the Persian martyrdoms known as *Vkayk' Arevelits'*.[55] At the trial or interrogation preceding the martyr's death, it was customary for the judge to exhort the Christian to save himself by denying Christ—as does Denshapuh to Yoseph.[56] Following condemnation, the martyr was subjected to incredible tortures described in exaggerated terms. Thus the Armenians are dragged over the rocks until not a piece of flesh remained on their bodies.[57] In prison the martyrs' future glory is foreshadowed by celestial light—as indeed was seen by the Persian magus who had charge of the Armenian prisoners.[58] Death finally comes by beheading with a sword, since the martyrs do not succumb to their tortures—hence the frequent references in Eḷishē's *History* to the theme of swords and necks: "the sword is yours, the necks are ours"; "the swords of the executioners were blunted, but their necks were not wearied"; "they offered their necks to the sword of the executioner"; "he saw that the sword was still glinting over the necks of the blessed ones."[59] Following the martyrs' deaths, their bones were highly valued by fellow-Christians. This is emphasized by Eḷishē (as also by Ḷazar) by means of the story of the secret Christian from Khuzastan, who plays a major role in the last chapter of the *History*. But Eḷishē rarely mentions other Christian martyrs by name, though there are veiled allusions to the martyrdom of Stephen in Acts, and of course to the martyrdoms in Maccabees, and there is one explicit reference to the Forty Martyrs of Sebaste, a story well known in Armenia.[60]

There is another hagiographical theme that is relevant to the present discussion. It is common for the account of the martyrdom to be based on a (fictional) eyewitness report.[61]

55. See references on p. 42, n. 5.
56. P. 169.
57. P. 161.
58. P. 145.
59. Pp. 40, 61, 123, 178.
60. P. 138.
61. See Delehaye, *Passions,* pp. 182–183.

Ełishē claims to have been an eyewitness himself of the events in Armenia that form the basis of his narrative and to have had an eyewitness account of the fate of the prisoners in Iran from a Christian from Khuzastan.[62] Since Łazar also gives a basically similar account of the martyrdom in Iran and describes Abraham's comings and goings between Armenia and the prisoners in Iran, there can be little doubt that the main lines of the story were familiar in Armenia by the end of the fifth century. The basic question is whether Ełishē's description of events within Armenia—the Sasanian oppression, the outbreak of resistance, the defeat at Avarayr, the guerrilla warfare, and the endurance of the women whose husbands had been killed or imprisoned—is in fact that of a contemporary eyewitness or a later version of events.

Ełishē's claim cannot simply be taken at face value. For other Armenian histories were written by men who claimed to be eyewitnesses, but are recognized to be later productions. Thus Agathangelos' account of the conversion of Trdat by Saint Gregory the Illuminator is accepted by everyone as a work of the fifth century at the earliest, not the verbatim reporting of Trdat's "scribe."[63] (As will be seen below, the theme of the "scribe" is adapted to Ełishē, who emerges in later Armenian tradition as Vardan Mamikonean's secretary.) The claims of Moses Khorenats'i to have been a pupil of Mashtots' and to have written his *History* in the fifth centry are firmly upheld in Soviet Armenia but recognized by nearly all scholars outside the USSR for the last several generations as false.[64] It is therefore impossible to accept Ełishē's *History* as a product of the second half of the fifth century merely because the author says that it is. Any assessment of its date must be based on other evidence, internal or external. So we shall have to return to this problem after our discussion of the sources used by Ełishē. For these may provide some clues as to the date before which it could not have been written.

Reference has already been made to some of the hagiographical themes attested to in Ełishē's *History*. Parallels to these

---

62. For Ełishē as eyewitness see p. 5, n. 7; for the man from Khuzastan as eyewitness see p. 182.

63. See the Prologue and Epilogue to Agathangelos' *History* for his claim to have been commissioned by Trdat; and the Introduction to Thomson, *Agathangelos,* for a discussion of the probable date of this work.

64. See Toumanoff, "On the date of the Pseudo-Moses," and Thomson, Introduction to *Moses Khorenats'i.*

may be found in other Armenian historians: Agathangelos, for example, who describes Gregory's torments and the martyrdom of the nuns by Trdat. But in addition to the more general characteristics shared by such works, there is one particular source that has provided Ełishē with many precise figures of speech. That is the Armenian version of the Syriac Acts of martyrs in fourth-century Iran compiled by Marutha of Maiperqat (who died before 420). The Armenian version is attributed to the Abraham mentioned by both Łazar and Ełishē as a prisoner after Avarayr, later released, who acted for many years as an intermediary between the Armenian captives and their homeland. Neither Łazar nor Ełishē says anything about his literary activity. The translation is first linked to Abraham by Thomas Artsruni, who wrote four centuries after these events. But there seems to be no internal reason to doubt that the translation from Syriac into Armenian was done in the second half of the fifth century.[65]

There are numerous verbal parallels between Ełishē and the *Vkayk' Aravelits'* (Martyrs of the East) that have been noted in the commentary. Here it will suffice to draw attention to a few significant themes. The stress placed on the worship of the sun as the key feature of the abjuration of Christianity is notable in both texts. But when renunciation of Christianity is not being emphasized, Ełishē devotes his attention rather to the cult of fire and its inanity. Features common to both texts include the threats made to Christians by the "pagan" Persians, who are notable for their "bloodthirstiness," and trampling by elephants.[66] There are several rhetorical parallels in the description of martyrdoms and in the imagery describing the wild behavior of the Persian king.[67] The bringing of converts to Christianity is described as "hunting"—though this metaphor also appears in Agathangelos.[68] The cult of the martyrs' bones is too common a feature for it to be significant here; but the exact verbal parallels in the description of the marvelous signs that frightened those guarding the dead martyrs' bodies indi-

---

65. For the text see *Vkayk'*; for a recent study see Ter-Petrosyan, *Abraham*, discussed in van Esbroeck, "Abraham le confesseur."

66. For worship of the sun see references on p. 17, n. 9; the Persians as "pagan" or "heathen," p. 16, n. 3; bloodthirstyness, p. 7, n. 2; trampling by elephants, p. 48, n. 4.

67. E.g., pp. 44, 61.

68. See references on p. 64, n. 9.

cate borrowing.[69] Likewise the eulogy of the blessed Abraham near the end of the *History* is based on that of Saint Shmavon in the *Vkaykʻ*, both in structure and vocabulary.[70]

Given the literary skill of Ełishē, it is surprising that comparatively few parallels with texts other than biblical or hagiographical ones can be discerned. There are certain rhetorical commonplaces, such as the simile of a storm at sea or the theme of the merchant, found in other Armenian writers as well as patristic sources. Ełishē's description of the spread of Christianity has parallels in John Chrysostom.[71] Most of his disquisitions on theology and on the nature of the world (as in the long Armenian response to Mihrnerseh's letter) can be paralleled in other early Armenian sources such as Eznik and Agathangelos. Dependence on non-Armenian sources is less common. But Ełishē used an Armenian version of a Greek Hermetic treatise, both for details of the physical world and for a statement attributed to "someone of old": "death not understood is death, death understood is immortality."[72] Another aphorism, "it is better to be blind in the eyes than blind in the mind," is taken verbatim from the Armenian version of the Wisdom of Ahikar; it has a parallel also in the Armenian version of the *Alexander Romance* by Ps.–Callisthenes.[73]

There is only one other non-Armenian author on whom Ełishē is dependent for more than an occasional phrase or figure. That is Philo, known to him through the Armenian version of his works. Ełishē never mentions Philo by name (neither does Moses Khorenatsʻi, who is also indebted to the Armenian texts of Philo),[74] but he does introduce a quotation from the *In Exodum* with the phrase, "as some of the eminent historians [pl.] said." From the *In Genesin* Ełishē has taken a reference to those who, not seeing the great king, offered obeisance to his nobles. The *De Providentia* provides an elaborate passage about a doctor who is in no way distracted by the pomp and show when he attends a royal invalid. And from the *De Vita Contemplativa* Ełishē has taken the simile of grasshoppers who live merely by breathing the air.[75] But it is to the *De Jona* that Ełishē is most

69. P. 180.
70. P. 189.
71. P. 29.
72. Pp. 14, 33.
73. P. 14.
74. See Thomson, *Moses Khorenatsʻi*, pp. 31–32.
75. Pp. 4, 166, 172, 202.

indebted: from it he has taken descriptions of the physical universe and the celestial globe of the sun, and also the image of the charioteer. This last was made famous by Plato, but Eḷishē's phrasing is closer to the passages in Philo.[76]

Unfortunately, however, it is not possible to use the evidence of Philo's influence via the Armenian version as an unequivocal proof for dating. The Armenian version of Philo, as that of the Hermetic treatise, belongs to a style of translating commonly known as "Hellenizing." For unlike the rendering of, say, John Chrysostom, the Hellenizing school is characterized by extreme literalness, and more especially by the formation of technical Armenian terms by breaking down Greek compounds, translating the separate parts, and then recombining the Armenian.[77] Although most such translations are of technical texts (for example, on philosophy, grammar, rhetoric, and scientific topics) and are plausibly associated with the Armenians studying in Greek universities;[78] and although many of them have been subjected to close scrutiny and a comparative schema has been worked out—that is, a schema of *relative* dating—the absolute dating of these translations is not generally agreed upon. So those who accept Eḷishē as an author of the fifth century perforce move back the beginning of "Hellenizing" translations to the fifth century. Such arguments, in fact, merely emphasize how little agreement there is about the dating of early Armenian texts. Indeed, in Eḷishē's *History* itself there are numerous examples of such "Hellenizing" vocabulary.[79] Thus the dating of this work will have to be decided on other grounds. But here two important critical studies of Eḷishē need brief review before any general conclusions can be offered.

The most comprehensive critical study of Eḷishē produced in the nineteenth century is that by Babgēn Kiwlēsērean. Written in 1896 but not published until 1909,[80] it brings together many of the problems raised by earlier scholars. In the first place Kiwlēsērean notes that explicit references to Eḷishē are not found before Thomas Artsruni (writing ca.900). The seventh-century Sebēos speaks of what had been written "by

76. Pp. 15, 166, 167.
77. For general studies of this "school" see Manandean, *Yunaban dprots'ē;* Muradyan, *Hunaban dprots'ē.*
78. See the Introduction to Lewy, *De Jona.*
79. See Akinean, *Eḷishē,* III, 348–349.
80. B. Kiwlēsērean, *Eḷishē, k'nnakan usumnasirut'iwn* (Vienna, 1909).

others." [81] But since he does not mention Łazar either, this does not mean that Ełishē's *History* was not in existence by his time. Kiwlēsērean goes on to indicate the spuriousness of most of the details about Ełishē given by later writers. In the pages that follow I have extended this inquiry to cover references to Ełishē and Vardan down to recent times. What is of interest for us is not so much the recognition that these traditions are mostly spurious (Kiwlēsērean faced a more credulous readership than scholars do today). We are here more concerned with the fact that medieval writers developed such legends for their own purposes—the most obvious being the tendentious desire of Thomas Artsruni to glorify his patrons and explain the minor role assigned to their family in Ełishē. However, there is material common to both Thomas and John Catholicos which does not appear in either Ełishē or Łazar, namely, the stories surrounding Shavasp Artsruni; these are attributed by Thomas— but not John—to Abraham the Confessor. So Kiwlēsērean assumes that Abraham did write an account of the war. But since Łazar and Ełishē associate Abraham with the story of the martyrdoms in Iran, there is no guarantee that Thomas is more veracious here in implying that Abraham left an abbreviated account of the revolt, than he is elsewhere when he patently distorts his sources. However, for Kiwlēsērean the overriding consideration in dating Ełishē is that Ełishē has elaborated on Łazar and not vice versa. Therefore the *History of Vardan and the Armenian War* could not have been written before the beginning of the sixth century. Even though the Armenian translation of Philo used by Ełishē is generally attributed to the end of that century, Kiwlēsērean does not consider this date so certain that Ełishē's *History* has to be placed even later.

Much more radical was the approach of Nerses Akinean, whose study appeared first in articles in *Handes Amsorya* and then in three volumes published in 1932, 1936, and 1960.[82] He saw in Ełishē—or at least in the *History* as it has come down to us—not merely a later version of events as opposed to an eyewitness account, but a reworking of an earlier version itself written after the revolt of the *second* Vardan Mamikonean in 572; according to Akinean, the original version has not sur

81. See below, at n. 92.
82. N. Akinean, *Ełishē vardapet ew iwr Patmut'iwnn Hayots' Paterazmi* (Vienna, 1932, 1936, 1960).

vived. One of the merits of Akinean's study is that he drew attention to the discrepancies between Ełishē's version of events and other non-Armenian sources. Thus the image of Yazkert in Ełishē is different from that in Łazar; it is also different from the picture in later Syrian and Arabic sources. These differences Akinean does not explain as one facet of Ełishē's purpose. Rather he looks into later Iranian history in order to find a person who fits the picture, and concludes that Khosrov I Anushirvan was the original for Ełishē's characterization. Basing his deductions on parallels that he finds in sixth-century history, Akinean concludes that the original (lost) work of Ełishē was written in the Armenian colony in Constantinople after 572 and was an account of *that* revolt, its author having been an eyewitness of the events in which the second Vardan Mamikonean played the major role. The Ełishē who is the author of the text as we have it now Akinean identifies with the author of various homilies dated to the seventh century. This revised *History of Vardan*, which dates to around 640, was an attempt to move back the account of Vardan II to the time of Vardan I.[83]

Although these arguments have the advantage of fitting all the traditions about Ełishē and the later confusions of the two Vardans into one (not so simple) scheme, they have the disadvantage that the literary coherence of the *History* is entirely lost. Akinean's premises are twofold: the descriptions are to be taken almost literally, so individuals and events of the sixth century must be found with which they can be matched; and the surviving text of Ełishē can be separated into two recensions, an original text and a revised edition. On this second score, Akinean's arguments seem whimsical and arbitrary to the present writer, who is unconvinced by the effort to see two quite separate hands at work. But since this argument really depends on the first, the prime question remains: Did "Ełishē" base his picture of Yazkert and the events of 450/1 on a variety of later persons and events, or did he deliberately strive to cast the Armenian war in a mold of his own choosing?

In the commentary to the translation below I have tried to show that Ełishē's imagery, although often evincing general biblical and hagiographical parallels, does have one particular model—the Maccabees. This in no way implies lack of creativity or originality. Quite the reverse. For Ełishē's *History* is not sim-

83. The two Vardans were not always carefully distinguished; see below.

ply a record of events as remembered by an eyewitness. This claim to *literal* veracity obscures the underlying purpose of the book, which is to offer an *interpretation* of the events described. The war is not to be explained as caused by personal rancor, as Łazar explained it, but on more general grounds. It illustrates difficulties faced by Armenians not merely in 450/1 but perennially, and these difficulties are basically of a religious nature. The main problem is the preservation of Armenian traditions (*awrēnkʿ*), which include religious practices but are more comprehensive than the term "religion" in a modern sense. For Ełishē, in the long run it is better to die than to compromise these traditions; to defend them and die for them is an act of spiritual virtue. In recent times it has become fashionable to describe Vardan as a nationalist; but, as we shall see, such a term is misleading, since Ełishē is not concerned with territorial autonomy. For Ełishē, Vardan's patriotism is directed toward a way of life in which one's political allegiance may indeed be given to a foreigner and a non-Christian, but in which one's personal moral (Christian) integrity cannot be compromised.

So the Armenian position was not one of preserving a separate, independent, sovereign state; nor was it one of a purely personal quest for salvation, such as the goal of the early Christian martyrs. The Armenian dilemma lay between these extremes. Ełishē saw many parallels with the position of the Jews vis-à-vis the Seleucid kings of Antioch as described in the books of the Maccabees, though, of course, the political circumstances were quite different. Ełishē does not entirely hide his knowledge of the Maccabees, but he does conceal the extent to which he was indebted to the Armenian version. For his purpose was not just to borrow a few expressive phrases in order to embellish his own story—as, for example, many Armenian historians did in their descriptions of battles.[84] Rather, he wanted to recreate the kind of situation in which the play of basic issues between the antagonists would become clear in general terms. So Ełishē's *History* takes a *specific* occasion—the revolt of 450/1 and its aftermath—and describes it in terms reminiscent of the Maccabees so that the general problems will emerge more clearly.

Thus because Ełishē's *History* gives us an interpretation—in which the speeches, letters, and edicts play an effective literary role and are not to be taken as verbatim reports—it has had

---

84. See above, n. 25.

a continuing appeal. Later generations down to the present can interpret the specific ebb and flow of the current situation in the same general terms as Ełishē. To put it more accurately, the general interpretation offered by Ełishē can be used by others and adapted to very different political, military, or social conditions. Hence the shifting "image" of Vardan through the centuries down to 1980. This "image" forms the subject of the second part of the introduction. And there is no reason to suppose that in the coming millennium Ełishē's *History* will not continue to be interpreted as circumstances require.

But how does this affect the more specific question of the dating of the text known as the *History of Vardan and the Armenian War,* attributed to a certain "Ełishē"? In the first place, does it predate Łazar's *History* or is it later? In recent years that problem has become more complicated than it was for Kiwlēsērean, for we now know that the text of Łazar as it has come down to us in the manuscripts and printed editions is a later embellishment of the original. Fragments of an earlier version have been discovered indicating that the text of Łazar known in the tenth century was very different.[85] However, the differences are more literary than substantive in a historical sense. So although we cannot rely on any specific detail in the text as going back to the original, there seems no reason to doubt that the basic story has not been greatly changed.

The main differences between Ełishē and Łazar have already been noted. Are there any clues as to who might be following whom? Other than the dubious comment of Thomas about Abraham, there is no suggestion that there existed another source for information about the revolt of Vardan outside the Histories of Łazar and Ełishē; and since there are numerous exact verbal correspondences between them, especially in long lists of names, it is indubitable that one of them knew the other. However, neither mentions the other—though this is not surprising, given the unwillingness of most early Armenian historians to name their sources.

Although Ełishē's account is the longer, this does not of itself indicate that the expansions are later, especially since Łazar has numerous episodes and details passed over by Ełishē. The most substantive difference between them is in their explanation of the occasion for the revolt. Łazar offers a specific,

85. See Dowsett, "The Newly Discovered Fragment," and Sanspeur, "Le fragment."

personal grudge as the catalyst for the potentially explosive situation. He is also more understanding of the difficult position in which Vasak found himself as governor of Armenia for the shah, especially since his sons were hostages at court, though he does not obscure Vasak's role as traitor. Both historians in fact use him as a foil for the patriotism of Vardan. If Ełishē was really an eyewitness and Łazar, writing in the next generation and well within living memory of the events, used Ełishē's *History*, it is indeed surprising that he did not put the persecution by Yazkert into larger perspective, for he thought of it as a sudden decision. It is Ełishē who has the broader view; as is clear from his rhetorical speeches and letters, he is more concerned with the general issues than is Łazar.

But not only is the *History* of Ełishē more easily understood as an expansive adaptation of Łazar than the latter's work as an abbreviation of Ełishē; the influence of translations from the "Hellenizing" period on Ełishē is explained by that order without doing violence to our knowledge of such translations and their probable sixth-century date. Although the present writer is unconvinced by Akinean's theories that the original version of this *History* described the revolt of 572 and that it was rewritten in the seventh century, he does agree with Akinean and Kiwlēsērean that Ełishē wrote after Łazar. There is no compelling reason to accept the "eyewitness" claim, and the literary aspects of the work are far more easily explicable if it is dated to the sixth century. The fact that Armenian tradition— but not until *after A.D. 1000*—places Łazar after Ełishē is of no relevance. That listing is natural enough, since Łazar describes events that occurred after the period described by Ełishē. Yet, as Stephen of Taron places Faustos Buzand after both of them, the order is fairly arbitrary.[86]

One final argument which would place Ełishē's *History* in the last decade of the sixth century or later needs to be reviewed: the parallels between this *History* and the *Ecclessiastical History* of John of Ephesus, which extends to 585. Only the last part of John's *History* has survived, in a Syriac version; but in that third book John has much to say about Armenia in the time of Shah Khosrov Anushirvan (531–579).

Ełishē claims that the Persian magi encouraged the shah in his attack on Christianity by arguing that his empire would be that much stronger if all his subjects professed the same reli-

---

86. Stephen, I, 1.

gion.[87] A similar argument is found in John of Ephesus: at II, 19 he says that he had heard from the Armenian Catholicos and bishops who had taken refuge in Constantinople in 572 an account of the Persian persecution in Armenia. According to the Armenians, the magi had told Khosrov Anushirvan that just as the Roman emperor imposed the same religion on his subjects, so should the shah in his empire. Naturally, the Armenian bishops had not been present at this audience; the speech is therefore an Armenian interpretation of motivation for persecution. It is certainly no argument for Ełishē's writing after reading John, since such a general motivation for persecution could apply to any period of Sasanian history, or be equally relevant for earlier persecutions of Christians in the Roman Empire itself. Indeed, the Armenian report to John in Constantinople could as well have been colored by their previous reading of Ełishē.

John then goes on to describe the Armenian attitude of political obedience coupled with adherence to Christianity. Here there is a parallel with the ending of the reply to Mihrnerseh's letter as given in Ełishē, where the Armenians declare themselves servants of the shah in all worldly matters but refuse to deny the only true God.[88] Similar arguments may be found in John II, 19, which describes the prelude to the revolt of 571. But the phrasing is of such a common nature, that dependence of Ełishē on John for this hagiographical topos is hardly demonstrable.

More interesting is the fact that in Ełishē the attitude of Yazkert to Christianity is ambiguous. In the first chapter he rages when the Christian faith is expounded; at the beginning of the second chapter he reviews all doctrines with a view to choosing the best; in chapter three he states that Christianity is on a par with the Mazdaean religion and claims that his father had found the Christian religion to be the most sublime of all.[89] These last two episodes are quite at variance with the general image of Yazkert as the cause of persecution. Such tolerance and praise for Christianity are only attested to in later shahs, as noted by Sebēos.[90] More especially, the description of the examination of scripture by the shah, his praise for Christianity, and his kind treatment of the Christian community have close

87. P. 9.
88. P. 40.
89. P. 83.
90. P. 149.

parallels with the description of Khosrov in John of Ephesus.

But close as those parallels are, they are not *verbally* identical. So it is unlikely that Ełishē was using John as a direct source. On the other hand, unless Ełishē had been familiar with this tolerance of Kawat (488–531) and his successor Khosrov in the sixth century, as reflected in Sebēos and John of Ephesus, it is difficult to imagine that he would introduce such themes, especially as they are unknown to Łazar. It seems, therefore, most unlikely that Ełishē's *History* can predate the sixth century.

Some stress has been placed on Ełishē's work as an interpretive history. It is because of that particular outlook on a revolt that went unnoticed outside Armenia that Ełishē has continued to be read and to exert an influence on later Armenian literature, art, and thought. And conversely, because in modern times Vardan plays such an important role in the Armenian national consciousness, the claim of his historian to have been an eyewitness is the more zealously upheld. It does not seem to the present writer that Ełishē's literary genius and the intrinsic value of his *History* are in any way diminished by the general considerations noted above. But be that as it may, the later influence of Ełishē and, more particularly, the interpretation of the "image" of Vardan in Armenian tradition are important enough to deserve further discussion.

After Łazar and Ełishē, the first Armenian historian to describe the war of Vardan is Sebēos. The *History of Bishop Sebēos on Heraclius,* as the Armenian text is commonly known—though without any early manuscript authority—poses certain problems in that several sections irrelevant to the main theme have been added at the beginning. Furthermore, there is some doubt whether the book is in fact identical with the *History* attributed to Sebēos in Armenian literary tradition. But for our immediate purpose it is sufficient that the text is in all probability a product of the seventh century.[91]

The Prologue to the *History* proper begins with a reference to the Iranian effort to abolish Christianity in Armenia after the Armenian monarchy had been abolished. The second paragraph reads as follows:

91. See the general introduction to Abgaryan's edition of Sebēos, which revises some of the opinions expressed in his *Sebeosi Patmut'yunĕ* of 1965.

Then the period of the reign of the evil-working Yazkert. How he wished to destroy the divine institutions. How the valiant Armenian nobles and the chief of the Mamikonean house, zealous for God, the Vardan called *Karmir* ["red"], united with their armed and lance-bearing companions and their troops, prepared and armed themselves for battle. They took in their hands the shield of faith, and put on the breastplate of strength—zeal for the divine word. You might say that before their very eyes they could see their crown sent from above. Therefore they despised death, thinking it better to die on the divine highway. How the Persian army attacked them in violent force; and how in their resistance they attained their martyrdom. How the holy martyrs of Christ were seized by the heathens and were martyred in Apr Shahr near the city of Niwshapuh in the place called T'eark'uni. All this has been written down by others.[92]

Although Sebēos refers to the accounts of "others" in the plural, he never mentions either Ełishē or Łazar by name. However, here he is following the former, for the passage describing Vardan's lance-bearing companions taking the shield of faith and the breastplate of strength is based on Ełishē, p. 112. But Sebēos has used the term *Apr Shah* rather than the Armenian *Apar ashkharh* of the earlier writers, and identifies the site of the martyrdoms near Niwshapuh as T'eark'uni, which is unknown to Ełishē or Łazar. The most interesting innovation is the epithet *karmir* ("red") applied to Vardan. Its significance is not explained, but it is picked up in modern Armenian literature.

In the next chapter of his *History,* Sebēos passes rapidly over the period from the revolt of Vardan to the second major revolt against Iranian oppression led by another Vardan Mamikonean in 572. On this occasion the Armenians attacked the Persian *marzpan* (governor) Surēn in Dvin and killed him. But the rebels were soon forced to withdraw. Vardan, accompanied by the Catholicos John II and numerous bishops and nobles, took refuge in Constantinople. There followed an attempt at enforced reunion of the Armenian and Byzantine churches, which had no lasting effect and was rejected by the majority of

92. Pp. 64–65 in Abgaryan's edition.

Armenians in Armenia.[93] But from the point of view of later Armenian knowledge of Vardan, it is important to note that the two separate revolts of 451 and 572, in both of which a Vardan Mamikonean played the leading military role, were sometimes confused. So before plunging into those confusions, it may be helpful to given Sebēos' version of the second revolt:

In the forty-first year of the reign of Khosrov, son of Kawat, Vardan revolted and ceased being subject to the rule of the Persians in concert with all the Armenians. Killing the marzpan Surēn unexpectedly in the city of Dvin, they took much booty and went to the Greek empire . . .

The emperor of the Greeks made a promise to the Armenians; he confirmed the same pact which the two kings, the blessed Trdat and Constantine, had made between them, and he gave them imperial troops in support. Taking this army, they attacked the city of Dvin, besieged it, and completely destroyed it, expelling the Persian army that was in it.

But suddenly there fell on them a great tumult. For they [the Greeks?] had set on fire and burned the church of Saint Gregory, which had been built near the city and which the Persians had made into a storehouse. Therefore they incurred a great tumult.

Then Mihran Mihrevandak attacked him [Vardan] with an army of twenty thousand and many elephants. A great battle took place on the plain of Khaḷamikh; they inflicted terrible losses on the Persian army, smote them with the sword, and seized all the elephants. Mihran escaped with a few [Persians] and they went to their own country.

This is the Vardan whom the Persian king called Anushirvan Khosrov attacked in person with a huge armed host and many elephants. Marching through the province of Artaz, he went through Bagrevand, passed the city of Karin, and continuing on his way he came to Melitene and camped opposite him.

In the early morning they rapidly disposed their forces and lines, and attacked each other in battle. The battle

93. On these events see Garitte, *Narratio*, pp. 175-225.

raged over the face of the land and waxed ferocious. But the Lord delivered the Persian king and all his troops to defeat. They were crushed before their enemies by the sword, and fled before them in great confusion. Not knowing the course of the flight, they came to the great river called Euphrates and threw themselves in. But the water rose and swept away the multitude of fleeing [soldiers] like a host of locusts. On that day few managed to slip away. But the king escaped by a hair's breath with a few [Persians], taking refuge with his elephants and cavalry. Fleeing through Aḷdznikʻ, he returned to his own country.

They captured the whole camp with the royal treasures. They seized the queen and her entourage, and took the tent and the precious golden litter which was adorned with precious stones and pearls that is called by them "the glorious litter." Also captured was the fire which the king always took around with him in his support; it was more highly honored than all other fires and called by them *Atʻash*. It was cast into the river with the *Movpetan Movpet* and numerous other magnates. Blessed is God always.[94]

At the beginning of the tenth century an entirely different story appears in which the Artsruni family plays a significant role. According to the historian of this family, Thomas Artsruni, not only did the ancestors of his patrons take a more prominent part in the battle of Avarayr than is mentioned by Ḷazar or Eḷishē, he also provides a reason for the "distorted" form of the story in Eḷishē. Furthermore, Thomas claims that another Artsruni, Shavasp, collaborated with the Persians in the suppression of Christianity for reasons of personal ambition; and in this story, Dvin plays a role. Thomas writes as follows (II, 1):

After the extinction of the Armenian monarchy from the house of the Arsacids, then Persian *marzpans* ruled the country. The princes of Greater Armenia fortified themselves in strong fortress-like caves in various places and regions, while the Persian tyranny waxed stronger and bands of tax-gatherers made forays with terrible cruelties.

At that time Shavasp Artsruni, brother of Aḷan

94. Pp. 67–69.

Artsruni's father Vasak, developed the idea of ruling over Armenia. In accordance with this foolish plan he went to the Persian king Peroz, accepted by self-induced error the mad, ash-worshiping Mazdaean religion, and asked the king for the principality of Armenia. [Peroz] fulfilled the request of his stupid vainglorious desire. Then he returned to Armenia, bringing with him as *marzpan* Vndoy, a Persian chief-magus. When they entered the country they disturbed the covenant of Christianity. Zealously they set their hands to ravaging and razing churches, destroying houses of prayer, overthrowing altars [devoted to] the sacrament that works salvation, completely demolishing the font of the glorious illumination of the Holy Spirit, bitterly and cruelly torturing the priests, ministers of the new covenants, and casting men and women into prison and torture in their onerous demands for taxes. Their purpose in this was to be able all the more easily to subvert [the Armenians] to renounce and abandon the holy faith of the pure Christian religion. Many more there were who with heroic endurance were martyred than who wavered, regarding as naught the seizure of their goods and possessions and cruel death. When the impious Shavasp Artsruni reached Artashat with the *marzpan,* they built at the city gate a temple to Ormizd and lit therein the fire of their erring worship. So the country was in great and dangerous distress.

This bitter news reached the great Vardan Mamikonean who fortified himself in [the castle] Jṙayl in the Taurus. Unable to endure such perilous hardships as had been inflicted, and roaring in his soul like an enraged wild beast over the destruction of the holy faith and the ruin of Armenia, he hastily sent a letter of entreaty to Tachat, lord of the Ṙshtunik', and Vahrich, lord of the Andzavats'ik', to inform them of what had happened. Immediately, without delay, they joined the great Vardan with their forces, bringing with them the troops from the mountains, no more than twelve hundred men; and with unexpected rapidity they suddenly attacked Shavasp and the *marzpan* Vndoy. As they were encamped at the junction of the Eraskh and Metsamawr, Shavasp Artsruni advanced against them. But on him fell the valiant Vardan, roaring like a lion or lion cub. Drawing his one-edged sword with force and rapidity, he sliced Shavasp in two.

33

But Tachat and Vakhrich, having surrounded the *marzpan* and his son Shiroy, captured them and brought them to Dvin. In the temple of Ormizd they had [the *marzpan*] consumed by his god in the flames of the blazing fire of the pyraeum; above the pyraeum they hung Shiroy on a gibbet. The garrison they drowned in the river or put to the sword, while the fugitives they pursued beyond the city of Nakhchavan; then they returned victoriously. They demolished the temple, and razing the site to the ground built with the same stones the great church of Saint Gregory in the place called Blur. There they transferred the Catholicos of Armenia, Giut. The Armenian nobles each built royal palaces for themselves and splendid estates; the city they defended with an encircling wall, and they brought peace to the land. The royal residence of Trdat they entrusted to Vahan Artsruni, for him to build a mansion [fit] for kings—acts in preparation since they planned to make him king over Armenia, as he was a spirited and powerful man, shrewd and wise, humble, liberal, and quick-witted. But after the Armenian nobles became disunited, they abandoned their plans for making Vahan king and went over to Vardan the Great. Following the nobles, Vahan too went [among the] first to Vardan to be given the governorship of Armenia. And they obeyed him all the days of Vardan.

But the Persian king went away to wage war against the Kushans at the Chor Pass, so the land of Armenia was free from Persian raids. The king was killed there by the Kushans, and Yazkert ruled in his stead. He began to assail the nobles of Greater Armenia most severely, as the records of previous historians indicate: the ravaging of Armenia, the multiplication of oppression, the numberless multitude of martyrs who died heroically for Christ, and the brave valor of the holy priests, the good fight they fought there in the great desert of Apar, and all the rest. I consider it superfluous to repeat what has already been described.

When the great battle took place between Saint Vardan and Mshkan and the Persian army on the plain of Avarayr in the province of Artaz, emboldened by God the Armenian troops, like holy and divine warriors, were martyred in Christ. There Vahan Artsruni, with splendid and outstanding bravery, fought side by side with Saint

Vardan, like a fire passing through reeds among the valiant Persian champions.

When the two sides had joined battle and the left wing of the Armenians began to be overcome, Saint Vardan, spurring his horse, turned the Persian champions to flight and strengthened the troops of his own division. Then Vahan Artsruni intervened; he turned the Persian forces opposing Vardan. Rapidly, a large number of Persian soldiers were struck down one by one, about 140 men. Raising his eyes, Saint Vardan saw the impious Vasak, lord of Siunik'. Rushing after him they attacked the strongly-armed battalion among the elephants. The valiant Vahan Artsruni supported [Vardan], and together they died— the valiant and elect noble warriors Vardan and Vahan. Gaining the name of martyrs, 696 men of the holy Armenian army were perfected in Christ. and this is narrated in the abbreviated account of Abraham the confessor.

But why the story of Vahan's martyrdom is not related in the book of the historian I shall indicate to your erudite intelligence accurately and without uncertainty.

The reference to Abraham is to the eyewitness of the martyrdoms in Persia.[95] The "historian" is Ełishē, which brings us to the second chapter of Thomas, Book II:

In the time of Peroz, king of kings, there was a certain Barsauma of the sect of Nestorius, who had the title of bishop and most forcefully pursued the Nestorian heresy. Slandering the Armenian nobles to Peroz, he worked many bloody crimes.

At that time the chair of Saint Gregory was proudly and splendidly held by Lord Christopher, Catholicos of Armenia. He wrote to the regions of Asorestan warning them not to associate with the Nestorians, and wrote in similar terms also to the congregation of the orthodox in Khuzastan. Furthermore, he wrote to the district of Derjan and the inhabitants, sovereign lords, and bishops of the valley of Khaltik'. Barsauma seized these letters by deceitful means and had them taken to King Peroz, saying: "All that the Catholicos of Armenia writes, proposes revolt against you and encourages the Armenian princes

95. Ełishē, pp. 187ff.; Łazar, p. 106.

to submit to the Greek emperor. So you must look to this matter." Vindicating himself, Barsauma came to Arznarziwn and the land of Mokkʻ in order to sow there the seeds of the Nestorian heresy. Our holy teacher Eḷishē at that time was dwelling in the land of Mokkʻ. Barsauma came to him asking for the book of Armenian history which he had written at the command of Saint Vardan, and he fulfilled his request. At that time the great prince of the Artsrunikʻ, Mershapuh, who was then fortified in the castle of Tmorikʻ, hearing about him [Barsauma] sent word that he was to leave that territory. He did not lay hands on him because of the Persian king, but merely sent messages with a warning threat. Angered at the ultimatum, [Barsauma] took vengeance in his resentful rage. He expunged from the history book all details concerning the deeds of the house of the Artsrunikʻ and everything describing the martyrdom of Vahan Artsruni.

Now the teacher Eḷishē was at that time dwelling in the province of Ṙshtunikʻ by the shore of the lake; at that spot the holy man of God, Eḷishē, fell asleep in Christ. So when the book was returned to the land of Mokkʻ, no one paid any heed to the matter, assuming that the teacher had composed it in that fashion. Elsewhere I shall indicate what action the Persian king took against the house of the Artsrunikʻ at the instigation of the impious Barsauma.

Having explained the omission from Eḷishē of the heroic exploits of his patron's ancestors—but omitting to reconcile his version with the account in Ḷazar—Thomas then adapts the story of Greek pressure on Vardan II to accept communion with the church of Constantinople (as found in Sebēos) to the situation of the Artsruni princes in the previous century. Book II, ch. 2, continues:

The emperor Marcian ruled the Greek empire after Theodosius II. He convened the Council at Chalcedon of 634 bishops, and in his reign Saint Vardan and Vahan Artsruni were martyred.

Now Vasak Artsruni, father of the saintly Aḷan, taking Tachat and his brother Goter, went to the emperor to avoid the troubles of the Persian disturbances and the ruin of the country. The emperor Marcian received them in a friendly and peaceful fashion, and promoted them to rank and honor with splendid dignities, since like brave

champions for Christ's churches and the holy orthodox
faith they had heroically shed blood and gained in addition the renown of confessors. But the emperor begged
these honorable men, Vasak, Tachat, and Goger [*sic*], who
were of the great nobility of the Artsruni house, to accept
the council with the [other] three holy councils. They replied: "Since we were continuously preoccupied with Persian raids we were deprived of the study of the holy scriptures in the choice of an authoritative confession of faith.
While we were in our own country, our leaders did not
allow us to accept those formulations in the definition of
faith. So we cannot agree immediately to flatter and
please your majesty as your imperial dignity demands.
But allow us to write to Armenia, to ask the Armenian
primates, and to receive replies."

This reproof they also put to the emperor: "When you
convoked the council, why did you not think it necessary
to summon anyone from Armenia for the sake of the unity
of faith?"

Marcian responded: "Because the Armenian leaders
were endangered by the Persian troubles." Then our
Artsruni magnates received permission to write to Abraham, bishop of the Mamikonean, who was a disciple of
Saint Sahak, and they informed him of the emperor's request. In response he told them not to yield or obey the emperor, and if any danger befell them to endure it just as
they had endured [past ones]. They took the letter and
laid it before the emperor. Then he, realizing that their
minds were firm and inflexible, did not trouble them but
left them to their own wishes, to live as might please them.
Staying there until the time of the emperor Leo I, Vasak
and Tachat died there and were splendidly laid to rest in
the cemetery of the Greek magnates.

This is not the place to enter into a discussion of Thomas
Artsruni's elaborations and adaptations of Armenian history
for the greater glory of his patron's ancestors. We may simply
note here that the story of the pressure put on Armenians to
conform to the Greek church is a reflection of events that occurred after the arrival in Constantinople of the second Vardan
Mamikonean. And the story of the letter to the Armenians in
Constantinople urging them to hold fast to the true faith is a
doublet of the story concerning the Catholicos John II, who

went to Constantinople in 572 and died there two years later.[96]
But Thomas's distortions cannot be attributed to ignorance.
Not only does he mention Ełishē by name, he borrows exten-
sively from Ełishē's imagery for his description of Muslim emirs
and Muslim depredations in Armenia.[97]

The coupling of Vardan with the story of Shavasp,
Vndoy, and Sheroy and events in Dvin is found also in John
Catholicos, writing at the beginning of the tenth century. Un-
like his younger contemporary Thomas, John does not mention
Ełishē by name, although he too has borrowed imagery from
the *History of Vardan*.[98] His account of the revolt led by Vardan
Mamikonean runs as follows:

> [After the abolition of the Arsacid monarchy in Ar-
> menia and the extinction of the line of Saint Gregory in
> the patriarchate] . . . each man acted as he pleased, peace
> was shaken, and good order tarnished.
>
> Then some of our nobles, deceived by the evil one, de-
> nied the Christian faith and subjected themselves to a
> heathen religion. Indeed, two of the greatest among them,
> Shavasp Artsruni and Vndoy from the city of Dvin, or-
> dered the temple of Ormizd and the house of fire-worship
> to be built. As chief pagan priest, Vndoy appointed his
> own son Sheroy, and he established laws from the Persian
> code, many terrible customs of evil deeds, full of obfuscat-
> ing and obscure foul teaching. Then, when the valiant
> Vardan, grandson of Sahak the Great, heard that the
> good order of the church had been extinguished and the
> yearly festivals had been neglected, he immediately gath-
> ered an army and attacking resolutely, fell like a thunder-
> bolt on the impious Shavasp and slew him with the sword.
> The *marzpan* Mshkan he put to flight, and capturing the
> foul Vndoy he put to the torch the fire-temple which he
> had built in Dvin and hung on the gibbet his son Sheroy
> on its altar. On the site of the altar he built a great church
> named after Saint Gregory and transferred there the see of
> the patriarchate, establishing therein the great patriarch

96. See Garsoian, "Le rôle," p. 136, for the letter sent to John.
97. These borrowings from Ełishē will be presented in detail in a
forthcoming study of mine.
98. See the notes to pp. 227, 256, of the 1912 edition of John Catholicos.

Giut. For the holy patriarch Yoseph had been carried off prisoner to the mines with the holy Levondians; and although he was still alive, yet the Armenian nobles did not consider it right to leave Christ's flock without a shepherd lest they be routed by the heathen wolves. Or else this was arranged by the command of Saint Yoseph himself. And thus he restored the fine order of the holy church. From then on the Armenians obeyed the leadership of the valiant Vardan until the day of his death. He waged many brave battles for the sake of his faith in Christ, and with many other companions was found worthy to receive the unfading crown [of martyrdom] from the immortal king, Christ.

After this the martyrdom of the holy Catholicos Yoseph took place, after he had held the throne of the patriarchate for eight years. With him the other bishops and priests who were companions of Levond and their deacons [were martyred] in Persia by the impious Peroz; they placed on their heads the crown of the martyrdom adorned by the all-holy hands of God.[99]

Unlike Thomas, who passes over the revolt of 572, John Catholicos mentions briefly the second Vardan Mamikonean, the death of the *marzpan* Suren in Dvin, and Vardan's withdrawal to Greek territory—all in words taken from Sebēos.[100]

Naturally, it was the second revolt, which culminated in an attempt at reunion of the churches, that is remembered in pro-Chalcedonian sources. Thus the Greek *Narratio de rebus Armeniae,* which is a translation of a lost Armenian text, refers to Vardan and the murder of Suren.[101] But it has no mention of the earlier Vardan or the revolt of 450/1 for that had no repercussions outside Armenia and was not of interest to a Chalcedonian reader.

The *History* of Stephen of Taron (Asołik), written soon after the year 1000, has no reference to the exploits of Shavasp Artsruni or Vndoy. Stephen distinguishes the revolts of 450/1 and 572, and gives a brief account of the former with an explicit reference to the *History* of Ełishē (Book II, ch. 2):

99. Pp. 58–60.
100. John, pp. 63–64; Sebēos, p. 67.
101. *Narratio,* §77.

After the death of Artashir, king of Armenia, the Armenian nobles assembled and appointed Saint Vardan as their *sparapet;* he was from the family of the Mamikonean, grandson of Saint Sahak. Sometimes they were subject to the Persian kings and sometimes in rebellion, as the *History* of Eḷishē *vardapet* teaches.

After the death of Surmak the Armenian patriarchs [*sic*] assembled; after a search they found a certain priest called Yoseph, who had been a pupil of the great Mesrop, from the province of Vayots' dzor and the village of Holotsim. At the command of Vardan they appointed him to the throne of the Catholicosate, [which he held] for two years. He held a synod in Shahapivan where they established canon laws with penalties. Now Saint Vardan held the Armenian nobles together for nineteen years; having waged war with Yazkert, king of Persia, he was killed for the holy covenant and the Christian faith on the field of Avarayr, in the province of Artaz.

Following the war of Vardan, two years later the holy Levondians with the patriarch Yoseph were martyred in the month of Hrotits', on the sixteenth day of the month, that is, July; on a Sunday. Having investigated this, we found that it occurred in the fifteenth year of Yazkert and the third of Marcian the Accursed.

After the death of Vardan the land of Armenia was in anarchy for ten years; persecutions and tumults multiplied, though Yazkert abated a little from his destructive intentions, threw the [blame for the] damage on the apostate Vasak, and ordered him to be dismissed in great dishonor. Then, when his son Peroz came to the throne, he released the Armenian nobles from their bonds.

The reference to the Council of Shahapivan poses a problem, in that other Armenian sources place it in the sixth year of Yazkert (i.e., in 444) and not in the brief span of Yoseph's patriarchate. But it is noteworthy that the eighth-century preamble to the canons of this council carries a reference to Vardan:[102]

[After the death of Mesrop the good order of the church was disrupted.]

102. *Kanonagirk',* I, 426.

Especially because at that time authority and leadership were no longer in the hands of the Mamikoneans, for they were cowed and reduced and subject to the proud Persian kingdom. Although they were oppressed, they roared and bellowed like young lions, Vardan Mamikonean and his relatives, with his brothers. Yet they remained as it were confined to their den; so they looked for help from above, since the malicious race of Persians was suspicious and fearful and did not give authority into their hands.[103]

More immediately interesting for our study of Ełishē, however, is the fact that Stephen of Taron is the first to place him in a chronological list of Armenian historians. In the first chapter of the first book of his *History*, Stephen lists his predecessors:

First and foremost the valiant Agathangelos, the historian of the amazing wonders and torments of Saint Gregory and of our coming to know God; then the great Moses [Khorenats'i], the equal of Eusebius, who is called the father of the rhetors (*k'ert'ol*); then Ełishē *vardapet*, who [wrote] about the Vardanank' and the tortures and martyrdom of the holy priests; then the history of the eloquent Łazar P'arpets'i . . .

The importance of this passage is that, by putting Ełishē after Moses, Stephen introduces us indirectly to the legends surrounding the date and personality of that most elusive of all Armenian historical writers. It is irrelevant here to reopen the debate concerning Moses and his date.[104] It is sufficient to note the late (undated) preface to the *Elegy on the Cross* that is attributed to the philosoher David "the Invincible," himself a figure of mystery and legend.[105] This preface claims (1) that David was a pupil of Sahak and Mesrop; (2) that he traveled widely, to places including Alexandria and Athens, in order to study philosophy and rhetoric and to make translations; and (3) that David was accompanied by Moses' brother Mambrē, by Mushē and Ełishē, Eznak (Eznik), and Ardzak Artsruni and Ałan.

---

103. A more elaborate story appears in some manuscripts; see ibid., p. 629. That is the version printed in Alishan, *Hayapatum*, pp. 159–160.

104. See above n. 64.

105. Text in David, *Matenagrut'iwnk'*, pp. 5–6.

For later Armenian historians, therefore, Ełishē becomes more clearly defined as a member of that group of pupils of Mashtots and Sahak who founded Armenian literature—a group first described by Korium, who wrote a biography of Mashtots, which was enlarged with the passage of time to include most of the great writers whose personal lives were unknown: Moses, David, and Ełishē.[106]

A closer connection between Ełishē and Vardan than that hinted by Thomas[107] is claimed in a brief life of undetermined date, which like most hagiographical documents lays especial emphasis on its hero's pious death. It is worth quoting here in full:

History of Saint Ełishē Vardapet

It is related of the blessed Ełishē *vardapet* that he was a soldier of Saint Vardan's and served him. He was faithful in all things divine and human, and lived and was brought up in piety and love of study. [He wrote about] the perils of all the events inflicted on Armenia by the Persians in those times, being well informed about the battles and victories, and persecutions of the church, and the virtue and valor of Saint Vardan and those who, united with him, were martyred for faith in Christ and were crowned, despising the Zoroastrian error of magism; and also the admonitions of the bishops and the confrontations, and martyrdoms, and struggles of the priests and of all the saints who fought and defeated the tyrant who had waxed haughty over all the holy churches. All this he described, and the words and deeds that accompanied them—which account of the blessed Ełishē one can learn from the history of the holy Vardanankʿ. He also composed canonical and exhortatory works for the holy church, and especially in his just conduct was pleasing to God and men.

After this he took up a monastic life and strict austerity, being diligent in fasting and prayer. He hastened to the desert as from the waves of the sea to a harbor, abandoning earthly things and pursuing heavenly things. He resolved to imitate the life and character of the first fathers and be zealous for their way of life. He strove to enter

---

106. This is enshrined in the Synaxarion under Hori 8 (September 17).

107. Thomas, II, 2.

through the narrow gate which leads to eternal life. Demonstrating the whole range of virtue, he separated himself from the cenobitic brothers and gained solitude, making his dwelling in the desert where the Lord of saints pays visit. His daily sustenance was herbs, and he devoted himself to prayer and supplications day and night, attentive to the advice of Paul, who says of the saints: they went about in garments of hide and skins of goat hair, in poverty, suffering, and pain, not valued by this world, wandering in the desert in caves and mountains and holes in the ground. Living such a life, the blessed Ełishē struggled against the temptations of Satan with divine power, and in everything was mighty and victorious. He dwelt in a certain cave, making continual progress. The cave is called "Ełishē's cave" after the name of Saint Ełishē, which is now known to everyone and is a testimony to the blessed one from generation to generation. Shepherds came and found the saint in the open air; and seeing a miraculous sign [worked] by the blessed one, they made the cave and the site famous. But he withdrew, wishing to hide himself, and came to dwell in the province of Ṙshtunikʻ in a certain cave near the shore of the lake, which was also called "the cave of Saint Ełishē". After many austerities and a strict regimen, which he carried out for a long time in the first cave and for a few years in the other, there the blessed one died. Who could describe the man's so numerous virtues with which he fought against the perpetual enemy: prayer, fasting, vigils, tears, living like a bodiless creature in the body, and defeating the demons' attacks with the victorious power of Christ? But now he is hidden with Christ and later will be revealed with him.

Then some men came and found him dead. From the evidence they recognized that he was a servant of Christ's, for it would not be right to hide the manifestation of the saint, which would exhort others as well to the same practices. When the affair became known, much investigation was conducted. Then it was verified and fully revealed that it was the Saint Ełishē who had dwelt in the first cave in the province of Mokkʻ. For him they built a tomb near the cave and transferred him to his place of rest—where many healings were performed.

When the prince of Mokkʻ heard of this, stirred up to a

noble zeal, since the blessed one's death had not taken place in his own land he came to his resting place for the sake of some cure. Lodging there, he exerted himself all night, having the saint as intercessor with God, that perchance he might be made worthy to receive a part of the blessed one's relics. Openly he was unable to approach and take a part of his relics because of the inhabitants of the land and the prince of Ṙshtunikʻ. So he purloined his cure clandestinely, like the woman described in the Gospels. Cutting off the head and hand he fled back to his own land. There was a great outcry about this, but peace prevailed by the grace of Divine Providence. For it pleased God that the saint's first dwelling place should be honored. Bringing the blessed one's relics, he built a martyrium near the cave where his first dwelling place had been, and he multiplied ever more greatly the honor paid to the place in which he had died. At that same spot the grace of Christ's benevolence was manifested through the holy anchorite, and those oppressed by foul demons received healing of each one's affliction. They all blessed God and celebrated as a great festival the day of the blessed one's death, to the glory and praise of the Father, and Son, and Holy Spirit, now and for ever.[108]

A briefer version of this story is found in the *Synaxarion* (Lectionary) of Ter Israel, and was thus current by the beginning of the fourteenth century.[109] But there two important additions are made. First, a precise date is given for Eḷishē's death: February 27—Meheki 21 in the Armenian calendar. Second, not only is Eḷishē's eyewitness testimony emphasized again, he is actually made the secretary (*dprapet*) of Vardan. This idea, based on the tradition that Agathangelos was Trdat's "scribe" (*grichʻ*),[110] becomes popular in more modern Armenian literature.

But before tracing later Armenian traditions about Eḷishē as a historian, it may be worth noting that his *History of Vardan* was known and quoted for reasons other than his account of Vardan and the revolt. Mkhitʻar Gosh (d. 1213), who assembled

108. Text in *Sopʻerkʻ*, no. 11.
109. Under Meheki 21 (February 27).
110. See above, n. 63; and cf. Sebēos, p. 47 (in the "Primary History").

the first compilation of secular law—as opposed to canon law, which was already being codified in the eighth century—quotes Eḷishē as evidence for the various ranks in the church. Drawing parallels between the nine orders of angels as expounded by Dionysius the Areopagite and the orders and ranks of the church and of the secular administration, Mkhit'ar notes that Eḷishē refers to the ranks of readers and psalmists. He is referring to Ḷevond's exhortation to the Armenian troops in which the latter mentions that "bishops, priests, deacons, psalmists, and readers of scripture, each in his own canonical rank" are ready to join in the battle.[111] But Mkhit'ar has no reference to Vardan Mamikonean or to the battle of Avarayr.

Somewhat earlier, Gregory of Narek (d. 1010) in his *Commentary on the Song of Songs* refers to the letter of the Persian king addressed to the Vardanank' (by a rhetorical figure meaning the Armenians).[112] Gregory is using this as an example of how even idolatrous kings cared for their charges. He could have had in mind either the short version of the letter in Ḷazar or the long one in Eḷishē, even though Eḷishē attributes the letter to the king's vizier Mihrnerseh rather than to the king himself. The nineteenth-century editor of the text is probably right in identifying this as a reference to Eḷishē, who was far more widely read and quoted than Ḷazar.

Not all references to Eḷishē are to the *History of Vardan*, for as the brief "History of Eḷishē" quoted above indicates, numerous homilies were also attributed to him. Thus, for example, the thirteenth-century historian Vardan refers to Eḷishē when speaking of the language in which the angels speak to God and among themselves.[113] But the *History of Vardan and the Armenian War* has no mention of that topic.

Nor, on the other hand, do references to Vardan necessarily imply a knowledge of or interest in Eḷishē. The Georgian historian Juanshēr in the *K'art'lis Tskhovreba* refers to Vardan as the father of Shushanik,[114] but he has no reference to Eḷishē or to the Armenian war. Curiously enough the Armenian adaptor of Juanshēr has omitted any reference to Vardan at all or to Yazkert's persecution.[115]

Just as the Georgian chronicles ignore the revolt of the Ar-

111. *Girk' Datastani*, pp. 139, 402: cf. Eḷishē, p. 113.
112. *Matenagrut'iwnk'*, p. 361.
113. *Hawak'umn*, p. 12.
114. I, 216.
115. Armenian text of 1884.

menians in 451, so also the historians of regions peripheral to central Armenia use Ełishē only for what is appropriate to their special concerns. So Moses Daskhurants'i devotes a long chapter to Vardan's campaign in the Caucasus;[116] but although he explains that Yazkert was persecuting Christians in Armenia as well as in Albania, he says nothing of Vardan's death, nor does he mention the battle of Avarayr. And similarly the later Stephen Orbelian, who was concerned with the history of the province of Siunik', devotes much attention to the deeds of the prince of Siunik', Vasak, and his downfall, but gives no details of the final conflict "in which Saint Vardan was crowned with other companions."[117]

By the twelfth century the chroniclers are introducing confusions into the story, although they quote Ełishē as their authority. Samuel of Ani, for example, makes Vardan the *marzpan* of Armenia who governed at the shah's orders for fifteen (or seventeen) years.[118] But Ełishē clearly indicates that Vardan was the *sparapet* (military commander) and that the governor, *marzpan,* was Vasak. Indeed the whole story as expounded by Ełishē with hero and villain becomes much less dramatic unless the one who leads the opposition to Vardan is the duly constituted authority in the land. Samuel also refers in his brief *Chronicle* to the martyrdom of the Ļevondeank' and to the horrible death of Vasak "according to Ełishē."[119] More interesting is the reference in the longer recension of the text to Ełishē as a disciple of the Armenian interpreters, that is, the pupils of Sahak and Mashtots, as Samuel follows the tradition established by Stephen of Taron.[120]

Writing about the same time as Samuel, or a little earlier, Nersēs Shnorhali is the only Armenian author to bring out explicitly the comparison between Vardan and his companions with the Maccabees that is so significant implicitly in Ełishē's *History*. In his *Lament on the Fall of Edessa*, Nerses writes that its inhabitants "died rather than be false to the covenant; they resembled the Maccabees and the war of the Vardanank'."[121]

It is curious that this comparison is not brought out more often. For quite apart from the theme in Ełishē and his reminis-

116. II, 2.
117. P. 61.
118. P. 70.
119. P. 71.
120. Brosset, *Collection,* II, 385.
121. *Ołb,* p. 63.

46

cences of the Armenian version of Maccabees, the basic story would have been quite familiar to Armenians. On Hrotits' 26 (August 1) was celebrated, as in the rest of Eastern Christendom, the feast of the Maccabees with appropriate readings.[122] In the collection of sermons or homilies known as *Charĕntirk'* the Maccabees had their place, remembered by passages from the Armenian version of Gregory Nazienzenus' *Homily on the Maccabees*.[123] And the full version of that homily had a wide circulation.[124] So the concept of the Maccabees as heroes and martyrs was familiar to Armenians. Faustos Buzand was the first author to mention them explicitly when he described the festival of those Armenians who died fighting the Persians: "they fell in combat like Judas and Mattathias Maccabee and their brothers."[125] Moses Khorenats'i has one reference to Mattathias, as he laments that no second-day Maccabee has arisen to deliver Armenia in his own time—although there are many unacknowledged references to the text of the books of the Maccabees in his *History*.[126] John Catholicos recalls the Old Testament heroes including Maccabaeus, and later echoes Moses' lament that no new Mattathias has arisen to save the Armenians from Antiochus.[127] Likewise, Thomas Artsruni compares the exploits of Gurgēn Artsruni against the Tachiks to those of Judas Maccabaeus against Antiochus.[128] Anania Shirakets'i mentions the Maccabees in his *Chronicle*,[129] as does the later Vardan,[130] while in his *History* Stephen Asołik adds a few more circumstantial details.[131] However, Nersēs Shnorhali is unique in his specific parallel between those Jewish heroes and the martyrs of Armenia.

The later Armenian historians do not add much to the picture of Ełishē that has already been developed. The strange story in Thomas Artsruni describing how the *History* of Ełishē was defaced by Barsauma has no echo in the centuries that followed. For Vardan,[132] Kirakos,[133] and others, Ełishē was a

---

122. Renoux, *Codex*, II, 214–217.
123. Van Esbroeck-Zanetti, "Le manuscrit," p. 156.
124. Lafontaine, "La tradition."
125. III, 1.
126. III, 68; see also the Introduction to Thomson, *Moses Khorenats'i*.
127. Pp. 258, 278.
128. III, 13.
129. In ed. of Abrahamyan, p. 370.
130. P. 28.
131. I, 1, 2.
132. P. 51.
133. P. 28.

pupil of Mashtots' and Sahak, author of the book that described the martial exploits of Vardan and his martyrdom (though the battle of Avarayr is not explicitly named), and also the author of various homiletic works. Vardan the historian adds the detail that Vardan Mamikonean fought forty-two battles with the Persians.[134] This seems to have its origin in a passage from the tenth-century Mesrop of Vayotsdzor, author of the *Life of Saint Nersēs*.[135]

The thirteenth-century Kirakos mentions the tent and altar of Trdat, used in the Armenian camp at the time of the holy Vardanank'.[136] This seems to be a unique reference to that tradition, but Kirakos does not connect it with Ełishē. As a historian Ełishē is placed between Moses Khorenats'i and Łazar by Kirakos,[137] as by Stephen of Taron,[138] whereas in the next century the chronicler Mkhit'ar of Ayrivank' places Ełishē after Łazar,[139] which strictly speaking would render invalid Ełishē's claim to have been an eyewitness. But it would be wrong to stress that minor variation, for Armenian chroniclers never cast any doubt on Ełishē's veracity or exhibit any suspicion that he was not one of the circle of students associated with Mashtots' and Sahak.

This is carried through into the eighteenth century in the various minor chronicles. But Step'anos Ṙōshk'ay adds the detail that Ełishē, pupil of Mesrop, studied in Athens. He was the secretary (*dprapet*, as above) of Vardan.[140] Step'anos also seems to think that Yoseph, Łevond, and the other martyrs died with Vardan and the 1036 at Avarayr.[141] But Step'anos has often confused or misunderstood his sources, for he claims that the later Vardan accepted Chalcedon in 553 at the time of the Fifth Ecumenical Council (held that year in Constantinople) rather than in 572.[142]

Vardan is also well known to Armenian poets. Thus Simeon Aparants'i refers to the bitter cup of death as was drunk by Vardan Mamikonean, in connection with the capture of

134. P. 53.
135. Quoted in Nalbandyan, *Vardanants'*, pp. 55–56.
136. P. 167. Cf. the Continuator to Thomas Artsruni, p. 504.
137. Pp. 6–7.
138. See above, at n. 86.
139. P. 25 in Brosset; p. 261 (§36) of the Armenian text.
140. Step'anos, p. 65; cf. above, n. 110.
141. P. 63.
142. P. 73.

Tabriz by the Turks in 1589.[143] And in his *Homeric Epic on the Pahlavuni and Mamikonean Families,* based on Lazar's *History,* Simeon several times refers to the heroic exploits of Vardan. He also mentions that Vardan, who slew the Persian *marzpan* Surēn, fled to Greek territorty and was honored by Justianos—which could render either Justin or Justinian.[144]

It is perhaps worth noting that Vardan is not a figure who appears very often in Armenian art (at least until modern times). On reliefs and sculptures that adorn medieval Armenian churches or on freestanding stelae he is never represented. There one finds purely religious figures—such as Christ, Mary, figures from the Bible, saints Armenian or non-Armenian—or the figures of donors and their entourages. King Trdat may seem an exception, but as the first Christian king his association with Saint Gregory gives him a special place. Vardan and similar secular heroes, despite their standing as martyrs for the faith, are not included in the comparatively small dossier of figures sculpted in stone.[145] Vardan does appear, however, on the famous reliquary made at Skevra in Cilicia in 1293. On the outside of the doors are depicted in larger size Saint Gregory the Illuminator and Saint Thaddaeus; in smaller size Saints Peter and Paul above, and below Saints Eustratius and Vardan. The only other Armenian figure on the reliquary is King Het'um II, also mentioned in the dedicatory inscription.[146]

Not until the later fifteenth century does Vardan appear in miniature painting. In several hymnaries the battle of Avarayr is portrayed in rather stilted fashion with Vardan in the van. These are copies of earlier miniatures that are unknown or that have not survived.[147] But in general Armenian painting does not indulge in secular scenes until the fourteenth century. Even then, Vardan and the battle of Avarayr do not play a particularly prominent role. More popular was the Alexander Romance.[148]

143. P. 75, line 17.
144. P. 127, ll. 1417ff.
145. For these stelae see Khatchatrian, "Monuments funéraires," and for sculpture in general Der Nersessian, *Armenian Art,* pp. 51–68.
146. See Der Nersessian, "Le réliquaire."
147. See Der Nersessian, "Miniatures."
148. See Der Nersessian, *Armenian Art,* pp. 230–233.

Since Armenian miniature painting was primarily oriented toward religious rather than national themes, the small number of occasions on which Vardan is depicted is not a true measure of the popularity or influence of Ełishē's *History*. So we should return to our survey of Armenian literary references to this theme.

The first significant history of Armenia published in the West was that of the Mekhitarist scholar M. Chamchean. His massive three-volume opus appeared in Venice in 1784–1786; in it he attempted a general history of the Armenians from their beginnings in remote antiquity down to his own time, primarily drawing upon Armenian sources.[149] Thus the revolt of 450/1 is described in the very words of Ełishē and Łazar, as Chamchean took for granted the authenticity and veracity of both authors.

Chamchean's *History* was of great influence for two reasons. In the first place an abridged version was translated into English and published in Calcutta in 1827, thus providing non-Armenian readers with a basic history of Armenia "from B.C. 2247 to the year of Christ 1780."[150] But, more important, Chamchean's method of weaving his sources into a continuous narrative provided a model for later Armenian historians down to the twentieth century. Thus. L. Alishan's *Hayapatum*, published in Venice in 1901, gives a description of the events leading up to the revolt of 450/1, the battle of Avarayr, and its consequences, which is but a string of connected quotations from Ełishē and Łazar.[151] And M. Ormanian's more elaborate *Azgapatum*, published in Constantinople in 1912, follows the same pattern.[152] Y. Gat'rchean, in his incomplete *World History* ("from the beginning of the world to our times") published in Venice in 1849 and 1852, evinced a broader point of view by attempting to put Armenian events into perspective. But for the period in question, he too simply combined the Histories of Łazar and Ełishē to produce a continuous narrative.

However, twentieth-century historical scholarship had to take into account the doubts about the date of Ełishē's *History* raised by the critical work of Babgen Kiwlēsērean and others

149. M. Ch'amch'eants', *Patmut'iwn Hayots'*, 3 vols. (Venice, 1784–1786).

150. J. Avdall, *History of Armenia by Father Michael Chamich*, 2 vols. (Calcutta 1827).

151. Hayapatum, pp. 160–183.

152. §235ff.

(as noted above).[153] On the other hand, Vardan's role in more popular thought and literature as a symbol of nationalism grew even more predominant than before. So to the poetry, prose, and drama of the nineteenth and twentieth centuries we should now turn.

L. Alishan (1820–1901) was famous not only for his scholarly works (such as *Hayapatum* mentioned above) but also for his patriotic poetry, much of it written before he was thirty. Among his most popular poems of the late 1840s is the *Bulbul Avarayri* (Nightingale of Avarayr), which depicts the close friendship between Eḷishē and Vardan, the travels of the former to Byzantium, Athens, and Alexandria, and the events leading up to the Armenian defeat on the field of Avarayr.[154] Raphael Patkanean (1830–1892) was influenced by Alishan's romantic poetry and devoted a long poem of his own to the theme *The Death of the Valiant Vardan Mamikonean* (in 608 lines).[155] Here, as in other works of Patkanean's the theme of patriotism predominates. Alishan had ended his *Bulbul Avarayri* with the line, "Armenia remembers her own Karmir Vardan."[156] However, Patkanean ends on the theme that Vardan loved "the soil of his motherland—the land of Armenia." The description of the soil (*hoḷ*) as motherland (*mayreni*) is interesting, for in Eḷishē, as in all classical authors, references to ancestral lands or customs are in a masculine form.[157]

In nineteenth-century Armenian drama also, patriotism was a major concern, especially for the Mekhitarists. Numerous themes from Armenian history provided material for plays glorifying the past: the pre-Christian kings of Armenia such as Eruand, Artashēs, or Tigran; the early Christian kings such as Trdat, Arshak, or Khosrov; significant religious figures such as the patriarch Nersēs as well as non-Armenian saints. Vardan and the revolt against Iran naturally figured among these patriotic themes. As early as 1799 Father Lukas Inchichean wrote a play entitled *The Flight of Vardan the Great*, and in 1818 Father

---

153. See nn. 80 and 82 above.
154. *Nuagkʻ*, III, 309–332.
155. Reprinted in *Erkeri Zhoḷovatsu* II, 17–35 (written in 1856).
156. But since Armenian has no distinction of *grammatical* gender, here "her" (*iwr*) could as well be rendered "his" or "its."
157. In classical Armenian *mayreni* could refer to one's descent on the mother's side.

Ephrem Set'ean wrote *The Worship of the Magi*. These were produced by and for a primarily religious audience.[158]

Of more secular appeal, though also written by a priest,
were the plays of Narbey—the pseudonym of Khorēn Galfayean, born in 1831 in Constantinople, who studied at the
Mekhitarist monastery of Saint Lazar in Venice. His main centers of activity as a playwright were Constantinople and Theodosia (in the Crimea). For Narbey too the characters in Faustos
Buzand's *History* (which deals with fourth-century Armenia)
were of particular appeal, but he wrote one play entitled *Vardan*.[159]

After the middle of the century the drama became an important part of eastern Armenian literary activity. In Tiflis
comedies and tragedies were produced, but themes from Armenian history remained popular. From this point of view Yakob
Karinean was the most significant figure. In 1860 his first historical play, *Shushanik* (daughter of Vardan Mamikonean married to the apostate Georgian prince, Varsken), was performed.
And his later plays include tragedies entitled *Nersēs the Great*
and *Vardan Mamikonean*. But later in the century playwrights
turned to more contemporary themes.[160]

The novel too provided an opportunity to present themes
and stories from the Armenian past in stirring fashion aimed at
arousing patriotic sentiments. The two most famous exponents
of this literary form in the nineteenth century were Tserents'
(pseudonym of Yovsep' Shishmanean, 1822–1888), who was
born in Constantinople, worked mostly in western Armenia,
but died in Tiflis; and Raffi (pseudonym of Yakob Melik' Yakobean, 1835–1888), who was primarily active in Tiflis, but
traveled in western Armenia. Most of Raffi's historical novels
deal with events closer to his own time than the days of Vardan. An exception is *Samuel*, which describes the revenge taken
by a son on his apostate father in the fourth century—but
again the theme is taken from Faustos Buzand. Tserents' wrote
several novels descriptive of Armenia under Muslim domina-
tion (after the seventh century) and about Cilician Armenia.
But the earlier period did not attract his pen.[161]

158. For brief descriptions of these writers see Chanashean, *Patmut'iwn*, pp. 45–48, 300.
159. Ibid. pp. 199–203.
160. Ibid. pp. 325–326.
161. For Raffi and Tserents' see the brief description in Inglisian, *Armenische Literatur*, pp. 236, 243–244.

It is significant that Vardan does not figure among the heroes of these novelists. Perhaps his well-known fate made him a more suitable subject for tragic playwrights. But even on the stage, the nineteenth century was more concerned with the secular figure—either the most ancient kings about whom little was known in Armenian sources, or the figures of the fourth century described in detail by Faustos Buzand. This was, of course, a dramatic period, marked by struggles between a fledgling church and pagan society, by the perennial social problem of princes striving to preserve traditional liberties against royal authority, and by the question of political orientation toward the Zoroastrian shahs or the Christian (though sometimes Arian) eastern Roman emperors.

Naturally, Vardan and the Armenian war, known from the Histories of Ełishē and Łazar, were not neglected or forgotten. But the theme was more popular with poets and dramatists than with prose writers. No doubt the emphasis in the classical historians on the purely religious aspect of this war, on the thirst for martyrdom rather than compromise, was out of step with the more secular and political interests of nineteenth-century writers anxious to provide their people with patriotic themes. Be that as it may, it is perhaps ironic that the figure of Vardan as a national hero plays as great a role in Soviet literature as it does in the pre-Marxist Armenian world.[162]

---

162. Particularly noteworthy is the novel *Vardanank'* by D. Demirchyan, published during the Second World War. On Demirchyan's work see Nalbandyan, *Vardanants'*.

53

Eḷishē

Vardan and the Armenian War

I have carried out the work that you ordered, noble sir.[2] You ordered [a work] about the Armenian war in which more than a few showed virtue.

Behold, I have composed it in the following seven chapters:

First: the time
Second: the course of events brought about by the Prince of the East
Third: the unity of the covenant[3] of the church
Fourth: the secession[4] of some who abandoned the covenant
[*p. 4*] *Fifth:* the attack of the Easterners[1]
Sixth: the resistance of the Armenians in war
Seventh: the continuation of the troubled state of affairs.

In these seven[2] chapters I have recorded and set down in complete detail the beginning and middle and end, so that you may read it without interruption and learn of the valor of the virtuous and baseness of the cowards[3]—not because of any lack in the fullness of your extensive worldly knowledge, but for an examination of the heavenly providence which in its fore-

1. David Mamikon is otherwise unknown. For the Mamikonean family see p. 43.

2. *Noble sir: k'aj.* See p. 9 for this title, frequently applied to royalty.

3. *Covenant: ukht.* For this term, a key theme in Ełishē, see the Introduction. For the etymology see Benveniste, "Elements parthes," p. 30. In addition to "pact" or "covenant," *ukht* can also be rendered "clergy" (κλῆρος), as on pp. 23, 54, 64, 81, and 92.

4. *Secession: erkp̣aṙakut'iwn,* as in 1 Macc. 3:29 of the disaffection (διχοστασία) caused by Antiochus. For the influence of the books of the Maccabees on Ełishē see the Introduction.

1. *Easterners.* With reference to the Persians this term occurs only here in Ełishē. In the book of Judges (6:3, 33; 7:12) it refers to enemies of Israel defeated by Gideon, whose example Ełishē cites on p. 109. The expression "East" for Persia is very common in early Armenian historiography.

2. *Seven.* For the problem of the division of chapters see p. 114, n. 6.

3. *Cowards: yets kats'elots'n.* Cf. pp. 81, 99, where there are overtones of "shirkers" or "deserters" or 2 Macc. 1:7, where revolt from Judaism is expressed.

knowledge dispenses the compensations of both sides and by visible means presages the invisible.

But why would you, who are so versed in the knowledge of God, command me rather than command those far better qualified? As it seems to me, and to you and to those who have occupied themselves with philosophy,[4] this is a token of heavenly love and not of earthly vainglory;[5] just as some of the eminent historians said: "Harmony is the mother of blessings, discord the parent of evils."[6]

So considering the holy love inspiring your command, we did not hesitate nor were we discouraged on contemplating our own ignorance. For holiness is many things, including support to weakness—as is prayer to knowledge and holy love to the common advantage.

Receiving this [support] with your command, we willingly accepted this task, which is consolation to friends, hope to the trusting, and [*p. 5*] encouragement to the valiant as they eagerly assault death, seeing before them the victorious general[1] who is not malevolent or hostile to anyone but teaches all his own invincible power. Behold, he accepts as a valiant hero[2] whoever so desires. And because the title of heroism is multifaceted, he distributes manifold grace to everyone; and that superior to all we recognize to be the holy love [inspired] by a guileless mind.

This simplicity bears the image of that heavenly [simplicity]; as we perceive it in you, we forget our own nature. Indeed, we are raised up with you in flight; like high-soaring birds we pass through all the harmful tempestuous atmosphere; and gradually absorbing the pure upper air, we receive knowledge for the salvation of our souls and the glory of the all-victorious church.[3] Hence may the multitude of holy ministers joyously

4. Cf. Wisd. of Sol. 6:15.
5. *Vainglory: p'aṙasirutʻiwn.* Cf. p. 76.
6. The quotation is based on Philo, *In Exodum,* II, 64; cf. also *Chaṙkʻ* (ed. 1892), p. 190.

---

1. *General: zawraglukh,* i.e., Christ. For the use of this term in a Christian sense see Lampe, *Lexicon,* s.v. στρατηγός.
2. *Hero: nahatak.* This is an important expression in Ełishē as it has overtones of martyrdom and the defense of the faith. In this sense it renders the Greek ἀγωνιστής, for which see Lampe, *Lexicon,* s.v., and Murray, *Symbols,* p. 198 (where Syriac usage is also described). Cf. the Armenian title of the *Vkaykʻ,* which refers to the martyrs as *surb nahatakkʻ.* For the etymology of *nahatak* see Meillet, "De quelques mots parthes."
3. On this image cf. p. 110.

58

perform the service of their office to the glory of the Father of all; therewith may also the Holy Trinity rejoice and be glad in his own untroubled essence.[4]

So then, having received this command from your generous person, let us begin where it is right to begin, although not eagerly do we bemoan the misfortune[5] of our nation. Indeed, not willingly but with tearful laments[6] we shall describe the many blows which we suffered and of which we ourselves were an eyewitness.[7]

4. *Essence: ēut'iwn.* On this term see Thomson, *Teaching*, p. 11, with further refs. there.

5. *Misfortune: t'shuarut'iwn;* cf. Moses Khorenats'i, III, 68, for the same theme.

6. Tearful laments for the misfortunes of Christians and their land are a common feature of the *Vkayk'*.

7. *Eyewitness: aknates* (as in Agathangelos, §14, Moses Khorenats'i, II, 10). Eḷishē claims to be an author contemporaneous with the events he describes; see also pp. 15, 99. But for the date of composition of this *History* (at least in its present form) see the Introduction.

CHAPTER ONE

The Time

O N the extinction of the Arsacid line[1] the race of Sasan the Persian ruled over Armenia. They governed their empire by the religion[2] of the magi,[3] and frequently fought against those who would not submit to the same religion; beginning from the years of King Arshak, son of Tiran,[4] they waged war up to the sixth year of Artashēs, king of Armenia, the son of Vramshapuh.[5] And when they had deprived him of his kingdom, rule passed to the Armenian princes. For although the tribute[6] went to the Persian court, yet the Armenian cavalry was completely under the control of the princes in time of war. Therefore piety was freely practiced with head held high[7] in Armenia from the beginning of the rule of Shapuh, king of kings, up to the second year of Yazkert, king of kings, son of Vram.[8] But him Satan made his accomplice,[9] and spewing out

1. This phrase has verbal parallels with Agathangelos, §18.
2. *Religion: awṙenkʻ.* For this term see the Introduction.
3. *Magi.* On this term see Nyberg, *Manual* II, p. 122.
4. *Arshak:* king of Armenia, 350–367. *Tiran:* king of Armenia, 339–350.
5. *Artashēs:* king of Armenia, 423–428 (when he was deposed). *Vramshapuh:* king of Armenia, 392–414.
6. *Tribute: gandz,* lit. "treasure." For the various terms used in Ełishē for taxes see p. 23.
7. *Head held high: bardzraglukh.* Cf. p. 82, where Yazkert returns from battle "not" *bardzraglukh.*
8. Yazkert II is intended here. His first regnal year began on 4 August 438; see Nöldeke, *Sassaniden,* p. 435. See Koriun, p. 43, for the "second Yazkert, son of Vram."
9. The same epithet is applied to Vasak, p. 138 at n. 7. Cf. also p. 171, n. 3, for Yazkert as a friend of Satan.

all his accumulated venom[10] filled him like a quiver with poisonous arrows.[11] He began to wax haughty in his impiety; by his roaring he blew winds to the four corners of the earth; he made those who believed in Christ to appear as his enemies and opponents; and he tormented and oppressed them by his turbulent conduct.[12]

[*p. 7*] Since confusion[1] and the shedding of blood[2] were dear to him, therefore he was agitated within himself: "On whom[3] shall I pour out my poisonous bitterness, and where shall I loose my multitude of arrows?" In his great folly, like a ferocious wild beast[4] he attacked the land of the Greeks. He struck as far as the city of Nisibis[5] and ruined in his assault[6] many Roman provinces; all the churches he put to the torch, he amassed plunder and captives, and terrified all the troops of the land.

Then the blessed emperor Theodosius,[7] since he was peace-loving in Christ, did not wish to go out to oppose him on the field, but he sent to him a man called Anatolius,[8] who was the commander[9] of the East, with many treasures. And the Persians who had fled [from Persia] because of their Christianity and who were in the imperial city he arrested and handed over to him. Whatever he [Yazkert] said at that time, he

10. Cf. *Vkayk'*, pp. 171–172.

11. *Arrows:* cf. Eph. 6:16. For the simile of Satan with his quiver see Lampe, *Lexicon*, s.v. βελοθήκη.

12. This passage and the following paragraph were adapted by Thomas Artsruni (pp. 181–182) to describe the behavior of Jafr.

1. *Confusion: khṙovut'iwn.* As on p. 23 of the "dissension" brought on Armenia, or p. 95 the "tumult."

2. *Shedding of blood: ariwnheḷut'iwn*, as in Isa. 59:7. Cf. *Vkayk'*, pp. 22–23, for a similar description of the kingdom of Persia.

3. *On whom: yo,* which could also mean "wither."

4. The simile is common: cf. *Vkayk'*, p. 23.

5. Nisibis was given up to the Persians in 363 after the death of Julian. There is no other source which suggests that it was attacked by Yazkert; see *PW*, v. 33, col. 752. Ḷazar p. 74, notes that there had been a long peace before 450.

6. *Assault: aspatak,* used of marauding raids. See Hübschmann, *Grammatik*, p. 108.

7. Theodosius II, 408–450.

8. Procopius, *Wars* I, 2, describes an embassy of Anatolius to Vram (shah 421–439). For Anatolius, Theodosius's general of the East (τὸν τῆς ἔω στρατηγόν), see further *PW* I, 2072–3, and cf. Moses Khorenats'i, III, 57.

9. *Commander: sparapet.* Here the term refers to a Greek office (see preceding note); for its Armenian application see Toumanoff, *Studies*, p. 211. On p. 196 it is used to refer to an Iranian office.

[Theodosius] carried out according to the former's desires; thus he restrained him from much anger, and he returned to his own city of Ctesiphon.[10]

When the impious[11] ruler saw that his wickedness had succeeded, he began to increase his plotting, as one throws more wood onto a blazing fire.[12] From being a little suspicious he became thoroughly fearless; therefore he caused many to fall away from the holy covenant[13] of the Christians—some by threats, some by imprisonment and tortures, and some he put to a terrible death. He confiscated goods and possessions and tormented everyone with great dishonor. [*p. 8*] And when he saw that they had been scattered to many regions[1] he summoned to a council his perverse ministers,[2] who were bound to idolatry by indissoluble links, burning and heated like a furnace[3] to consume the community of the holy church.

For such people were living in their lifetimes as it were in gloomy darkness; their souls were captive in their bodies like a living man in a tomb;[4] on them the ray of Christ's pure light shone not at all.[5] Just as bears in their dying pangs fight more powerfully at their last gasp and wise men retreat and flee from them, such is the end which befell their rule.[6] If they are struck they do not feel it; if they strike they are unaware of doing so; and when no outer enemy is found they wage war against themselves. Appropriate is the prophet's saying concerning them: "A man in his hunger will go about and eat half of himself."[7] In like fashion the Lord himself says: "Every house and

10. For the form *Tizbon* see Christensen, *Iran,* p. 379; he also gives a brief description of the Iranian capital.

11. *Impious: anawrēn,* a very common epithet in Ełishē for the Persians. For *awrēnk'* as "religion" see the Introduction.

12. The simile is from Ezek 24:10.

13. *Covenant: ukht.* See p. 3, n. 3.

1. For the spread of Christianity cf. p. 17.

2. *Perverse: dzakhakołmann,* lit. "of the left-hand side," i.e., "sinister." Cf. *dzakhołaki* on pp. 24, 184, or *dzakhoł,* p. 88. In Byzantine tradition demons always appeared on the left side; see C. Mango, *Byzantium* (New York, 1980), p. 152.

3. Cf. Dan. ch. 3 passim, or 2 Macc. 4:38 of Antiochus.

4. The body as a tomb is reminiscent of the σῶμα-σῆμα in Plato, *Gorgias,* 493a.

5. Cf. Luke 11:34–36.

6. For the simile of bears, cf. Isa. 59:11, and Prov. 28:15 for the comparison of bears and wicked rulers. "Dying pangs" (*awrhasakan*) as in Isa. 59:10 and Ełishē, pp. 42, 64, 118.

7. Isa. 9:20: but Ełishē does not follow the biblical text closely.

kingdom which is divided against itself is unable to stand firm."[8]

So why do you beat around, why do you struggle, why do you burn, why do you flame up, why are you not extinguished? Why do you summon to council those who have drawn your spirit out of you, brought your soul to corruption, and dragged your corruptible body to the dust like a foul, discarded corpse? Do you in fact wish that the desire of your impiety be hidden? But when it is revealed, look, and you will know its final outcome.

[*p. 9*] The magi said:[1] "Valiant king,[2] the gods[3] have given you your empire and success. They have no need of human honor; but if you convert to one religion[4] all the nations and races in your empire, then the land of the Greeks will also obediently submit to your rule. But do you, king, immediately fulfill one counsel of ours. Raise an army and gather a force; march to the land of the Kushans;[5] assemble all nations and bring them through the Pass,[6] and there make your dwelling. When you detain and enclose them all in a distant foreign land[7] the plans of your desire will be fulfilled; and as it seems to us in our religion,[8] you will rule over the land of the Kushans, and the Greeks will not venture forth against your power—on condition you exterminate the sect[9] of the Christians."

This counsel seemed pleasing to the king and to the magnates, who were of the same mind. He wrote edicts[10] and sent

---

8. This is based on Matt. 12:25; Mark 3:24-25; Luke 11:17, without following any text exactly.

---

1. There is a parallel to this speech in John of Ephesus, II, 19; see Akinean, *Ełishē*, I, 175.

2. *Valiant king: arkʿay kʿaj*, a standard mode of address; cf. pp. 13, 45, 84, and 128, and Thomson, *Moses Khorenatsʿi*, III, 17, n. 4, or *Vkaykʿ*, p. 133.

3. *Gods: astuatskʿ* as opposed to *dikʿ* (n. 12 below).

4. *Religion: awrēnkʿ*, see the Introduction.

5. *Kushans.* The term is often used inexactly in Armenian texts. See Thomson, *Agathangelos*, §19, 20, and *Moses Khorenatsʿi*, II, 2, n. 4, and 67, n. 3; Trever, "Kushani," and Maenchen-Helfen, *Huns*, pp. 457-458.

6. *Pass: Pah durn*, i.e., the Chor Pass at Derbent.

7. *Distant foreign land: heṙawor awtarutʿiwn;* cf. refs. on p. 132.

8. *Religion: den.* This term is used by Ełishē only of the Persian religion, not Christianity; cf. p. 24. For the etymology see Hübschmann, *Grammatik*, p. 139.

9. *Sect: ałand.* Commonly used of heretics (as in Acts 5:17, to render αἵρεσις); its use for Christians (in the mouth of Persians) is rare; but cf. Ełishē, pp. 179, 180, and *Vkaykʿ*, pp. 220, 224.

10. *Edicts: hrovartaks*, "official letters"; see Hübschmann, *Grammatik*, p. 184, and Perikhanian, *Sasanidski sudebnik*, p. 476.

many messengers to every region of his empire. And this is a copy of the edict:

"To all the nations of my empire, to Aryans and non-Aryans,[11] may the greeting of our benevolence be multiplied for you. Be well, and we ourselves are well by the help of the gods.[12]

Without causing you any trouble we marched into the land of the Greeks, and without warfare by our loving benevolence we subjected the whole land to us in servitude. Do you celebrate and [*p. 10*] be unstinting in rejoicing. But immediately accomplish this command which we impose:

"We have decided in our infallible judgment to march to the land of the East, to subject the empire of the Kushans to us with the help of the gods. When you see this edict, straightway without impediment gather cavalry before us and meet me in the land of Apar."[1]

In this form the edict reached the lands of the Armenians, Georgians, Albanians,[2] Lp'ink',[3] Tsawdēik',[4] Korduik',[5] Aldznik',[6] and many other distant parts which were previously not accustomed to travel that road. A force of nobility and lesser nobility was assembled from Greater Armenia and retainers[7] from the royal house; likewise from Georgia, and Albania, and the land of the Lp'ink', and still others from all the districts of the south near the borders of Tachkastan,[8] the Roman Empire,

---

11. For Armenia described variously as part of Ērān or Anērān, see Garsoian, "Prolegomena," col. 194-195.

12. This sentence is paralleled in Trdat's edict, in Agathangelos, §131. "Gods" (*dik'*) is used in the Bible of pagan gods as opposed to God, *astuats*.

---

1. *Apar:* see Hübschmann, *Grammatik,* pp. 20-21, Markwart, *Eranšahr,* pp. 74-75. On p. 158 Ełishē describes the area as "the upper land" (*verin ashkharhk'*), a proper etymology; see Nyberg, *Manual* II, 22, s.v. *Apar.*

2. I.e., the *Ałuank'* of the eastern Caucasus, for whom see Trever, *Albanii.*

3. *Lp'ink';* north of the Ałuank'. See Trever, *Albanii,* p. 48.

4. *Tsawdēik':* in southwestern Armenia; see Hübschmann, *AON,* pp. 321-322.

5. *Korduik':* in southern Armenia; see Hübschmann, *AON,* pp. 333-334.

6. *Ałdznik':* in southwestern Armenia; see Hübschmann, *AON,* pp. 248-251.

7. *Nobility, lesser nobililty, retainers: azat, azatordi, ostanik.* On these terms see Toumanoff, *Studies,* pp. 124-126, and bibliography in Adontz/Garsoian, *Armenia,* p. 523, n. 84.

8. I.e., the region of the Tachiks, the Arabs of northern Mesopotamia. See Hübschmann, *Grammatik,* p. 86, for the etymology. From its original

Korduk', Dasn,[9] Tsawdē, and Arznarzn,[10] people who were all believers and baptized into the one catholic and apostolic church.

Innocently unaware of the king's duplicity,[11] they marched from each one's land obediently and with loyal intentions in order to fulfill their military service with sincere faith. They brought with them the divine holy testaments, with many [*p. 11*] ministers[1] and priests. But they bade farewell to their lands, not as in expectation of life, but as if [they were to] pay the debt of death, commending their souls and bodies to each other. For although the king's plan had not been revealed to them, yet suspicions were in everyone's mind. Especially when they saw the power of the Greeks broken before him, they were greatly stricken in their thoughts.

But because they were obedient to the holy testaments of God, they continually recalled the commands of Paul: "Servants, be obedient to your bodily masters; be not false servants and deceitful, but serve [them] faithfully as if [serving] God and not men. For the recompense of your just labors comes from the Lord."[2]

Setting out from their lands with all this goodwill and commended to the Holy Spirit, they presented themselves [to the king], hastily fulfilling his orders and doing everything according to his wishes. The king greatly rejoiced as if the desires of his thoughts[3] had been accomplished. And behold he acted with them just as the ministers of his impiety had advised.

So when the king saw all the armed soldiers and the multitude of the force of the barbarians who had loyally come to the royal service, he was even more happy in front of the mag-

---

meaning of "Arab" (as Syriac *Tay*), *Tachik* later came to mean "Muslim," and was applied to Arabs, Persians, or Turks.

9. *Dasn:* in southern Armenia; see Hübschmann, *AON,* pp. 320–321.

10. *Arznarzn:* in southwestern Armenia; see Hübschmann, *AON,* pp. 321.

11. *Duplicity: erkdimi mits,* cf. pp. 16, 162.

---

1. *Ministers: pashtawnēayk'.* This is a term of general meaning (e.g., p. 68), but here means "deacon" as opposed to "priest," as on pp. 69, 100, and *Vkayk',* p. 112. For its use referring to Persian ministers of state, see pp. 18, 86.

2. This is a conflate of Eph. 6:5, 7, and Col. 3:24, with allusions to the book of Proverbs.

3. For the "king's will" as a "commonplace of the Shapur martyrdoms" see Brock, "Candida," p. 178, n. 3.

nates and all the host of his army. Outwardly[4] he hid the desires of his mind, and unwillingly bestowed lavish presents on them. He marched immediately against the kingdom of the Huns, whom they call Kushans;[5] but [*p. 12*] after fighting for two years he was unable to make any impression on them. Then he dispatched the warriors to each one's place, and summoned to his presence others in their stead with the same equipage. And thus he established the habit from year to year and built there for himself a city to dwell in, beginning from the fourth year of his reign up to the eleventh.[1]

And when he saw that the Romans remained firm in their pact which they had with him, and that the Khaylndurk[2] had ceased to cross the Pass of the Chor,[3] and that in every region his empire lived in peace, and that he had put the king of the Huns into even greater straits since he had ruined most of his provinces and had prevailed over his rule, then he sent messengers throughout all the fire-temples[4] of his land, he increased the sacrifices of fire with white bulls and hairy goats,[5] and he assiduously multiplied his impure cult.[6] He honored many of the magi and the greatest of the chief-magi with crowns and distinctions. He gave a further command that all the goods and possessions of the Christians in Persia should be seized.

Thus he waxed haughty and overweening; in his arrogance he exceeded the nature of man, not merely in the matter of physical warfare, but he began to think of himself as one superior to the nature of his ancestral rank. Therefore he deceit-

---

4. *Outwardly: i verin eress*, cf. pp. 22, 135, and *Vkayk'*, p. 123.
5. *Kushans. The identification of the Kushans and Huns is a commonplace in Armenian historiography; see the refs. on p. 9, n. 5.*

---

1. I.e., from 441/2 to 448/9.
2. For the Khaylndurk' see Marquart, *Eranšahr*, pp. 56, 98.
3. *Chor*, i.e., the pass near Derbent.
4. *Fire-temples: atrushans.* For the etymology see Hübschmann, *Grammatik*, p. 110; cf. Christensen, *Iran*, p. 157, and *Vkayk'*, pp. 210, 227. Ełishē uses various terms for the Zoroastrian fire-temples: e.g., *krakatun* ("house of fire"), pp. 70, 175; *tun pashtaman kraki* ("house of fire worship"), p. 69; cf. πυρσολατρεία in *Narratio*, p. 30. In Łazar one finds *tun mokhranots'in* ("house of ashes"), pp. 39, 53, 62, and 85; for "ash worship," cf. Gray, "Two Armenian Passions of Saints," p. 373, n. 1; and the references in Brock, "Candida," p. 179, n. 3.
5. Cf. Agathangelos, §22, for the sacrifice of white bulls and goats, and the crowns. For the white bulls see Widengren, *Die Religionen Irans*, p. 439.
6. Cf. Ezek. 7:8 for the "impure cult."

fully hid his intention; but, as it appeared to the wise, he placed himself in the rank of the immortals.[7] He grew [*p. 13*] furious at the name of Christ, when he heard that he had been tortured and crucified, had died and been buried.[1]

As in this fashion he madly raved from day to day in the same designs, one of the youngest of the Armenian princes debated with him and said: "Valiant king,[2] whence did you learn to speak such things about the Lord?" The king answered: "They have read your erring Scriptures before me." Then the young man replied, saying: "Why, O king, did you have them read only to that place? But have the reading prolonged and you will hear of his resurrection, his appearance to many, his ascension to heaven, his sitting at the right hand of the Father, the promise of his Second Coming when he will effect the miraculous resurrection of all, and the summary compensation of his just judgment."[3] When the king heard this he was deeply smitten,[4] but outwardly he laughed and said: "All that is fraud." The soldier of Christ replied and said: "If his bodily sufferings are credible to you, even more credible to you should be his awesome Second Coming."

When the king heard this he blazed up like the fire of the furnace in Babylon, until his own people around him were consumed like the Chaldaeans.[5]

Then he poured out all the fury of his ire on that blessed man, whose name was Garegin.[6] Bound hand and foot he was given over to torture for two years, and deprived of his princely rank, he received sentence of death.

---

7. *Immortals:* cf. the titles of Shapuh in Moses Khorenats'i, III, 17, and the Greek title of Shapur in the inscription at Naqš-i-Rustam of Shapur I: ἐκ γένους θεῶν; Honigmann and Maricq, p. 11. For Yazkert's overweening pride, cf. p. 82.

1. Cf. p. 15 for Yazkert's interest in and knowledge of the Christian faith. Note that the Armenian creed omits "died" in the series "tortured, crucified, buried."

2. For the title see p. 9, n. 2.

3. For similar credal statements cf. pp. 27, 39–40, and 87.

4. *Deeply smitten, i khor khots'eal,* as on p. 49, and *Vkayk'*, p. 122.

5. Cf. Dan. 3:22.

6. A Garegin is mentioned on p. 120 among those Armenians who died at the battle of Avarayr.

CHAPTER TWO

The Course of Events Brought About
by the Prince of the East

THOSE whose souls are sluggish in heavenly virtue[1] are great cowards in their physical nature. Such a man is shaken by every wind, troubled by every word, and trembles[2] at every contingency; he is a dreamer in his lifetime, and at his death is despatched to irretrievable destruction.[3] As someone said of old: "Death not understood is death, death understood is immortality."[4] Who does not know death, fears death; but he who knows death does not fear it.

All these evils enter man's mind from lack of knowledge. A blind man is deprived of the rays of the sun, and an ignorant man is deprived of a perfect life. It is better to be blind in the eyes than blind in the mind.[5] As the soul is greater than the body, so is sight of the mind greater than that of the body.

1. *Sluggish in heavenly virtue.* This basic theme is picked up again on the last page (p. 203). Throughout Ełišē the contrast between the sluggish (t'ulats'eal) and those who remain firm (pind) is emphasized; cf. *Vkayk'*, pp. 36–37. For sluggish natures cf. Philo, *In Exodum*, II, 19. Heavenly virtue is emphasized several times in Ełišē, as on pp. 89, 100, and 122; see esp. Phil. 3:20: our virtue (aŕak'inut'iwn) is in heaven.

2. *Shaken . . . trembles,* cf. the description of Yazkert, p. 82, or of the chief-magus, p. 146.

3. *Irretrievable destruction: angiwt korust,* a popular phrase in Ełišē, cf. pp. 36, 91.

4. This quotation is from the Hermetic treatise published by Manandyan in *Banber Matenadarani* 3, p. 311. On that work see also de Durand, "Un traité hermetique," and Mahé, "Les Définitions."

5. This is taken verbatim from the Armenian version of the *Wisdom of Ahikar,* ed. Martyrosyan, I, 88, 186, and 253 (Erevan, 1969); ed. F. C. Conybeare et al. p. 207 (1913). Cf. also Ps.-Callisthenes, §131: Alexander upbraids the bard Ismenias for being koyr ach'aw ews ew mtawk'. For blindness to the truth cf. pp. 111–112.

If someone is very affluent in worldly wealth but is very poor in his mind, such a man is more pitiable than most others—as indeed we see not only in ordinary men but even among the very greatest. If a king does not have wisdom that is equal to his throne, he is unable [*p. 15*] to shine in his rank.[1] And if this is so with bodily matters, how much the more so in a spiritual sense!

The soul is the life of the whole body, but the mind steers both body and soul.[2] Just as it is for a man, so it is for the whole world. A king has to give account not only for himself, but also for all those for whom he was the cause of destruction.[3]

Although we are not permitted to censure princes, yet we cannot praise the man who will fight with God. However, I shall not delay in describing the course of events which was brought about by him against the holy church—not with the intention of denouncing, but neither being silent in giving a truthful account of events. Not spurred to conjecture or sparked to rumor; but I myself was there in person and I saw and heard the sound of the arrogant voice.[4] Like the strong wind which agitates the great sea, so he shook and convulsed the whole host of his army. He made a review[5] of all doctrines,[6] and compared magism[7] and divination[8] and all the doctrines of the empire. He also deceitfully introduced Christianity and said with raging mind: "Question, examine, see. Let us choose and hold which is best."[9] And he hastened

1. *Rank: vichak,* as on p. 90 n. 4.

2. This Platonic simile of the charioteer (*kařavar*) probably came to Ełishē via Philo; cf. *De Jona,* p. 597, for the *kařavar.* See also below, pp. 34, 167. Eznik, §3, expands the idea, introducing the chariot, the horses, and the *kařavar.*

3. For the responsibility of the sovereign for his subjects see pp. 26, 46, 131, 165, and 171, and in general Christensen, *Iran,* p. 297, and Lambton, "Islamic Mirrors," pp. 421–422, and *Letter of Tansar,* p. 67. The theme is used in Ełishē as an argument by the shah to enforce Zoroastrianism lest he incur the anger of the gods.

4. For Ełishē as an "eyewitness" see p. 5, n. 7.

5. *Review: handēs,* cf. p. 44. For the etymology and other examples see Hübschmann, *Grammatik,* p. 179, and Meillet, "Sur les mots iraniens."

6. *Doctrines: usmunkʻ,* as on p. 19, 27, 52, 60, and 83, lit. "teachings."

7. *Magism: mogutʻiwn.* For the form *mog* see Nyberg, *Manual* II, s.v. *magū.*

8. *Divination: kʻawdēutʻiwn* (derived from "Chaldaean"?). See Hübschmann, *Grammatik,* pp. 318–319.

9. For Yazkert's interest in Christianity, cf. p. 13. There are parallels in later shahs; see Sebēos, p. 149 (for Khosrov) and esp. John of Ephesus, VI, 20, for public discussions.

quickly to fulfill what was in his mind.

But on every side the Christians in the army recognized the fire which was secretly burning and intending to consume the mountains and [*p. 16*] plains together. They too were warmed by the inextinguishable fire and valiantly prepared themselves for the trial of his hidden stratagems.

Then, with voices raised, with psalms, and spiritual songs,[1] and glorious preaching, they began to worship openly and publicly in the great camp.[2] Fearlessly and without hesitation, they willingly instructed whoever came to them. And the Lord prospered them with signs and miracles, for many of the heathen[3] army who were ill received healing.[4]

But when the impious[5] ruler realized that his perverse plan had been revealed and that the flames of the fire which he had prepared had become known to the fearers of God before anyone had blown on it, then he began to wound his own evil mind with hidden arrows and he saw incurable wounds inflicted on his soul and body.[6]

Now he flashed and writhed like a poisonous snake, now he stretched himself and roared like a furious lion.[7] He rolled, twisted, and sprawled in his double-faced[8] intention, striving to fulfill his desired plans. Since he was unable to seize and arrest them—because they were not gathered together in one spot near him—he therefore began to give precedence to the junior over the senior,[9] to the unworthy over the honorable, to the ignorant over the knowledgeable, to the cowards over the brave. Why should I enumerate the details? All the unworthy he promoted and all the worthy he demoted, until he had split father and son from each other.

Although he worked this confusion among all nations, he

1. As in Col. 3:16.

2. *Camp: banak.* See Nyberg, *Manual* II, s. v. *būnak.*

3. *Heathen: hetanosakan.* There were many non-Persians in the army. Interestingly enough, Ełishē frequently calls Persians "heathens" (e.g., pp. 22, 69, 73, 95, 101, and 120), as they are called in the *Vkayk'* (e.g., p. 56). The parallel with the ancient Jews fighting the "heathen" is brought out on p. 109. Cf. also Moses Khorenats'i, III, 55, where the Persian prince Shapuh is likened to the "heathen" of Ps. 32:10.

4. For the Armenians healing the foreign sick, cf, pp., 180, 196.

5. Cf. p. 7, n. 11.

6. *Wounds . . . body:* cf. p. 185.

7. Cf. *Vkayk',* p. 111.

8. *Double-faced: erkdimi;* see p. 10, n. 11.

9. *Junior, senior: krser, awag,* terms which could refer to age or rank; see Toumanoff, *Studies,* p. 113, n. 181, and Adontz/Garsoian, *Armenia,* p. 344; cf. also pp. 20, 62, 153, 194, and 200.

especially strove against the land of Armenia. For he saw that they were very ardent in their piety, especially those of the Armenian nobility, [*p. 17*] and they sincerely observed the holy preaching of the apostles and prophets. He deceived some of them with gold and silver, and many with other liberal gifts—some with estates and large villages, some with honors and great principalities. And still further vain hopes he offered to their souls. In this way he was continuously enticing and exhorting: "If only, he said, you accept the religion[1] of magism and sincerely convert your error to the splendid truth of the religion of our gods, I shall make you the equal of my beloved nobles in grandeur and in dignity,[2] and shall even make you surpass them."[3] In such fashion he deceitfully humbled himself before all, speaking with them on the pretext of love, but hypocritically so that he might be able to seduce[4] them according to the former advice of his counselors. Thus he acted, beginning from the fourth year of his reign up to the eleventh.[5]

However, when he saw that his secret cunning[6] had been in no way effective but that his opponents waxed the greater—for he saw Christianity daily increasing and spreading throughout all the regions of the distant road through which he was passing[7]—he began to languish, to waste away,[8] and to lose his spirits from sighing. He unwittingly revealed his secret plans. He gave a public command: "Let every nation and language under my authority abandon each one's erring religion and only cleave to the worship of the sun,[9] offering sacrifices and calling it god, [*p. 18*] and serving the fire. In addition to all this, let them fulfill the religion of magism and be negligent in nothing."

1. *Religion: awrēnkʻ.* See the Introduction.

2. *Dignity: awagutʻiwn.* See p. 16, n. 9, for *awag*.

3. Such a promise of rank and money if the youngest brother would abandon his "ancestral customs" is stressed in 2 Macc. 7:24. Cf. The exhortation on p. 169 below.

4. *Seduce: orsal,* a term with overtones of trickery. Cf. pp. 37, 64, 95, and Mark 12:13, Luke 11:54.

5. I.e., from 441/2 to 448/9. But there is no reference in Łazar or the Canons of Shahapivan (444/5) to any persecution during this period.

6. *Cunning: hnaragitutʻiwn,* a term used in Wisd. of Sol. (9:14; 14:12; 15:4) to describe man's foolish devices.

7. For the eastward spread of Christianity in this period see p. 60, n. 3.

8. *Languish, waste away: hashel, mashel,* as 3 Macc. 6:11, or *Vkaykʻ,* p. 80.

9. *Worship the sun.* This is the basic rite of Zoroastrianism according to Ełishē; see also pp. 50, 64, 85, 162, 183, 185, and 195; for its importance as an abnegation of Christianity see also *Vkaykʻ,* pp. 37, 116ff, 169.

These words a herald proclaimed in the great camp,[1] and he imposed strict injunctions on everyone. He also hastily despatched messengers to all the distant nations, and imposed the same orders on them all.

Then at the beginning of the twelfth year of his reign,[2] he gathered a force infinite in multitude and attacked the land of the T'etals.[3] When the king of the Kushans saw this, unable to oppose him in battle he retreated to the regions of the impregnable desert and lived in hiding with all his troops. But [the Persian king] assailed his provinces, regions and lands, captured many fortresses and cities, amassed captives, booty, and plunder, and brought them to his own empire. Then, still engaged in the same vain plans, he was strengthened in his erring intention and said to his impious ministers: "With what shall we repay the gods for this great victory, in which no one was able to oppose us in battle?"

Then in unison the magi and astrologers[4] raised their voices and together said: "The gods who gave you empire and [*p. 19*] victory over your enemies have no need to seek visible honors from you, but [they wish] that you remove all the erroneous teachings of men and bring them to the single honorable Zoroastrian religion."[1]

This statement seemed pleasing to the king and all the magnates, especially to those foremost in their religion. When council had been held, this opinion prevailed.

Then he held within the Pass[2] the host of cavalry of the Armenians, Georgians, Albanians,[3] and of all who believed in the holy Gospel of Christ. The garrison of the Pass was given strict instructions to allow through those who were coming eastward to us,[4] but to block the way for those going from the East to the West.

When he had restrained and confined them in this secure and inescapable prison—and in truth I said secure and ines-

---

1. *Camp: karawan,* "an army as mobilized and ready for war," Nyberg, *Manual* II, s.v. *kārvān.*

2. I.e., 449/50.

3. The MSS read *Italakan* or a close variant thereof. For the *T'etalk'* see Markwart, *Erānsahr,* pp. 59, 67. Sebēos, p. 73, emphasizes the proximity of the T'etalk' and the Kushans (on whom see p. 9, n. 5).

4. *Astrologers: k'awdeayk',* see p. 15, n. 8.

---

1. *Zoroastrian religion: awrēns zradashtakan,* as also on p. 143. For the Armenian *Zradasht* (Zoroaster) see Hübschmann, *Grammatik,* pp. 41–42 (with refs.), and p. 162, n. 6 below.

2. *Pass: Pah duṙn,* as on p. 9, n. 6.

3. On p. 63 Ełishē numbers the Albanian cavalry at ten thousand.

4. *Us:* i.e., the Persian king who gave the order.

capable, for there was no place to flee or hide because the enemy dwelt all around—then he laid hands on them and by means of severe tortures and various torments maltreated many of them and pressed them to deny the true God and confess the visible elements. But the soldiers in unison, with noble minds, bravely and forcefully cried out together saying: "Heaven and earth are witnesses[5] to us that we were never tardy in the king's service, nor did we ever mingle cowardice with our noble valor.[6] These inflictions on us are without reason and merciless."

And the noise of their complaint increased until the king himself [*p. 20*] with his own eyes saw their denunciation of their treatment, but he immediately affirmed with an oath: "I shall not let you go until you have accomplished all the intent of my orders."

So his malicious[1] servants received authority to put four soldiers from the aristocracy[2] to torture. First they condemned them to many torments, then imprisoned them in the same bonds. But the others he deceitfully left alone for a while, throwing the blame for all the harm on those imprisoned. This he did by the advice of Satan.

Twelve days later he commanded a banquet to be given, more liberally than the daily custom, and he summoned many of the Christian soldiers. When they were ready to take their seats,[3] he granted a place at the table[4] to each one of them; he conversed with them in a friendly and gentle way in accordance with his former manner so that perhaps they might be persuaded to eat sacrificial meat,[5] which had never been lawful

5. *Heaven and earth are witnesses:* cf. p. 87, and *Vkayk'*, p. 97. The phrase is biblical; see Deut. 4:26, 31:28.

6. Cowardice and valor and the Armenians' duty figure also in the speeches on pp. 87, 102. The theme is based on Judas' exhortation in 1 Macc. 9:10, where the Armenian text (*och' khaṙnests'uk' zanun vatut'ean meroy ĕnd arut'iwns k'ajut'ean*) lies behind Ełishē's *och' khaṙneal vatut'iwn ĕnd arut'iwn k'ajut'ean.*

1. *Malicious: ch'arasēr* ("loving evil"), a term frequently applied by Ełishē to the Persians, e.g., pp. 42, 44, and 51. On p. 24 it is applied to Haraman/Arhmn, the evil principle (cf. p. 71, n. 5: *ch'aramits'*).

2. *Aristocracy: i bun awagats',* see p. 16 n. 9.

3. *Gah* means "seat" or "rank" (as on p. 101). For the written lists of precedence called *gahnamak* see Toumanoff, *Studies,* pp. 229ff., and Adontz/Garsoian, *Armenia,* pp. 191ff.

4. For seating at the table see the numerous Armenian texts quoted in Adontz/Garsoian, *Armenia,* pp. 214ff.

5. *Sacrificial meat: mis zoheal.* For the prohibition see Acts 15:29. A more liberal attitude is found in 1 Cor., ch. 8 and 10:25–28. For the later Chris-

for Christians to eat. Although they all refused, he did not force them but ordered that they be offered their usual food, and he increased the merrymaking in the palace with ever more wine.

As they were leaving the royal chamber, some of them were arrested, their hands bound behind them, and the cords [of their trousers] sealed and carefully tied—some for two days, some for three. They also suffered many other [*p. 21*] ignominious torments, which we did not consider suitable to put in writing. Some of them were exiled, deprived of their noble rank, and humiliated.

Again many detachments from among these [peoples] were sent to a distant land to wage war against the king's enemies in the inaccessible desert. There many died by the sword. [The Persians] reduced everyone's set pay[1] and afflicted them with hunger and thirst. They ordered their winter quarters to be in the harshest places and rendered them dishonorable and base in the eyes of all.

But they, for love of Christ, bore all these fortunes very joyfully for the sake of the great hope which is prepared in advance for those who keep the commandments and endure.[2] The more evil increased their dishonor, the more they were strengthened in the love of Christ. Especially because many of them had studied the Holy Scriptures from their youth, they consoled themselves and encouraged their companions; and like a tower[3] of light they practiced their worship and increased it.

Therefore many of the heathen,[4] to whom their voices seemed sweet and pleasant, encouraged them and spoke words of consolation to the effect that it was better for a man to suffer[5] even death than to deny such a religion.

[*p. 22*] However, although in their love of Christ they were

---

tian attitude see Lampe, *Lexicon,* s.v. ειδωλόθυτον, and for Armenian evidence see p. 64, n. 12.

1. *Pay: t'oshak.* See Hübschmann, *Grammatik,* p. 155.
2. This sentence is an amalgam of 1 Cor. 2:9; Col. 1:5; and James, 5:11.
3. *Tower: ashtarak.* The tower is a common symbol of the church and of hope and piety; see Lampe, *Lexicon,* s.v. πύργος.
4. *Heathen: het'anos,* cf. p. 16, n. 3.
5. *Suffer: chgnel,* a term with overtones of struggle and endurance, frequent in Ełishē and the books of the Maccabees.

very happy and joyful in the inner man,[1] their outward appearance was very miserable in their exile. Such noble soldiery had attained miserable ignominy, and their ancestral[2] freedom was in cruel subjection to a murderous[3] tyrant who exceeded the traditions of heathens in the shedding of blood and did not at all suppose that there might be revenge for all this in heaven.[4]

Likewise he did not remember anyone's earthly services; and what is worse than all else in the human condition, since there were some of the princes who had nourished his brothers with their mothers' milk,[5] these he condemned even more than all the others.

In addition to all this he contrived even further wickedness. He sent one of his trusted servants, called Denshapuh,[6] on a mission to Armenia. He came at the royal command, bringing the great king's greetings, and made a census[7] of the whole land of Armenia with soothing hypocrisy [as if] for the alleviation[8] of taxes[9] and the lightening of the burden of the cavalry.[10] Although outwardly he dissimulated, yet within his plans were revealed as evil.

1. Cf. Rom. 7:22.

2. *Ancestral: hayreni.* See the introduction for the importance of this expression.

3. *Murderous: mardakhoshosh,* as Antiochus in 2 Macc. 9:28. For the parallels between Antiochus and Yazkert see the Introduction.

4. Cf. Heb. 10:30.

5. This refers to the common practice whereby young nobles were brought up in the houses of other noble families, a custom both within Armenia and also practised between Armenia and Iran. The child was called *san* and the tutor *dayeak* (for which see Nyberg, *Manual* II, s.v. *dāyak*); cf. pp. 43, 162, "foster brothers," and p. 197, n. 9, "tutor" and "protégé," p. 201, "nurse." On the whole question see Widengren, *Feudalismus,* ch. 3.

6. *Trusted servant,* Denshapuh: *hawatarim tsaṙay.* Lazar, p. 64,[30] also calls Denshapuh *hawatarim.* Eḷishē, p. 143, gives Denshapuh the title of *hambarakapet* (as in Lazar, p. 104[19]), "in charge of the stores," for which term see Christensen, *Iran,* pp. 102 and 283 (where Denshapuh is described). On p. 169 below, Denshapuh says he spent eighteen months in Armenia.

7. *Census: ashkharhagir,* as in Luke 2:1. No other Armenian source refers to a census in Yazkert's time, and Akinean, *Eḷishē,* II, 483ff., notes that the only attested census in Iran was in the sixth century.

8. *Alleviation: t'oḷut'iwn,* possibly "relief" or "remission"; cf. p. 70; it can also mean "amnesty," as on p. 85, 94, 121, and 124.

9. *Taxes: harkk'.* For the various types of taxes and the terms used see below, p. 23, n. 9.

10. For the Armenian military obligations to the shah, cf., pp. 10 and 44.

First: he cast the freedom of the church into slavery.[11]

Second: he included in the same census the Christian monks living in monasteries.[12]

Third: he increased the tax burden on the country.

[*p. 23*] *Fourth:* by slander he pitted the nobility against each other, and caused dissension[1] in every family.

He did all this in the hope of breaking their unity, scattering the clergy[2] of the church, driving away the monks, and wearing out the peasants,[3] so that in their great poverty they might unwillingly turn to the religion of the magi.

And even more pernicious was the fifth. The governor (*hazarapet*)[4] of the country had been regarded as a father and overseer[5] by the Christians of the land, but he incited accusations against him, deprived him of office, and in his place brought a Persian to the country. In addition he also brought a chief-magus[6] as judge[7] of the land, so that they might corrupt the glory of the church.

11. For taxes imposed on the "freedom" of the church, cf. *Vkayk'*, p. 104. The term "freedom" (*azatut'iwn*) here has the connotation of untaxed patrimony; see Perikhanian, "Notes sur le lexique iranien," p. 15; and cf. p. 46 below.

12. *Monks, monasteries: miaynakeats', vanorayk'. Miaynakeats'*, lit. "living alone," could also mean "hermit," but the reference to monasteries here makes the sense clear. However, on pp. 57 (there, *menakeats'*), 95, 131, 189, and 200, "solitaries" or "hermits" could be intended. On p. 199 "monks" seems more likely. On p. 52 the term *menanots'* is used, clearly implying a monastery; but on p. 60 *miaynanots'* might be rendered "hermitage."

1. *Dissension: khrovut'iwn;* cf. p. 7, n. 1.

2. *Clergy: ukht,* for which term see p. 3, n. 3. It is not always clear from the context whether the meaning "covenant" or the narrower meaning "clergy" is intended.

3. *Peasants: shinakank';* for this term see p. 52, n. 6.

4. *Hazarapet.* For this office see Toumanoff, *Studies,* pp. 205–206, n. 234, and Adontz/Garsoian, *Armenia,* p. 340. Here the governor of Armenia is intended, an office different from the "great hazarapet of the Aryans and non-Aryans," p. 28, which renders the Iranian *Vzurghramatar.* For "Aryans and non-Aryans" see p. 9, n. 11.

5. *Overseer: verakats'u,* which renders προϊστάμενος in Rom. 12:8 and προστάτις in Rom. 16:2. The term is used by Koriun of the pupils that Mashtots' left in the regions he had visited to oversee the missionary work (e.g., pp. 27, 29, and Moses Khorenats'i, III, 54). Cf. also below, p. 29, n. 4.

6. *Chief-magus: mogpet,* Iranian *mōbadh;* see Christensen, *Iran,* pp. 112–113, and Boyce, *Zoroastrianism,* p. 65. This was not the supreme rank (*mōbadhan mōbadh*), so the plural is common (e.g., p. 24).

7. For a chief-magus as judge, see refs. in Adontz/Garsoian, *Armenia,* pp. 511, n. 34 and 35, and Gnoli, "Politica religiosa," p. 249. Cf. also Eḷishē, p. 51, and p. 71, n. 1 for *awrēnsdir.*

However, although all these actions were so cruel, no one yet openly laid hand on the church. Therefore nobody opposed him despite the severity of the taxes. For where it was suitable to take up to a hundred *dahekan*,[8] they took twice as much. Likewise they taxed both bishops and priests, not merely of inhabited lands but also of desolate areas. So who indeed could describe the severity of dues and taxes, excises and levies[9] on the mountains and plains and forests? They did not act in accordance with royal dignity but raided like brigands, until they themselves were greatly amazed as to whence all this treasure came and how the country remained prosperous.[10]

When they saw that despite all this they were unable to cow [the Armenians], [*p. 24*] then they openly ordered the magi and chief-magi to write a letter in keeping with their perverse religion.[1] And this is a copy of the letter:

"Mihrnerseh,[2] Great Vizir[3] of Iran and non-Iran,[4] many greetings to Greater Armenia.

"You must know that every man who dwells under heaven and does not accept the Mazdaean religion[5] is deaf and blind

8. *Dahekan.* For the etymology see Hübschmann, *Grammatik*, p. 133. It is used to translate various Greek terms for coins. On p. 187 Ełišē contrasts it with *dram*. For its value as 4.53 grams of gold see Manandian, "Les poids," p. 327; and cf. Moses Khorenats'i, II, 50, for gold *dahekans* scattered at weddings.

9. Dues (*mutk'*), taxes (*sakk'*), excises (*bazhk'*), levies (*hask'*): for this passage see Adontz/Garsoïan, *Armenia*, pp. 363-364, and further references ibid., p. 525, n. 93. The article by T. Avdalbegyan, "Has, sak u bazh," has been reprinted in his *Hayagitakan Hetazotut'yunner*, pp. 362-413 (Erevan, 1969).

10. *Prosperous: shēn:* cf. pp. 123-124 for the noun *shinut'iwn* (prosperity). *Shēnk'* in this same paragraph is rendered by "inhabited lands," and for *shinakank'* ("peasants") see n. 3 above.

1. *Perverse religion:* for *dzakhołaki* see p. 8, n. 2, and *den*, p. 9, n. 8.

2. For Mihrnerseh see Christensen, *Iran*, pp. 272-273.

3. *Great Vizir: vzurk hramatar.* For the title see Hübschmann, *Grammatik*, pp. 182-183, and Adontz/Garsoïan, *Armenia*, p. 340. *Vzurk* is used to describe a class of nobles, see p. 84, n. 3, and *hramanatar* is common in Armenian (e.g., Faustos Buzand, III, 14, of the bishop Daniel, or Thomas Artsruni, pp. 167, 169, of Muhammad).

4. *Iran and non-Iran: Eran ew Aneran.* The usual Armenian expression is *Arik' ew Anarik'* ("Aryans and non-Aryans") as on pp. 9, 28. On the position of Armenia as part of Eran or of Aneran see p. 9, n. 11.

5. *Mazdaean religion: awrēnk' deni mazdezn.* For the terms *awrēnk'* and *den* see Thomson, "Maccabees," p. 336; and for *mazdezn* see Hübschmann, *Grammatik*, p. 190, and Benveniste, "Le terme iranien *mazdayasna*," *BSOAS*, 33 (1970): 5-9. Ełišē more frequently uses the expressions "religion of the

and deceived by the demons of Haraman.[6]

"For before heaven and earth existed the great god Zrvan[7] sacrificed for a thousand years and said: 'Perhaps I shall have a son, Ormizd by name, who will create heaven and earth.' And he conceived two in his belly,[8] one from making sacrifice and one from saying 'perhaps.' When he knew that there were two in his belly, he said: 'To the one who emerges first I shall give my rule.'

"But the one who had been conceived from his doubt tore open the belly and came out. Zrvan said to him: 'Who are you?' He said: 'I am your son Ormizd.' Zrvan said to him: 'My son is luminous and sweet-smelling, you are gloomy and evil-loving.'[9] And when he had wept very bitterly, he gave him his rule for a thousand years.[10]

[*p. 25*] "When he begat the other son he called him Ormizd. He took the rule from Arhmn and gave it to Ormizd, saying to him: 'Up to now I sacrificed to you, now do you sacrifice to me.' And Ormizd created heaven and earth, but Arhmn worked evil in opposition.

"And creation is thus divided: the angels are Ormizd's, but the demons Arhmn's. And everything good, both in heaven and here, is Ormizd's and everything harmful done there and here Arhmn worked. Likewise, whatever is good on earth Ormizd did, and whatever is not good Arhmn did. Just as Ormizd made man, Arhmn made diseases, illnesses, and death.[1] All

---

magi" or "magism" (*mogut'iwn*). Note the expression *ayladen*, pp. 159, 179, in the mouth of a Persian for a non-Zoroastrian.

6. *Haraman:* a variant of Arhmn; see the references in Hübschmann, *Grammatik,* pp. 26–27. For Arhmn's role see the following pages.

7. The following myth of Zrvan is expounded in detail (with some variations) in Eznik, §§145ff., where he claims that the teaching is oral and not written. For a comparison of the accounts and other evidence concerning the myth see Mariès, "Le *De Deo* d'Eznik," and Bianchi, "Alcuni aspetti abnormi del dualismo persiano," pp. 149ff.

8. According to Eznik, p. 145, the two were conceived in the womb of their mother (*jargandi mawr iwreants'*). No further reference to a female is made by Eznik, so one could interpret the passage to mean that Zrvan was both father and mother (which Eznik does not do).

9. *Evil-loving: ch'araser;* see p. 20, n, 1. In Eznik "foul-smelling" (*zhandahot*).

10. Nine thousand years in Eznik.

---

1. *Diseases, illnesses, and death: zakhts ew zhiwandut'iwns ew zmah,* as in Eznik, p. 72. Eznik does not elaborate on the kinds of good and evil created by Ormizd and Arhmn in his description of the myth.

misfortunes and disasters that occur, and bitter wars, are the creations of the evil side; but success and empires and glory[2] and honors and health of body, beauty of face, eloquence and longevity—these receive their existence from the good one. And everything which is not like that has been mixed with a creation of the evil one's.

"All men are in error who say: 'God made death, and evil and good derive from him.' Especially as the Christians say: 'God is jealous. Because of the eating of a single fig from the tree[3] [*p. 26*] God made death, and subjected man to that punishment.' Such jealousy not even man has for man, let alone God for men. For who says this is deaf and blind and deceived by the demons of Haraman.[1]

"Again there is another error: 'God who created heaven and earth came,' they say, 'and was born of some woman called Mary, whose husband was Joseph.' But in truth he was son to a certain Banturak by an illicit intercourse.[2] And many have gone astray after such as man.

"If the Romans[3] have ignorantly gone astray in their great folly and have been deprived of our perfect religion, they have brought their own ruin upon themselves. But why are you infatuated with their error? Do you hold the same religion that

---

2. Cf. Eznik, §154, for the contrast of misfortunes (*tʻshuarutʻiwnkʻ*) with success and glory (*yajoḷutʻiwn* and *pʻarkʻ*).

3. In Gen., ch. 3, the species of tree is not named, though v. 7 mentions fig leaves as garments. The *Apocalypse of Moses*, p. 20, refers to the tree as a fig. Akinean, *Eḷishē, II*, 607, quotes an unpublished commentary on the Pentateuch by Vardan Areveltsʻi (thirteenth century) to the effect that some regarded the fruit of the tree as a fig, others as a grape. For the grape and the tree of life in Syriac thought (Afrahat and Ephrem, who were known in Armenia) see Murray, *Symbols*, pp. 114ff., and for the olive and tree of life, ibid., pp. 320ff. Gregory of Narek (*Matenagrutʻiwnkʻ*, p. 289) calls the fruit of the tree of life an apple, with regard to Song of Sol. 2:3.

---

1. Cf. the first paragraph of this letter.

2. *But in truth ... intercourse*. This is found only in *A* and is probably an interpolation. However, *Pʻandurak* is mentioned on p. 38 and attested by the MSS. The tradition that Jesus was the son of Πανθήρ is attested in Origen, *Contra Celsum*, I, 32, and later writers (e.g., Epiphanius, *Adversus Haereses*, 78:7); it may derive from a (deliberate?) misunderstanding of ὁ υἱὸς τῆς παρθένου.

3. *The Romans: ashkharh Hoṙomotsʻ*, "the empire (land) of the Romans." More usually Eḷishē refers to the Roman (Byzantine) Empire as "the land of the Greeks" (*Yunatsʻ*). There is sometimes ambiguity as to whether *Hṙovm* means Constantinople (the New Rome) or Rome in Italy; cf. p. 72.

your lord has, especially because we have to give account for you before God.[4]

"Do not believe your leaders whom you call Nazarenes,[5] for they are very deceitful. What they teach in words they do not practice in deeds. 'To eat meat,' they say, 'is not a sin,' yet they themselves do not like to eat meat. 'It is right to marry,' but they themselves do not wish even to look at a woman.[6] 'It is a great sin,' they say, 'to accumulate riches,' but they praise poverty excessively. They honor misfortune and despise success; they mock [*p. 27*]the name of fortune and greatly scorn glory. They love simplicity of clothing, and honor the dishonorable more than the honorable. They praise death and condemn life. They dishonor the births of men and praise childlessness. And if people were to listen to them and not approach their wives, the end of the world would soon arrive.

"But I did not wish to put all the details in writing for you, because there are many other things that they say. But what is even worse than what we have just written, they preach that God was crucified by men, that he died and was buried, then rose and ascended to heaven. Should you yourselves then not have made a judgment concerning such unworthy doctrines? Demons, who are evil, are not seized and tortured by men, let alone God, the Creator of all creatures. This is shameful for you to say, and these words are most incredible to us.

"So there are two possibilities before you: either answer this letter word for word, or come to court and appear before the great assembly."

The names of the bishops who gathered in the province of Ayrarat and composed a reply to the letter:

4. *Account: hamars*, as in Heb. 13:17. For the theme of the shah's responsibility see p. 15, n. 3. Cf. also p. 171, n. 2.

5. *Nazarenes: Natsrats'ik'*. As on p. 158 the term is here used of the leading Christians; on p. 179 it refers to Christians generally. For the term Ναζαραῖος applied to Christian ascetics see Lampe, *Lexicon*, s.v. (but there is frequent confusion between Ναζιραῖος [referring primarily to the Nazirites] and Ναζωραῖος [referring to Nazareth]. It is important that Ełishē only uses the term in the mouth of a Persian. Its use is therefore parallel to the Syriac *Naṣraye*, which was used by Persians of the native Christians, whereas the Greek deportees were called *Krestyane*. See Brock, "Some Aspects of Greek Words in Syriac," pp. 91–95. The word *Natsrats'i* is not found in other early Armenian authors. Cf. the use of "sect" in the mouth of Persians, p. 9, n. 9.

6. Cf. p. 46 for the Persian derision of celibacy, and Faustos Buzand, V, 27, for an anecdote giving the Armenian (ascetic) viewpoint.

Joseph, bishop of Ayrarat[1]
Sahak, bishop of Tarawn[2]
Melet, bishop of Manazkert[3]
Eznik, bishop of Bagrevand[4]
[*p. 28*] Surmak, bishop of Bznunik'[1]
Tachat, bishop of Tayk'[2]
T'at'ik, bishop of Basean[3]
K'asu, bishop of Turuberan[4]
Eremia, bishop of Mardastan[5]
Euḷal, bishop of Mardoyali[6]
Anania, bishop of Siunik'[7]
Mushē, bishop of Artsrunik'[8]
Sahak, bishop of Ṙēshtunik'[9]

1. For Joseph see Garitte, *Narratio,* pp. 94–96. Ḷazar (p. 44) makes it clear that he was a priest, although he held the throne of the Catholicos, Eḷishē does not call him Catholicos or patriarch but "bishop" (also pp. 43, 71), "leader" (*ishkhan*) of all the Christians (p. 169), "supreme in rank" (p. 178). Ayrarat is a major province of northern Armenia; see Hübschmann, *AON,* pp. 278–283, 361–366.
2. *Tarawn:* a province west of Lake Van; see Hübschmann, *AON,* pp. 325–327.
3. *Manazkert:* a town north of Lake Van; see Hübschmann, *AON,* pp. 449–450.
4. *Bagrevand:* a province in central Armenia; see Hübschmann, *AON,* p. 363. This Eznik is generally identified with the pupil of Mashtots' mentioned in Koriun (pp. 30–31), author of the *De Deo* (see L. Mariès in the Bibliography), who was instrumental in persuading Proclus of Constantinople to send his *Tome* to Armenia (see Tallon, *Livre des Lettres,* pp. 50–53).

1. *Bznunik':* on the northwestern shore of Lake Van; see Hübschmann, *AON,* pp. 328–329; and for the family, Toumanoff, *Studies,* p. 216.
2. *Tayk':* in northwestern Armenia; see Hübschmann, *AON,* pp. 276–278, 357–361; for its importance as an Armenian/Georgian borderland see Toumanoff, *Studies,* pp. 450–456.
3. *Basean:* in northern Armenia; see Hübschmann, *AON,* pp. 362–363.
4. *Turuberan:* northwest of Lake Van; see Hübschmann, *AON,* pp. 251–254, 322–331.
5. *Mardastan:* east of Lake Van; see Hübschmann, *AON,* pp. 343, 451.
6. *Mardoyali:* in northwestern Armenia; see Hübschmann, *AON,* pp. 327, 451.
7. *Siunik':* a major province south and southeast of Lake Sevan; see Hübschmann, *AON,* pp. 263–266, 347–349.
8. *Artsrunik':* on the south shore of Lake Van; for the family see Toumanoff, *Studies,* pp. 199–200.
9. *Ṙshtunik':* on the southwestern shore of Lake Van; for the family see Toumanoff, *Studies,* p. 213.

Basil, bishop of Mokk'[10]
Gad, bishop of Vanand[11]
Eḷisha, bishop of Amatunik'[12]
Eḷbayr, bishop of Andzavatsik'[13]
Eremia, bishop of Apahunik'[14]

All these bishops[15] and many chorepiscopi[16] and honorable priests from many places, and the holy clergy[17] of the church, with one accord and in unison, gathered in the capital city of Artashat,[18] in concert with the greatest princes and all the people of the land, and wrote an answer to the letter.

"Bishop Joseph and his united colleagues from the greatest to the smallest, to Mihrnerseh, the great *hazarapet* of the Aryans and non-Aryans,[19] with very peace-loving intentions—may greetings be multiplied to you and all the great army[20] of the Aryans.

10. *Mokk'*: south of Lake Van; see Hübschmann, *AON*, pp. 254–255, 331–333.
11. *Vanand:* in northern Armenia; see Hübschmann, *AON*, pp. 363–364.
12. *Amatunik'*: in eastern Armenia; on the family see Toumanoff, *Studies*, pp. 197–198. Eḷisha (Eḷin Ḷazar, p. 45) did not write this *History*.
13. *Andzavats'ik'*: south of Lake Van; on the family see Toumanoff, *Studies*, pp. 198–199.
14. *Apahunik'*: north of Lake Van; on the family see Toumanoff, *Studies*, p. 199.
15. Ḷazar (pp. 44–45) gives the list in quite a different order; but the only divergence in names is that Ḷazar omits Eulalius of Mardoyali and includes Zavēn of Mananaḷi. (Note that Eḷishē omits the further list of nobles who attended the Council, merely referring to the "greatest princes," *metsamets nakharark'*.) The bishoprics are all in Persian Armenia, i.e., on or east of the demarcation line (roughly Amida/Erzerum) drawn by Theodosius I and Shapuh II in 387; on that see Garitte, *Narratio*, p. 64, and Toumanoff, *Studies*, p. 152, n. 6.
16. *Chorepiscopi: k'orepiskopsk'*: on this rank see Lampe, *Lexicon*, s.v. χωρεπίσκοπος, and for Armenian evidence the Indexes to the *Kanonagirk'*. Cf. also p. 57 below.
17. *Clergy: ukht;* see p. 3, n. 3.
18. *Capital city: t'agaworanist teḷi*, lit. "place of royal residence." On pp. 80, 99 the same term is used of royal estates in Armenia and on p. 93 of Constantinople. Artashat was founded by Artashēs in the second century B.C. (see Manandian, *Trade*, pp. 44–46) and remained the Arsacid capital after the time of Tigran. But the Armenian monarchy had been abolished by the mid-fifth century. This title is unknown to Faustos, Agathangelos, and Ḷazar; Moses Khorenats'i (II, 49) describes Artashat as *ark'ayanist*. Ḷazar does not name the place where the bishops assembled.
19. Cf. Mihrnerseh's title on p. 24. For the rank of *hazarapet* see p. 23, n. 4.
20. *Army: spah*, not used elsewhere in Eḷishē; cf. *spay* in Ḷazar, p. 51. See Hübschmann, *Grammatik*, p. 239.

"From our ancestors we have retained the divinely-instituted custom of praying for the life of the king[21] and ceaselessly requesting God [*p. 29*] for long life for him, so that he may rule in peace his universal empire, which has been entrusted to him by God, and so that in its extended peace we too may complete our lives in well-being and piety.

"Concerning the letter which you addressed to our land—in an earlier time one of the chief-magi, who was greatly versed in your religion and whom you regarded as superior to ordinary mortals, believed in the loving God, the Creator of heaven and earth, and he explained and expounded your religion to you word for word. And since they were unable to refute him, he was stoned and put to death by King Ormizd.[1] If you consider it reliable to hear our words, in many places of your own country his book[2] is to be found: read and you will be informed.

"But as for our religion—it is not obscure nor is it preached in some corner of the land, but it is spread throughout the whole world, across the sea, the dry land, and the islands;[3] not only in the West, but also in the East, the North, the South and in between [the world] is densely filled with it. It does not have its surety in a man, to be spread through the world by a protector,[4] but has its confirmation in itself. It does not appear sublime[5] from comparison with the depravity of others, but from heaven above it derives its infallible charter[6] and not through a mediator—for God is one and there is none other beside him, neither older nor younger.

"God did not receive the beginning of his existence from

21. Cf. 1 Pet. 2:13, 17; Heb. 13:1-7. The point is emphasized on p. 163; cf. also Agathangelos, §52.

1. This Persian martyr is unknown to Lazar. Ełishē, pp. 143ff., describes the conversion of a Persian learned in the Zoroastrian religion who was exiled, but "in an earlier time" would mean during the reign of Ormizd II (307-310).

2. *Book: girkʻ.* This means the account of his martyrdom, as the story of Gregory (later expanded into "Agathangelos") was known as "the book of Saint Gregory," Lazar, p. 1.

3. There are parallels with this sentence in the Armenian version of John Chrysostom's *Commentary on Matthew*, p. 9.

4. *Protector: verakatsʻu;* cf. p. 23, n. 5.

5. *Sublime: veh.* Cf. p. 83, where Christianity is described (by Yazkert!) as the most "sublime" of all religions. On p. 165 Sahak ironically calls the pagan gods "sublime beings."

6. *Charter: awrēnsdrutʻiwn,* lit. "legislation." The term is frequently used in later Armenian writers of Islam; see p. 71, n. 1.

anyone, but he is [*p. 30*] eternal in himself; he is not in any place but is his own place;[1] he is not in any time but time derives from him; and he is prior not only to heaven but also to the thoughts of men and angels. He is not shaped into a material appearance nor is he subject to the vision of the eye; he is not merely impalpable to the hand, he is not even graspable by anyone's mind—not merely among mortals, but also among the incorporeal angels. But if he himself wishes he is comprehensible to minds worthy of him, though he is not visible to the eyes or understanding, not to earthly [minded] creatures but to those who believe truly in God.[2]

"His name is Creator of heaven and earth. But as he is self-existent, prior to heaven and earth, so is he self-named. He himself is timeless, but when he wished he made a beginning of existence for his creatures, not from something but from nothing.[3] For he alone is "something"[4] and everything else received its being from him. Not that after he had taken thought then he created [creatures],[5] but before he created, in his foreknowledge[6] he saw the creatures. Just as now, before a man has done anything good or evil, men's deeds are clear to God, likewise then also, before he had created, he was aware of the uncreated beings, not as a confused jumble,[7] but the forms of each of their parts were arranged and ordered before him, both of men and of angels, and the forms of whatever was going to be in a form.

"And because he is a creative power, his benevolence was unable to prevent our wickedness, as indeed happened;[8] but we have as judge [*p. 31*] the creative right hand. The hands which established heaven and earth, inscribed also the stone tablets[1]

---

1. *God ... place.* This is closely paralleled in Philo, *Chaŕkʿ*, p. 119 (1892), and in the Hermetic text, ed. Manandyan, p. 305. The whole paragraph is similar in argument to the long speech of Callistratus in *Vkayabanutʿiwnkʿ* I, 664ff.

2. Cf. *Teaching of St. Gregory,* esp. §355, 359.

3. For the term *ochʿinchʿ* "nothing," see Mariès, *Etude*, pp. 89ff.

4. *Something: inchʿ.* See Mariès, *Etude*, pp. 59ff.

5. Cf. Eznik, §§ 349–350.

6. Cf. 1 Pet. 1:2.

7. *Confused jumble: khaŕn i khuŕn,* as in Eznik, §350.

8. This is a major theme in the *Teaching,* e.g., §262. For God's benevolence, cf. also Eznik, §52.

---

1. Cf. Exod. 24:12. But *pʿorogretsʿin* ("inscribed") is not a biblical term, nor does it occur in the Armenian text of Philo, *In Exodum,* II, 41, which explains the writing on stone.

and gave us a book[2] containing the laws of peace and salvation, so that we might know the one God, Creator of things visible and invisible—not different as if one were good and the other evil, but one and the same wholly good.

"But if it appears to you that anything evil exists among God's creatures, speak out boldly so that perchance you may learn the true good. You said the demons are evil; there exist also good spirits,[3] whom you and we call angels.[4] If they wish, the spirits are good, and if they wish, the angels become evil. This also can be seen among men, and especially in the sons of a single father: there is one who is obedient and submissive to his father, and there is one who is more evil than Satan. Likewise a single man can be seen to be divided into two: sometimes evil and sometimes good; and the one who was good, the same became evil; it has occurred that he again returned to the good, yet his nature is one.

"But as for your saying that because of a single fig God created death, a piece of parchment is even less significant than a fig: if the king's order is marked on it, whoever tears it receives death as punishment. But is it then right to call the king evil? Far from it; I say no. But by using an example I am instructing others. God would have been jealous at that time if he had not commanded not to eat from the tree. But if he had previously cautioned, he therein revealed the mercy of his natural love. Then man by despising [the command] received the punishment of death.

"Now as for your having said that God was born from a woman, it was not right for you to turn away or flee from that; for behold Arhmn and Ormizd were born from a father [*p. 32*] and not from a mother—to which if you really turned your mind even you would not accept. And there is something else still more laughable than this: the god Mihr is born from a woman,[1] as if anyone would have intercourse with his own parent.

2. *Book: dprut'iwn*, as in Exod. 32:32 and 33; it is also used of the "book of life" in Phil. 4:3 (cf. p. 120 below).

3. *Spirits: devk'*, as for "demons." For the *devk'*, cf. p. 46, and demon worship, p. 91.

4. Cf. Philo, *In Genesim*, IV, 188: the δαίμονες are called angels by the sacred word of Moses.

1. Mihr was not mentioned in Mihrnerseh's letter, but Ełishē may have in mind the very name *Mihr*nerseh. He mentions Mihr (Mithra) twice

"But if you set aside for a while the arrogance of your authority and enter into a debate[2] in a friendly way, I know that despite everything else you are a very wise man and did not consider as superfluity [what was said] about the birth of our Lord from the Holy Virgin, that you understood heavenly salvation to be much more important than the creation of the world from nothing, and that you attributed the transgression to man's freedom and the liberation from servitude to God's benevolence.

"For when you hear that God created this whole world from nothing, understand that creatures were born at his word. So God, who begat this great body without pain, thenceforth is compassionate to it like a father. He who is himself incorruptible begat creatures without corruption; but the latter fell of his own will and was rendered corruptible, and by himself was no longer able to stand on his feet. Because he was from earth and had acted for and by himself, he returned to the same nature. And since it was not from the foreign power of some evil being that he received punishment, but from his own laziness in not obeying the benevolent command, his subject part was chastized by the death which he suffered in his own person.

[*p. 33*] "Now if the evil god created death, what reality[1] does death appear to have? None at all. But it destroyed the creatures of the good God. If this is so, it is not possible to call the latter good, but imperfect[2] and corruptible. And the god whose creatures are corruptible and destructible cannot be called an indestructible God. So cast away these foolish babblings.[3]

"One world does not have two lords, nor one creature two gods. If two kings were presumptuous enough to arise for one

---

(pp. 165, 185) as a god whose impartiality makes him suitable to use in oaths. On p. 35, Ełishē repeats the claim that he had a mortal mother. For other refs. to Mihr in early Armenian literature see Agathangelos, §790; Moses Khorenats'i, III, 17.

2. *Debate: payk'ar.* Cf. pp. 170, 175 for debates before martyrdom. Hübschmann, *Grammatik,* p. 220, notes that the word means a "contest by sword or pen."

---

1. *Reality: goyats'ut'iwn,* as on p. 34, "being," or p. 111, "creation." For the term see Thomson, *Teaching,* pp. 11–12.
2. *Imperfect: kisagorts;* on p. 187 it means "half-tilled."
3. *Babblings: barbajank',* as in Eznik §359 of the Marcionite doctrines.

country, that country would be destroyed and the kingdoms would collapse.[4]

"This world is material, and the elements are different and opposed to each other.[5] The Creator of these opposites is one, and he brings them into harmony by persuasion. Just as he crushes and softens the heat of fire by the chill of air, and the cold solidity of the air by the warmth of fire—so too he grinds up the fine earth and kneads it with the moisture of water, while the natural tendency of water to flow downwards he solidifies and hardens by the binding effect of earth.[6]

"For if the elements were joined together, perhaps one of the less intelligent might suppose that these were God incorruptible, and abandoning the Creator might offer worship to his creatures. [*p. 34*] Therefore, he who created this [world] took care in advance that men, noticing the mutual hostility of the corruptible elements, might understand that its leader[1] alone is incorruptible and that he is one, not two—the same Creator of the former elements, by whom all things were fashioned at his creative command.

"The four seasons in their cycle fulfill their material tasks; the four of them look to the will of their attentive Creator. They are unconsciously yoked to their obligatory work, not encroaching on each others' established order.[2] Here is a clear explanation, easily comprehensible in the ears of all. That which is fire, in its being and essence[3] is mixed with the three other parts. The warmth is found more in stones and iron, and less in air and water, while it itself never appears alone. The nature of water is separate, yet it also exists in mixtures of the other three parts, more so in plants and less in air and fire. But air penetrates fire and water, and through water [penetrates] food that causes growth.

---

4. Cf. p. 167. The passage is based on Matt. 12:25; Mark 3:24; Luke 11:17.

5. For this paragraph compare Eznik, §2, 32, and Anania Shirakats'i, *Yaḷags erkri*. There are parallels to the theory of the four elements in the Hermetic text, ed. Manandyan, pp. 299[20ff.], 311[20ff.].

6. Cf. p. 175 for the mingling of the indissoluble elements.

---

1. *Leader: Kaṙavar,* "charioteer," as on p. 15, n. 2.

2. Cf. *Teaching,* §267 and refs. there.

3. *Being and essence: goyats'ut'eamb ew zawrut'eamb.* For *goyats'ut'iwn* see p. 33, n. 1; for *zawrut'iwn* see Thomson, *Teaching,* p. 12, and cf. p. 110 below where it is used of the Trinity.

"So are these elements mingled, and they exist[4] as one body and do not destroy each other's nature. They never cease [*p. 35*] in their opposition, looking to the one unmingled Lord who arranges and orders their mixtures with a view to the nature of all living things and the prolongation of the stability of the whole world.

"Now if God cares thus for the irrational world, how much more [does he care] for the rational world—men.

"As for what one of your very learned men said, that the god Mihr was born from a mortal mother[1] and is king as divine offspring and is a partner of the seven noble gods,[2] if it is right to believe in that fable—which in your religion you claim to be actually real—we no longer believe in fables but are pupils of the great prophet Moses. With him God spoke in the bramble on Sinai,[3] and face to face he set down the law and gave it to him. He made known to him this material world as created and his own immaterial essence as Creator of these elements from nothing. And he revealed to him that this earth with its earthly beings and heaven with the heavenly beings were the works of his hands.[4] The inhabitants of heaven are angels, and the inhabitants of earth men. Man and angel alone are rational, while God is above heaven and earth.

"All creatures carry out the commands he orders without reasoning, and never do they cross the limit imposed on them. [*p. 36*] Only man and angel have been left free in their own will, for they are rational. If they abide by his command they are immortal and sons of God. He gave all creation into subjection—earth to men and heaven to the angels. But if they disobey and transgress the commandment, they will be opposing God and will receive disgrace and be deprived of each one's

4. *Exist: goyats'eal.* For the stem see the previous note. For the pl. *goyats'ealk'* as "things that exist" see p. 166, n. 6, and Eznik, §354.

---

1. Cf. p. 32, n. 1.

2. Or perhaps "a noble partner of the seven gods." For *hamharz* (partner, assistant, adjutant) see Nyberg, *Manual* II, s.v. *ham-harz;* the term is used in a military sense below, pp. 77, 96, and 116. The term "seven" (*ewt'nerord*) is in the form for "seventh." For the seven gods (the Amesha Spentas) see, e.g., Boyce, *Zoroastrianism,* pp. 21ff. (That seven main cult centers in Armenia are mentioned by Agathangelos [see Thomson, *Agathangelos,* p. xl, n. 65] is not revelant to the Iranian tradition.)

3. See Exod., ch. 3.

4. For God's revelation to Moses of the nature of the physical world, cf. *Teaching,* §306–311. Philo, *Vita Mos.,* II, 48–52, interprets the law as the image of the cosmos.

honor, so that his dominion may appear blameless and the transgressors be put to shame at their transgressions.

"But if you err in ignorance, I who have secure knowledge am unable to follow your error. If I become a pupil of your lack of learning, the two of us would go to irretrievable destruction[1]—and perhaps I worse than you because I have as witness to me the very voice of God: "A servant, he says, who does not know the will of his lord and does something worthy of the bastinado is beaten, but less";[2] whereas he who is informed of the king's will and transgresses in his presence, is greatly punished without propitiation.

"So I beg you and all those under your authority: do not be greatly tormented with me, nor I less so with you. But let me and you and all your host with your valiant king so study divine Scripture that we may escape those torments, scorn hell, avoid the inextinguishable fire, [*p. 37*] inherit the kingdom, and in this transitory life possess unending glory that passes not away.

"But accept what you dread and you will straightway learn the truth.

"One of the host of immortal angels left heaven in revolt.[1] Coming to our world, with treacherous words and a false promise, he proferred an unrealizable hope to the untested, inexperienced, and newly created man, as to a child,[2] turning his mind upwards so that by eating of the fruit of the tree—which he had been commanded not to approach—he might become god. So he forgot God's command, was tricked into following that erring deceit, and lost the glory of immortality that he possessed; nor did he gain the dream of his hope. Therefore, expelled from the place of life, he was cast into this corruptible world, in which you too now dwell and senselessly err following the new counselor—no longer by eating of the forbidden tree but by calling creatures god, worshipping the dumb elements, offering food to demons who have no stomachs, and neglecting the Creator of all.[3]

"The evil counselor is not satisfied but wishes to outdo

---

1. *Irretrievable destruction: angiwt korust,* as on p. 14, n. 3.
2. Luke 12:48.

---

1. For this paragraph cf. *Teaching,* §278ff.
2. Eḷishē frequently uses the expression "as a child" in ref. to being deceived (e.g., p. 42 and refs.); this is no evidence for the idea of Adam being a child (for which see Murray, *Symbols,* pp. 304–306).
3. Cf. *Teaching,* §522ff.

himself in committing evil. For the demons do not lead anyone to destruction by force, but they sweeten sins for man's desires and by blandishments[4] seduce[5] the unlearned into error—just as many men [urge] their friends to theft and brigandage, not doing anything by force but by false deceit causing them to commit many evil deeds, [leading] some to sorcery,[6] [*p. 38*] some to fornication, and others to innumerable other impure acts. Through just judges they pay the penalty of death—not that the judges of a good God are beneficent and those of an evil one malevolent; for it is often the case that evil deeds are done by good men, and then wholly good deeds by the most wicked men.

"The righteous judges who judge evildoers are not called evil and tormentors but very good and benevolent. Their nature is one, and not two; but from one of them acts of two kinds derive—disastrous for some and munificent for others. And if it is the case among men that [judges] protect the kingdom by means of punishment through royal authority, how much more does God [protect] the whole of this world, he who wishes life for everyone and not death. So where transgression increased, he inflicted all with death; but where there was attentive obedience, he bestowed gifts of immortality.

"He is the true God, Creator of us all, whom you blaspheme with your impudent and unbridled mouth in fearless and unquivering arrogance. Abandoning the saving name Jesus Christ, you call him the son of P'andurak[1] and suppose him to be a deceiver; you corrupt and dishonor the heavenly salvation to the destruction of yourself and of the whole world. For this you will pay the eternal penalty of torments, condemned to the unquenchable fire [*p. 39*] of hell with all your companions—the first, middle, and last.

"But we acknowledge God in this fashion, and in the same we believe without doubting:

"God who made this world, the same came and was born from the Holy Virgin Mary, as the prophets previously indicated, without any bodily intervention. Just as he made this

4. *Blandishments:* see p. 126, n. 1.
5. *Seduce: orsan,* as on p. 17, n. 4. Cf. also *Teaching,* §280.
6. *Sorcery: kakhardut'iwn.* On this charge, frequently made against Christians in hagiographical literature, see p. 42 and further refs. there.

---

1. *P'andurak.* See p. 26, n. 2. Here the ref. is not an interpolation; the MSS read variously P'andurak, P'ant'urak, P'akt'urak, while *A* has Bant'urak as on p. 26.

massive body, the world, from nothing, likewise without any bodily mediator he took flesh from the unsullied Virgin—truly and not in a shadowy appearance. He was truly God and became truly man. In becoming man he did not lose his divinity, nor in remaining God did he spoil his humanity, but [he remained] the same and one.[1]

"But because we were unable to see the invisible or approach the unapproachable, he came and submitted to our humanity so that we might attain his divinity.[2] He did not think it any disgrace to put on this body created by himself, but he honored as divinely fashioned his own creation. Not gradually did he bestow on it the honor of immortality, as with the incorporeal angels, but all at once he put on the entire [human] nature,[3] with body, soul, and spirit, and united[4] it to his divinity—a unity and not a duality.[5] Consequently we acknowledge the divinity as one, who existed before this world and is the same today.

"This Jesus Christ, who in his own body redeemed the whole world, came willingly to death. And, as the Godhead knows, he was formed from the immaculate Virgin, was born and wrapped in swaddling clothes, was placed in [*p. 40*] a manger, brought the magi from the East to worship him, was nourished as an infant with milk, grew up and reached thirty years of age,[1] was baptized in the Jordan River by John, son of the barren woman.[2] He performed great signs and miracles among the Jews, was betrayed by the priests, was condemned by Pontius Pilate. He was crucified, died, was buried, rose on the third day, appeared to the twelve disciples and to many others—more than five hundred. He moved among them for forty days, ascended from the Mount of Olives to heaven before his own disciples, and came and sat on the Father's throne. He

---

1. Cf. *Teaching*, §378–381.

2. This is the classic Athanasian statement, see notably *De Incarnatione*, §54.

3. *Put on . . . nature:* for this statement, cf. *Teaching* §515, and for patristic evidence Lampe, *Lexicon*, s.v. ενδύω.

4. *United:* cf. *Teaching*, §369.

5. For the one nature see refs. in Thomson, *Teaching*, p. 20. For the Armenian rejection of a "duality" see, e.g., the commentary of Tallon (*Livre des Lettres*) to the *Apats'oyts'* (Demonstration) attributed to John Mandakuni in the *Girk' T'łt'ots'*, pp. 29–40.

---

1. Cf. Luke 3:23. But the Armenian of Ełishē seems to mean that Jesus grew *for* thirty years.

2. *Son of the barren women: amlordi;* cf. Luke 1:36.

promised to come a second time with fearsome power to raise the dead, to renew the whole world, to make a just judgment between the just and the sinners, to give rewards to the worthy, to punish evildoers who do not believe in all these benevolent acts.[3]

"From this faith no one can shake us, neither angels nor men, neither sword nor fire nor water, nor any kind of cruel torture.

"All our possessions and properties are in your hands and our bodies stand before you; do [with them] whatever you will. If you leave us with this same faith we shall not exchange you for another lord on earth, nor in heaven shall we exchange for another god Jesus Christ—than whom there is no other God.[4]

"Now if after this extensive testimony you ask further questions, behold we have given[5] our entire bodies into your hands. Do immediately whatever you wish: tortures from you, submission from us; the sword is yours, the necks are ours.[6] We are no better than our ancestors, who on behalf of this witness laid down their possessions, properties, and bodies.[7]

[*p. 41*] "For if we were immortal and it was possible for us to die for the love of Christ, it would be right [to do so], because he was immortal and so loved us that he accepted death in order that by his death we might be saved from eternal death. And if he did not spare his own immortality, we—since we become mortal by our own will—shall willingly die for his love so that he may willingly endow us with his own immortality; we shall die as mortals so that he may accept our death as that of immortals.

"But do you ask us no further questions after all this, for the covenant of our faith is not with a man that we may be deceived like children,[1] but is indissolubly with God—from whom it is impossible to be divided or separated, not now, not

3. Cf. pp. 147–148 for a similar credal statement.
4. There are parallels to this paragraph in *Vkayk'*, pp. 118, 119, and John of Ephesus, II, 19.
5. *We have given: kamk' tueal,* a very unusual perfect formation.
6. *Sword . . . neck.* The final beheading of martyrs is a standard theme in hagiography; see Delehaye, *Passions,* and cf. below, pp. 61, 123, and 158.
7. The ref. is probably to those Armenians who died fighting Persia in the fourth century; e.g., Faustos, III, 11 where the "martyrs" are likened to the Maccabees.

1. *Deceived like children:* a common idea in Ełishē, cf. pp. 37, 87, and 163; there are parallels in *Vkayk'*, as on p. 169, and *Vkayabanut'iwnk'*, I, 572.

in the future, not forever, not forever and ever."

To this great pact[2] all the multitude assented, from the greatest to the smallest. With a solemn oath[3] they bore witness that they would remain true to it in life and death.

When the letter reached the court and was read in the great hall[4] in the presence of the whole host of the army,[5] many were they who on hearing it praised the answer. Although they were frightened for awe of the government, yet secretly they bore witness of their praise to one another, astonished more at its bold fearlessness than at its eloquence. [*p. 42*] Many of the cowed began to recover strength; and the same whispering was heard from all lips.

But the malicious[1] chief-magus with the great *hazarapet*[2] breathed calumny, and inflamed the king like an inextinguishable fire. He began to gnash his teeth like one fatally wounded.[3] In public he raised his voice in the great assembly[4] and said: "I know the wickedness of the many men who do not believe in our religion and have gone irrevocably astray after sorcery.[5] I have decided that I shall not exempt anyone from the worst tortures until they, though unwillingly, abandon such an erroneous religion. Even if someone is among those very close to me I shall inflict the same on him."

Then the embittered old man[6] interposed and said to the king: "What is the reason for this great dejection of yours? For if the emperor does not transgress your command and the Huns remain subject to you, what man is there on earth who could

2. *Pact: hawanut'iwn.* Although this might mean "declaration of faith," the meaning "pact" comes out strongly from its use in 1 Macc. 8:30; 12:10; 2 Macc. 9:26.

3. *Solemn oath: ansut erdumn,* as on pp. 66, 199, where "sealing" is emphasized.

4. *Hall: khonastan,* a hapax in Armenian; see Hübschmann, *Grammatik,* p. 160.

5. *Army: karawan,* see p. 18, n. 1.

1. *Malicious,* as on p. 20, n. 1.

2. I.e., Mihrnerseh; for the term *hazarapet,* see p. 23, n. 4.

3. *Fatally wounded:* cf. p. 8, n. 6.

4. *Assembly: hraparak,* cf. pp. 27, 136. For the term see Meillet, "etymologies arméniennes, VIII."

5. *Sorcery.* Cf. p. 37, n. 5 and p. 158. Such charges against Christians were very common; cf. Agathangelos, §203, *Vkayk',* pp. 81, 112, and 123, and in general Delehaye, *Passions,* pp. 181–182.

6. *Embittered old man: tsern darnats'eal,* i.e., Mihrnerseh, as on pp. 88, 91. But on p. 158 the expression is applied to the chief-magus, who had been converted to Christianity.

oppose your order? Give an imperial command within[7] and whatever you say will be carried out immediately."

Then the king summoned the chief-scribe[8] and commanded him to write an edict[9]—not in the usual fashion but in angry terms as if to hateful and vile people, not at all recalling the great services of these loyal men[10] but merely summoning by name the men whom he knew personally.[11] Their names were:

> Vasak, from the house of Siunik'[12]
> [*p. 43*] Nershapuh, from the house of the Artsrunik'
> Artak, from the house of the Řeshtunik'
> Gadeshoy, from the house of the Khořkhořunik'[1]
> Vardan, from the house of the Mamikonean[2]
> Artak, from the house of Mokk'
> Manēch, from the house of the Apahunik'
> Vahan, from the house of the Amatunik'
> Giut, from the house of the Vahevunik'[3]
> Shmavon, from the house of the Andzevatsik'

These princes[4] were summoned by name to the royal court. Some of them were already by him in the army, others were in the garrison of the Huns in the north, and some of the princes he had left in Armenia.

So although they did not happen to be all united in one place, nonetheless they realized in advance the plot of the

7. *Within: i nerk's,* i.e., to the palace officials.
8. *Chief-scribe: dprapet.* For his duties and status see Christensen, *Iran,* pp. 129–130.
9. *Edict: hrovartak,* as on p. 9, n. 10.
10. Cf. p. 10.
11. *Personally: yakanē yanuanē,* lit. "by eye and by name," a common expression; cf. pp. 42, 43, 92, 120, 162, and 200.
12. Vasak of Siunik', the acting governor (*marzpan,* see p. 63 below) of Armenia, is the villain of Ełishē's *History,* the foil to the patriotic martyr Vardan.

---

1. *Khořkhořunik':* on the northwestern shore of Lake Van; for the family see Toumanoff, *Studies,* pp. 208–209.
2. Except for the title of the *History,* this is the first reference in Ełishē to his hero. For the Mamikonean family see Toumanoff, *Studies,* pp. 209–211.
3. *Vahevunik':* for this family see Toumanoff, *Studies,* p. 215.
4. This list is identical with that in Łazar, p. 47. For these lists see the discussion in Adontz/Garsoïan, pp. 188ff., and Toumanoff, *Studies,* pp. 246ff.

wicked tyrant,[5] and they thought of themselves, including the most distant, as close to one another in one spot.

Strengthened by the holy bishop[6] Joseph in the same faith, they journeyed from each one's place to the royal court. They made great haste for the sake of their brothers, and sons, and dear foster friends,[7] who were in sore affliction. Therefore they committed themselves to death, not hesitating like ignoble cowards; but they bravely strengthened themselves,[8] that perchance they might be able to save them from severe torments.

When they arrived at the royal court they appeared before the king on the holy Easter Saturday.[9] But although they saw their own brothers in [*p. 44*] great trouble and affliction—who had steadfastly endured[1] for the sake of Christ's name—they did not show sad or solemn faces in public. And the more they appeared joyful to everyone, the more the lovers of evil[2] were astonished.

It was the rule in former times, when the cavalry from Armenia went to the court under some distinguished general, for him (the shah) to send a man to meet them, to greet them,[3] and inquire about the welfare of Armenia; he would do the same twice and three times and in person review[4] the force. Before

---

5. *Wicked tyrant:* reminiscent of p. 22 (at n. 3), with overtones both of the Maccabees and of the common hagiographical description of the persecutor.

6. But Łazar calls Joseph a *priest;* see p. 27, n. 1.

7. *Foster friends: dayekasnund bnakatsʿ.* See p. 22, n. 5 for the significance of fostering in Armenia. Here the sentence is reminiscent of 2 Macc. 15:18, where the Jews were fearful for "their wives and children and blood brothers, for the *dayekatsʿ bnakatsʿ* of the citizens related to them" (where the Armenian differs from the Greek).

8. *Cowards . . . strengthened themselves: vatasirt, pndetsʿin zandzins.* The contrast is frequent in Ełishē; here there are reminiscences of the Armenian text of 1 Macc. 3, v. 56 (where the *vatasirt* are sent home; cf. also Judg. 7:3) and v. 43 (where the Jewish soldiers prepare for battle).

9. In 450 Easter Sunday fell on 16 April.

---

1. *Steadfastly endured: shgnealkʿ ēin pndapēs.* Both terms have many parallels in the books of the Maccabees; the verb *chgnel* is also widely used in hagiographical literature of a martyr's endurance.

2. *Lovers of evil:* a common term in Ełishē for the Persians; see p. 20, n. 1.

3. Cf. Łazar, p. 172[15]. On this whole ceremony Christensen, *Iran,* p. 205, notes the article by Patkanian, "Essay," in *JA* (1866), p. 112; but Patkanian merely cites this passage.

4. *Review: handēs tesanēr;* cf. p. 15, n. 5.

they went out to war he would greatly thank them for coming to him, and in front of his companions[5] and all the magnates he would praise them all and recall the services of their ancestors and rehearse the brave deeds of each man.

But on that day he remembered nothing at all of these customs, but like an evil demon[6] he did not cease provoking and stirring up a winter snowstorm.[7] He resembled the tumult of the surging wave-tossed sea; not insignificantly and superficially, but from the bottommost depths he rose in a mass of foam,[8] thundering like a dragon[9] and roaring like a wild beast, shaking his whole worldwide empire[10] as if it would crash and scatter in its entirety over the hills, hollows, and valleys to destroy completely the beauty of the extensive plains.

He raised his voice in a bellow and said: "I have sworn by the sun,[11] the great god who with his rays illuminates the whole universe [*p. 45*] and with his warmth gives life to all existing things,[1] unless tomorrow morning, at the rising of the splendid one, each of you bends his knee to him with me, confessing him as god, I shall not cease to bring upon you every form of affliction and torture until you fulfill the desires of my commands, though unwillingly."

But the Christians, firm in Christ, were not chilled by the icy blasts of winter or burned by the scorching heat, nor did they tremble at the fearsome voice or hesitate at the threats of tortures. But looking up they saw the power of Christ coming

---

5. *Companions: at'oṙakits'*, lit. "(those who) shared the throne." The term is used of a coemperor (Moses Khorenats'i, III, 19) or of a coadjutor bishop (Faustos, IV, 15; Moses, III, 57). A more exact parallel to the Iranian context is found in Esther 1:14, where it is used of the seven foremost princes of Persia (οἱ πρῶτοι παρακαθήμενοι); cf. also p. 49, n. 3.

6. *Evil demon: ch'aradev*, an epithet frequently applied by Ełishē to the Persian king; cf. pp. 46, 164.

7. *Snowstorm: buk'*; cf. Moses Khorenats'i, II, 36, 62.

8. For the simile of a sea-storm cf. the opening paragraphs of Agathengelos.

9. *Thundering like a dragon: vishapadzayn*. For the *vishap* in Armenian mythology see the refs. in Thomson, *Moses Khorenats'i*, I, 30, n. 17. In the Armenian Bible the *vishap* is a beast of the sea.

10. *Thundering . . . empire:* this is closely paralleled in *Vkayk'*, p. 112.

11. For oaths by the sun cf. p. 47, *Vkayk'*, p. 215, Moses Khorenats'i, II, 19 and refs. in n. 6. For oaths by Mihr see p. 185 below, and Moses Khorenats'i, III, 17, n. 7, Sebēos, p. 78. See in general for Iranian oaths Bailey, *Problems*, pp. 40, 59.

---

1. Cf. pp. 165–166 below for the image of the sun, and the refs. there to Philo.

to their aid, and approaching with joyful faces and modest words they replied to the king.

"We beg you, noble sovereign,[2] give ear to our words and listen kindly to what we have to say.

"We remind you of the time of Shapuh, king of kings, who was the father of your grandfather Yazkert and to whom God gave Armenia in subjection under the same religion as that by which we still live today.[3] Our fathers and great-grandfathers rendered him service and loyally fulfilled all his commands, often receiving generous presents from him. From those times until [your accession] to your ancestral throne we have performed the same service, but perhaps more so for you than for your predecessors."

By saying this they indicated that their valiant deeds in military service had been superior to those of their ancestors. Indeed the amount of revenue and dues and all the other taxes[4] of the country going to the court was greater than in the time of his father.

[*p. 46*] "Likewise on the holy church, which was free in Christ from the beginning according to the custom of our ancestors, you also imposed taxes.[1] And we, in our loyalty to your rule, did not oppose you. Now why has this anger been stirred up against us? Tell us the reasons for the maltreatment. Is our religion the cause of our being without merit[2] in your sight?"

But the wicked demon,[3] full of all deceit, turned his face to one side and said: "I consider it harm to receive into the royal treasury the tribute of your land, and your valiant deeds useless. For you have ignorantly gone astray from our true religion and have dishonored the gods; you have killed fire and defiled water;[4] you have buried the dead in the ground and corrupted

2. *Noble sovereign: ark'ay k'aj;* see p. 9, n. 2.

3. Ref. is here made to the division of Armenia in 386/7 into an Iranian sphere and a smaller Byzantine one; for secondary literature see Garitte, *Narratio,* p. 64, and Toumanoff, *Studies,* p. 152, n. 6. Shapuh is Shapuh III (383–388).

4. *Revenue, dues, taxes: mutk', sakk', hark.* For these terms see p. 23, n. 9.

1. Cf. p. 22, n. 11 for the "freedom" of the church.

2. *Without merit: anvastak.* The term *vastak* is frequently used by Eḷishē of the duties and services that the Armenians paid the shah.

3. *Wicked demon:* see p. 44, n. 6.

4. *Killed fire:* cf. the long passage on killing fire below, pp. 174ff. For the cult of fire and water cf. Moses Khorenats'i, II, 33.

the earth; and by not performing pious duties,[5] you strengthen Haraman. And what is worst, you do not regularly approach your wives.[6] The demons have great joy when you disregard and do not observe all the institutions of the magi. I see you as sheep scattered[7] and lost in the wilderness. And I have great scruples that perhaps the gods, in their anger at you, will take vengeance from us.[8] But if you wish to live and save yourselves and be sent back in honor, do what I have said immediately."

Then the blessed princes in unison raised their voices and said before everyone: "Do not, O king, do not say that again to us. For the church is not the creation of man or the gift of the sun; not only is the latter not god, [*p. 47*] but it is not even alive as you in your confusion[1] suppose. Churches are not the gifts of kings, or the invention of skill, or the discovery of the wise, or the booty of valiant soldiers, or the false deceits of demons. Similarly, whatever you say of earthly beings, whether grand or ignoble, nowhere is a church [created] by them to be found. But it is a gift of grace from the great God, not given to some individual man, but to all rational peoples whose lot it is to dwell under the sun. Its foundations have been placed on a firm rock; powers below cannot shake it or powers above move it. What heaven and earth cannot topple, let no man boast of conquering.[2] So, in whatever manner you wish to treat us, do so. We are all ready for every contrivance of torments and tortures that you have threatened, ready not only to be tortured but even to die.[3] And if you were to ask the same questions again, you will hear from each one of us more than the present reply."

Then the king became more bitter than gall.[4] He spewed forth the sea[5] of the willful bile[6] in his stomach; from his nose

5. *Pious duties: k'rpikar.* For the term see Nyberg, *Manual* II, s.v. *kirpak,* and Asmussen, "Einige Bemerkungen"; cf. also p. 137 below.
6. Cf. pp. 26–27 above.
7. Cf. Matt. 9:36; 26:31; Mark 14:27.
8. For this idea see p. 15, n. 3.

1. *Confusion: ayl ĕnd ayloy,* as on pp. 93, 130, and 146.
2. The description of the church in this paragraph is reminiscent of 1 Cor., chs. 1–3; cf. also Matt. 7:25; 16:18; Luke 6:48.
3. *Ready . . . die.* This sentence has parallels in 2 Macc. 7:2, where the seven brothers defy Antiochus.
4. Cf. Prov. 5:4.
5. Cf. Isa. 11:15.
6. Cf. Acts 8:23.

and mouth issued hot vapor[7] like thick smoke from a heated furnace. Unable to tame his heart he destroyed the strength of his body, pierced the overflowing vessel of his plans, and scattered and wasted all his deceitful thoughts. And what he had never intended to reveal to his friends, unwillingly he revealed before the servants of Christ in its details.

Three and four times he repeated his false oath to the sun, saying as follows: [*p. 48*] "You are unable to destroy my sure fortifications, nor shall I allow you to obtain immediately what you desire. But all of you and those in my army I shall exile in cruel bonds to Sagastan[1] through roadless parts, where many of you will perish on the journey from the heat, and the survivors will be thrown into secure fortresses and inescapable prisons. To your country I shall send an infinite army with elephants; your wives and children I shall have despatched to Khuzhastan;[2] your churches and what you call martyria[3] I shall destroy, raze, and obliterate. And if anyone is found to resist he will be trampled by wild beasts[4] and die a merciless death. All that I have said I shall perform and carry out on the survivors in your country."

Straightway he ordered the honorable princes to be expelled from his presence in great dishonor. He strictly commanded the chief-executioner[5] to guard them unbound in each one's lodging, and the perverse one took up his residence in unconsolable sadness.

But the true believers in Christ were not at all irresolute or

---

7. Cf. Sirach 22:30.

1. *Sagastan:* modern Sistan. For the province in Sasanian times see Marquart, *Erānšahr,* pp. 35–36. (Hübschmann, *Grammatik,* p. 71, considers Sagastan an error for Sakastan [as MSS *G Z Ē Tʿ I*], but the reading in Moses Khorenatsʿi, III, 55, confirms the reading of the majority of the MSS.)

2. *Khuzastan:* see Marquart, *Erānšahr,* p. 27. In *Vkaykʿ,* p. 113, it is the place of exile and martyrdom for the bishop Shmavon of Ctesiphon.

3. *Martyria: vkayaran,* a chapel dedicated to the cult of a martyr (*vkay*), normally containing relics. Cf. Faustos, IV, 23, or Agathangelos, §768. In general see Lampe, *Lexicon,* s.v. μαρτήριον, III.

4. On trampling by elephants as a punishment see *Vkaykʿ,* p. 43; Boyce, *Letter of Tansar,* p. 48; Christensen, *Iran,* p. 304.

5. *Chief-executioner: dahchapet,* for which see Hübschmann, *Grammatik,* p. 133, and Harmatta-Pekary, "Decipherment," p. 470. The *dahichkʿ* were responsible for the guarding of prisoners as well as their torture or execution; see p. 160 below.

doubtful[6] of the earlier counsel of their holy teachers, but they sought further ways how they might extricate themselves and their loved ones from this great tribulation. After frequent attempts, they offered great promises with the prospect of money to the magnates who had helped them at the royal court, and they expended on them no little treasure at that time.

When their inescapable prison[7] was closed on all sides, then recalling the example of Abraham, they cried and said in their hearts: "We have all offered our brothers and sons [*p. 49*] and all our dear ones and placed them bound like Isaac on the holy altar;[1] receive, O Lord, our willing sacrifice and do not give your church to the ridicule and mockery[2] of this lawless prince."

One of the king's privy counselors[3] secretly had an indissoluble love for Christ,[4] for he had been baptized in the living font,[5] and he was greatly concerned with saving the lives of these unfortunate ones. When he became fully aware that the king was intending to inflict on Armenia all the evils he had threatened, he advised a few of them, though not all, of a means whereby they might save themselves from tribulation for a while.

While they were gathering a force which would banish[6] them to a foreign exile of no return,[7] as they had banished many princes from Georgia,[8] at that very time arrived a bearer of bad news from the regions of the Kushans, to the effect that a detachment had separated from the enemy and had ruined

---

6. *Irresolute, doubtful: erkmtut'eamb t'erahawatēin,* as in Matt. 14:31 of Peter sinking. But cf. also p. 109, where the ancient heroes of Israel were not irresolute, or p. 99, where the Armenians were not doubtful. (But p. 89, n. 4, where some were).

7. *Inescapable prison: anel argelan,* as on p. 19 of the region beyond the Chor Pass.

---

1. Cf. Gen. 22:9.

2. Cf. Ps. 43:14.

3. *Counselors: khorhrdakits',* as in Ezra 7:14 of the king's seven σύμβου-λοι; cf. also p. 44, n. 5.

4. For Christians at the Sasanian court see Akinean, *Elishē,* II, 536, and Christensen, *Iran,* ch. 6.

5. Cf. Titus, 3:5.

6. *Banish: shkot'ak;* cf. pp. 159, 162.

7. *Of no return: andardz,* reminiscent of Job 16:23, where it refers to death.

8. The first exile of Georgian princes attested to in other sources occurred in 484; see Akinean, *Elishē,* I, 357ff.

many royal provinces. This proved a great help to them from heaven.[9] The impious one quickly and urgently sent off the cavalry, and he himself in haste followed closely behind. Deeply wounded[10] in his intentions, he shattered his earlier firm oath.

When the fearers of the Lord saw this, with great hope they prayed and said in unison: "O Lord of all, who knows the secrets of men's hearts and before whom all invisible thoughts are revealed, who does not require witness from the visible as your eyes see what we have not yet done[11]—now before you we pour out our requests. Receive, [*p. 50*] O Lord, our secret prayers and make us delight in your commands, so that the evil one, who has dared to fight against you through the power of the impious one,[1] may be put to shame. Shake, O Lord, the crooked[2] plans of the deceitful one and obstruct the desires of his impiety; lead us back with peaceful minds to the holy church, that it may not be suddenly attacked and cruelly ruined by the enemy."

Having in their souls made this indissoluble covenant with God that they would remain firm in their former resolution, they sent in as messenger the same adviser[3] of theirs, as if the desire of his impiety would be fulfilled.

When the king heard this he very greatly rejoiced, thinking the gods[4] had come to his help and had toppled and destroyed the firm resolve of God's servants. And behold they offered adoration to the sun,[5] honoring him with sacrifices and with all the rites[6] of the magi.

The madman was unable to understand that the unshadowed light of the sun of righteousness[7] was absorbing and consuming his dark plots, and that they were destroying and

---

9. *Help . . . heaven;* reminiscent of 3 Macc. 5:28.
10. *Deeply wounded;* cf. p. 13, n. 4.
11. Cf. Ps. 138:16.

---

1. *Evil one, impious one: ch'arn, anawrēnn;* i.e., the devil and Yazkert, cf. p. 7, n. 11.
2. *Crooked: kamakor,* reminiscent of Isa. 27:1, referring to the serpent (*vishap awdzin*), as Mihrnerseh is described on p. 88.
3. I.e., the Christian counselor mentioned on p. 49.
4. *Gods: dik';* see p. 9, n. 12.
5. For the adoration of the sun see p. 17, n. 9.
6. *Rites: awrēnk',* for which term see the Introduction.
7. Cf. Mal. 4:2. For Christ as the "sun of righteousness," cf. *Teaching,* §566.

ruining all his perverse desires.[8] Blinded by the revelation of
the truth he in no way comprehended the deceitful ruses by
which he was tricked. He showered them with earthly gifts and
restored to them all their honors and ranks, promoting them
and making them distinguished throughout his entire worldwide empire. With unbounded liberality he bestowed on each
one of them estates and towns [*p. 51*] from the royal treasury.
He called them dear friends, and in the arrogant presumption[1]
of his perverse mind he thought that the truth could be
changed for falsehood.

Having done this he gathered a large force of cavalry to escort them, and not a few magi; more than seven hundred
teachers[2] he sent with them, and over them he appointed a certain great prince as chief-magus.[3] Humbly and beggingly he
ordered them: "By the time I return in peace from this war, you
will have performed and accomplished everything according to
my will." And thus with éclat and honor[4] he sent them off[5] on
the long journey to Armenia. He himself sent joyful tidings to
many fire-temples,[6] and indicated in writing to the magi,
chief-magi, and all the magnates of every region of his dominions how "by the help of the gods I have carried forward my
noble work."

But then those impure ones, rising up from each one's
gloomy lair,[7] were impatient to fulfill the command at once.
He [the king] sent word to distant lands that they should immediately march to the West. And before they had arrived in
the great land of Armenia, they threw sticks[8] and drew lots as
to which group [of magi] would undertake the instruction of

---

8. This sentence is reminiscent of Phil. 2:15. But there are parallels
with the feigned adoration of the sun in *Vkayk'*, p. 123; see p. 102, n. 3.

1. Cf. 3 Macc. 2:1.

2. *Teachers: vardapet.* For this term in Armenian tradition and for
parallels between the *vardapet* and the Iranian *mobed* see Thomson, "Vardapet." Lazar, p. 54, does not give the number of magi. Cf. p. 70 below for
three hundred more.

3. For the chief-magus (*mogpet*) as governor see p. 23, n. 7.

4. *Thus with éclat and honor: ayspēs shk'ov ew patuov;* cf. 2 Macc. 3:28:
aynch'ap' shk'ov ew patuov, describing the vision of Heliodorus.

5. *Sent them off: aṙajnordēr,* which means "led," although it is not suggested that Yazkert went in person.

6. *Fire-temples: atrushan,* see p. 12, n. 4.

7. *Rising . . . lair;* cf. Judg. 9:35 of the wicked Abimelech.

8. *Threw sticks: p'ayt ěnkenuin. P'ayt* (lit. "wood") in this sense of drawing lots is not attested to elsewhere, but cf. the Persian *chob andakhtan.*

which people. For they had received a general command from the court [to instruct] not only Armenia but also Georgia, Albania, and the land of the Lp'ink', Aḷdznik', Korduk', Tsaudēik' and Dasn, and wherever else in the Persian empire they secretly observed Christianity.[9]

In a mad onslaught they hastened to plunder the treasures of the holy churches, and then like demons they began to fall on one another. A large force was gathered, and the malicious Satan[10] appeared among them like a general, [*p. 52*] ceaselessly exhorting them all and urging them to make haste. He fixed a time, six months, and they spared no efforts [in fulfilling] the royal command.

"From Navasard to Navasard,"[1] he said,[2] "in every place that is under the authority of the great king, church services shall be suppressed, the doors of the holy temples shall be shut and sealed, the sacred vessels[3] shall be numbered and taken to court, the singing of psalms shall be silenced, the readings of the true prophets shall cease. Priests shall not be allowed to instruct the people in their own homes, and the believers in Christ, men and women who dwell each in their own monasteries,[4] shall change their garments for secular attire.[5]

"Furthermore the wives of the princes shall receive the magi's instruction. Sons and daughters of the nobility and peasantry[6] shall study the precepts of these same magi. The laws of holy matrimony which they received from their forefathers according to Christian ritual shall be abrogated and abolished; instead of one wife they shall take many, so that the Armenian nation may increase and multiply. Daughters shall

---

9. Cf. the list of Christian lands on p. 10.

10. *Malicious Satan;* i.e., the chief-magus. For "malicious" see p. 20, n. 1.

---

1. *Navasard:* the first month of the Armenian year; see Hübschmann, *Grammatik,* p. 202. For the Armenian system of dating see Grumel, *Chronologie,* pp. 140–145; in 450 the Armenian year began on 6 August. Here the more general idea of a whole year is intended; cf. p. 53, n. 2.

2. *He said.* Although this speech seems to be delivered by the chief-magus, the final paragraph of the chapter might imply that the king gave these instructions.

3. *Church services . . . vessels:* parallel expressions for persecution in *Vkayk',* p. 112.

4. *Monasteries: menanots';* see p. 22, n. 12.

5. *Attire: kargk',* a term usually applied to rituals, as on p. 85.

6. *Nobility and peasantry: azatk', shinakank'.* For these two basic divisions of Armenian society see Toumanoff, *Studies,* p. 124–127. Cf. also pp. 57, 131.

be [wives] for fathers, and sisters for brothers. Mothers shall not withdraw from sons, and grandchildren shall ascend the couch of grandparents.[7]

"Sacrificial animals[8] shall not be killed without being offered [to the gods], be they sheep, goats, cattle, fowl, or pigs. Dough shall not be kneaded without a veil.[9] Excrement and dung shall not be thrown into fire. Hands shall not be washed without urine.[10] Otters, foxes, and hares shall not be killed. [*p. 53*] Snakes and lizards, frogs and ants, and all other various kinds of insects shall not be left,[1] but promptly shall be brought forth in appropriate numbers according to the royal measure. And whatever other duties there are, either of offerings or sacrifices, shall be performed according to the yearly festival rites and the due amount of ashes.

"Everyone shall fulfill all that we have said for a period of time up to the completion of a year;[2] and to everything else they shall address themselves in the future."

When the magi and chief-magi received all these instructions, day and night they hastened to Armenia. And in their great joy they were never wearied by the length of the journey.[3]

7. For marriage of blood relations in Zoroastrian Iran see Christensen, *Iran,* pp. 318–320, and Boyce, *Zoroastrianism,* pp. 97, 111. The practice was bitterly attacked by Armenian clerics; see, for example, Faustos, IV, 4, and the frequent references to it in Armenian canon law, *Kanonagirk'.*

8. *Sacrificial animals: patruchak,* which renders "sheep" at 1 Kings 25:11; 2 Kings 17:29.

9. *Veil: pandam;* see Hübschmann, *Grammatik,* p. 254, *Mundtuch.* For a modern illustration see the cover of Boyce, *Zoroastrianism.*

10. For bull's urine as a ritual purifier see MacKenzie, *Dictionary,* s.v. *gōmēz* (Armenian, *gumēz*).

1. *Snakes . . . insects.* This passage was adapted by the thirteenth-century chronicler Mkhit'ar of Ani, p. 40, to refer to the pre-Islamic cults adopted by Islam.

2. *The completion of a year: minch'ew i glukh tarwoy.* The MSS *B G D E ZH L KH K H* read *tarwoyn* ("the year"). But the phrase seems to refer back to "from Navasard to Navasard" (p. 52, n. 1)—i.e., for the period of a whole year.

3. See p. 58 for their arrival and the problem of dating.

CHAPTER THREE

Concerning the Unity of the Holy Covenant[1] of the Church

ALTHOUGH we are unable to mention all the evils which were inflicted on the Armenian contingent[2] in the army, yet we do not wish to remain silent and hide their cruel afflictions. But we shall give a summary[3] so that we may join our voices[4] to those who bitterly lamented us, and so that you too, as you listen, may shed not a few tears over the misfortune of our nation.

For behold, in the great Persian camp, those of the various nations who were believers in Christ's holy Gospel, when they saw the evil submission of the Armenians were sorely pained, collapsed, and fell on their faces. Many of them, grieved[5] in deep mourning, smitten in their souls, and with bitter tears, came and reproached the nobles and greatly blamed the clergy.[6]

Execrating them all they said: "What will you do with your Holy Testaments or where will you take the vessels[7] of the

1. *Covenant: ukht.* For this key expression in Ełishē see the Introduction.
2. *Contingent: gund.* For the technical meaning of this term see Adontz/Garsoïan, p. 181. Cf. also p. 96, n. 4 below.
3. *Summary: pʻokʻr i shatē,* as in Moses Khorenatsʻi, II, 67, giving a "summary" of Agathangelos.
4. *Join our voices: dzaynakitsʻ.* The only biblical parallel is at 3 Macc. 4:6, also in the context of mourning.
5. *Grieved: tʻaltseal.* Cf. 2 Macc. 3:16 for the grief (*tʻaltsutʻiwn*) of the high priest.
6. *Clergy: ukht kʻahanayutʻean,* "covenant of the priesthood." For the use of *ukht* as clergy (translating κλῆρος) see p. 3, n. 3.
7. *Vessels: spas,* equivalent to the Greek σκεῦος. Cf. p. 174 for the vessels of the Zoroastrian cult.

Lord's altar? Will you really forget your spiritual blessings or remain impervious to the voices of the prophets? You have shut your eyes to reading and closed your ears to hearing.[8] [*p. 55*] Will you not recall what should be indelible in your minds? What will you make of the commands from the Lord: 'Who denies me before men, him shall I too deny before my Father who is in heaven and [before] the holy angels?' "[1]

"You were teachers of the apostolic preaching; will you now become pupils of erring deceit?[2] You were teachers of the truth; will you now teach the wily deceit of the magi? You were preachers of the creative power; do you now confess the elements of gods? You were reprovers of falsehood; will you now become even more mendacious than falsehood? You were baptized in fire and spirit;[3] will you now be immersed in ash and dust?[4] You were nourished with the living flesh and immortal blood;[5] will you now be blackened with the smoke of sacrifices and impure filth?[6] You were a temple of the Holy Spirit;[7] will you now become an altar for demons? You had put on Christ from your youth;[8] will you now be stripped of glory and dance like demons[9] before the sun?

"You were heirs of the kingdom;[10] you have now made yourselves heirs to hell. It was they who were threatened with

8. Cf. Isa. 6:10; Matt. 13:15.

1. A conflate of Matt. 10:23 and Luke 12:9.
2. This paragraph has some parallels with the lament in Moses Khorenats'i, III, 68.
3. Cf. Matt. 3:11; Luke 3:16.
4. Cf. 2 Macc. 13:8, where the holy fire is contrasted with the death of dust. But here "ash" has overtones of Zoroastrianism; see p. 12, n. 4 for the "ash-worship," and cf. p. 176 below.
5. Cf. John 6:53ff.
6. Cf. p. 176 below for the smoke and soot of fire worship. Agathangelos, §523, refers to the foul smoke and soot of sacrifices to idols. The "smoke" (*chencher*) recalls 2 Macc. 7:5 and the death of the first brother.
7. Cf. 1 Cor. 6:19.
8. Cf. Rom. 13:14 and Gal. 3:27.
9. This recalls the picture of desolation in Isa. 13:21. For the use of *kak'aw* ("partridge") for a strutting dance see Greppin, *Bird Names*, p. 84; cf. also p. 64 below. Here the use of *kak'awel* in 2 Macc. 5:7 (when the Jews were forced to join in Greek rites) may be in Ełishē's mind. The term is also used of Salome in some medieval poems on the beheading of John the Baptist; see *Bazmavēp*, 1850, p. 52; 1851, p. 343.
10. Cf. James 2:5. Many of the biblical allusions in these paragraphs are so commonplace that it is difficult to point to a single text as the source.

the unquenchable fire;[11] why have you been burned and seared[12] with them? For them the undying worm[13] is being fattened; but now you have fattened your own bodies as food for it. The outer darkness[14] is being kept impenetrable for them; why did you, clothed in light,[15] accompany them to the same darkness? They long since had become blind; why will you become blind following the blind? They had dug the pit; why did you fill it in advance?[16] When will you learn the myriad [*p. 56*] names of their gods, of which not one exists anywhere? Lightened of heavy burdens, you have taken up of your own accord a heavy burden;[1] freed from servitude,[2] you have perversely entered into inescapable bondage.

"If only you knew and it was clear to you that heaven mourned for you and earth grieved beneath your feet.[3] The angels above have become angered with you, and from earth the martyrs have become furious at you. I pity, I pity your loved ones, but more I pity your own selves. For if a man had saved you from servitude, and you then of your own accord put yourselves in servitude to another, you would provoke your first lord to great anger. But now how will you treat the divine command: 'I am God and there is no other beside me, nor will any other after me be God. I am a jealous God. I shall punish the sins of fathers on sons up to the seventh generation'?[4] But if the just sons are subject to punishment for their fathers' sins, when the sons themselves sin, will they not at one and the same time answer for both their own and their fathers' [sins]?

"You were our strong wall of refuge;[5] when danger approached we went to you for safety. But now that great fortress

11. Cf. Mark 9:42.
12. Cf. James 3:6.
13. Cf. Mark 9:47.
14. Cf. Matt. 8:12.
15. Cf. Rom. 13:12.
16. Cf. Matt 15:14 and Luke 6:39.

---

1. Cf. Ps. 37:5.
2. Cf. Rom. 8:21.
3. Cf. Jer. 4:28. There are more elaborate parallels in *Vkayk‘*, p. 57.
4. This is an elaborate conflate of Exod. 8:10, 20:5; Deut. 5:9; Isa. 44:6; Mark 12:32. The punishment of sins to the seventh generation is not attributed to God's own words in the O.T.; but cf. the seven punishments of Cain in Gen. 4:24.
5. A common expression in the O.T., especially associated with Jerusalem.

has been destroyed to its foundations. You were our boast[6] against the enemies of truth;[7] but now you are our shame before those same enemies. Up to the present, for the sake of your true faith, they spared us a little; but now because of you they judge us mercilessly. You will have to give a reckoning before God's fearful tribunal not only for yourselves[8] but also for many others whom they will torment because of you."

This and more besides they said to the greatest of the nobility,[9] [*p. 57*] piling pain on pain. The latter were unable to reveal or indicate their intention, but it was impossible to remain silent and make no response. Choked, they burst into intense weeping. With them the embittered audience[1] also all mourned inconsolably.

Then the priests who were there in the army, unable to endure the anger of their hearts, separated themselves from the princes and all the troops and sent a messenger by horse in haste to Armenia. With the sad news in his mouth and with his collar rent,[2] he reached the group of bishops;[3] bursting into profuse tears, he related all the details of the tortures, but he did not reveal to them the secret plans.

Then the bishops scattered to each one's diocese, and they sent chorepiscopi[4] to the villages and estates and to many castles in the mountainous provinces. They urged the populace to assemble—the men and women, peasants and nobles,[5] priests and monks. They exhorted and strengthened them, and made them all soldiers of Christ.

Their prime resolve was decided thus: "Let the hand of

6. Cf. Isa. 62:7; Zeph. 3:19–20 (of Jerusalem; cf. preceding note).

7. *Enemies of truth:* a common expression in Ełishē; cf. pp. 65, 89, 113, and 192.

8. Cf. Rom. 14:12; 2 Cor. 5:10.

9. *Greatest of the nobility: metsametsk' awagani.* The same phrase is used of Persians in *Vkayk',* p. 213. For *awag* see p. 16, n. 9; the form *awag-ani* is a collective plural, see Meillet, *Esquisse,* §53.

1. *Audience: lsołk' ew tesołk',* lit. "those listening and seeing."

2. *Collar rent: zawdzis pataṙeal;* cf. 1 Macc. 5:14 for this phrase in a similar situation. But it is common in Armenian to indicate grief; cf. also p. 78.

3. Although Yuzbashyan and Ter-Minasyan translate this as "synod of bishops," there is no other ref. to a specific "synod" after the gathering on p. 41, which had taken place a considerable time earlier. The same phrase *i zhołovs* is used on p. 169[2] to mean a group or company, which is my justification for that translation here.

4. *Chorepiscopi:* see p. 28, n. 16.

5. *Peasant and nobles:* see p. 52, n. 6.

blood brother be upon his relative who may transgress the covenant of God's ordinance. Let not a father spare his son, nor a son respect his father's dignity. Let a wife strive with her husband, and a servant turn against his master.[6] May the divine Law rule over all, and by the same Law may transgressors receive the punishment of their condemnation."

When this had been so confirmed and established, they all mustered [*p. 58*] armed and helmeted, girt with a sword and shield in hand,[1] not only valiant men but also virile women.

Now the Armenian troops with all their auxiliaries[2] and the crowd of magi arrived in Armenia in the fourth month,[3] at an important town called Angl.[4] They pitched camp together and settled in; from all sides they gathered there, forming an innumerable multitude.

After twenty-five days the chief-magus himself and the magi arrived with a great force in order to break down the doors of the church on a Sunday. He intended to put the proposed action to the test. But the holy priest Levond, in concert with his leading supporters[5] and many clergy, stood ready at the spot. Although he was not informed of the intentions of all the princes, nor of the strength of the chief magus's force, he did not wait for all the bishops, nor did he give way for a mo-

---

6. *Let not a father ... master:* an inversion of Col. 3:18–22.

---

1. The helmet, sword, and shield are too reminiscent of Eph. 6:17 to be taken as a literal description of the Armenian men and women. Since Ełišē's purpose is to describe this war as a battle for spiritual values, his style is too often redolent of biblical and theological themes to be relied upon as the unadorned version of an eyewitness.

2. *Auxiliaries: awgnakankʻ,* as on p. 59 of the assistants of the chief-magus. The Armenian term translates the Greek βοηθός.

3. *Fourth month.* This must mean the fourth month after setting out (on a very long journey, p. 53). In 450 the fourth month of the Armenian year, Trē, ran from 4 Nov. to 3 Dec., and the fourth month of the Sasanian era began five days earlier (calculations based on Grumel, *Chronologie,* and Nöldeke, *Sasaniden*). The Armenians had reached the Iranian court at Easter time (April, 450), but Ełišē does not say how long it took them to decide to feign apostasy, or for the shah to gather his expedition (p. 51). But according to Łazar, p. 60, the magi were already in Armenia before the hot season. And many military exploits by Armenians are described by Ełišē following the arrival of the magi before Marcian came to the throne (August, 450), p. 73. On the chronology see the Introduction.

4. *Angl:* in the province of Tsałkotn, north of Lake Van, different from the Angl in western Armenia on the upper reaches of the Tigris; see Hübschmann, *AON,* p. 399.

5. *Supporters: khorhrdakitsʻ,* "like-minded," "sharer of counsel"; cf. p. 49, n. 3.

ment to the impious ruler,[6] but he brought a great tumult on the army and magi. Grasping stones,[7] they aimed their blows at the skulls of the magi and chief-magus, forcing them to flee to their camps. They themselves offered the Liturgy in the church and continued the Lord's service throughout the whole Sunday.

After this dangerous disturbance, from all parts of Armenia a crowd of men and women reached the place. [*p. 59*] There one could see the great agony of doubt. Some let forth torrents of tears which flowed from their eyes like streams; others let forth loud shrieks as if they would shake the heavens; while others took courage and ran to arms, preferring death to life. Some of the holy clergy of the church took the Gospel in their hands and addressed prayers to God. Others desired the earth to open that it might become their tomb. Thus they brought fearful anguish on the chief-magus. He frequently begged his assistants[1] to rescue him from death and bring him back to the court safe and sound.

In the matter for which he had come he pressed them, saying: "Let me write and indicate to the great king that he should abandon such a project as this. For even if the gods themselves were to come to our aid, it would be impossible for the religion of magism[2] to become firmly established in Armenia, as I have tested the unity of the covenant of the church. For even if the soldiers of this country were magi, these [Armenians] would not spare them in the slaughter—not only the outsiders but also their brothers and sons and all their relatives, and even their own selves.[3] These men, who do not fear imprisonment, are not afraid of tortures, have no reverence for wealth, and—what is the most extreme evil of all—prefer death to life.[4] Who is there who can oppose them?

[*p. 60*] "I had heard from our ancestors that in the days of Shapuh,[1] king of kings, when that doctrine of yours began to

6. *Impious ruler: anawrēn ishkhan;* cf. p. 7, n. 11.

7. *Stones: virgs;* as at 2 Macc. 1:16, where (Persian) priests attacked Antiochus as he entered the temple of Nanea.

1. *Assistants: awgnakank';* see p. 58, n. 2.

2. *Religion of magism: awrēnk' mogut'ean;* for *awrēnk'* see the Introduction.

3. Cf. 2 Macc. 15:18, where wives and children, brothers and relatives are of less concern than the preservation of Jerusalem.

4. Preferring death to life is a common theme in Ełishē (e.g., pp. 72, 98, 124, and 197) and Maccabees (e.g., 2 Macc. 6:19; 3 Macc. 1:14).

1. It is not clear which Shapuh is intended: Shapuh III (383–388)

increase and spread and fill the whole of Persia, and even reach the east beyond, those who were the teachers[2] of our religion enjoined the king to prevent the religion of magism from being completely exterminated from the land. So he gave a strict order that Christianity should be silenced and brought to a halt. Yet the more he wished to restrain and prevent them the more they increased and expanded, reaching even the land of the Kushans, and to the south spreading as far as India.[3]

"They were so fearless and audacious in Persia that in every city of the land they built churches which surpassed in splendor the royal palace. They also built what are called martyria[4] and decorated them in the same fashion as the churches; and in every uninhabited spot they constructed hermitages.[5] Although no assistance from anywhere was apparent, they increased and multiplied and grew in material prosperity. We had no idea of the causes of their wealth, but this much we truly understood—that the whole world was following their teachings.

"Although the king lay forcible hand on them,[6] arresting and torturing many of them, slaughtering even more and becoming embittered and soured, yet he was unable to diminish their number. Furthermore, although he locked and sealed the doors of the churches throughout the whole land of Persia, they made every house a church and practised their religion everywhere. Each one considered himself a shrine,[7] and they reckoned bodily temples [*p. 61*] superior to material ones. The swords of the executioners were blunted, but their necks were not wearied.[1] The plunderers of their possessions labored, and the booty daily increased and multiplied. The king was

---

who is mentioned above on p. 45, or Shapuh II (310–379) in whose reign there were severe persecutions; see Christensen, *Iran*, pp. 263ff. Yet this paragraph seems to imply a spread of Christianity later than the fourth century. See n. 3 below.

2. *Teachers: vardapet*, as on p. 51, n. 2.

3. For the spread of Christianity to the land of the Kushans (Huns) see the reference in Akinean, *Ełishē*, I, 221–222; and more generally the several articles of J. M. Fiey listed in the Bibliography.

4. *Martyria: vkayaran*, as on p. 48, n. 3.

5. *Hermitages: miaynanots'*; see p. 22, n. 12.

6. Cf. Isa. 5:25, where God lays hand on the wicked.

7. *Shrine: vkayaran* as in n. 4 above. The idea is reminiscent of Paul; e.g., 1 Cor. 6:19.

1. *Swords, necks:* see p. 40, n. 5.

enraged, and the executioners waxed cruel in their anger.[2] But these were awake and joyful, and happily accepted all torments, willingly enduring all the confiscation of their belongings.

"When the king saw that they were rushing to death like holy sheep to the heavenly salt,[3] he stopped and cut short their torments. He commanded the magi and chief-magi that no one should molest them in any way, but that they should remain undisturbed in their own doctrines without fear—magus and Zandik[4] and Jew and Christian, and whatever other many sects[5] there were throughout the Persian Empire. So the land gained secure peace and all disturbances and commotions ceased, for at the agitation of our land the West had been even more stirred up and all Tachkastan had been disturbed with them.[6]

"This we know by report. But what I have seen with my own eyes seems to me even more significant than the former. Now you who are *marzpan*[7] of this land, you must be sure to write and indicate to the court the strength of their union and how fearlessly they set at naught the royal commands. If we had not hastened to take flight, they would not have allowed a single one of us to escape. And if unarmed people [*p. 62*] were so powerful, should they unexpectedly join forces with soldiers, who would be able to oppose their resolute assault?

"I was indeed unaware of the mutually indissoluble covenant of this church.[1] For it is one thing what a man hears and

---

2. These three sentences have numerous parallels in the rhetorical descriptions of persecutions in *Vkayk'*.

3. *Heavenly salt:* for this theme in patristic exegesis see Lampe, *Lexicon,* s.v. ἅλς, esp. B6.

4. *Zandik: Manichaeans,* see Eznik, §148, and in general Christensen, *Iran,* ch. 4. For the etymology see Hübschmann, *Grammatik,* p. 149, and Nyberg, *Manual* II, s.v. *zandī.* However, the Armenian text of *Vkayk',* p. 231, translates "Manichaeans" with *manik'ets'i.*

5. *Sect: kesht,* as on p. 83 (in general sense) and p. 144 (of Persian doctrines). For the etymology see Hübschmann, *Grammatik,* p. 167, and Nyberg, *Manual* II, s.v. *kēs.*

6. For Tachkastan see p. 10, n. 8. It is not clear what disturbances in the "West" (i.e., the Roman Empire) are intended.

7. *Marzpan:* governor of a border province, in this case of Persian Armenia. For this office see Christensen, *Iran,* pp. 131–134, and for further Armenian references Hübschmann, *Grammatik,* p. 193. Cf. the description of Armenia as a frontier (*marz*) on p. 62. The *marzpan* is not named here, but Vasak of Siunik' is intended (cf. p. 42, n. 12).

---

1. The indissoluble (*ank'ak*) covenant of the church is a basic theme in Eḷishē; cf. p. 50, and in general the Introduction.

another what he sees for sure with his own eyes. You who were nourished from your childhood in that religion and truly knew the firmness of those men, that without the shedding of much blood they would not allow us to lay hands on their churches, why did you not explain all this faithfully before the king? Since you were the most senior[2] of all the nobles and he had entrusted this whole country to you as *marzpan*, why did you not take greater pains? For at other times you were wise, and I knew it; but in this matter you did not act wisely. Otherwise it would be assumed that you were in agreement with them and it was at your advice that they acted thus against me and against the army.

"Now if this is so and you do not wish to hold to magism, do not in any way be frightened of the king. I shall write and explain to the court, to the *Movpetan movpet*,[3] and to the chancellor,[4] *and to the great hazarapet*[5] that they must persuade the king to leave them alone in accordance with his former edict and to let them act according to their own will, so that gradually they may become accustomed to the religion of magism and those who accept it may be seen to have fulfilled the king's command willingly. For this land is a frontier.[6] [*p. 63*] Perhaps when they work any harm they may be scattered and lost to foreign lands. But when this country is emptied of its population, then on you especially greater trouble will be inflicted by the court."

The *marzpan* replied to the chief-magus, saying: "All the words of advice which you have spoken are true. What at first we did not understand, you saw, and now we regret it greatly. But do what I say and it will seem good to you. Be a little patient and keep your thoughts from most [people], except those men to whom I tell you to reveal them, until I can gather a force to bring support. Then perhaps I shall be able to split the covenant of the church. And if I manage that, I know that I can fulfill the king's command."

2. *Senior: awag;* see p. 16, n. 9.

3. *Movpetan movpet;* the highest official in the Zoroastrian clergy; see Christensen, *Iran*, pp. 111–113, and Hübschmann, *Grammatik*, p. 195.

4. *Chancellor: darandardzapet,* a high court official; see Nyberg, *Manual* II, s.v. *handarzpat,* and Hübschmann, *Grammatik*, p. 179, for further Armenian refs. For the Iranian office see Christensen, *Iran*, pp. 94, 108, 130, and 515. On p. 165 below the *anderdzapet* is named Movan, as in Lazar, pp. 88, 97, and 102. The spelling is variously *andardzapet* or *anderdzapet.*

5. *Hazarapet:* see p. 23, n. 4; Mihrnerseh is intended, cf. p. 24.

6. *Frontier: marz;* see Hübschmann, *Grammatik*, p. 193, and cf. *marzpan*, p. 61, n. 7.

Then raising cavalry[1] from the land of Siunik' he increased his own forces for the support of the magi and chief-magus. Then he said: "Now send a letter to the court that the cavalry in Albania, which numbers ten thousand,[2] may come to winter quarters in Armenia. When we have them to hand there is no one who can subvert the royal command."

The chief-magus replied and said to the *marzpan:* "Your counsel is again contrary to my suggestion. For if we use force against this country it will be destroyed, and we too shall not escape damage—harm to ourselves and especially loss[3] to the king."

But the *marzpan* had no desire to heed him, for he had sincerely accepted the Persian religion. Then he began to deceive some with money and others with blandishing words. By threatening all the common people[4] in fearful words, he disheartened them. He continually increased the [*p. 64*] allowances[1] of the banqueting-hall, he extended the music of jollity, stretching out the nights in drunken singing and lascivious dancing.[2] He amused some with music and pagan songs,[3] and heaped great praise on the king's religion. He had brought from the treasury a mass of wealth and he secretly distributed bribes[4] to each person on the pretext of giving gifts and honor; and very deceitfully he enticed innocent men and drew them to himself.

But when the holy bishops saw all this they were even more fervent and animated for their union. With shrewd wisdom they divided the army into two. And especially when they

---

1. *Cavalry: hros,* not attested to elsewhere in Ełishē; for the etymology see Bedirian, "Système." In the next sentence "cavalry" is the translation of the usual *ayrudzi* (lit. "man and horse").

2. For a discussion of the military potential of the various Armenian noble houses see Toumanoff, *Studies,* pp. 234ff., and cf. below p. 96, n. 1.

3. *Loss: zean,* not attested to elsewhere in Ełishē; for the etymology see Hübschmann, *Grammatik,* p. 150.

4. *Common people: ṙamik,* a general term for those not belonging to the "free" *(azat)* class, i.e., peasants (comprising the vast majority of Armenian society) and artisans; see Toumanoff, *Studies,* p. 127.

---

1. *Allowances: ṙochik,* see Hübschmann, *Grammatik,* p. 234, and Nyberg, *Manual* II, s.v. *rōc* ("day").

2. *Lascivious dancing: i kak'aws lktut'ean;* for *kak'aw* see p. 55, n. 9, and cf. Agathangelos, §180 for dancing *(zparsn parel ew zkak'awsn yordorel)* at the intended wedding of Trdat and Rhipsimē.

3. For banquets and singing cf. Moses Khorenats'i, II, 68; III, 55.

4. *Bribes: kashaṙ,* cf. p. 174, where God's tribunal is called *ankashaṙ* ("incorruptible").

realized for certain that the impious prince of Siunik[5] had inflicted mortal wounds on his soul,[6] they turned away in horror and avoided him.

One evening the entire group of the clergy[7] held council. Summoning the commander[8] of the army to the council for questioning and investigation, they realized the firmness of his mind, and that he had not in the least failed in his love for Christ. After praying together over him, they received him again into [the fold of] virtue. Through him they brought[9] many to the same union; those who had not broken away from the former union came and joined them, a force of many troops. And they became even more removed from the magi and the chief-magus and the impious Vasak.

But the latter had so demented and dulled the mind of the chief-magus that he was unable to understand the consequences of his deeds. He began to distribute the magi among the houses of the nobles, to arrange vast allowances,[10] to sacrifice beasts,[11] forcibly to oblige baptized men to eat sacrificial meat[12] and to worship the sun.[13] [*p. 65*] After such filthy practices began to multiply throughout the whole country, even the wives of the Lifeguards[1] dared to extinguish the church lamps on Sunday and to tear the garments of the nuns.[2]

---

5. Vasak is called "impious" (*anawrēn*) because he had accepted magism; see p. 7, n. 11 for *anawrēn* as applied to Yazkert.

6. Cf. Isa. 59:10 for "mortal" and "soul."

7. *Clergy: ukht*, see p. 3, n. 3.

8. *Commander: sparapet*. For the term see p. 7, n. 9. At this time the office was held by the prince of the Mamikonean family, therefore Vardan Mamikonean is meant.

9. *Brought: orsats'an*, lit. "hunted"; see p. 17, n. 4. The term is often used for bringing converts to Christianity: cf. *Vkayk'*, p. 127, where the martyr Shmavon is addressed: *ov Shmavon orsord, or orsats'aw zastuatselēn orsn;* or Agathangelos, §81, where Christ "catches" (*orsastsʻē*) men for heaven.

10. *Allowances:* as in n. 1 above.

11. *Beasts: patruchaks;* see p. 52, n. 7.

12. *Sacrificial meat: mis yazatsoy*. The only biblical use of *yazel* is in 1 Macc. 1:50 where the command "to sacrifice" sets off the revolt. For Christian abstention from sacrificial meat see refs. on p. 20, n. 5. The prohibition is repeated in *Kanonagirk'* I, 160; II, 149, 152.

13. For the worship of the sun see p. 17, n. 9.

---

1. *Lifeguards: pʻshtipan;* see Hübschmann, *Grammatik*, p. 255, and Nyberg, *Manual* II, s.v. *pustēpān*. Christensen, *Iran*, p. 390, notes that they formed the royal honor guard.

2. *Nuns: hawatawor kanants'n*. For this meaning of *hawatawor* (lit. "faithful, believing") see the *Nor Baṙgirk'* s.v.

When all the holy bishops saw this grievous clamor, taking the Gospel in their hands,[3] without asking they entered the general's quarters[4] where were gathered all the Armenian troops.

They raised their voices and said: "We beg you all by this Holy Gospel—if at your advice the *marzpan* and chief-magus are committing these impious crimes, first cut off our heads[5] and then seize the church. But if they are committing these evils against your will, today let your vengeance be sought from them."

Those who were inside the general's quarters stood up, and raising their voices in unison to God said: "O Lord who knows the hearts of all,[6] you have no need of witness from men;[7] if we have intentionally strayed from you, you yourself know that well. Today judge us according to our sins. But if we stand firm in the covenant of this Holy Gospel, you Lord be our helper[8] today and give the enemies of truth[9] into our hands that we may deal with them according to our will."

When they had said this they all put their heads to the ground and were blessed with the Gospel by the bishops.[10]

[*p. 66*] But one of the princes who was present and took part in their council did not join them in their great act of witness. Straightway he was stoned by them on the spot,[1] and great fear fell on all.

Then they all burst into such a raging fury that the bowels of all the onlookers trembled; they considered as naught the king's gifts and trampled under foot his fearsome commands.[2] They ran quickly to their weapons and spent the entire night arming and organizing. At dawn they divided their force into three parts and fell on the [enemies'] army. The first group from the east, the second group from the west, and the third

3. For taking the Gospel, cf. p. 59.
4. *Quarters: vankʻ*, used for example in 1 Kings 17:54 of David's "tent."
5. *Heads: paranotsʻ*, lit. "necks"; cf. p. 178 for the same expression.
6. Cf. Acts, 1:24.
7. Cf. John 5:34.
8. Cf. Heb. 13:6.
9. See p. 56, n. 7.
10. Lit.: "by the gospel and by the bishops." Cf. p. 66, n. 4 for oaths on the Gospel.

1. Łazar, p. 61, names the renegade Zandalan, for whom see Adontz/Garsoian, *Armenia*, p. 442, n. 21.
2. This sentence has numerous precise verbal parallels with the Armenian text of 1 Macc. 2:24, which describes the zeal of Mattathias.

group from the north surrounded and fenced in the host of the [Persians'] army. Many they killed, and even more notable warriors they captured and threw into strong prisons under their own command. Gathering to one place the plunder and booty of the army they guarded them as if at the king's command.

When they arrested the *marzpan* he was for joining them with an oath to remain firm in the covenant; he repented of his earlier falling away from them. He fell in penitence at the feet of the holy bishops and tearfully begged that he should not be rejected and cast from them. Two and three times he repeated an inviolable oath[3] on the Holy Gospel before them all; he put it in writing, sealed it, and bound it to the Gospel.[4] He begged that it be left to God to seek vengeance and that they not take it upon themselves as men to kill him.[5]

Now although they well knew his deceitful hypocrisy [*p. 67*] and that he would falsely return to his old error,[1] they were in no way anxious to seize him because of his former transgression, but they left his condemnation to the Holy Gospel.[2]

Those who had come to plunder the holy treasures of the church unwillingly surrendered themselves and their plunder to the holy bishops and the entire army. The king's command was rendered null and void.[3] Having succeeded by the power of God, men, women, and all the common people[4] cried out in thanks: "We are ready for persecution and death[5] and every affliction and torture for the sake of the holy churches which our forefathers entrusted to us by the power of the coming of our Lord Jesus Christ, whereby we were reborn to the one hope of faith by baptism in Christ Jesus.[6] In the same fashion we wish

3. *Inviolable oath: ansut erdumn;* see p. 41, n. 3.
4. For oaths on the Gospel cf. pp. 92, 122; see in general Lampe, *Lexicon,* s.v. εὐαγγέλιον, G3. For sealing with rings cf. p. 132; for a collection of seals from Dvin see K'alant'aryan, "Knk'adroshmner."
5. Cf. Rom. 12:19.

1. Cf. p. 121.
2. Cf. Rom. 2:1.
3. This sentence has precise verbal parallels with 1 Macc. 2:48, which describes Mattathias saving the law.
4. *Common people: r̄amik;* see p. 63, n. 4.
5. *Ready . . . death:* a common theme in Ełishē with parallels in Maccabees; further refs. on p. 73, n. 10.
6. This last phrase is a conflate of 1 Pet. 1:3 with the theme of John 3:5.

to renew ourselves by torments and blood. For we recognize the Holy Gospel as our Father, and the apostolic Catholic church as Mother.[7] Let no evil partition come between us to separate us from her."

Thenceforth the lord seemed no greater than the servant,[8] or the pampered[9] noble[10] than the rough[11] villager,[12] and no one was behind another in valor. One willing heart was shown by all—men and women, old and young, and all those united in Christ. For all together put on the same armor and donned the same breastplate of faith in Christ's command; with one belt of truth men and women girded their waists.[13]

Thenceforth gold was cast away, no one took silver for himself, and without avarice they despised and disparaged the honorable garments [worn] for adornment and distinction. Likewise, each one's possessions were accounted as nothing in the eyes of their possessors. They regarded themselves [*p. 68*] as dead corpses, and they dug each one his own grave. Their lives were reckoned as death, and their death as certain life.[1]

But this acclamation was continuously voiced: "Let us only die valiantly, let us merely inherit fame and spirit, so that Christ may be alive in us; it is for him easy to renew again from dust both us and all those who fell asleep before, and to recompense each one according to his deeds."[2]

Voicing these and more similar arguments, consoling themselves[3] and one another, once more the soldiers prepared

7. For the Gospel as Father see Lampe, *Lexicon*, s.v. πάτηρ, 2; for the church as Mother, ibid, s.v. μητηρ, 2b, and Murray, *Symbols*, pp. 142 ff.

8. *Lord, servant: tēr, tsaṙay;* for these terms in Armenia see Toumanoff, *Studies,* p. 117. But here there are overtones of Pauline imagery. For *tsaṙay* as "subject" see p. 131, n. 6.

9. *Pampered: p'ap'kats'eal;* this term is usually applied to women; but cf. p. 194, n. 4. It has overtones of luxury; see esp. p. 200.

10. *Noble: azat;* see p. 52, n. 6.

11. *Rough: vshtats'eal,* with overtones of "afflicted, miserable"; cf. p. 49, and esp. p. 81, where it is contrasted with *p'ap'kasun* (see n. 9 above).

12. *Villager: geljuk;* not attested to elsewhere in Ełishē or in Łazar. See Moses Khorenats'i, II, 3 for their status, and I, 6, 12 for them as purveyors of old tales. For modern studies of this class see Adontz/Garsoian, *Armenia,* pp. 333, 362, and bibliography on p. 263*.

13. *Breastplate, belt, girded:* cf. 1 Thess, 5:8; Eph. 6:14.

1. *Death, life:* cf. p. 14; but it is a theme common to Ełishē and the Maccabees.

2. Cf. Rom. 2:6; Phil. 3:21.

3. *Consoling themselves: mkhit'arelov zandzins,* as in 1 Macc. 12:50 of the Jews preparing for battle.

their arms. The prayerful were unceasing in their prayers, and those fasting assiduous in their fasts. The voices of the ministers[4] ceased not day and night from [reciting] the holy psalms. The readers of the divine Scriptures never paused at any hour, neither did the expounders of the consolation of heavenly teaching.

Then once more they attacked the fortresses and towns which the Persians held in various strong places in the country. They destroyed and razed their dwellings: first the great [city] Artashat[5] with its villages. They took the following inaccessible fortresses: the cities of Garni, Ani, Artagerk', and their villages;[6] Erkaynordk' and Arkhni and their villages; Bardzrabol, Khoranist, Tsakhanist,[7] [*p. 69*] the secure Olakan,[1] and its villages with it; Arp'aneal,[2] the town of Van,[3] and its villages with it; Greal and Kapoyt, Orotn and Vashakashat.[4]

All of these places with each one's villages and farms, troops and commanders, they captured and destroyed in the same year; they led away into captivity the men and women with their possessions and belongings, their valuable treasures and goods. They destroyed and razed their buildings and burned down the houses of fire-worship.[5] They cleansed away the impurity of idolatry[6] and removed the furniture and effects of the fire-temples, placing them in the holy churches; through the holy priests they dedicated them to the service of the Lord's altar. In place of the vain pagan[7] cults, which they destroyed

---

4. *Ministers;* see p. 11, n. 1.
5. See p. 28, n. 18.
6. Artagerk' is in north central Armenia; see Hübschmann, *AON*, p. 409. But there are two Garnis (in northeastern and northwestern Armenia) and two Anis (in north central and northwestern Armenia); see Eremyan, *Hayastan*, s.v.
7. These five sites are not otherwise attested to.

---

1. Olakan is west of Lake Van in Tarawn; see Hübschmann, *AON*, p. 326.
2. The river Arp'aneal flows from Siunik' into the Araxes; the town is not otherwise attested to. See Eremyan, *Hayastan*, s.v.
3. On Lake Van; see Hübschmann, *AON*, p. 469.
4. Greal and Vashakashat' are otherwise unattested to. Kapoyt and Orotn are in Siunik'; see Hübschmann, *AON*, pp. 438, 462.
5. *Houses of fire-worship: tuns pashtaman kraki;* cf. the term πυρσολατρεία in *Narratio*, §30, and commentary, ibid. p. 97. More frequent in Elishē is the term *atrushan* (as in the next sentence), for which see p. 12, n. 4.
6. Cf. the ref. to the Jews purifying their land, p. 109.
7. For "pagan" (*het'anos*) applied to Persians see p. 16, n. 3.

everywhere, they set up the saving cross of Christ,[8] they raised the all-holy altar, and reverently celebrated the vivifying Sacrament. They installed deacons[9] and priests in those places. Sustained by hope, the whole land rejoiced in unison.

While they were carrying out all this great and virtuous task of heroism, a divine grace appeared over them all. For without orders from the Armenian army, from the eastern part of the country some[10] attacked the land of Atrpatakan[11] and caused much damage in various places, seizing and looting, and razing many fire-temples.

[*p. 70*] Those who attacked the great fortresses fell on the enemy, making the sign of the cross. It even happened that the walls of two tremendous castles collapsed[1] without anyone approaching them, so that all the inhabitants of the land were terrified by the great miracle and themselves with their own hands set fire to the fire-temples;[2] disavowing the religion of magism, they confessed in the Holy Gospel.

And other tremendous successes were accomplished through the soldiery. For where there was no expectation that anyone would remember the name of God, terrifying shocks befell them and everyone told his neighbor of these unprecedented visions and wonders. Likewise the stars in heaven appeared shining with greater brilliance than was their usual nature.[3] And all the youths of the land were as bold as mature warriors.[4]

8. Reminiscent of Gregory's activity as described in Agathangelos, §781–816.

9. *Deacons: pashtōneaykʿ;* see p. 11, n. 1, for this rendering.

10. *Some:* Akinean, *Ełishē,* I, 341ff., takes this to be an invasion by Turks; but from the context Armenian attacks would be the most likely meaning.

11. *Atrpatakan:* southeast of Lake Urmia, an area smaller than the modern Azerbaijan; see Hübschmann, *Grammatik,* pp. 23–24.

1. *Walls, collapsed:* a conflate of Josh. 6:5 and 20 (of Jericho).

2. *Fire-temples: kratatun;* see p. 69, n. 5, and p. 12, n. 4.

3. Akinean, *Ełishē* I, 344ff., associates these earthquakes and shining stars with phenomena reported by Michael the Syrian and others as occurring in the second half of the sixth century. But it may be doubted whether these vaguely described events are more real than the standard run of miracles in hagiographical texts; they are more easily accounted for as rhetorical embellishments. Cf. the following note.

4. Cf. 2 Macc. 15:17, where the exhortation of Judas makes men out of boys. The term *paterazmoł* ("warrior") is used also on p. 189 of the martyrs, and has many parallels in the O.T.; cf. also *Vkaykʿ,* p. 32.

Many days later the *hazarapet*[5] of Albania arrived with the holy bishop of that country, and urgently exhorted the soldiers, saying: "The Persian army which was in the land of the Huns[6] has returned and reached our land, and many more cavalry from the court have also arrived. In addition to all this, they have brought with them another three hundred magi as teachers;[7] they have created discord in the country and have brought some over to themselves. They desire to lay hands on the church, and at the king's command they put pressure on everyone, saying: 'If you willingly accept his religion, you will receive gifts and honors[8] from him and you will gain relief of taxes[9] from the treasury. But if you do not do this willingly, we have a command to build fire-temples in villages and towns, to place inside them the fire of Vṙam,[10] [*p. 71*] and to appoint magi and chief-magi as arbiters[1] for the entire country. And if anybody resists and opposes he will be punished with death; and the wife and children of such people will be exiled to [work] the royal estates.' "[2]

When the Armenian army heard this bitter news, they were in no way discouraged or weakened[3] in bravery. But there

5. *Hazarapet:* see p. 23, n. 4.

6. For Persian expeditions against the Huns cf. pp. 12, 42, and Marquart, *Erānšahr*, p. 56.

7. For magi as teachers (*vardapet*) see p. 51, n. 1. The number three hundred is reminiscent of the three hundred elephants and the damage they caused in *Vkaykʻ*, p. 180.

8. *Gifts and honors:* the same promise is made in *Vkaykʻ*, p. 169, if the Christians will only worship the sun.

9. *Relief of taxes,* as on p. 22.

10. *Fire of Vṙam:* this was the highest, most sacred form of fire-worship; see Boyce, *Zoroastrianism*, pp. 64, 108–110, and Duchesne-Guillemin, *Religion*, pp. 77ff.

1. *Arbiters: awrēnsdir.* Cf. p. 176 for this term applied to magi; later Armenian writers frequently use it of Muhammad. For the magi as judges, see p. 23, n. 7. The term *awrēnsdir* is widely used in a Christian context, following James 4:21; see Lampe, *Lexicon*, s.v. νομοθέτης. Cf. also *awrēnsdrutʻiwn*, p. 29, n. 6.

2. For work on royal estates cf. pp. 133, 183, and 187, and Perikhanian, "K vprosy." *Exiled: anashkharhik,* as on pp. 115, 162; the term has overtones of slavery, as in 1 Macc. 3:41 and 3 Macc. 7:5, its only biblical occurrences.

3. *Discouraged or weakened: tʻulatsʻeal lkʻan,* as also on pp. 105, 109. The terms are common both in Ełišē and Maccabees, see p. 14, n. 1; cf. also *Vkaykʻ*, p. 49.

was a gathering of people of the entire country to debate this bad news brought to them by the envoys. Unanimously giving them encouragement, they dismissed them; their purpose was to deal with them [the Persians] deceitfully for a while, so that they might be hindered from their wicked intentions and not lay hand on the holy covenant of their church. With the power of God they held council, seeking a way out of the problem.

Then they sent in haste one of the great princes of the Gnuni family, Atom,[4] to the West in order to reveal all these evil plans of the malicious[5] king of the East, and at the same time to describe their own brave valor, which they had proved by deeds—by trampling on the fearful order [of Yazkert] and inflicting great slaughter on the magi—and to seek from him [the emperor of the West] aid and support, even entering his service[6] should he so wish.

This is a copy of the letter[7] which they wrote to the Emperor Theodosius:

"The bishop Joseph, with many of my cobishops[8] and the whole Armenian army; Vasak the *marzpan* and Nershapuh Ṙmbosean,[9] with the *sparapet*[10] and all the greatest princes, to the illustrious emperor Theodosius—may our greeting be upon you and all your troops,[11] you who with your peaceful benevolence rule over land and sea; and there is no person on earth who can oppose your irresistible empire.[12]

4. For Atom see also pp. 99, 133, and 193, and Łazar, p. 45. The *Martyrdom of Saint Atom* (see Gray, "Two Armenian Passions,") bears little relation to what is said about him in Ełishē, although the *Martyrdom* has many verbal reminiscences of this *History*. For the Gnuni family see Toumanoff, *Studies*, p. 205.

5. *Malicious: ch'arimats'*, as on p. 124 of Vasak. Cf. the frequent *ch'arasēr*, p. 20, n. 1.

6. *Service: tsaṙayut'iwn:* cf. the Pauline exhortation, p. 11, and the frequent use of the term to mean subjection to the shah, e.g., p. 9, or the Greeks, p. 93.

7. *Letter: hrovartak*, as on p. 9, n. 10.

8. For Joseph as a bishop see p. 27, n. 1. For the title "cobishop" see Lampe, *Lexicon*, s.v. συνεπίσκοπος.

9. *Nershapuh Ṙmbosean*, The name Ṙmbosean (of unknown origin, see Adontz/Garsoian, *Armenia*, p. 463, n. 70) is not found in Łazar, but he frequently refers to Nershapuh as an Artsruni.

10. *Sparapet:* i.e., Vardan Mamikonean, see p. 64, n. 8.

11. Similar greeting in the Armenian letter to Mihrnerseh, p. 28.

12. *Irresistible empire: anargel tērut'iwn*, as in 3 Macc. 6:19 of the Greeks.

[*p. 72*] "According to our infallible records[1] concerning your courageous ancestors, having occupied Europe they crossed over and also ruled the regions of Asia from the borders of Sēir to the limits of Gaderon;[2] and there was no one who rebelled or escaped their control.

"Within that vast dominion they called Armenia a great and beloved territory.[3] For that reason our ancestor Tiridates[4] remembered your earlier affection: when in his youth he fled from his murderous uncles who had assassinated his father,[5] he lived and was brought up in the land of the Greeks; made king by you, he ruled over his ancestral land. Likewise, having received faith in Christ from the holy archbishop of Rome,[6] he illuminated the benighted regions of the North,[7] which now the darkness-loving sons of the East wish to wrest away from us.

"Relying on your noble valor, some of their commands we have opposed and many more we are ready to continue opposing. We have chosen death in piety rather than life in apostasy.[8] If you extend further help to us we will have gained a sec-

1. *Infallible records: ansut yishatakarank'.* Akinean, *Eḷishē*, III, 67, n. 8, mentions several later examples of the same phrase. What Armenian record Joseph refers to here is obscure. *Yishatakaran* could mean "memory."

2. *Sēir to Gaderon:* Sēir is frequently mentioned in the O.T.; it is in Sinai. Gaderon is to the north of Media. As Akinean (*Eḷishē*, III, 67, n. 10) comments this is based on Hippolytus (*Chronicle*, §§82–83), where he describes the expansion of the races of Japheth from the borders of Media to Gaderon and names those nations which have writing: Iberians, Latins, Spaniards, Greeks, Medes, Armenians. Gaderon also renders "Cadiz."

3. *Territory: dastakert;* for the use of this term see Sarkissian, "Les deux significations."

4. *Tiridates: Trdatios,* a curious hybrid of the Armenian *Trdat* with a Greek ending. For the many various forms of the name see Garitte, *Documents,* pp. 237–238.

5. *From ... father: i hayraspan mardakhoḷkhoḷ hawreḷbarts'n iwrots'.* That Trdat's uncles assassinated his father is contrary to the tradition in Agathangelos, which is repeated by all later Armenian writers. For the importance of this comment in Eḷishē see Toumanoff, "The Third Century," p. 262. The adjective *mardakhoḷkhoḷ* is reminiscent of the term *mardakhoshosh* applied to Yazkert and taken from 2 Macc. 9:28. See p. 22, n. 3.

6. This seems to refer to the visit of Trdat to "the city of the Romans" as described in Agathangelos, §874; but this occurred after the conversion of Trdat. It is noteworthy that Eḷishē never refers to Gregory the Illuminator, unlike Ḷazar.

7. For Armenia as a country in the "North" see Koriun, p. 24; Agathangelos, §175, 741, 742; Moses Khorenats'i, I, 10, 17; III, 68.

8. This is a basic theme for Eḷishē with verbal borrowings from the Maccabees, see refs. on p. 59, n. 4.

ond life and avoided death. But if you delay even a little, the heat of their furnace will perhaps reach many other countries."

After they had come into the presence of the great king and had read the supplication of Armenia and the records of their ancestors, many books were introduced and read, in which they found the same firm covenant.

While the blessed Theodosius was questioning the whole Senate,[9] anxious to find a peaceable solution to the matter and greatly concerned [*p. 73*] lest the churches of the East be ravaged by the impious heathen,[1] at that very time the end of his life suddenly befell him.[2] This put a serious obstruction in the way of procuring help.

In his stead the emperor Marcianus[3] came to the throne. The king was influenced by his evil counselors Anatolius, who was the commander-in-chief,[4] and Elpharios the Syrian[5]—both vile and wicked men, and ungodly[6] to boot—so he was unwilling to heed the united pact of the Armenians, who with all their strength were opposing the wickedness of the heathens. But this ignoble man thought it better to preserve the pact with the heathen[7] for the sake of terrestrial peace, than to join in war[8] for the Christian covenant.[9] Therefore he quickly despatched that same Elpharios as ambassador to the Persian king and contracted a firm pact with him that he would not support the Armenian forces with troops, arms, or any form of assistance.

When this had been so concluded and hope of human help had vanished, the holy bishops began to reassure themselves

---

9. *Senate: sinklitos;* see Hübschmann, *Grammatik,* pp. 379–380.

1. *Heathen:* for the Persians as "heathen" see p. 16, n. 3.
2. On 28 July 450.
3. *Marcian:* emperor from 25 July 450 to 26 January 457.
4. *Commander-in-chief: sparapet;* see p. 7 for Anatolius and this office.
5. *Elpʿarios:* a corruption of Florentius; perhaps the same official as the *Praefectus praetorio Orientis,* 428/9 and 438/9; see Paully-Wissowa, s.v. *Florentius 13.* Łazar, p. 74, calls him *"Pʿlorent,* a senior member of the court." Both Anatolius and Florentius are mentioned in *Novel* IV, 1 of Theodosius, dated to 438; see C. Pharr, *The Theodosian Code,* s.v. *Novel* IV, 1.
6. *Ungodly: anastuats,* as on p. 138 of the Persians.
7. For this pact see p. 7.
8. *Join in war: paterazmakitsʿ linel,* with the implication of joining (*-kitsʿ*) the Armenians. Neither Ełishē nor Łazar says anything about the menace posed in 450 to Constantinople by Attila.
9. *Covenant: ukht,* with ref. to the earlier covenant between Armenia and the empire (p. 72).

and the Armenian army. Although they were aware of their own small numbers and of the alliance of the two kings, they were not discouraged or shaken, but were emboldened in their former pact and said: "We are ready to kill and to die.[10] It is easy for God to work through a few the business of many,[11] and through despised [persons] to accomplish the greatest deeds."

Although they did not have a king as leader nor any support from abroad, nevertheless [supported] by their own valor and the consolation of their holy teachers, [*p. 74*] all the nobles immediately assembled in one spot with the troops from each one's house. There were also many additional cavalry there from the royal house.[1]

They divided all their forces into three sections. The first section they gave to Nershapuh Ṙmbosean, and charged him with defending the country near the borders of Atrpatakan. The second section they entrusted to Vardan, the Armenian general,[2] with orders to cross the Georgian frontier against the *marzpan* of Chor, who had come to destroy the churches of Albania. The third section they entrusted to Vasak, the prince of Siunikʻ, who in his innermost heart had not abandoned his covenant with the heathen. He chose and took with him those whom he knew to be weak in their faith:

The prince of the Bagratunikʻ[3] with his forces,
The prince of the Khoṙkhoṙunikʻ[4] with his forces,
The prince of the Apahunikʻ[5] with his forces,
The prince of the Vahevunikʻ[6] with his forces,

10. Readiness for death is a common theme in Eḷishē and the Maccabees; see also pp. 67, 76, and 113, and cf. 2 Macc. 7:2 (*patrast emkʻ . . . i meṙanel,* as here).

11. This is based on 1 Macc. 3:18 (Judas's encouragement to his small force before defeating a large enemy army), with exact verbal parallels in the Armenian.

1. *Royal house: arkʻuni tun,* as also in n. 11 below; cf. the "royal" estates (pp. 80, 99) or the "royal" capital (p. 28), although the monarchy had been abolished a generation before the events here described.

2. *Chor:* see p. 12, n. 3; on p. 75 the *marzpan* is called Sebukht. Ḷazar, p. 64, refers to Nikhorakan Sebukht. For the names see Hübschmann, *Grammatik,* pp. 59–60, 72.

3. This is the first reference in Eḷishē to the Bagratuni family, for which see Toumanoff, *Studies,* pp. 201–203.

4. See p. 43, n. 1.

5. See p. 28, n. 14.

6. See p. 43, n. 3.

The prince of the Palunik[7] with his forces,
The prince of the Gabeḷeank[8] with his forces,
The prince of Urts[9] with his forces.[10]
And many other troops from the royal house[11] he brought over
to his side and some lesser[12] nobles from other families. With
deceitful cunning[13] he lay in wait[14] in the strongholds of his
own land with the fictitious excuse that he would rapidly move
to attack the Persian army in order to expel them from Albania.

[*p. 75*] But from his securely hidden lair he quickly sent
messengers to the Persian army: "Behold I have broken the
unity of the Armenians' covenant and have split their army
over three areas. The first section I have sent far off to the regions of Her and Zarevand;[1] the second section is under my
control and I shall not allow them to do any harm to the royal
army. And all the other fighting men in the country I have
dispersed and scattered throughout all the central part of the
land. The third section I sent to Albania under Vardan, a small
force[2] and not numerous. Face him boldly and do not hesitate[3]
at all to give battle. I know that they will be defeated by your
great force."

This he wrote and explained to the *marzpan*, whose name
was Sebukht.[4] When he heard all this encouraging news from

---

7. For the Palunik' family, which held land in Turuberan and also
east of Lake Van, see Toumanoff, *Studies*, p. 212.

8. For the Gabeḷeank' family see Toumanoff, *Studies*, pp. 220–221.

9. For Urts, on the left bank of the Araxes in Siunik', see Toumanoff,
Studies, p. 222.

10. This list appears in Ḷazar, p. 67; but there the Gabeḷeank' are replaced with the Abeḷeank' and the princes are given personal names.

11. *Royal house;* as in n. 1 above.

12. *Lesser: sepuh;* see Toumanoff, *Studies*, pp. 114–115, 126, and 130,
and Christensen, *Iran*, p. 95, for this term. It refers to rank; cf. p. 16, n. 9.

13. *Deceitful cunning: khoramank khabēut'iwn*, a common phrase in Eḷishē;
cf. pp. 86, 92.

14. *Lay in wait: daranamut linēr*, as in 2 Macc. 14:22 of Judas's men; and
cf. *Vkayk'*, p. 78.

---

1. *Her and Zarevand:* provinces to the northwest of Lake Urmia; see
Hübschmann, *AON*, p. 338.

2. *A small force: sakawadzeĩn*, as in 1 Macc. 3:17 of the Jews under
Judas.

3. *Do not hesitate: mi zangiter*, as in 1 Macc. 3:22 of Judas's exhortation
to his small force.

4. Cf. p. 74, n. 2.

Vasak and was assured that the Armenian general was advancing on him with a small number of troops, he did not remain in the region of Chor, but gathered all the host of his army and rapidly crossed the great river called Kura.[5] He encountered him near the borders of Georgia, opposite the city of Khalkhal, which was the Albanian kings' winter residence.[6] After crossing with all his troops, he drew them up to enclose the entire plain; they were armed and equipped in total readiness for battle against the Armenian army.

Now when the valiant Vardan and all the troops with him saw the host of the heathen army in readiness and looked at their own [*p. 76*] small number—although they were very much less numerous than the enemy they were not at all dismayed by their great number, but together in unison raised their hands to heaven in supplication, saying:[1]

"Judge, Lord, those who judge us; fight with those who fight against us; with your arms and shield help us.[2] Shake and make tremble the vast host of these impious ones. Scatter and overthrow the evil unity of your enemies before your great saving sign;[3] and give into the hands of these few the glory of victory over that immense host. Not in the pride of vainglory for profitless exploits or with an avaricious greed for acquiring transitory grandeur do we make this prayer, but in order that all those who do not heed the preaching of the Holy Gospel may realize and know that you are Lord of life and death, and that through you come victory and defeat. We are ready to die[4] for love of you; but if it happens that we slaughter them, we shall be avengers[5] of the truth."

Saying this, they closed ranks[6] and attacked. Having bro-

5. Kura: the river dividing Armenia and Georgia; see Hübschmann, *AON*, pp. 358, 370.
6. Khalkhal: north of Lake Sevan; see Hübschmann, *AON*, p. 272. According to Agathangelos, §28, it was winter quarters for the Armenian king. Lazar, p. 65, merely says Khalkhal was in the land of the Albanians.

---

1. This paragraph repeats the themes and allusions of the preceding page. The following prayer echoes the intent of Judas' prayer before the defeat of Nicanor, 1 Macc. 7:41.
2. Cf. Ps. 34:1–2.
3. I.e., the Armenians carry the cross before them into battle; cf. Thomas Artsruni, p. 244.
4. *Ready to die:* see p. 73, n. 10, for this basic theme.
5. *Avengers: vrēzhkhndir,* a term usually applied to God, but used in 2 Macc. 4:2 of the patriotic Onias.
6. *Closed ranks: khumb arareal,* as in 2 Macc. 12:15 of Judas' attack after the invocation of God.

ken the right wing, they threw it back onto the left. They put all to the sword over the face of the plain and turned them in flight as far as the secure regions of the forests along the deep precipices of the Lop'nos River.[7] There some warriors of royal blood, related to the king of Baḷas,[8] offered resistance; they unseated from his horse and killed one of the Armenian nobles, Mush of the Dimak'sean family, and wounded Gazrik.[9]

[*p. 77*] At that spot Arshavir Arsharuni[1] raised his eyes,[2] roared like a lion, and attacked wildly, striking and slaying Vurk, the valiant brother of the king of the Lp'ink'.[3] Many of his aides-de-camp[4] he killed with him. Thus they all alike struck each man his opponent[5] to the ground. And from the great impetuosity of the attack, there were many more drowned in the river than were felled by the sword on dry land. From the great number of fallen corpses the pure waters of the river turned to blood, and none of them at all was able to escape and hide in the thick forests of the plains. But one of the enemy soldiers crossed the great river on the back of his horse with his armor.[6] Saved from the battle by the skin of his teeth,[7]

7. *Lop'nos:* north of Lake Sevan.

8. *Baḷas:* on the lower Kura; see Marquart, *Erānšahr,* pp. 119–120, Hübschmann, *AON,* p. 412; Honigmann and Maricq, pp. 80–87.

9. For the Dimak'sean family see Toumanoff, *Studies,* p. 204. Cf. Łazar, p. 65, for the death of Mush. Gazrik Dimak'sean is mentioned by Eḷishē on p. 100 as being among the loyal Armenians; the only Gazrik mentioned by Łazar (pp. 45, 58) was of the Abeḷeank' family.

1. For the Arsharuni family (also known as Kamsarakan) see Toumanoff, *Studies,* p. 206; Arshavir Arsharuni is mentioned below on p. 99 as being among the loyal Armenians; and an Arshavir is mentioned on p. 116 as a commander at the battle of Avarayr. In his description of this episode, Łazar, p. 65, calls Arshavir a Kamsarakan, and the Arshavir at Avarayr an Arsharuni, p. 72.

2. *Raised his eyes: dētakn i ver ambaṙnayr,* as of Mushkan at the battle of Avarayr, p. 117 below, and of Eleazar at the battle of Bethzacharia in 1 Macc. 6:43.

3. For the Lp'ink' see p. 10, n. 3. Vurk is not otherwise attested to save for the corresponding passage in Łazar, p. 66.

4. *Aides-de-camp: hamharzs;* see p. 35, n. 2.

5. *Opponent: akhoyean,* lit. "champion," as on p. 113. It is used by Łazar to describe Goliath, *Letter,* p. 189. For the sense of "opponent" cf. Thomas Artsruni, p. 244.

6. This sentence is reminiscent of the escape of Trdat from battle, who swam the Euphrates in armor carrying(!) his horse. See Agathangelos, §202, and Moses Khorenats'i, II, 79.

7. *By the skin of his teeth: mazapur,* lit. "saved by a hair," a very common expression in Armenian.

he brought the sad news to the remnants of the army who had fled into the great capital.[8]

Then the Armenian troops, having won a great victory, turned to plunder the dead.[9] They gathered much booty from the [enemies'] camp and stripped the fallen corpses. They accumulated much silver and gold, armor and decorations of valiant men and brave horses.

Then they attacked with no little ardor the fortresses and towns which the Persians held in Albania. After a fierce struggle they set fire to their strongholds, and wherever they found them in various fortresses they put to the sword numerous magi who had come ready to bring ruin[10] to the country; these they threw out as carrion for the birds of heaven and beasts of the earth.[11] They purified the sites of all impure[12] sacrifices, and saved and delivered the churches from their terrible affliction.

[*p. 78*] Many of the Albanian nobles and of the general peasantry for the sake of God's name had scattered and spread out among the fortresses of the Caucasus[1] Mountains; when they saw the success of the enterprise which God had effected through the Armenian army, they too assembled and joined their forces. Together and in concert they shared in the heroic task. Then they marched against the pass of the Huns,[2] which the Persians were holding in force. They captured and destroyed the fortifications, slaughtered the troops quartered inside, and made over the pass to Vahan, who was from the royal family of Albania.[3] During all these brave exploits not a single

---

8. *Capital: shahastan;* any capital of a province or district, see Hübschmann, *Grammatik*, p. 209. Here Partav is probably intended.

9. *To plunder the dead: diakaput,* from *di* ("corpse") and *kaput* ("plunder"). Not used elsewhere in Ełishē, but common in early Armenian historians, e.g., Moses Khorenats'i, I, 15 of Semiramis's troops. Cf. 1 Macc. 4:17, where Judas tells his troops not to think of plunder or *kaput diakanats'n.*

10. *Ruin: gayt'aklut'iwn,* the "scandal" of the Gospels. It is used on p. 92 of backsliders. For the situation here cf. 1 Macc. 5:4, where it describes the humiliating defeat of the Idumaeans by Judas.

11. Cf. Ps. 78:2 for these precise words; but similar expressions are very common in the O.T.

12. *Purified . . . impure:* this has verbal parallels with 1 Macc. 13:48, where Simon purifies Gazara from idolatry.

---

1. *Caucasus: Kapkoh;* for this Iranian form see Hübschmann, *Grammatik*, p. 45. In early Armenian sources the usual form is *Kawkas.*

2. I.e., the Chor.

3. Vahan of Albania is not otherwise attested to, save in the corresponding passage in Łazar, p. 66.

one of them fell wounded, save one blessed man who died like a hero[4] in the great battle.

Then the man to whom they had entrusted the pass they sent as ambassador to the land of the Huns and to many other barbarian nations who were allied with the Huns in order to come to an understanding with them and make a pact that the alliance would be kept indissoluble. When these [nations] heard all that had occurred, they immediately rushed to the spot and saw with their own eyes the victory that had been won. They did not hesitate to enter into a pact with an oath in accordance with the ritual of their own religion;[5] they also took a Christian oath to keep a firm alliance with them.

When this had been completed and mutually confirmed and while they were still peacefully settled in that spot, a bearer of sad news arrived from Armenia, beating his forehead and tearing his collar[6] because of the rebellious[7] Vasak: "He has abandoned the Christian covenant and ruined many places in Armenia, notably the royal winter residence, [*p. 79*] which was the army's quarters. He has also seized, destroyed, and set afire Gaṙni[1] and Eramunk'[2] and the great estate of Draskhanakert;[3] Vardanashat[4] and the fortress of Awshakan;[5] P'aṙakhot,[6] Sardeank',[7] the town of Dzoḷakert,[8] and the fortress of Arma-

4. *Died like a hero: katarets'aw nahatakut'eamb.* For *nahatak* see p. 5, n. 2. The verb *katarel* in certain contexts means "to be martyred" (e.g., p. 105 of the Maccabees, p. 119 of the Vardanank'), in which sense it is a calque on the Greek τελειοῦσθαι or the Syriac *eshtamli.* For this use see Lampe, Lexicon, s.v. τελειόω,8.

5. *Religion: awrēnk';* for this term see the Introduction.

6. Cf. p. 57, n. 2.

7. *Rebellious: apstamb,* as on p. 82. Although Eḷishē uses this term only of Vasak's religious backsliding, the abstract noun "rebellion" or the verb "to rebel" are used of the Armenian political rebellion against the shah.

1. *Gaṙni:* see p. 68, n. 6.

2. *Eramunk':* otherwise unattested to.

3. *Draskhanakert:* an area on the upper left bank of the Akhurean river, see Hübschmann, *AON,* p. 423.

4. *Vardanashat:* otherwise unattested to, probably in Ayrarat.

5. *Awshakan:* a town north of Vaḷarshapat; see Hübschmann, *AON,* p. 479.

6. *P'aṙakhot:* near the foot of Mount Masis; see Hübschmann, *AON,* p. 477.

7. *Sardeank':* otherwise unattested to.

8. *Dzoḷakert:* south of the Araxes in Ayrarat; see Hübschmann, *AON,* p. 476.

vir;[9] the town of Kuash,[10] Aruch, Ashnak,[11] and all Aragat-sotn;[12] the province of Artashat[13] with Artashat itself and all the villages and towns in its neighborhood. He has put to flight all of your families and expelled them from their homes. He has also laid hands on the holy churches and seized the holy altar vessels.[14] He has led away captive priests' families, bound them and imprisoned them. He has extended his ravaging and ruin over the entire country. The army on the borders of Atrpata-kan did not arrive in time to support the interior of the country, while the army which had remained there fled from the lawless one and moved off to the frontier.[15] But they still keep with you the covenant of unity in Christ's love. Of those with him, a few have fled to their own places, but most have followed after his impiety."

They set out from that place to return with all speed to Armenia, [*p. 80*] bearing a vast booty and immeasurable wealth. In joyful gladness they sang aloud: "Acknowledge the Lord, for he is good; for his mercy is eternal. He has struck great nations and slain mighty princes. For he is good; for his mercy is eternal."[1] Singing this psalm right to the end, in their prayers they offered praises to the Holy Trinity. Their general himself took responsibility for the rear ranks;[2] posting guards to the front and rear and the sides, he brought the army back safe and sound in thirty days[3] near to the borders of their native land.

9. *Armavir:* on the Araxes in Ayrarat; see Hübschmann, *AON,* p. 405, and for the history of this early Armenian capital, Manandian, *Trade,* pp. 36ff.

10. *Kuash:* at the foot of Mount Aragats; see Moses Khorenats'i, III, 22.

11. *Aruch* and *Ashnak:* not otherwise attested to. From the context they would seem to be near Kuash.

12. *Aragatsotn:* lit. "foot of Aragats"; see Hübschmann, *AON,* p. 403.

13. *Artashat:* see p. 28, n. 18.

14. *Churches . . . vessels:* cf. p. 52, n. 3.

15. For the three armies see p. 74.

1. Cf. Ps. 105:1; 106:1; 135:1, 17–18. In 1 Macc. 4:23ff., where the return of Judas is described, similar phrases from the psalms are quoted as a song of thanksgiving.

2. *Rear ranks: kats' ew mnats'.* A phrase used in 1 Macc. 5:53 to translate τοὺς ἐσχατίζοντας, with overtones of "straggling."

3. *Thirty days:* i.e., from the Chor Pass. The only other precise time for a journey given by Ełishē is on p. 130: two months and twenty days from Armenia to the shah's winter quarters.

News reached the apostate[4] Vasak and the princes in his company of the heroic valor of Vardan's force in Albania, and also of their alliance with the Huns. Before they encountered each other, taking advantage of night he fled for refuge into the secure areas of his own territory.[5] Departing in such great haste, all the captives and plunder that he had brought from the province of Ayrarat as well as his own property he unwillingly abandoned in his flight.

Because wintertime had arrived and the enemy troops had seized the provisions,[6] he [Vardan] was unable to supply all his forces in one area; so he spread them through various provinces of the land for their winter quarters. He commanded them to be ready and equipped for spring. A few of the group of senior nobles he kept in support, and he seized and occupied the royal estates.[7]

[*p. 81*] He sent numerous forces into the land of Siunik', capturing and destroying many provinces. He put him [Vasak] and all the troops with him into such straits that they were forced to eat donkeys and dead horses in the extremity of their hunger. And many sufferings did he inflict on the apostate. Finally a synod of holy bishops and of all the clergy[1] deplored with bitter tears the cruel tribulations, which forced men and tender[2] women to go barefoot without a mount,[3] and many children to fall and hit the rocks along the paths.[4]

Since the fearers of God had gained such success, all the bishops and priests commanded the country to spend the whole month of K'alots'[5] making supplications to God with fasting and prayers, and to celebrate the victory in the war on the holy

---

4. *Apostate: urats'eal.* Note the importance that Ełishē places on Vasak's apostasy from the Christian covenant as well as his political treachery; cf. pp. 72, 81, 92, and 98.

5. I.e., Siunik'.

6. *Provisions: ŕochiks;* see p. 64, n. 1.

7. *Royal estates: t'agaworanist tełis;* see p. 28, n. 18.

---

1. *Clergy: ukht,* as also below of the clergy in Constantinople; see p. 3, n. 3.

2. *Tender: p'ap'uk;* see esp. p. 200. For its application to women cf. p. 67, n. 9.

3. *Barefoot without a mount:* cf. p. 201 for this as a special hardship for women; there is a parallel in *Vkayk',* p. 161.

4. *Children . . . paths:* from Nah. 3:10, describing the fate of the captives from Nineveh.

5. *K'alots':* the fifth month of the Armenian year, beginning in 450 on 5 December, and ending 4 January 451.

festival of Christ's Epiphany,[6] so that this splendid commemoration might be indissolubly linked with the divine and immortal feast day.

And all these visitations[7] of God, which had been splendidly made manifest on Armenia's behalf, the holy bishops set in writing and had sent to the land of the Greeks, to the holy clergy in the capital, so that they in their prayers might beg God that "we might conclude our enterprise as we have begun it."[8]

Releasing one of the foremost Persian captives and bringing him before the nobles, they conversed with him and indicated all the damage that had been done: the destruction of their lands, the slaughter of the royal troops, and the other [disasters] which lay ahead. As they explained all this to him, the accusations[9] of both sides, of the virtuous and of the shirkers,[10] concurred: how for no reason and unjustly[11] he [the king] had constrained them [*p. 82*] to abandon their ancestral religion;[1] the treachery of the rebel[2] Vasak; how he had deceived the king by speaking for the Armenians[3] that they would accept magism; for although no one had made an agreement with him he had made false insinuations[4] on his own.

When they had made all this completely clear, they sent him off as a messenger to present their case[5] and to contrive some means that perchance they might be able to extricate their brothers from their tribulation.

6. I.e., 6 January, following the early practice of Jerusalem; see Renoux, *Codex armenien Jerusalem 121*, p. 182.

7. *Visitation: ayts'elut'iwn*, a term widely used of God's providence, rendering the Greek ἐπισκοπή. For the Armenian situation here cf. 3 Macc. 5:2.

8. The last two verbs are in the first person; for a similar expression see p. 87.

9. *Accusations: ambastanut'iwn;* for the etymology see Nyberg, *Manual* II, s.v. *hanbasānēnītan.*

10. *Shirkers: yets kats'elots'n;* see p. 4, n. 3.

11. *For . . . unjustly: i zur ew tarapartuts',* as in 1 Macc. 2:37, where the Jews accept death. Cf. also p. 185 of the death of the Armenian martyrs.

1. *Ancestral religion: hayreni awrēnk'.* For the importance of this phrase and the parallels with the Maccabees see the Introduction.

2. Cf. p. 78, n. 7.

3. *For the Armenians: Hayots' baniw;* for this use of *baniw* cf. *Vkayk',* p. 41.

4. *False insinuations: sutakaspas,* as in Prov. 26:22; 28:23; cf. Moses Khorenats'i, II, 60; III, 60, where the term is used of hypocrites or impostors.

5. *To present their case: yaḷers apabanut'ean. Apa-banut'iwn* is also attested to in Philo (*Nor Baŕgirk',* s.v.), translating the Greek ἀπο-λογία.

But meanwhile, the messengers of the impious Vasak had previously reached [Persia] with the sad news of the terrible disaster that he [Vardan] had brought upon the royal army, and claiming that the whole blame lay on the holy clergy. For such was the desire of the impious one—to destroy the unity of the bishops with the nobles. But of this he was not yet aware—that the soul and body may be separated for a while, as can be seen in nature;[6] but such [separation] is impossible for those who have entered a covenant in love of God.

So the man went to the winter quarters of the king and repeated all this in his ears, making him shake and quiver.[7] He lost all his strength, especially because he had returned from the war in the East humiliated[8] and not with head held high.[9] When he had received accurate confirmation from this last messenger who had come to him, he threw all the blame for his enterprises on his counselors. Then he cooled from his raging anger because the mouths of his evil advisers, who had been urging him unceasingly to cruel acts, had been silenced. He was humbled from his lofty pride, and he restored his wild heart to human nature.[10] He looked and saw himself full of weakness. He realized that he could not complete everything he wished to do. [*p. 83*] Therefore he ceased his haughty aggression, and quieted his raging cries.

He who had loudly thundered and by even more fearful commands had made those far and near quake,[1] began to speak softly and to entreat everyone, saying: "What harm have I done, and what crime have I committed against [any] nation, or people, or individual? Are there not many creeds[2] in the land of the Aryans, and is not the cult of each one openly [performed]?[3] Who has ever forced or compelled [anyone] to accept

6. For Ełišē's views on the separation of soul and body see pp. 8, 15–16.

7. *Shake and quiver;* cf. p. 14, n. 2.

8. *Humiliated: kamakor,* as in 2 Macc. 9:1 of Antiochus returning from Persia, or 2 Mac. 11:12 of Lysias returning from Bethsura.

9. In contrast with the Armenians as described on p. 6.

10. Cf. p. 12, n. 7.

1. *Thundered, quake:* as on p. 44.

2. *Creeds: usmunkʿ;* for which see p. 15, n. 6.

3. *Openly (performed): yaytni;* perhaps merely "clear, manifest." The only Armenian reports of explicit tolerance for Christianity in Iran date from after the reign of Yazkert. For the tolerance of Kawat (488–531) see

the single religion of magism? Especially with regard to the Christian religion, just as they have been firm and true to their own religion,[4] in such measure have they seemed to us superior to all [other] sects.[5] No one can find any fault with their select religion. But I consider [it] equal and on a par with our Mazdean religion,[6] just as it was respected in the time of our ancestors—as I myself remember in my father's[7] time when he sat on this noble throne. When he began to examine and scrutinize all creeds and had understood them well, he found the Christian religion to be the most sublime[8] of all. Therefore [the Christians] were honored at the royal court and were blessed[9] by him with liberal gifts; they freely traveled throughout the whole land. Likewise the leaders of the Christians, whom they call bishops, he treated as worthy of presents and offerings. [*p. 84*] And he entrusted to them as reliable officials[1] the distant borderlands;[2] and never did any mishap befall the great affairs of state.

"You never recalled a single one of these facts, but continuously wearied my ears by speaking all sorts of evil about them. See—you have made me do what I did not wish, and great damage has occurred on the borders between two implacable enemies. While we were on a distant campaign, before we had brought any military operation to a successful conclusion, you raised war against me in my own house, the result of which will

---

Sebēos, p. 149, and the letter of Babgen in *Girkʿ Tʿltʿotsʿ*, p. 43. For the tolerance of Khosrov I (531–579) see ibid., p. 60.

4. *Religion:* here *den*, in contrast to the more usual *awrēnkʿ*. *Den* is used only of the Persian religion or in the mouth of a Persian; see Thomson, "Maccabees," pp. 336ff.

5. *Sects: kesht;* see p. 61, n. 5.

6. *Mazdaean religion: den mazdezantsʿ;* see p. 24, n. 5.

7. Yazkert's father was Vram V (421–439), who persecuted Christians (!); see Akinean, *Eḷishē*, I, 226.

8. *Sublime: veh.* On p. 29 the Armenians themselves describe Christianity as *veh*. For the use of the word with *den* in a Zoroastrian contex see Nyberg, *Manual*, II, s.v. *vēh*.

9. *Blessed: erahikkʿ.* Akinean, *Eḷishē*, I, 237, unconvincingly emends this to *eranikkʿ* and makes it refer to Nestorian Christians, natives of Eran.

---

1. *Officials: ostikan.* For the term see Hübschmann, *Grammatik*, pp. 215–216, and Nyberg, *Manual* II, s.v. *ōstikan*. Cf. p. 181 below. For the use of Christian bishops as ambassadors see Garsoian, "Le role de l'hierarchie." Here there is a verbal parallel with 1 Macc. 12:34.

2. *Borderlands: marz;* as on p. 62, n. 6.

be even worse than [war] against outside enemies."

Such words and more like them he addressed to the nobility, laying the blame for these faults on the chief-magus and magi. All the great and honorable nobles[3] who were sitting in the Council and attending to his disingenuous[4] speech bent down in shame and stared at the ground, unable to lift up their heads.

But a few of them, humoring[5] him, spoke as follows: "Yes, noble king,[6] it is just as you have said. But now you can successfully arrange everything. There is nothing which is beyond the reach of your will, for the gods have granted you power to do everything you wish.[7] Do not be distressed or grieve yourself or afflict the minds of us all. Perhaps there may be an easy solution to the matter. Be long-suffering, and patiently leave these men to their Christianity; through them you will bring these obstinate ones[8] to submission."

[*p. 85*] This speech seemed pleasing to the king. He immediately summoned before him those in his army, of all nations, who observed Christianity and whom he had forcibly prevented from daring to worship God in his presence. For those who had opposed him, he had tortured and prevented from open worship; and some he had made worship the sun against[1] their will, inflicting much sorrow[2] on all the soldiers.

But that day he commanded them to remain firm[3] in their Christian religion according to their former usage, without hesitation. However, those who were sinners did not wish immediately, without much repentance, to come and join the Christian

---

3. *Great and honorable nobles: vzurkkʿ ew patuakan nakhararkʿ.* For *vzurk* see p. 24, n. 3, and for this class of nobility in general see Christensen, *Iran*, p. 105.

4. *Disingenuous speech: yeḷyeḷuk lezu:* as in Prov. 17:20; cf p. 124 (there translated as "fickle"), and 3 Macc. 5:22 of the king's mind (*mits*).

5. *Humoring: zmits hachelov*, as in 2 Macc. 11:14 of Lysias humoring Antiochus.

6. *Noble king: arkʿay kʿaj;* see p. 9, n. 2.

7. Similar sentiments in the mouths of Yazkert's advisers on pp. 9, 19.

8. *Obstinate ones: stambaks*, as on pp. 184, 185; it is frequently used of Christians also in *Vkaykʿ*. For the etymology see Nyberg, *Manual* II, s.v. *stambakēh.*

---

1. See p. 17, n. 9.

2. *Inflicting much sorrow: nstoytsʿ i sug trtmutʿean*, parallel to 1 Macc. 12:52 of Israel mourning for the captured Jonathan.

3. *Remain firm: hastatun kal*, very frequent in Paul's epistles.

ranks; [so] the king ordered them to be forcibly seized and taken to their churches, and he let the priests deal [with them] according to their rites[4] as they might judge best. The allowances[5] that had been cut off he restored to each one; the seats at the table[6] that had been denied them he ordered to be restored; and he did not prevent their continuous access to the palace. He re-established everything according to its former usage. He humbled himself and spoke with them in a friendly way according to his previous custom.

When he had completed all these arrangements, in their presence he sent edicts of amnesty[7] throughout the whole area of his empire concerning the Christians:

"If any is in bonds, by royal command he is to be released. If anyone's possessions have been usurped, they are to be returned to him. Likewise lands, whether patrimonial, or gifted, or purchased,[8] that anyone has seized, we have ordered to be returned."

[*p. 86*] When he had informed them of all this, he requested from them a testimony of [his] sincerity[1] for Armenia; and with an oath he subscribed to a covenant in their presence, with the approbation of all his magnates, to the effect that: "I shall not harbor the least resentment or desire to seek vengeance. Just as previously you practised your religion in good faith,[2] henceforth practise it even more so. But only do not withdraw from our service."

All this he put in writing and made known in Armenia and many other lands which practised the Christian religion.[3] But secretly and deceptively he made haste to send messengers

---

4. *Rule: karg,* as on p. 52, n. 5. "Usage" in the same paragraph below is the translation for *kargeal.*

5. *Allowances: ṙochik;* see p. 64, n. 1.

6. *Seats at the table: bazmakan;* see p. 20, n. 4.

7. *Amnesty: tʻoḷutʻiwn;* cf. p. 22, n. 8. This edict (*hrovartak,* p. 9, n. 10) is quite different from that described in Ḷazar, pp. 67–68, as *"sut"* (false).

8. *Patrimonial, gifted, purchased: hayreni, pargewakan, kʻsakagin;* for such types of property see the discussion in Toumanoff, *Studies,* p. 119, and Adontz/Garsoian, *Armenia,* p. 347.

---

1. *Sincerity: hawatarmutʻiwn.* Cf. Esther 6:3, where the Armenian text (but not the Greek, Hebrew, or Syriac) speaks of Mordecai's "faithfulness" to King Ahasuerus.

2. *In good faith: chshmartutʻeamb;* lit.: "in truth."

3. Cf. p. 10 for other regions in the Caucasus where there were "believers and baptized" Christians.

to the emperor Marcian.[4] When he had verified that the Romans had refused to help the Christians, either with militasry assistance or in any other way, he reverted to his earlier wicked views. Since he put the responsibility for the success[5] of events on his own ministers, he thus assumed that they could carry out everything in accordance with his previous intentions.

But although the Armenians had received the king's deceitfully flattering letter, which outwardly contained the good news of life[6] but inwardly the bitterness of death, yet they were amazed at its defective reasoning and said to each other: "How brazen is his treacherous deceit![7] For after two and three attempts he was rebuffed, but he is not ashamed. Even though he is aware of our indissoluble unity, he is impudent and shameless nonetheless; by harassing [us] he intends to weaken our courage.

"But should we believe his inconsistent[8] order? What benevolence have we seen directed to all the churches in Persia? For he who is himself wicked cannot be good to another. And he who himself walks in darkness cannot guide another by the light of truth.[9] For just as justice does not derive from [*p. 87*] injustice, so neither does truth from falsehood; nor from a turbulent[1] mind does there come any expectation of peace.

"However, we live by God's power and have been strengthened by faith[2] in the hope of Christ—who came and took from the Holy Virgin the flesh of our nature, and by uniting[3] it with his indivisible divinity received into his own body

4. On p. 73 Ełishē says that Marcian had already sent an ambassador to Yazkert.

5. *Success: yajoḷutʻiwn*, as in all the MSS. But the edition *A* reads *anyajoḷutʻiwn* ("failure"). Ter-Minasyan and Yuzbashyan follow *A* and translate it as "put the blame for failure on his ministers." But Ełishē seems to be referring to Yazkert's future hopes rather than his past failures, hence the subjunctive mood "they *could* carry out" (*katarestsʻen*).

6. Cf. 2 Tim. 1:1.

7. Cf. p. 74, n. 13.

8. *Inconsistent: anhastat;* cf. Łazar, p. 142[27], the "inconstant" nature of women.

9. Cf. p. 8 of Yazkert and "such people" who live in darkness.

1. *Turbulent: khṙovasēr;* cf. p. 7, where *khṙovutʻiwn* is dear to Yazkert.

2. Cf. 2 Cor. 1:23.

3. *Uniting: miatsʻeal;* for this term in a Christological context see Thomson, *Teaching*, §369, 592. For these credal statements cf. above p. 39-40.

the sufferings of our sins. In that same [body] he was crucified, buried, and resurrected; he appeared to many, was raised up in the presence of his disciples to his Father and sat at the right hand of the power. The same we believe to be the true God, and we wait for him to come in the Father's glory and power to raise all the dead, to renew the old Creation, and to render summary judgment on the just and the sinners.

"We shall not be deceived like children,[4] go astray like the ignorant, or be tricked like the witless; rather, we are ready for every test. We beseech God and ceaselessly beg his great mercy that we may complete what we have begun[5] with valor and not with cowardice.[6] For already East and West have come to know that you oppose God and pointlessly kill us despite all our services. Heaven with its angels and earth with its inhabitants bear us witness[7] that we have not failed in our duty even in our thoughts. Yet instead of rendering us gifts and blessings you wish to deprive us of the true life, which is impossible and will never occur.

"Should we now trust his unworthy mouth, which forces heinous apostasy? Will he today become the preacher of good tidings without doing any good deed? [*p. 88*] We are unable today suddenly to accept the involuntary confession of one who has blasphemed Christ and forced believers to deny him. He who swore in his vain and erring cult to bring every evil upon the ministers of the church now has come to offer sham[1] thanks, desiring thereby to pour out all his wickedness on us. We do not believe him, nor shall we accept his false command."

But when he realized that he could not break the firmness of their unity, then he despatched from his presence the old man full of bitterness,[2] in whom lurked Satan with all his power, and who had perpetrated much slaughter. The food he had craved since childhood was the pure flesh of the saints, and the drink of which he was never sated was the blood of the innocent.[3] To the evil of this man he added his own lethal com-

---

4. Cf. p. 41, n. 1.
5. Cf. p. 81, n. 8.
6. Cf. p. 19, n. 6 for the theme of valor and cowardice.
7. *Heaven, earth, witness:* cf. p. 19, n. 5.

---

1. *Sham: goḷanalov.* For the use of this verb in the sense of "deceptively," see the *Nor Baṙgirkʿ*, s.v. *goḷanal.*
2. I.e., Mihrnerseh; see p. 42, n. 6 for this epithet.
3. There is a similar idea in *Vkaykʿ*, p. 112. Cf. also Jer. 19:4 for the blood of the innocent.

mand: he gathered under his command troops from every land and sent with him many companies[4] of elephants.

Approaching the borders of Armenia, he entered the town of Pʻaytakaran[5] and spread all his troops around the city in careful preparation for his malicious plans. The old poisonous snake[6] entered the fortified retreat,[7] very deceitfully disguising himself so as not to be feared. He threatened the distant by fearful roaring and those near by hissing and crawling like a snake. He was the prince and commander[8] of the whole Persian Empire. His name was Mihrnerseh, and there was no one at all who could escape his clutches. Not only the greatest and the least, but even the king himself obeyed his command; and now he had undertaken the latter's sinister[9] schemes.

4. *Companies: eramak,* as on p. 114. For the term see Hübschmann, *Grammatik,* p. 147.

5. *Pʻaytakaran:* on the eastern border of Armenia between the Kura and Araxes rivers; see Hübschmann, *AON,* pp. 267–270.

6. *Snake: vishap.* Cf. p. 173, where the term is applied to Satan (see refs. given there), or *Vkaykʻ,* p. 226, for a chief-magus insulted as a *vishap.* For the *vishap* in Armenian tradition see refs. in Thomson, *Moses Khorenatsʻi,* I, 30, n. 17.

7. *Retreat: orj:* lit. "den" or "lair," continuing the image of the snake.

8. *Commander: hramanatar;* see p. 24, n. 3.

9. *Sinister: dzakhoḷ:* cf. p. 8, n. 2.

CHAPTER FOUR

Concerning the Secession[1] of the Prince of Siunikʻ and His Companions

P to this point I have not at all hesitated to describe the afflictions of our nation which were cruelly inflicted upon us by the foreign enemies of the truth.[2] They were few who struck us but very many struck by us, for we were still united and agreed.[3] Although some secretly had deceitful vacillations,[4] yet to the eyes of outsiders our unanimity seemed imposing, so they were unable to resist [us] in two or three places.

So then, where discord[5] penetrates, at the breaking up of unity heavenly virtue[6] also departs; and when there is self-interest, weeping and mourning greatly increase. For when the limbs, which previously were part of a man's undefiled body, are severed and fall away, one turns to tears before the corpse beside him. One is filled with even more bitterness over the man who dies in both soul and body. [*p. 90*] And if this is the case for a single person, how much more so for a whole nation!

But here our lament is not only for one nation but for [many] nations and countries which I shall present and speak of in order, though without a joyful mind. It is unwillingly that I shall describe these many—how some of them lost their own true lives and were the cause of destruction for many others, for

---

1. *Secession: erkparakutʻiwn;* see p. 3, n. 4 for the importance of this term in Eḷishē.
2. *Enemies of the truth:* cf. p. 56, n. 7.
3. *United and agreed: miabankʻ ew hawasarkʻ;* cf. 3 Macc. 6:25: *i hawasar miabanutʻenē.*
4. *Vacillations: erkmtʻutʻiwn:* cf. p. 48, n. 6.
5. *Discord: erkparakutʻiwn,* as at n. 1 above.
6. *Heavenly virtue:* for this theme see p. 14, n. 1.

some merely of visible things, for others of things both visible and invisible. And this is the worst of all: the gate to destruction[1] which they opened God alone has the power to close. That possibility surpasses the bounds of man.

This wicked Mihrnerseh, since he was previously well informed of Vasak's impiety, now sent and summoned him to his presence. As he had earlier broken away from and abandoned the union of the Armenians, he came and presented himself. He confirmed his own faithfulness[2] and the illegal rebellion[3] of the Armenians. He also exaggerated and told of things the Armenians had not done, wishing to insinuate himself into the favor of that wicked one.

Although inwardly he greatly despised him, yet in outward appearance he respected him and presented him with the greatest worldly gifts. He promised him greater authority than that he possessed, and raised him to vain hopes that were even above his own station—to the effect that he might aspire even to royal status[4] if only he could find a way to destroy the unity of the Armenians' covenant and ensure the fulfillment of the king's wishes in that land.

[*p. 91*] When he [Vasak] had agreed to everything including following his wishes, the embittered old man[1] knew that he was benumbed[2] and deranged and had broken away from the firm unity of the [Armenians]. He was greatly consoled in his miserable mind and thought that he would thus be able to seduce[3] them all to irretrievable destruction.[4] He attributed this knowledge to his own cunning,[5] quite unaware of the fact that he [Vasak] on his own had separated and cut himself off[6] from the holy church and had removed and estranged himself from Christ's love.[7]

For he had forgotten the coming of the Son of God and

1. Cf. Matt. 7:13.
2. *Faithfulness: hawatarmut'iwn;* see p. 86, n. 1.
3. *Rebellion: apstambut'iwn;* see p. 78, n. 7.
4. *Status: vichak;* as on p. 15, n. 1.

1. I.e., Mihrnerseh; cf. p. 42, n. 6.
2. *Benumbed: t'mbreal,* as on p. 146 of the chief-magus.
3. *Seduce: orsal;* as on p. 17, n. 4.
4. *Irretrievable destruction;* as on p. 14, n. 3.
5. *Cunning;* as on p. 17, n. 6.
6. *Separated and cut himself off: ziwr andzn zateal ew orosheal;* as in Gal. 2:12 of James separating himself from the gentiles.
7. Cf. Eph. 4:18.

did not recall the preaching of the Holy Gospel. He was not dismayed by threats or consoled by promises.[8] He renounced the font which had conceived him,[9] nor did he remember the receptive[10] Holy Spirit which had begotten him.[11] He dishonored the honorable[12] body by which he had been sanctified,[13] and he trampled on the living blood[14] by which he had been redeemed from sin. He annulled the deed of adoption[15] and with his own hands broke the firm seal of the ring.[16] He left the number of the blessed and caused many to rebel with him.

Perversely he accepted and adopted devil-worship.[17] He became a vessel of evil,[18] and Satan filled him with every deceit.[19] He took him [Satan] as a shield, put him on as armor, and became as it were a soldier fulfilling his will.[20] He fought against the wise with cunning and against the knowledgeable with craft—openly against the innocent and secretly against the prudent. He seized and drove many from the band of Christ,[21] joining them to the troops of demons. Into many other places he stealthily insinuated[22] himself, and like a snake[23] en-

8. I.e., of heaven and hell.

9. The font is normally associated with birth or life; cf. Titus 3:5.

10. *Receptive: ěnkaluchʻ;* this can also be translated as "betrothed," a term used of Joseph or Christ; see Lampe, *Lexicon,* s.v. μνηστήρ.

11. For the Spirit and *rebirth,* see Lampe, *Lexicon,* s.v. ἀναγέννησις. But for the Spirit as *womb* (rather than begetter) see Agathangelos, §830, and Winkler, "Tauftradition."

12. *Honorable: patuakan,* normally associated with the saving blood, as in 1 Peter 1:19.

13. Cf. Heb. 10:29; but there sanctification is by the blood; see preceding note.

14. *Living:* cf. John 6:51 (of bread).

15. Cf. Col. 2:14 for the annulled deed—i.e., Christ annuls the O.T.

16. The "seal" refers to baptism; but here there are also overtones of the seal made by Vasak's ring, p. 66.

17. *Devil-worship: diwapashtutʻiwn;* cf. p. 46 for the "demons" (*diw*) of Zoroastrianism. The term is used by Eznik, §346, of paganism at the time of Christ's birth.

18. *Vessel of evil: aman chʻarin,* perhaps, "vessel of the evil one" (Satan). The same term is used of Diocletian in Agathangelos, §141.

19. Cf. Acts 13:10.

20. A curious twisting of Pauline epithets: see Eph. 6:14, 16, and 2 Tim. 2:3.

21. *Band: gund;* the band of Christ is a common expression in the *Teaching.*

22. *Insinuated himself: gołabar* ("like a thief") *sołatsʻaw,* as in Gen. 1:26, picking up the theme of the snake.

23. The theme of the snake (see also previous note) recalls both Mihrnerseh on p. 89 and Diocletian in Agathangelos, §141 (see n. 18 above).

tered the fortified places. Opening a breach[24] he snatched away and openly seized many of the nobles and very many of the peasants, and some others who were so-called priests. [*p. 92*] Here are the names of his associates:[1]

> The prince of the Ṙshtunik, called Artak
> The prince of the Koṙkhoṙunikʻ, called Gadisho
> The prince of the Vahevunikʻ, called Giut
> The prince of the Bagratunikʻ, called Tirotsʻ
> The prince of the Apahunikʻ, called Manech
> The prince of the Gabeḷeankʻ, called Artēn
> The prince of Akē, called Ēnjuḷ
> The prince of Urts, called Nerseh
> The prince of the other [branch] of the Palunikʻ, called Varazshapuh
> A lesser noble of the Amatunikʻ, called Manēn.

And many other noble men, whom they called *ostanik,*[2] from the royal house.

He caused his entire land to apostatize[3] completely, not merely the mass of the laity but also many of the holy clergy. He accomplished his evil deeds notably through false priests, a priest called Zangak, a priest called Peter, a deacon called Sahak, and a deacon called Mushi.[4] These he sent to innocent men, to deceive and trick them. They swore on the Holy Gospel,[5] saying: "Christianity will be graciously permitted to everyone by the king." In this fashion through deceptive trickery[6]

---

24. *Breach: khram;* a term with many biblical parallels.

---

1. There are differences in the following list from that in Ḷazar, p. 67, describing Vasak's accomplices. Ḷazar had seven names, in order: Tirots, Gadisho, Manēch, Giut, Varazshapuh, Artēn (but of the Abeḷeankʻ family, as also on p. 74, n. 8), Nerseh. The first in Eḷishē's list, Artak Ṙshtuni, is mentioned on p. 43, as are Gadisho, Giut, Manēch; but Tirotsʻ, Artēn, Ēnjuḷ, Nerseh, Varazshapuh and Manēn he does not mention elsewhere. Akē is east-southeast of Lake Van; see Hübschmann, *AON*, p. 344. The other families and places have been mentioned before.

2. *Ostanik:* "retainers"; see p. 10, n. 7. Ḷazar merely says "other from among the *ostaniks*"; Eḷishē adds "from the royal house" as a gloss.

3. *Caused to apostatize: apstambetsʻoytsʻ yuratsʻutʻiwn;* for these terms see p. 78, n. 7, and p. 80, n. 4.

4. Zangak, Peter, and Sahak, but not Mushi, are also mentioned by Ḷazar, p. 68. He calls Sahak *"Dzaynoḷ"* (i.e., having a (loud) voice) and Peter *"Erkatʻi"* (i.e., of iron), and says they came from the province of Siunikʻ.

5. For oaths on the Gospel see p. 66, n. 4.

6. *Deceptive trickery: khoramank khabēuteamb;* see p. 74, n. 13.

they removed many from the holy union and brought them to join the bands of the apostates.

He brought together all who had stumbled[7] and made a force of many soldiers. He wrote [their names] and presented many of them in person[8] to the great *hazarapet;*[9] he greatly boasted of his brave valor, how [*p. 93*] he had instructed them in deceitful error; and he made the Armenian army appear divided and disunited.[1]

Having been successful in all these evil actions, he also broke the union of Georgia with Armenia;[2] he did not allow the Albanians to advance and he held back the land of Aḷdznik[3] in the same fashion. He wrote an epistle to the land of the Greeks, falsely confusing[4] matters for them; it was addressed to a man called Vasak, one of those Mamikoneans who were in service to the Greeks.[5] In this time of trouble he was the *sparapet*[6] of Lower Armenia[7] and faithful to the Roman army on the Persian border, but in his actions was beyond the pale of God's religion. The former Vasak found this latter Vasak to be an accomplice in the great crimes in which they both united.

He wrote and pretended continuously that all the Armenians were united behind him. The furtive Vasak had this letter taken to the emperor's capital[8] secretly with great caution,

---

7. *All who had stumbled: amenayn gayt'akḷut'iwn;* see p. 77, n. 10.

8. *In person: yakanē yanuanē;* see p. 42, n. 11.

9. I.e., Mihrnerseh; for the term see p. 23, n. 4.

---

1. *Disunited: erkts'eḷ,* lit. "of two sorts"; no other occurrence of the word is attested to in the *Nor Baṙgirk'.*

2. For Vasak in Georgia, cf. p. 135.

3. Aḷdznik' is in southwestern Armenia, see p. 10, n. 6. Eḷishē is indicating Vasak's activity from one end of the Caucasus to the other.

4. *Confusing: ayl ĕnd ayloy:* as on p. 47, n. 1.

5. For the Mamikonean holdings in western Armenia see Toumanoff, *Studies,* pp. 209ff. For the term "service" (*tsaṙayut'iwn*) cf. p. 71, n. 6. See further n. 7 below.

6. *Sparapet:* see p. 7, n. 9.

7. *Lower Armenia: storin Hayots'* [for *storin* B reads *tohmin* (family) and D *erkrin* (land)]. This expression occurs only here in Eḷishē; it is not found in Ḷazar. On this passage see Adontz/Garsoian, *Armenia,* p. 414, n. 66, where it is shown that there could not have been an Armenian *sparapet* of Roman troops earlier than 529, and suggested that Vasak may be a reminiscence of the Vasak mentioned by Procopius, *Wars,* II, 3, in 539. But Toumanoff, *Studies,* p. 194, n. 209, indicates that there was a line of the Mamikonean house in Ekeḷeats' at the time in question. *Storin* would render the Latin "Inferior," here meaning "Inner Armenia."

8. *Capital: t'agaworanist k'alak';* see p. 28, n. 18.

so that he estranged[9] the minds of the holy bishops from them [the Armenians] and caused all the Greek forces to doubt the covenant.

He deceived and tricked particularly through the false priests, pretending that they were honest men. He had the Gospel and cross[10] brought and by these means hid all his own satanic falsehood. He ranked himself and all the party of apostates among the pious, and put himself out to be more sure than all the Armenian troops. He swore and [*p. 94*] affirmed and produced all the orders of amnesty[1] from the palace.

It pleased the Greek Empire to hear this happily, but through him they were subverted[2] even more.

He acted likewise with the garrisons[3] in all regions of the country, in Tmorik'[4] and in Kordik', in Arts'akh[5] and in Albania, in Georgia and in the land of Khaltik'.[6] He sent word, urging that no one should offer [the loyal Armenians] refuge.

In proportion to his great wickedness the occasion brought him even more success, for no outside assistance at all was forthcoming for the Armenian army except from those Huns with whom they had a treaty.[7] But on their account he assembled the mass of the Aryan cavalry, barring and closing the Gates[8] to their passage. For he did not give the Persian King any pause at all but sent summons for many troops to the Chor Pass; he gathered the entire [forces of] Georgia, the troops of

9. *Estranged: utsats'oyts'*, a rare verb; cf. Job 39:16 of the bird which is estranged from its offspring.

10. For the Gospel, cf. p. 66, n. 4, and for the cross, p. 76, n. 3.

1. *Amnesty: t'olut'iwn;* see p. 85, n. 7.

2. *Subverted: yeleal tapalets'an*, a phrase frequent in the Bible of a building crashing down from its foundations.

3. *Garrisons: amrakank':* a term that can be used of a garrison (as also on p. 127) or of the fortifications (as on p. 126).

4. *Tmorik':* in southern Armenia; see Hübschmann, *AON*, p. 334.

5. *Arts'akh:* to the east and southeast of Lake Sevan; see Hübschmann, *AON*, p. 266.

6. *Khaltik':* in northwestern Armenia; see Hübschmann, *AON*, p. 200, 277.

7. Cf. p. 78 above and p. 127 below. But not all the Huns were allied with the Armenians. At the battle of Avarayr (p. 115) a contingent fought in the Persian army.

8. *Gates: drunk'*, used of the Dar-i-Alan, but here the Chor Pass is intended.

146

the Lp'ink' and Chiḷbk',[9] Vat, Gav,[10] Gḷuar,[11] Khras[12] and Hechmatak,[13] P'askh and P'oskh,[14] P'iwk'uan[15] and all the forces of T'avasparan,[16] from the hill and plain and all the mountain strongholds.[17] Some he constrained by money and liberal distributions of royal treasures,[18] and others by the threat of the king's command.

Accomplishing all this in accordance with the king's order. he wrote daily reports to the great *hazarapet* of Persia, who was lurking [*p. 95*] hidden[1] in the city of P'aytakaran. From then on he dared to show himself to many nations, terrifying some and distributing gifts to others in a friendly way. Having summoned Vasak to his presence with all the princes of his party, he gave many gifts from the treasury to them and to the soldiers who were in his enterprise. He also brought before him the apostate priests, indicating and assuring that "through these I shall seduce[2] the [others] to break away from the united covenant." When the *hazarapet* heard this, he was very grateful to the priests[3] and held out to them the hope that "if the victory is ours, I shall bestow on these the property[4] of the other priests and shall indicated to the king their great services."

In this fashion he brought disturbance and confusion to Armenia, with the result that he split many blood brothers

9. *Chiḷbk':* to the northeast of the Lp'ink', on whom see p. 10, n. 3.

10. The location of Vat and Gav is unknown.

11. There is an area Gḷuark' just south of the Lp'ink'; see Eremyan, *Map*.

12. *Khras:* perhaps Khsruan on the Caspian south of the Chor?

13. *Hechmatak:* on the Caspian north of the Chor.

14. *P'askh, P'oskh:* southeast of the Dar-i-Alan.

15. The location of P'iwk'uan is unknown.

16. *T'avasparan:* on the Caspian just north of the Chor.

17. It is significant that *eleven* areas are named: Lp'ink' to T'avasparan, because on p. 198 Eḷishē refers to "eleven kings of the mountains."

18. This clause has verbal parallels with the Armenian of 1 Macc. 3:28–30, describing Antiochus' effort to raise troops.

1. *Lurking hidden: ḷawḷeal ew t'ak'uts'eal*, a phrase that occurs twice in 3 Macc.

2. *Seduce: orsats'ayts'*; cf. p. 17, n. 4.

3. *The priests:* as *B D* and the editions *A T²*; but *D L K* read: "them both," i.e., the two Vasaks (?). Ter-Minasean reads "them both," but Yuzbashyan translates "tekh iereev" as the sense implies.

4. *Property: keank'*, which also means "life"; note the ambiguity on p. 115, n. 3. For the meaning "property" see Adontz/Garsoian, *Armenia*, p. 362.

from each other, did not leave father and son united, and wrought tumult[5] in the midst of peace.

In his own province there were two nephews of his in the holy covenant of virtue. He wrote a report about them to the court; he received authority over their property and expelled them from the land so that they might never return. He persecuted and put to flight all the monks[6] of the land who cursed his inflexible impiety. He accomplished all this wickedness against the truth and informed the irreligious heathen[7] of what they did not know, namely, by what means he might be able to remove the Christian clergy[8] from Armenia.

When Mihrnerseh saw all this evil in him, he put his hopes in him more than in himself. He inquired and discovered how many men [*p. 96*] there were in Armenia in the total host of Vardan's army. When he learned from him that there were more than sixty thousand,[1] he asked for even more information about each one's individual prowess: how many wore full armor, how many were archers without armor,[2] and likewise concerning the infantry with shields.

When he heard the total number of the army, he was even more anxious to learn how many leaders there were of the brave champions, so that he might prepare three against each one of them, let alone all the rest. He also inquired from him about each of the standards:[3] into how many companies[4] they divided the army, which of them were generals,[5] which commander would attack from which side, what were the names of each one's adjutants,[6] how many trumpeters would sound in

---

5. *Tumult: khṙovutʻiwn*, as on p. 7, n. 1.
6. *Monks: miaynakeatsʻ*, as on p. 22, n. 12.
7. *Irreligious heathen: anawrēn* (see p. 7, n. 11) *hetʻanoskʻ* (see p. 16, n. 3).
8. *Clergy: ukht*, see p. 3, n. 3.

---

1. For the number of troops that Armenian noble houses could put into the field see Toumanoff, *Studies*, pp. 234ff.; and cf. above (regarding Albania), p. 63, n. 2.

2. *Without armor: merk aṙantsʻ zinu;* for *merk* as meaning "unarmed" cf. Moses Khorenatsʻi, I, 24, n. 5.

3. *Standards: drawsh.* For the etymology see Nyberg, *Manual* II, s.v. *drafs,* and Hübschmann, *Grammatik,* pp. 146–147. For types of Armenian flags see Faustos, IV, 3 (quoted in Adontz/Garsoian, *Armenia,* p. 519, n. 57), and Hatsʻuni, *Hay Drōshnerě.*

4. *Companies: gund;* for this term see p. 54, n. 2.

5. *Generals: saḷar;* only here in Eḷishē; see Hübschmann, *Grammatik,* p. 235, for the etymology and further refs.

6. *Adjutants: hamharz;* see p. 35, n. 2.

the company. Would they make an entrenchment or camp in the open? Would they oppose battleline to battleline or set all their forces against one spot? Which of them would be hesitant, and which of them would fight to the death?

After he had been informed by him about all this, he summoned all his generals, and in his presence commanded them all to heed his advice. He entrusted all the troops with their commanders to one of the nobles,[7] whose name was Mushkan Niusalavurt.[8]

He himself then marched to the East and presented himself before the great king, informing him of the course of events, of his own [*p. 97*] cunning wisdom, and of Vasak's deceitful subterfuge, namely, how he had wished to hide his original impiety because he had broken and divided the Armenian army.

When the great king heard all this from the mouth of the great *hazarapet*, he was inwardly embittered and uttered an inviolable oath: "If that impious[1] one survives the great war, I shall make him drink the cup of bitter death[2] in great dishonor."[3]

7. *Nobles: awag;* see p. 16, n. 9.
8. Łazar, p. 69, mentions two Persian generals, Mushkan Niusalavurt and Dołvech; the latter does not appear in Ełishē.

---

1. *Impious: anawrēn;* see p. 7, n. 11.
2. Cf. Isa. 51:17, 22
3. For Vasak's end see below, p. 139.

CHAPTER FIVE

For a Second Time the Armenians Oppose the Persian King in War

T HE love of God is superior to all earthly greatness[1] and makes men as fearless as the incorporeal hosts of angels—as can be seen very many times in many places from the very beginning [of the world]. Men who were armed with the love of God for a weapon[2] shrank at nothing in dread, as would cowards who are feeble-hearted.[3] Their own death or loss of possessions, the massacre of their loved ones or the captivity of their families, the leaving of their native land to be enslaved[4] abroad—all these misfortunes they reckoned as nothing if they could only remain united with God and if only they were not deprived of him. They reckoned him to be more satisfying than all apparent greatness, having chosen thus in their hearts. Apostasy they accounted as death,[5] and death for God's sake as everlasting life; to serve[6] [p. 99] on earth as freedom for their lives, and they recognized exile as familiarity with God.

So did we observe with our own eyes[1] at that time that the

1. Cf. Rom. 8:38–39.
2. Cf. Eph. 6:11ff.
3. *Feeble-hearted: vatasirtkʿ;* see p. 43, n. 8 for the parallel with the Maccabees.
4. *Enslaved: strkutʿiwn.* For slavery in Armenia see the refs. in Toumanoff, *Studies,* p. 128, n. 222. *Strkutʿiwn* is not used elsewhere by Ełishē; here the emphasis is on "abroad" (*yawtarutʿean*), as in the last line of the paragraph—"exile."
5. For death, life, and apostasy cf. p. 72, n. 8.
6. *To serve: tsaṙayel,* which picks up the theme of slavery, at n. 4 above.

1. For Ełishē as "eyewitness" see p. 5, n. 7, and the Introduction.

land of Armenia fought with similar heroism.[2]

Now when Vardan the Great saw the discord[3] of his country, he experienced no hesitation or doubt. Although he well knew that many others of those still united with him were vacillating,[4] he took heart and encouraged his soldiers, for he had a firm hold on the royal estates,[5] in union with the nobles who had not abandoned the holy covenant. He commanded all the troops to muster at the city of Artashat; in place of those who had deserted[6] and followed the prince of Siunik' he appointed in their stead their brothers, or sons, or nephews, handing over to them each one's troops, since he still controlled the whole country.

In haste they all reached the battlefield with each one's troops and in full preparedness, these and all who had remained loyal:

Nershapuh Artsruni
Khorēn Khorkhoruni
The *sparapet* himself[7]
Artak Paluni
Vahan Amatuni
Giwt (from the house) of the Vahevunik'
T'at'ul Dimak'sean
Arshavir Arsharuni
Shmavon Andzavats'i
Tachat Gnt'uni
Atom Gnuni
[*p. 100*] Khosrov Gabelean
Karēn Saharuni
Hmayeak Dimak'sean
And another Dimak'sean, Gazrik
Nerseh K'ajberuni
P'arsman Mandakuni
Arsēn Ēndzayats'i
Ayruk Slkuni

2. *Heroism: nahatakut'iwn;* an important theme in Eḷishē; see p. 5, n. 2.
3. *Discord: erkparakut'iwn,* as in the title of ch. 4; see p. 3, n. 4.
4. *Hesitation, vacillating: t'erahawatut'eamb, erkmtut'iwn;* as on p. 48, n. 6.
5. *Royal estates: t'agaworanist teḷik',* as on p. 80, n. 7.
6. *Deserted: yets kats'elots'n;* the same phrase is used on p. 82[1] of "abandoning" the ancestral religion.
7. I.e., Vardan Mamikonean.

Vrēn Tashrats'i
Aprsam of the Artsrunik'
The royal *shahkhoṙapet*[1]
Khurs Srvandzteats'
The K'oḷeank'
The Akēats'ik'
The Trpatunik'
The troops of the Ṙshtunik'[2]
And all the royal officials,[3] each with his troops.

All these joined forces for war on the plain of Artaz[4] for a muster[5] of sixty-six thousand men, infantry, and cavalry.

In their company came the holy Yoseph and the priest Ḷevond, with many other priests and even more deacons.[6] For these too had no hesitation in coming with the others to war; since they considered the struggle to be in no way for a material cause but for spiritual virtue,[7] they desired to share the death of the valiant martyrs.

The *sparapet*, in the company of the nobles, began to address the troops, saying:[8]

1. For the *shahkhoṙapet*, "equerry," see Adontz/Garsoian, *Armenia*, p. 442, n. 21.

2. In the above list the following are named in Eḷishē for the first time: Khorēn, Artak, T'at'ul, Tachat (Gnt'uni; for the family see Toumanoff, *Studies*, pp. 204–205), Khosrov, Karēn (Saharuni; for the family see Toumanoff, *Studies*, p. 214), Hmayeak, Nerseh (K'ajberuni; for the family see Toumanoff, *Studies*, p. 206), P'arsman (Mandakuni; for the family see Toumanoff, *Studies*, p. 212), Arsēn (Ēndzayats'i; for the family see Toumanoff, *Studies*, p. 220), Ayruk (Sḷkuni; for the family see Toumanoff, *Studies*, p. 215), Vrēn (Tashir is in northern Armenia; see Hübschmann, *AON*, pp. 354–355), Aprsam, the *shahkhoṙapet*, Khurs (Srvandzteats'; for the family see Toumanoff, *Studies*, p. 221), the Koḷeank' (for this family see Toumanoff, *Studies*, p. 221), the Trpatunik' (for this family see Toumanoff, *Studies*, p. 221).

3. *Officials: gortsakal;* for this term see Adontz/Garsoian, *Armenia*, pp. 185, 354, and 519, n. 63.

4. Artaz is in east-central Armenia; see Hübschmann, *AON*, p. 344. It is usually called a "province," as in Ḷazar, p. 69[25], in his version of these events. Ḷazar adds that they came close to the village of Avarayr, but Eḷishē mentions the precise site of the battle only in retrospect, on p. 188, n. 9.

5. *Muster: handēs;* for this term see p. 15, n. 5.

6. For *pashtoneay* as "deacon" see p. 11, n. 1.

7. *Spiritual virtue:* a main theme in Eḷishē; see p. 14, n. 1.

8. In Ḷazar (p. 71), Vardan addresses the troops just before the battle, *after* Ḷevond; but Ḷazar does not report the address of the Persian general to his troops.

"You and I have participated in many battles. Sometimes we have valiantly beaten the enemy, and sometimes they have defeated us. [*p. 101*] More often, though, we have been the victors than the defeated. But all these were for earthly distinction,[1] as we fought at the command of a temporal king. Whoever fled was regarded as a coward in the land and suffered a merciless death. But he who advanced bravely acquired a reputation for valor and received great gifts from the temporal and mortal king. So now we have many wounds and scars on our bodies, and many acts of valor have been performed for which we received great rewards. Yet I regard those acts of valor to be worthless[2] and profitless[3] and I count as naught the many rewards, since they all will pass away.

"Now if we accomplished these deeds of valor for a mortal commander, how much more [will we do] for our immortal king, who is Lord of the living and the dead[4] and who will judge every man according to his works?[5] So even if I were to attain a very advanced age, yet we would still have to leave the body to enter the presence of the living God, from whom we shall be separated no more.

So I beseech you, my valiant comrades,[6] especially because many of you have surpassed me in valor and are superior in ancestral rank.[7] But as of your own free will you have appointed me your leader and general, may my words seem sweet and agreeable to the ears of both the greatest and the least. Do not be afraid of the multitude of the heathen;[8] do not turn your backs to the fearsome sword of a mortal man;[9] for if the Lord

---

1. *Earthly distinction: marmnoy* (lit. "of the body") *partsank'. Partsank'* ("glory, boasting") is a favorite theme of Paul's; here Ełishē contrasts personal fame with that of 2 Cor. 10:17: "Let he who will boast, boast in the Lord." The following paragraph picks up and completes the argument.

2. *Worthless: anarg;* reminiscent of Ps. 57:8, of water which runs away. But it also has overtones of worldly distinction, as on p. 16[18], "the unworthy."

3. *Profitless: anawgut;* as in Wisd. of Sol. 3:11: the "profitless" labors of those who despise wisdom.

4. Cf. Rom. 14:9; 2 Tim. 4:1.

5. Cf. 1 Pet. 1:17.

6. *Comrades: nizakakits';* see Nyberg, *Manual* II, s.v. *nēzak* ("spear"). In the Bible the term occurs thirteen times—but only in Maccabees.

7. *Rank: gah,* see p. 20, n. 3.

8. For Persians as "heathen" see p. 16, n. 3.

9. *Mortal man: ařn mahkanats'ui;* the same adjective is used in the Armenian text of 2 Macc. 7:16, where the fifth son is sarcastic about Antiochus. For Yazkert as Antiochus see the Introduction.

puts victory in our grasp we shall destroy their power so that the cause of truth may be exalted. And if the time has come [*p. 102*] to end our lives in this battle with a holy death, let us accept it with joyful hearts—provided only we do not mingle cowardice with valor and bravery.[1]

"Especially since I cannot forget—remembering how I and some of you on that occasion cheated and deceived the lawless prince like an insignificant young child[2] by outwardly[3] fulfilling his impious wishes—but the Lord himself bears us witness how in our secret thoughts we remained united with him. You yourselves well know how we sought means of comforting our friends who were in great tribulation, so that we might struggle together against the impious prince for our ancestral and divinely-bestowed religion.[4] And since we were unable to help them, let it also be impossible that for the sake of human love we exchange God for men.

"Now the Lord himself has helped us with his great power in two or three battles so that we acquired the repute of valor,[5] cruelly smote the royal forces, mercilessly slew the magi, cleansed from various places the impurity of idolatry, overthrew the king's impious command, calmed the fury of the sea; the mountainous waves became smooth, the high-piled foam disappeared, the ferocious wrath ceased. He who thundered[7] above the clouds humbled and abased himself more than is his natural custom on speaking with us. He who wished by the [mere] word of his command to accomplish his evil designs on the holy church, now struggles [to do so] with bow and lance and sword. [*p. 103*] He who supposed that we put on Christianity like a garment, now [realizes] that as he cannot change

1. For the theme of cowardice and valor and parallels with speeches in Maccabees see p. 19, n. 6.

2. *Deceived . . . child:* see p. 41, n. 1.

3. *Outwardly: i verin eress.* Although the phrase is common in Ełishē (e.g., pp. 11, 22, and 135), the situation here is parallel to *Vkaykʻ*, p. 123, where Goshtazd speaks of "deceiving you and fulfilling your wishes, because outwardly I worshiped the sun but not sincerely." The situation in Ełishē refers back to p. 50.

4. *Ancestral . . . religion:* for this theme and parallels in the Maccabees see the Introduction.

5. *We . . . valor: zanun kʻajutʻean zharangetsʻak;* cf. p. 101[4-5], *kʻaj anun zharangēkʻ*, of fighting *for* the shah.

6. Cf. p. 69, with similar wording.

7. For the similes of waves, foam, and thunder cf. p. 44.

the color of his skin,[1] so he will perhaps never be able to accomplish his designs. For the foundations of our [Christianity] are set on the unshakable rock, not on earth but above in heaven where no rains fall, no winds blow, and no floods rise.[2] Although in the body we are on earth, yet by faith we are established in heaven[3] where no one can reach the building of Christ[4] not made by human hands.[5]

"Stand firm in our sure general,[6] who will never forget your heroic[7] deeds. My valiant men, this is a great thing that God has worked through us,[8] in which God's power is greatly revealed. For if by slaughtering others for the sake of the divine religion we have gained glory[9] for ourselves, and bequeathed the valiant name of our family to the church—and the expectation of reward stems from the Lord,[10] preserved for each one of us according to the willingness of his heart and the achievement of his deeds[11]—how much more [would we gain] if we were to die for the great witness of our Lord Jesus Christ,[12] which even the heavenly beings would desire were it possible. And since these rewards are not appropriate for everyone but only for him who is prepared by the benevolent Lord, this has befallen us not from any just deeds [of our own] but from the liberal bestower of gifts,[13] as he indeed said in the Holy Testament: 'Where sin abounded, there the grace of God was even more abundant.'[14]

"Very apposite is the injunction of this saying. As we apeared to men most impious,[15] in double measure shall we appear the most righteous to men and angels and the Father of all. For on the day when men heard that we were implicated in

1. Cf. Jer. 13:23.
2. Cf. Matt. 7:25; 16:18.
3. Cf. Col. 2:7.
4. Cf. Eph. 4:12.
5. Cf. 2 Cor. 5:1; Heb. 9:11.
6. I.e., Christ, not Vardan. For the exegesis of Christ as "general" see Lampe, *Lexicon*, s.v. στρατηγός, 4.
7. *Heroic: nahatakut'ean;* see p. 5, n. 2.
8. *Us:* lit.; "our human nature."
9. *Glory: partsank';* see p. 101, n. 1.
10. Cf. 1 Cor. 3:8; Heb. 11:26.
11. Cf. 2 Cor. 8:11–12.
12. Cf. 2 Tim. 1:8.
13. Cf. Heb. 11:6.
14. Rom. 5:20.
15. I.e., after the (feigned) apostasy; see p. 55.

an impious deed, many tears were shed in the holy church and even more among our dear ones. Even our comrades in their anger threatened [*p. 104*] us with the sword, wishing to inflict a bitter death on us, and our servants fled from us in horror. Distant people[1] who had heard the repute of our Christianity, since they were unaware of our intentions lamented and bewailed us unceasingly, in their ignorance heaping many blasphemies on us. And I shall mention something greater than all this: not only men on earth, but also the angels in heaven turned their faces from us so as not to look on us with saddened countenance.[2]

"Behold the time has come for us to cast off every suspicion of infamy.[3] Then we were afflicted in soul and body like grieving mourners.[4] But today we are joyful, happy, and yet sober in both respects at once, for we see the benevolent Lord with us in the lead. Our commander is no man but the general of all martyrs.[5] Fear is a sign of doubt.[6] Long ago we rejected doubt, likewise let fear flee from our minds and thoughts."

In these terms the virtuous general addressed the whole host. Furthermore he exhorted and encouraged each of them in private, filling all the wants of the indigent. Whichever soldier lacked something he provided from his own [resources] or his companions'. He supplied arms to the one who had no arms; he clothed the one who needed clothes; he gave a horse to the one who lacked a horse. With liberal pay[7] he contented them all, showing himself very cheerful to everyone. In accordance with military practice[8] he continually repeated to them the records[9] of valiant men, [*p. 105*] for he himself had been learned in the Holy Scriptures from his youth. Taking up the brave model of the Maccabees, he read it out to them all, telling them in fluent

1. I.e., the "various nations" of p. 54.
2. As on p. 56.
3. *Suspicion of infamy: keḷt anun*, as in 2 Macc. 6:25, in Eleazar's speech where he rejects deceit for the sake of a brief moment of life.
4. But on p. 54 it is the Armenians who grieve at Vardan's apostasy.
5. See p. 103, n. 6.
6. *Doubt: t'erhawatut'iwn;* see p. 28, n. 6.
7. *Pay: ṙochik;* see p. 64, n. 1.
8. *Practice: karg;* see p. 85, n. 4. It is interesting that Eḷishē thinks primarily in biblical terms (Vardan being "learned in the Holy Scriptures") for the practice of exhortations before battle.
9. *Records: yishatakarank',* as on p. 72 of the Armenians' ancestors. On p. 81 *yishatakaran* refers to a liturgical festival; cf. Faustos, III, 11, the *yishatak* of the Maccabees. See also p. 105, nn. 1, 3.

words of the outcome of events—how they fought and struggled against the king of Antioch for their God-given religion.[1]
For although they had been martyred[2] in that [battle], yet the
fame of their valor has survived to this very day, not only on
earth[3] but also eternally in heaven. Likewise he recalled to the
soldiers how the relatives of Mattathias had split away[4] from
the union, returned to the king's service, built temples,[5] offered
impure sacrifices, abandoned God, and had received the punishment of death from the holy covenanters.[6] But Mattathias
and his companions had not weakened or slackened;[7] rather,
they became even firmer[8] and plunged into war for an extended period. So he spoke; and there on the plain he pitched
camp, installed the troops, and gradually built up the cavalry
from all sides.

A few[9] days later the Persian general set out with his whole
heathen[10] host, marched to Armenia, and reached the province
of Her and Zarevand. Halting in that province, he pitched his
camp, dug ditches, erected a rampart, surrounded it with a
wooden palisade, and vigilantly fortified it like a city. Detach-
ing a large force from his army, he raided many provinces
seeking plunder.

1. *God-given religion: astuatsatur awrēnkʻ;* as on p. 102 at n. 4. For the
theme of the Maccabees see the Introduction. The parallel between Armenians and Maccabees was earlier stressed by Faustos Buzand, III, 11, and
later by Thomas Artsruni, III, 13.

2. *Martyred: kataretsʻan;* see p. 78, n. 4.

3. For the festival of the Maccabees in early Armenia see Renoux,
Codex II, 353. It was celebrated on 1 August of the Greek calendar, corresponding to Hrotitsʻ 26 in the later Armenian synaxarion of Ter Israel.

4. *Split away: kʻakteal bazhanetsʻan,* terms frequent in Ełishē (cf. p. 3[9] of
the secession from the covenant, p. 66[16] of Vasak's falling away, p. 95[6] of
the apostate priests) based on Maccabees, e.g., 1 9:8; 2 13:17.

5. *Temples: mehean,* only here in Ełishē; for the etymology see Meillet,
"Termes religieux."

6. Cf. the death of the Armenian who did not join the covenanters, p.
66.

7. *Weakened or slackened: lkʻeal tʻulatsʻan;* cf. p. 43[23] of the Armenians, or
Vkaykʻ, p. 116. The verb *lkʻanel* is very common in the books of the Maccabees.

8. *Became firmer: pndetsʻan,* as of the Armenians, p. 43[23].

9. *A few:* following the renderings of Ter-Minasean and Yuzbashyan;
all the MSS read "many (*bazum*) days later," but *A* has *ochʻ bazum* ("*not
many*"). This fits the sense better.

10. *Heathen:* although the Persians are often described as "heathen"
(cf. p. 16, n. 3), here non-Persians may well be included; see p. 115 for the
foreigners in the Persian army.

When the Armenian troops heard of this they chose from the whole army a junior noble[11] of the Amatuni family, Aṙandzar by name,[12] [a man] full of wisdom and valor. He opposed [the Persians] with two thousand men, slew [*p. 106*] the majority of their force, and threw back the survivors in flight to their camp. He himself returned safe and sound, so that day was a festival of great rejoicing[1] for the Armenian army.

Then once more the apostate Vasak had recourse to subterfuge in accordance with his former duplicity. He went around with the false priests whom we mentioned above,[2] through them claiming to be on an official royal mission; with an oath he confirmed that they could observe Christianity.

Although he did this for many days, he was unable to break their union, especially the holy covenant of the church, which the soldiers had not abandoned.

The blessed priest Levond, receiving permission from his holy companions, from the great Yoseph and all the magnates, from the priests and generals, opened his mouth[3] and spoke out loudly before the angelic [soldiers].[4]

"You all remember our forefathers who [lived] before the birth of the Son of God at each one's time.

"For when the Evil One caused our expulsion from the divine garden, we were exposed to merciless condemnation for our sins of transgression which we had unworthily committed in our desire for freedom. We brought upon ourselves the force of the Creator's anger, and moved the merciful Judge to take impartial vengeance on his creatures. He even ordered the sea

11. *Junior noble: sepuh;* see p. 74, n. 12.

12. *Aṙandzar:* also mentioned on p. 193 as a prisoner in Persia after the war. On his foray here described cf. Łazar, p. 69.

---

1. *Festival of rejoicing: tawn urakhut'ean,* as in 1 Macc. 1:67, where the Armenian is quite divergent from the Greek.

2. Cf. p. 92.

3. For this speech cf. Łazar, p. 70. Łazar refers to St. Gregory's sufferings in his exhortation and has no reference to specific heroes of the O.T. But Eḷishē never refers to the Illuminator of Armenia, and is particularly interested in the parallels between the Armenians and the warrior leaders of ancient Israel. This speech in Eḷishē owes much to the dying speech of Mattathias in 1 Macc., ch. 2. See further below, p. 109, n. 3.

4. *Angelic (soldiers): hreshtakk',* lit. "angels" or "messengers," Ter-Minasean and Yuzbashyan translate as "envoys" (*patgamavor, poslanets*). But "angels" seems more appropriate to the context, for the soldiers are about to be martyred. Cf. Cyril of Jerusalem, *Catecheses,* 16:20: martyrs turn their faces to the judge, but in reality are in heaven.

of heaven to flow over the dry land, and the firm ground of earth was rent, causing the same from the opposite side.[5] The upper and lower [waters] became instruments of torture for us, taking vengeance on our transgressions without mitigation.

"So the just Noah remained as the only perfect one in the human race; [*p. 107*] he softened the severity of the Lord's anger and became the prime cause of the growth and multiplication of mankind. Abraham too was proved virtuous in his trial, offering in return to God with his own hands the gifts he had received from him. Therefore God accepted him as a model, for he saw in him a type of the invisible coming of the Son of God,[1] the apprehension of the incomprehensible, the sacrifice of the immortal, who by his own death abolished the power of death.[2] And if death is destroyed by death, let us not fear to share Christ's death; for with whom we die, with the same we shall also live.[3]

"Remember, valiant [comrades], the great Moses;[4] before he had reached manhood the mystery of pious heroism[5] was revealed to him in the years of his youth. The house of the Egyptian king offered him service and unwillingly fostered and nourished him.[6] At the time of the people's deliverance from oppression he became a mediator[7] between heaven and earth and at the same time was named god[8] over the Egyptians. For where the Holy Mystery waxed strong, in his own person he took vengeance on the Egyptians. And where the divine revelation was upon him, through his rod[9] he worked great miracles. Because of the holy zeal he possessed, he smote the Egyptian and buried him in sand.[10] Therefore [God] bestowed a great name on him and established him as leader of his people. The main thing is that he was justified by the shedding of blood and

---

5. Cf. *Teaching*, §296.

1. For Abraham as a type of the Incarnation see *Teaching*, §300, 302.
2. Cf. Heb. 2:14.
3. This is a paraphrase of 1 Cor. 15:22.
4. For Moses cf. *Teaching*, §305–306.
5. *Heroism: nahatakut'iwn*, see p. 5, n. 2.
6. Cf. Exod. 2:11.
7. Cf. *Teaching*, §306ff.
8. In Exod. 2:14 Moses is called "prince" and "judge" (*ishkhan, datawor*). For Moses described as "god" in patristic exegesis (notably Gregory of Nyssa) see references in Lampe, *Lex.* s.v. θεός, K 2.
9. Cf. Exod. 4:2–4.
10. Cf. Exod. 2:12.

was called the greatest of all prophets[11] for slaughtering not only the outer enemies but also his kin, who had exchanged God for the calf in the desert.[12]

"If from afar he displayed such zeal for the coming of the Son of God, how much more should we—who were eyewitnesses and greatly enjoyed the heavenly gifts of his grace[13]—be zealous [*p. 108*] for the recently revealed truth. As he lay down his life in death for our sins and absolved us from the insupportable condemnation, let us too lay down our lives in death[1] for his immortal power, lest we be inferior to those zealous ones.

"Remember the great priest Pinehas, who by slaughter removed the profanation in the hour of battle, and confirmed the priesthood by oath from generation to generation.[2] Do not forget the holy prophet Elias, who was unable to endure the sight of Achab's idolatry. In his righteous zeal he slew eight hundred with his own hands and offered two fifties as tinder for the unquenchable fire.[3] Having sought retribution, he was raised from earth to heaven in an incomprehensible and awesome chariot.[4] You have attained an even greater fate, for no longer is a chariot sent from heaven for your ascension but the Lord of chariots and horses himself,[5] meeting you with his mighty power and holy angels,[6] will cause wings to grow on each of you,[7] so that you may journey with him and share his city.

"What else can I repeat before you valiant warriors, for you are more versed and learned than I in the Holy Testaments? David in the time of his youth slew the great mountain of flesh[8] with a stone, quite unfearful of the giant's fearsome

---

11. For this title applied to Moses see Lampe, *Lexicon*, s.v. προφήτης, Q.

12. Cf. Exod. 32:27–28.

13. Cf. Heb. 6:4.

---

1. Cf. 1 John 3:16.

2. Cf. Num. 25:6–8, 13.

3. Cf. 3 Kings 18:19; but there eight hundred and fifty false prophets are slain. Is the "two fifties" a confusion with the two fifties of true prophets in the same ch., vv. 4, 13?

4. Cf. 4 Kings 2:11.

5. Cf. Isa. 43:17.

6. Cf. 2 Thess. 1:7.

7. For the growing of wings see *Teaching*, §605–606; but that men may become like the angels is a very common theme.

8. *Mountain of flesh: blurn mseḷēn;* cf. the description of Bēl in the *Primary History* (Sebēos, p. 50; Thomson, *Moses Khorenats'i*, p. 361), or the description of King Pauros struck by Alexander, Ps-Callisthenes §219 (p. 134 of the Armenian text).

sword.[9] He scattered the forces of the foreigners[10] and saved his army from death and the people from enslavement. He became the first[11] of the kings of Israel and was called the father of the Son of God.[12] He was [so] called for the needs of the time; while you, truly born of the Holy Spirit, are sons of God and heirs of Christ.[13] Lete no one [*p. 109*] deprive you of your portion, or estrange[1] and alienate you.

"Remember all the earlier generals of Israel: Joshua, Gideon,[2] Jephthah,[3] and all the others who were of the true faith. They smote and slew the armies of the heathen,[4] and purified the land from their foul idolatry.[5] On account of their unwavering righteous conduct—as they never hesitated[6] in their intentions—the sun and moon, which have no ears, heard and fulfilled their command.[7] The sea and rivers[8] made a path

9. Cf. 1 Kings, ch. 17.

10. *Foreigners: aylazgi*, i.e., the Philistines (as passim in the OT); later Armenian texts often use this term for Muslims.

11. *First: andranik*, lit. "eldest." Saul was the first king of Israel, 1 Kings, ch. 10; David, already king of Judah, became the first king of both Israel and Judah, 2 Kings 5:4.

12. Cf. Matt. 21:9; 22:42; John 7:42.

13. Cf. Rom. 8:14, 17.

1. Cf. Heb. 12:8.

2. Gideon, Judg. chs. 6–7, fought against the children of the East, *areweleayk'*, which is the name given the Persians by Ełishē; see p. 4, n. 1.

3. With Jephthah Ełishē closes his list of O.T. heroes. This list has very significant parallels with those of 1 Macc., ch. 2 (=M); Ecclus., chs. 44–45 (=E); and Heb., ch. 11 (=H):

Noah:		E	H
Abraham:	M	E	H
Moses:		E	H
Pinehas:	M	E	
Elias:	M	E	
David:	M	E	H
Joshua:	M	E	
Gideon:			H
Jephthah:			H

Heb. 11:32ff was included in the readings on the festival of the Maccabees; see Renoux, *Codex*, p. 353.

4. Cf. the parallel with Persians as "heathen," p. 16, n. 3.

5. *Foul idolatry:* as on p. 69, of fire-worship.

6. *Hesitated: erkmtets'in*, see p. 48, n. 6.

7. Cf. Josh. 10:13, where Joshua overcame the Amorites.

8. The river refers to the crossing of the Jordan, Josh, 3:16; the sea is the Red Sea, Exod. 14:21.

before them, contrary to their usual nature. The high walls of the city[9] at a mere sound collapsed and were destroyed in requital for the just religion. And all the others who performed acts of valor in each one's age in accordance with their faith were praised by men and justified by God.

"So the Lord is the same[10] from the beginning up to today and forever, for age after age and beyond all eternity.[11] He becomes neither new nor ancient, grows neither young nor old. The immutable nature of God does not change.[12] As he himself said through the mouth of the holy prophets: 'I am, I am;[13] I am the same from the beginning forever. I give not my glory to another or my deeds of valor to sculpted [images].'[14]

"As we know all this, brethren, let us not slacken or be dispirited,[15] but [*p. 110*] with firm heart and constant faith let us eagerly attack the enemy who has risen up against us. Our hope appears to us as double: if we die, we shall live; and if we put to death,[1] the same life lies before us. Let us recall the Apostle's saying: 'Instead of the joy which lay before him, he patiently endured death—even the death of the cross. Therefore God raised him even higher and gave him a name above all names, that at the name of Jesus Christ every knee might bow—of things in heaven and things on earth and things below the earth.'[2]

"For he who is truly united to the love of Christ sees with the eyes of the Spirit the invisible but clear light of the rays of the spiritual sun,[3] which every hour and every day shines more brilliantly over everyone. With crystal purity it attracts the contemplation of those with unsullied and holy sight; penetrating heaven[4] it brings them close to the unapproachable vision,

9. I.e., Jericho, Josh. 6:20.
10. Cf. Ps. 102:26–28; Heb. 1:12.
11. Cf. Heb. 13:8 (of Christ); cf. *Teaching*, §378.
12. Cf. Eznik, §3.
13. Cf. Exod. 3:14.
14. Isa. 42:8; 48:11–12.
15. *Slacken, dispirited: mi tʻulutʻeamb lkʻanitsʻimkʻ;* as on p. 105, n. 7 of the Maccabees, or p. 71, n. 3 of the Armenians.

1. *Put to death: meṛutsʻanel;* it occurs in Eḷishē only here and on p. 113 of the clergy ready to fight alongside the soldiers. For the theme of life and death, cf. p. 73, n. 10. Cf. also 1 Macc. 4:35: "they were ready to live or die."
2. Cf. Phil. 2:7–10.
3. For Christ as the spiritual sun see p. 50, n. 7.
4. Cf. p. 5.

and through its power inclines them to the worship of the three Persons of the united Being.[5] So he who has trod the divine ladder,[6] reached the palace on high, and seen all its greatness, he alone will inherit unfading joy and blissful consolation.[7]

"So, my honorable lords, after rising to such a height let us not fall back to earth, but let us make a firm stand here on high. [*p. 111*] Although we may look down on the lower region of this earth, we see it filled with all kinds of corruption and foul impurities. For what miseries and anguish do not befall the calamity-prone inhabitants of earth—the misfortunes of the poor and their innumerable troubles, the violent exactions of the tax-gatherers, the oppression and ill-usage of tyrannical neighbors, hunger and thirst in accordance with our natural needs? The icy blasts of winter and the burning winds of summer, premature sickness and mortal illnesses continually torment men. Fear of foreign [enemies] and dread of inner [enemies] ceaselessly come upon them. [Some] desire an untimely death but do not attain it, while there are many who ferret and search and are delighted when they find it.[1] But those who seem to us to have successfully obtained wealth and spend this imperfect life in luxury[2] and enjoyment, arrogant and haughty in the transitory affairs of the world, these are the ones who are blind to the true life.[3] What indeed are the evils not committed among them? With their wealth is mingled the rapine of the possessions of the poor, with their pure marriages foul lewdness. Having strayed from the true life they worship as God whatever they have chosen to enjoy.

"Is not the whole world the Creation[4] of the Maker of all? Now what they worship and honor is but a part of its substance. So are parts in subjection to parts?[5] For if one part of the

5. *Persons, Being: hatuatsk', zawrut'iwn.* For *zawrut'iwn* ("power") in this sense see Thomson, *Teaching,* p. 12 and §383. But *hatuats* is not a traditional Armenian term for the three Persons of the Trinity, although it is found in Gregory of Narek (d. 1010); e.g., at the end of *Prayer* 11.
6. *Ladder: astichank';* on the idea of a ladder symbolizing ascent to heaven see Lampe, *Lexicon,* s.v. κλῖμαξ; cf. also Gen. 28:12 and Philo, *In Gen.,* IV, 29.
7. Cf. John 16:20.

1. Cf. Job 3:20–22.
2. *Luxury: p'ap'kakan;* on this term see p. 67, n. 9.
3. See p. 14 for the theme of being blind to truth and light.
4. *Creation: goyats'ut'iwn;* see p. 33, n. 1, for this term, and p. 30 for Ełishē on creation.
5. Cf. p. 33. The sense requires that this sentence be a rhetorical

world [*p. 112*] is corruptible, then all the other parts must be corruptible. Likewise, from among these parts distinctions should be discerned. Now the best is clear to all, and he who can understand is the most select of the parts. So if this is the case, those worshipers are superior to all the cults of the heathen that they revere and to the irrational elements they detestably serve. They do not worship the living God who took the form of a man,[1] but they offer worship to creatures—for which sin there is no propitiation at the just tribunal.[2]

"Let us then abandon the dark thoughts of these erring ones. Let us reckon them as more unfortunate and miserable than all men, especially because they are blind by intention and not by constraint and will never find the true road. But since we have seen the heavenly light with open eyes, let not the outer darkness befall us. For to those who were in darkness has come the true light.[3] The blind have been deprived of life, but you who received [the light] with faith are sons and not bastards, friends not enemies, sharers and inheritors of the supernal and spiritual city.[4]

"The leader of our salvation[5] is here. Here he bravely fought to the death and taught the same to his fellow warriors and companions,[6] the Apostles. Blessed by faith, you too will again appear with them today in opposition to the invisible enemy; armed with breastplates[7] [you will] oppose the allies of Satan's work. In one way or another you will bring both sides to defeat, as the Lord himself did [*p. 113*] for the world. It

---

question, although the editor of the Armenian text does not provide a question mark. Yuzbashyan provides an exclamation mark.

1. *Who took the form of a man: or i mard kerparanets'aw*, lit. "who was formed into a man." Cf. Proclus', *Tome* (*Girk' T'łt'ots'*, p. 3): *kerparanets'aw ibrew mard.* In the *Teaching* the expression "who took the form of mankind" is preferred; §377: *ar zmardkan kerparans*, or §381: *ar zkerparans marmnoy* (of flesh).

2. Cf. 2 Cor. 5:10; 1 John 2:2.

3. Cf. Isa 9:2; John 1:4–9, and p. 111, n. 3.

4. This last sentence is a conflate of Rom. 11:28; Heb. 3:1; 11:16; and 12:8.

5. Cf. Heb. 2:10.

6. *Fellow warriors and companions: nizakakits' gortsakits';* note the parallels with the Armenians; *nizakits'* on p. 101, n. 6, with parallels in Maccabees, and *gortsakits'* on p. 80[21].

7. *Armed with breastplates: patenazēn zrahiwk'.* The only biblical use of *patenazēn* is in 1 Macc. 6:39 of Lysias's cavalry. *Zrah* in this context recalls Paul, Eph. 6:14, and 1 Thess. 5:8.

seemed that he had died, but he then bore off the prize of complete victory; he threw down the champion,[1] won the battle, scattered the enemy, amassed plunder, restored the captives, and distributed gifts to all his friends in proportion to each one's valor.[2]

"You all know that in former times, when you went out to war you had the custom that priests would always be in the camp; and at the hour of battle, relying upon their prayers, you would leave them in a safe place. But today bishops, priests and deacons, singers of the psalms and readers of Scripture, each in his own canonical rank,[3] like armed men ready for battle, wish to attack with you and smite the enemies of the truth.[4] Even if they may be killed by them, yet they will not be afraid of that because they prefer to die than to kill.[5]

"It is as if they had gained double vision: with the eyes of faith they see the stoning of the prophets,[6] and with the eyes of the body the valor of your heroism.[7] Moreover, we see that you have this double [vision]. For you see the torments of the holy Apostles and the murders of all the saintly martyrs by whose death the holy church was strengthened; the shedding of their blood was [a cause of] boasting for those above and those below. Now until the Second Coming the same heroism will be performed under torment."

[*p. 114*] All this the holy priest Łevond spoke that night; he ended with a blessing, saying "Amen." Setting up an altar they

---

1. *Champion: akhoyean*, see p. 77, n. 5. Here the parallel to David smiting Goliath is Christ smiting Satan. The juxtaposition may be based on the Armenian text of Ephrem, *Commentary on the Diatessaron*, IV, 12.

2. The last phrase has verbal parallels with Acts. 4:35 (distributed, all, in proportion).

3. *Canonical rank: kargeal kanonaw;* cf. p. 85, n. 4. These same five ranks: bishops (*episkopos*), priests (*erēts'*), deacons (*sarkawag*), singers of psalms (*saḷmosergoḷ*), and readers of Scripture (*grakardats'*) are listed in the Armenian Canon 64 of the Apostolic Canons II attributed to Clement (see *Kanonagirk'*, I, 92). For the last two ranks see Lampe, *Lexicon*, s.v. ψάλτης and ἀναγνώστης; they are also mentioned in the Armenian text of Canon 90 of the Second Nicene Canons, *Kanonagirk'*, II, 87. It is noteworthy that Mkhit'ar Gosh quotes this passage with ref. to the Ps-Dionysian orders of the church that are parallel to the orders of angels and of secular administration, *Girk' Datastani*, p. 139, ch. 225.

4. Cf. p. 56, n. 7.

5. Cf. p. 110, n. 1.

6. Cf. Matt. 23:37; Luke 13:34.

7. *Heroism: nahatakut'iwn*, common of martyrs, cf. p. 5, n. 2; so here there is a further parallel with the death of Stephen, Acts 7:58.

celebrated the most holy Liturgy.[1] They also put up a font, and throughout the night baptized any catechumens[2] in the army. In the morning these received Holy Communion[3] and were clothed with light as on the Lord's great festival of holy Easter.[4]

With much joy and great happiness the whole host of the army cried out, saying: "May our death equal the death of the just and the shedding of our blood that of the blood of the holy martyrs. May God be pleased with our willing sacrifice[5] and not deliver his church into the hands of the heathen."

After this,[6] when the general of the Persian army saw that there were no messengers left to deceive them and that his expectation and hope of separating them from the indissoluble union had failed, then he summoned the impious Vasak and all the apostate nobles from Armenia who were with him. He questioned them to discover what means of victory there might be. On being informed about each man's individual valor,[7] he summoned many of the generals under his authority and or-

---

1. *Liturgy: khorhurd,* lit. "Mystery," a standard expression for the Liturgy; see Lampe, *Lexicon,* s.v. μυστήριον.

2. *Catechumens: erakhay.* For regulations concerning the Baptism of catechumens see (for example) the Armenian text of Canon 14 of Nicaea, *Kanonagirkʿ,* I, 126–127.

3. *Received Holy Communion: surb awrinatsʿ haḷordetsʿan;* lit. "participated in the holy *awrēnkʿ.*" For this use of *awrēnkʿ* as the consecrated elements cf. Faustos, V, 28; for *awrēnkʿ* as "religion" see the Introduction.

4. I.e., normally Baptism would be restricted to Holy Saturday. According to Łazar, p. 69, this was the Friday evening before Pentecost, which in 451 fell on 4 June.

5. *Willing sacrifice:* a liturgical expression referring to Christ's death.

6. There has been much debate as to whether a new chapter begins here. No manuscript has a new chapter heading here, though most of them indicate some break; see apparatus p. 114 in the edition of Ter-Minasean. However, on p. 122 only MS *B* has "sixth [chapter]," all others reading "seventh." The list of chapter headings on pp. 3–4 does not solve the problem as the titles for chapters 6 and 7 could refer to Avarayr and its aftermath (in which case the long section on the martyrdoms in Persia would not be part of the schema expounded in the Introduction), or they could refer to the battles *after* Avarayr and the continuing troubles during the captivity of the Armenians in Persia. Furthermore, the actual chapter headings do not correspond to the titles on pp. 3–4.

I have kept Ter-Minasean's numbering of the chapters (i.e., a total of seven including the long final section) because the final section does not seem to be an adjunct to a separate book but an integral part of the story, picking up numerous themes adumbrated in the earlier chapters. For these themes see the Introduction.

7. Cf. the inquiries of Mihrnerseh, p. 96, with identical phrasing.

dered them to bring forward the companies[8] of elephants. These [*p. 115*] he divided into various groups, and he assigned to each elephant three thousand armed men in addition to all the other troops.

He addressed the greatest nobles at the king's behest, saying: "Each of you remember the command of the great king and set as your goal the fame of bravery. Choose death over a cowardly life.[1] Do not forget the oil, the crown, the laurels, and the liberal gifts[2] which will be granted you from the royal treasury. You are lords each of your own province, and you possess great power. You yourselves know the bravery of the Armenians and the heroic valor of each one of them. If perchance you are defeated, though alive you will be deprived of the great property[3] you now have. Remember your wives and children, remember your dear friends. Perchance you will be trampled by your enemies[4] from abroad and be joined in grief by your friends at home."

Likewise he reminded them of their many companions who had fled; although they survived the battle, they had received the penalty of death by the sword. Their sons and daughters and their entire families had been banished,[5] and all their ancestral lands taken from them.

Such were his words, and even more strongly did he emphasize the royal orders. He set in order the whole army and extended his battleline all the way across the great plain. He disposed the three thousand armed men to right and left of each elephant, and surrounded himself with the elite of his warriors. In this fashion he strengthened the center[6] like a pow-

---

8. *Companies:* see p. 88, n. 4.

---

1. This is a theme emphasized for the Armenians; see p. 19, n. 6 for the parallel in Maccabees.

2. *Crown . . . gifts:* the crown has Christian overtones of the martyr's crown (e.g., p. 150), but cf. the Iranian crowns on p. 12. Laurels (*uṙ*) are a commonplace in biblical and classical texts. The liberal gifts are reminiscent of p. 83.

3. *Property: keankʻ*, for which see p. 95, n. 4. Here the play on the meaning "life" is evident.

4. *Trampled:* reminiscent of the trampling by elephants, p. 48, n. 4. But "trampling (*otnhar*) by enemies" is a common biblical expression.

5. *Banished: yanashkharhiks gretsʻan* (lit. "enrolled among the banished"). For *anashkharhik* see p. 71, n. 2. Does this paragraph refer to the Persian defeat and flight described on p. 77?

6. *Center: gund matean.* For this term see Nyberg, *Manual* II, s.v. *Mātiyān;* it refers to the center of an army.

erful tower or an impregnable castle. He distributed banners,[7] unfurled flags,[8] and ordered them to be ready at the sound of the great trumpet.[9] The contingents of the Aparhatsik',[10] the Katishk',[11] [*p. 116*] the Huns[1] and the Gelk',[2] and all the rest of the army's elite he assembled in once place, and commanded the force on his right-hand side to be ready to oppose the Armenian general.

Then the brave Vardan advanced, questioned the nobles,[3] and with their unanimous advice disposed his generals.

The first division he entrusted to the prince of Artsrunik', with the great prince of Mokk' in support.[4] Many other nobles he appointed as adjutants[5] to these two, and deployed the mass of the troops on the wings to either side.

The second division he entrusted to Khorēn Khoṙkhoṙuni, with Ĕntsayin[6] and Nerseh K'ajberuni in support.

The third division he put under the command of Tat'ul Vanandats'i,[7] and ordered Tachat Gnt'uni to support him with many brave warriors to both sides on their wings.

He took upon himself the command of the fourth division, with the valiant Arshavir[8] and his own blood brother Hamazaspean[9] in support.

---

7. *Distributed banners: nshans bashkhēr,* as in 2 Macc. 8:23; 13:15. For *nshan* ("sign") see Hübschmann, *Grammatik,* pp. 205–206. On p. 16 it has the meaning of "miracle."

8. *Flags: drawsh,* see p. 96, n. 3. For the raising of flags at the attack see Christensen, *Iran,* p. 206.

9. For an attack at the sound of the trumpet cf. 1 Macc. 9:12.

10. *Aparhats'ik':* i.e., the people of Apar, for which see p. 10, n. 1.

11. *Katishk':* in the region of Herat; see Marquart, *Erānšahr,* p. 77.

---

1. In previous references to the Huns they are described as subject to the shah, p. 42; at war with the shah, pp. 12, 70; or allied with the Armenians, p. 80.

2. *Gelk':* i.e., the people of Gilan; see Hübschmann, *Grammatik,* pp. 34–35.

3. *Nobles: awagani;* see p. 56, n. 9.

4. *In support: nizakits';* see p. 101, n. 6. The same term is used in the three following paragraphs.

5. *Adjutant: hambarz;* see p. 35, n. 2.

6. This is the only ref. to Ĕntsayin K'ajberuni. For the family of the Ĕntsayink' see p. 120.

7. This is the only ref. to Tat'ul.

8. This is Arshavir Arsharuni (see p. 77, n. 1), as is clear from Łazar, p. 72.

9. This is the first ref. to Hamazaspean; he is mentioned once again, p. 193, among the nobles imprisoned in Persia.

He deployed his battleline, spreading (the troops) across the whole surface of the plain opposite the Aryan army on the bank of the river Tłmut.[10]

When these preparations had been completed and both sides were filled with passion and enflamed with wrath, they rushed on each other with the force of wild animals. Their melee caused a roar like the thundering in turbulent clouds, and the echoing of their shouts [*p. 117*] made the caverns of the mountains shake. From the multitude of helmets and shining armor of the soldiers light flashed like rays of the sun. The glittering of the many swords and the waving of the massed lances were like fearful lightning from heaven. For who is able to describe the tremendous commotion of the terrifying sounds or how the clashing of shields and the crack of bowstrings deafened everyone's ears?

There one could see the commotion of the great conflict and the anguish of the immense anxiety on both sides as they resolutely attacked each other. For the dull-witted became mad and the cowards deserted; the brave advanced fearlessly and the heroes roared. Forming a solid group, the whole host blocked the river. The Persian army, fearing the difficulty of (crossing) the river, began to stir in its place. But the Armenian army crossed over on horseback and attacked in great force. As the two sides collided with a crash, many wounded fell to the ground, rolling in the agony of death.[1]

In that great tumult the valiant Vardan looked up and saw that the elite of the bravest warriors of the Persian army had dislodged the left wing of the Armenian force. With great vigor he attacked the spot and broke the right wing of the Per-

---

10. *River Tłmut;* a tributary of the Araxes in central Armenia; see Hübschmann, *AON*, p. 476. The name means "muddy."

---

1. Like many other descriptions of battle scenes in Armenian historians (see Thomson, "Maccabees") this one owes much to imagery in the Armenian version of the books of the Maccabees:

wild animals, as in 2 Macc. 12:15, Judas's attack on Caspin.
rays, glittering, as in 2 Macc. 1:22, 32.
waving, lances, as in 2 Macc. 11:8.
tremendous commotion, as in 2 Macc. 3:21; 6:9; and 10:28.
anguish, anxiety, as in 3 Macc. 4:4.
collided, as in 1 Macc. 7:42; 10:49.
rolling, death, as in 1 Macc. 3:24; 5:34; and 6:42.

Łazar's account of the battle (p. 72) is brief and less circumstantial; he attributes the Armenian defeat primarily to defection.

sian army, throwing it back on the elephants; surrounding them, he cut them down back to the same place. Such confusion he brought upon them that the center broke and abandoned their fortified position, even the most valiant taking to flight.

Then Mushkan Nisalavurt lifted his eyes[2] and saw that some of the Armenian troops had broken away from the main force and remained behind in the valleys of the mountains. [*p. 118*] Therefore, raising a shout, he urged on the Aryan soldiers around him, who had halted opposite Vardan's division. At that spot the two sides both were prepared to acknowledge defeat, as the corpses had fallen so thickly as to resemble piles of rough stones.[1]

When Mushkan Nisalavurt saw this he waited for the elephants of Artashir,[2] who was sitting on [one of] them in a high watchtower[3] as if in a fortified city. At the sound of the great trumpets[4] he urged on his troops and surrounded him [Vardan] with the troops of the front line.

Now the stalwart Vardan with his valiant companions worked no little carnage in that very place where he himself became worthy to suffer perfect martyrdom.[5]

As the battle continued, the day began to go down and night drew on. Many reached the point of death,[6] especially as the bodies had fallen so thickly that they lay in dense piles like logs hewn in the forest.[7]

There one could see so many broken lances and snapped bows that the holy bodies of the blessed ones could not be distinguished, and there was a frightful press[8] of those who had fallen on both sides. The survivors had run off and scattered in the safe valleys of the plateau. Whenever they came across one

2. *Lifted his eyes,* as on p. 77, n. 2.

---

1. Cf. Isa. 27:9.

2. This Artashir is not mentioned elsewhere.

3. *Watchtower: ditanots‘,* see Hübschmann, *Grammatik,* p. 141. Cf. the turret on the backs of elephants, described in 1 Macc. 6:37.

4. *Trumpets: galarap‘oł,* as opposed to the simple *p‘oł* of p. 115, n. 9. *Galarel* means "to roll, bend." This noun is very rare.

5. *Martyrdom: nahatakut‘iwn;* see p. 5, n. 2. Łazar in his account of Avarayr, p. 72, places great emphasis on the Armenians' desire for the crown of martyrdom.

6. *Point of death: awrahasak‘ mahu;* see p. 8, n. 6.

7. Cf. Isa. 27:9, as in n. 1 above.

8. *Press: khuchap,* as in 2 Macc. 14:44 on the death of Razis.

another, they again fell to mutual slaughter.[10] This bitter work
continued without respite until the setting of the sun.

[*p. 119*] Since it was springtime the flowering meadows[1]
became torrents of many men's blood. Especially when one saw
the vast mass of fallen corpses,[2] one's heart would break[3] and
one's bowels shrivel up[4] on hearing the groaning[5] of the in-
jured, the crying[6] of the hurt, the rolling and crawling of the
wounded,[7] the fleeing of the cowards, the hiding of the deserters, the dismay[8] of the fainthearted, the wailing[9] of the effemi-
nate, the lamentations[10] of dear ones, the bewailing of relatives,
the woe and grief of friends. For neither side was victorious and
neither side was defeated; but heroes attacked heroes[11] and
both sides went down to defeat.

But because the Armenian general had fallen in the great
battle, there was no longer any leader among them around
whom the remaining troops could rally. Although there were
many more who survived than died, nonetheless they had been
widely scattered and had escaped to various secure parts of the
country; they had seized many provinces and castles which no
one could capture.

These are the names of the valiant martyrs who died[12] on
the field:

From the family of the Mamikoneans, the valiant Vardan
with 133 men

10. For mutual slaughter and flight cf. 2 Macc. 12:22 on the defeat of
Timotheus by Judas Maccabeus. (The parallel here is not so much verbal,
as with other refs. to the Maccabees noted above, but rather one of situation.)

1. There is a verbal parallel to flowering meadows in spring in *Vkayk'*,
p. 130.
2. For torrents of blood and the plain covered with corpses cf. Jth.
6:3–4, with some verbal parallels to this passage.
3. Cf. Ezek. 21:7.
4. Cf. Gen. 43:30.
5. Cf. Isa. 38:14.
6. Cf. 3 Macc. 4:7.
7. Cf. Nah. 3:3.
8. Cf. 2 Macc. 12:22.
9. Cf. Isa. 26:17.
10. Cf. Jer. 31:15.
11. As in Moses Khorenats'i, I, 29, of the battle between Azhdahak
and Tigran.
12. *Martyrs, died: nahatakk', katarets'an;* see p. 5, n. 2, and p. 78, n. 4.

From the family of the Khořkhořunikʻ, the resolute
Khorēn, with 19 men

From the family of the Palunikʻ, the brave Artak with 57
men

From the family of the Gntʻunikʻ, the wonderful Tachat[13]
with 19 men

From the family of the Dimakʻsean, the wise Hmayeak
with 22 men

From the family of the Kʻajberunikʻ, the splendid Nerseh,
with 7 men

[*p. 120*] From the family of the Gnunikʻ, the young
Vahan[1] with 3 men

From the family of the Ēntsayinkʻ, the just Arsēn with 7
men

From the family of the Sruandzit, the forward-looking
Garegin[2] with two blood brothers and 18 men[3]

These 287 heroes with the nine great nobles were martyred
on the field. In addition to these 287 another 740 men from the
royal house and from the house of the Artsrunikʻ[4] and from the
houses of the other nobles inscribed their names in the book of
life[5] on that day in the great battle. Altogether they were 1,036.

But on the side of the apostates and heathen[6] there fell on
that day 3,544 men.[7] Nine of them were of the most eminent

---

13. For a mausoleum supposedly erected to Tachat Gnʻuni see
Hasratian, "Amarass," p. 255.

---

1. This Vahan is mentioned only here; for the Gnuni family see p. 71,
n. 4.

2. It is not clear whether this is meant to be the same Garegin mentioned on p. 13, who in 450 was handed over to two years of torture. The
adjective "forward-looking" (*yaṙajadēm*) is used of Isaac in Gen. 26:13.

3. Ełishē's list of named nobles is the same as Łazar's, p. 72. However,
Łazar gives no description of the individuals save the epithet "blessed"
(*eraneli*) passim, nor does he give the number of companions who perished
with each. Although there are some biblical parallels for the numbers (e.g.,
19: 2 Kings 2:30 of David's servants; 22: 1 Chron. 12:28 of those who join
David; 18: 1 Chron. 26:9 of the strong men of Meshelemiah) they do not
seem to have any relevance for this situation.

4. This ref. to the Artsrunikʻ led the later historian Thomas Artsruni
to expand in greater detail on the role of his patrons in this rebellion.

5. Cf. Phil. 4:3, and p. 31, n. 2.

6. *And heathen:* i.e., Persians; these two words are not found in any
MSS, but in the edition *A*. They are required by the sense, as the rest of the
paragraph makes clear.

7. The totals of fallen are identical with those in Łazar, p. 73.

nobility,[8] for which reason Mushkan Nisalavurt was exceedingly hurt. Particularly when he saw that the terrible casualties of his own forces were three times worse than the Armenians', his strength and powers failed[9] and he could not calm his troubled mind, since the outcome of the battle was not what he had expected.[10] When he saw the great number of fallen on his own side and reckoned them up, and when he discovered how many more of his men had fallen than in the Armenian army, he was especially disturbed—even more so on account of the notable men whom the king knew personally. For fear of the king he could not describe events accurately, yet again he was unable to conceal them, as such a great battle could not be hidden.

[*p. 121*] While his thoughts were on this and his mind was troubled, Vasak the apostate, who had survived by hiding himself among the elephants, came up to console his distress. He indicated to him deceitful means whereby he might be able to attack the strongholds by guile. He sealed sworn declarations with the royal imprint[1] and with his own witness and that of the false priests in his company. The latter he sent as messengers to announce pardon[2] for the insurrection, and he indicated that permission had been granted to restore the church and that all conditions were to be reestablished in their former order. Although the king's command had been definitely given—because his power had indeed been broken as he had been struck on two sides—nonetheless the Armenian troops were unable to believe the king's order immediately because of the treachery of Vasak, whose deceit they had frequently recognized.[3]

8. *Nobility: patuawork‘*, lit. "honorable"; cf. p. 84, n. 3, where the cognate *patuakan* is used.

9. *Strength, failed: zawrut‘iwn, bekaw;* cf. Jer. 51:30 of the "mighty men of Babylon."

10. Cf. 1 Macc. 4:27 of Lysias' disappointment that the Jews had not been defeated as the king had ordered (with verbal parallels).

1. *With the royal imprint: ark‘uni hramanaw;* the same expression as on p. 115[3], where it is translated "at the king's behest." *Hraman* would normally mean an "order" (see Nyberg, *Manual* II, s.v. *framān*), but here a royal signature stamp seems to be implied. However, "command" and "order" (both *hraman*) later in the paragraph do refer to a command coming from the shah.

2. *Pardon: t‘oḷut‘iwn*, as on p. 85, n. 7.

3. For the disbelief of the Armenians and their recognition of Vasak's treachery, cf. pp. 66–67, 86ff.

CHAPTER SIX

In Which the Virtue[1] of the Armenians Is Again Set Forth and the Impiety[2] of Vasak Is Shown To Be Even More Wicked

THEN he (Vasak) again incited Mushkan Nisalavurt and all the Aryan nobility. Taking troops, he reached the fortress in which a detachment of the Armenian army with the holy priests had taken refuge; they joined battle around the castle. Since they were unable to make any impression on them [the Armenians], they resorted to oaths, that they should come down under a pact without [the Persians] engaging in any deceit. Two and three times they had the Gospel brought.[3] But although the priests agreed to go down and present themselves, many of the soldiers were unable to trust Vasak's false pact, since Mushkan Nisalavurt had begun to follow Vasak's wicked advice.

One of the brave Armenian soldiers who had fled to the castle for refuge, Bak by name,[4] went up onto the wall and reviled the impious one. [*p. 123*] In front of the Persian general he rehearsed all the evils that he had brought upon Armenia. On hearing this, many confirmed the truth of the charge—not only from the Armenian side, but even more of the Persian soldiers. That same night Bak left the fortress with seven hundred men,[1] without them being able to lay hands on him.

1. *Virtue:* see p. 14, n. 1.
2. *Impiety: anawrēnutʿiwn;* see p. 7, n. 11.
3. For oaths on the Gospel, cf. p. 66, n. 4.
4. Bak is otherwise unattested to.

1. Cf. 4 Kings 3:26, where the king of Moab attempts to escape from a

But those who remained within the fortress, although they well knew that their [the Persians'] oaths were false, had no provisions inside.[2] When they had unwillingly gone down and presented themselves, he ordered two hundred and thirteen of them to be killed. They all cried out, saying: "We thank you, our Lord God,[3] that while the churches are still flourishing and the temples of martyrs are still undestroyed, and the holy covenant of the church is still unbroken and undefiled,[4] you have made us worthy of your heavenly calling.[5] May our death equal the death of the brave heroes, and our blood be mingled with the blood of the fallen wounded. May the Lord look favorably on his churches and this host of willing victims who are mounting this holy altar."[6] Having said this the two hundred and thirteen men were martyred on the spot.

Now the holy priests who were in the castle—the blessed Yovsēp and Levond with their numerous companions—also offered their necks to the sword[7] of the executioner, uttering the same words as the two hundred had spoken. For the blessed ones had no expectation at all of bodily life, but were wisely seeking to be a means for the prosperity of the whole land. Therefore they addressed a complaint[8] to the court and threw the whole blame on the impious Vasak. When Mushkan Nisalavurt heard of this, he was unable to impose the death penalty on them. [*p. 124*] But after inflicting the bastinado[1] on Yovsēp and Levond, [the Persians] ordered them to be kept under strict

---

battle with seven hundred men. But as with the figures of those killed at Avarayr, no ulterior significance may be intended.

2. *Provisions: hambar;* cf. 1 Macc. 6:49, where the besieged in Bethsure give up for lack of provisions. For *hambar* see Hübschmann, *Grammatik,* p. 178.

3. *We thank you . . . : gohanamk zkʻēn . . .*; this phrase (with liturgical parallels) commonly begins the prayer of martyrs immediately before death. Cf. Agathangelos §75 (and Thomson, *Agathangelos,* §75, n. 2), 207; *Vkaykʻ,* p. 207; and p. 149 below.

4. *Undefiled: aṙakʻinatsʻeal,* which picks up the theme of p. 122, n. 1.

5. Cf. Eph. 4:1 and Heb. 3:1.

6. Cf. p. 114 for these sentiments. "Victim" is the translation for *zuarak* ("bullock," see Hübschmann, *Grammatik,* p. 303), which is very common in the O.T.

7. *Necks, sword:* see p. 40, n. 6.

8. *Complaint: boḷokʻ.* For this right of appeal to the shah see Christensen, *Iran,* p. 296. Cf. Paul in Acts 25:11: καίσαρα ἐπικαλοῦμαι: *i kaysr boḷokʻem.*

---

1. *Bastinado: gan;* see Benveniste, "Elements parthes," p. 35, and cf. the same term in Luke 12:48, quoted on p. 36 above.

guard because they had addressed a complaint to the court. The other priests they sent off to each one's own place with orders for the recovery and peace of the country.[2]

But the Armenian populace, who were aware of the fickle[3] orders of the king and of the malevolent[4] apostate Vasak, had no faith in the false pardon; rather, they encouraged one another, saying: "What need have we of life in this transitory world,[5] or why should we see the sun after [the death of] our friends? For even if our brave heroes fell in the great battle, and many wounded rolled in torrents[6] of blood on the plain, and all their bodies became carrion for birds[7] and food for animals,[8] and our honorable nobles were brought down to miserable indignity, abandoned their dominions, and are suffering grievously, and all our delicate Armenian women[9] have fallen prey to dangerous afflictions and terrible deprivations—we shall not obey your deceitful commands or submit to your impious princes."

Then they each abandoned their villages, towns, and estates. Brides left their chambers and grooms their rooms;[10] old men fell from their chairs and infants from their [mothers'] bosoms.[11] Young men and maidens and the whole populace of men and women went out and occupied the safe parts of the desert and the secure places of numerous mountains. They considered it better to live like beasts in caves but in piety, than to live luxuriously in their own houses but in apostasy.[12] Without

---

2. *Recovery and peace: shinutʿiwn ew khaḷaḷutʿiwn;* the terms often occur together, as on p. 188, or Agathangelos, §130.

3. *Fickle: yelyeḷuk,* as on p. 84, n. 4.

4. *Malevolent: chʿarimatsʿ;* as on p. 71, n. 5, of the king.

5. *What . . . world:* as *Vkaykʿ,* p. 110.

6. *Rolled in torrents of blood: tapaletsʿan yariwn yapazhoyz,* as in the threat of the king to Shmavon, *Vkaykʿ,* p. 119, or Moses Khorenatsʿi, III, 28 at n. 4, with parallells in Ps.-Callisthenes.

7. Cf. Ps. 78:2.

8. Cf. Jer. 16:4; but the expression is frequent in the Bible.

9. *Delicate Armenian women: pʿapʿkutʿiwn Hayotsʿ.* Although *pʿapʿuk* (tender, pampered) can refer to men, as on p. 67, n. 9, it is usually used by Eḷishē with regard to women, as of Susanna in Dan. 13:31. See also below, p. 200.

10. Cf. Joel 2:16.

11. Cf. Ps. 106:32, for old men sitting in chairs; infants in bosoms is a common theme, but I am not aware of parallels to the "falling" in this connection.

12. For the theme of living luxuriously in houses cf. Amos 6:4. For the contrast of piety and apostasy cf. above p. 72.

a murmur they endured their food of grass[13] and did not think of their usual victuals. Caverns in their reckoning were like ceilings in very tall buildings, and beds on the ground like painted arcades.[14]

[*p. 125*] Their whispered[1] songs were psalms, and the reading of the Holy Scriptures their ultimate delight. Every man was a church for himself, was himself a priest. Each one's body was a holy altar, and their souls an acceptable sacrifice.[2] For none of them dispairingly mourned those who had fallen by the sword;[3] no one bewailed and sighed over his close friends. Joyfully they endured the rapine of many possessions and did not even recall at all that they had owned prosperity. Patiently they suffered, and very bravely they endured their heroic struggle. But had they not seen with open eyes the joyous hope,[4] they would not have been able to act with such great virtue.

Many were from the families of the great nobility—brothers, sons, and daughters with all their friends in fortified[5] places: some in the benighted[6] land of Khaltik', many others in the South in the inaccessible strongholds of Tmorik', some in the thick forests of Ardzakh, and yet others in the center of the country had seized control of many fortresses. They all endured with great patience their many tribulations for the love of

---

13. Life like that of beasts and food of grass have verbal parallels in 2 Macc. 5:27 of Judas and his companions living in the desert.

14. The preceding sentence has numerous verbal parallels in *Vkayk'*, p. 38, especially life in caverns (*darap'ork'*) contrasted with lofty (*bardzraberdz*) arcades (*patshgamk'*). For *patshgam* see Hübschmann, *Grammatik*, p. 225. Beds on the ground and food of herbs also have parallels in Koriun (e.g., p. 10) of his ascetic companions. *Darap'or* is used in Faustos, III, 14 of Daniel's cell.

---

1. *Whispered: mrmnjunk'*, which has overtones of lament, as in Faustos, IV, 15. Cf. p. 202, for whispered psalms and readings.

2. Cf. Rom. 12:1; Phil. 4:18. For the themes of church, priest, altar, and sacrifices in these senses, see patristic refs. in Lampe, *Lexicon*, s.v. ἐκκλησία, H3; ἱερεύς, C5; βωμός, A3a; θυσία, 8; θυσιατήριον, A4e.

3. For the Armenian attacks on excessive "despair" (*anyusut'iwn*) at funerals cf. Faustos, IV, 4; V, 31; Moses Khorenats'i, III, 20; *Kanonagirk'*, I, p. 247.

4. I.e., the Second Coming of Christ; cf. 1 Thess. 2:19: *yoys ew khndut'iwn* (here: *yoysn khndalit's*). But note esp. the parallel with 2 Macc. 7:14: "we look for the hope of the rebirth and resurrection of the dead."

5. *Fortified: amrakan*, see p. 94, n. 3.

6. *Benighted: anloys*. In Agathangelos, §785, the demons fled there from Daranalik'.

Christ. This only did they beg of God—that they might not see the devastation of the holy churches.

But just as we have often shown the impious one's iniquity, [so again now] he urged and pressed the Persian army in the neighboring parts of the country to come in force to their aid by royal command.[7] Many cavalry arrived, making up the numbers of the fallen, so that the army was as numerous as before. They advanced to the center of the country and attacked the large fortress of the Blue Mountain.[8] but the defenders valiantly [*p. 126*] resisted, struck down many of the Persian troops, and threw the survivors back in flight to their camp. But they [the Persians] resorted to soft words,[1] wishing to subdue them by deceit.

Although no one had the confidence to go down to them lest they be cruelly betrayed into the enemies' hands, yet because of their oaths a priest, whose name was Arshēn,[2] was constrained to go down to them. He parleyed with them in an appealing and friendly way, indicating that the flight of the innocent was harmless. He entreated the apostate Vasak and begged him to remember his earlier allegiance[3] to the Christian covenant, hoping he might soften a little from his terrible cruelty. But he did not listen and paid no heed to his words. He bound and sent off the blessed man and those who had gone down with him. More particularly, when he saw what the commander [of the fort] was following his suggestions, he then began to send out marauders; the numerous people they found outside the fortress they led into captivity, and torch in hand they set fire to many places.

Now when those in the fortresses of Tmorikʻ heard of all the calamities wrought by the royal army, they reckoned there was no advantage in living inside the fortifications. They

---

7. *By royal command: arkʻuni hramanaw,* cf. p. 121, n. 1.

8. *Blue Mountain:* Akinean, *Ełishē* III, 272, adduces evidence from later writers indicating that this was in Eraskhadzor (the valley of the Araxes) in the province of Arsharunikʻ.

---

1. *Soft words: oḷokʻankʻ;* cf. 1 Macc. 11:49 of the citizens of Antioch entreating the king. The term is used several times by Ełishē, e.g., p. 37 of the demons seducing the unlearned by "blandishments"; p. 86 of the king's "flattering" letter; p. 132 of the king's "appeasing" letter.

2. *Arshēn:* he plays an important role in the last chapter. On the occasion of his martyrdom, p. 179, Ełishē says he was from the village of Eḷegeak in the province of Bagrevand; cf. Łazar, p. 101.

3. *Allegiance: karg,* lit. "rank, station."

bravely went out on the attack with the help of the garrison;[4] reaching the neighboring part of Persia they slaughtered [the inhabitants] mercilessly and made a bloody carnage.[5] The survivors they took captive and imprisoned in the local fortresses, and the buildings of the country they burned down, torch in hand.

Likewise, when those in the mountains of Khaltik' saw that [*p. 127*] the Persian army was fearlessly daring to descend on the fortresses of Armenia, in great strength they attacked the valley of Tayk'.[1] There they found a large detachment of royal troops who were intending to take captive the garrisons of the fortresses of the country and who were searching the area mercilessly, since they thought that the nobles' treasures were there.[2]

Now when (the Armenians) also saw that the churches in two villages had been set on fire, they were goaded into even greater fury.[3] They rushed to attack, and winning a decisive[4] victory, broke the strength of the Persian troops, slaughtered many of them, and expelled the survivors in flight from the country.

From this audacious attack only the blessed Hmayeak, brother of the Armenian general Vardan,[5] fighting with uncompromising[6] bravery, was heroically martyred[7] for the unity of the holy covenant. All the others escaped unscathed and pursued the fugitives.

After this outcome, the king's troops ceased occupying every place indiscriminately or seizing any more churches. Once more they began to ask the court [for orders].

---

4. *Fortifications, garrison: amrakank'*; see p. 94, n. 3.

5. *Mercilessly . . . carnage:* as in 2 Macc. 5:6 of Jason's massacre in Jerusalem (*yankhnay, gortsēr, kotorats* being verbal parallels).

---

1. *Valley of Tayk': dzoragawaṅ Tayots':* Tayk' (see p. 28, n. 2) is usually called simply "province" (*gawaṙ*), *dzor* means "valley," and the term *dzoragawaṙ* seems to be a hapax. However, Tayk' is on the river Chorukh.

2. I.e., that the treasures had been taken to the area of Armenia farthest from Persia, not that Tayk' was a depository for royal treasure like Ani (as in Agathangelos, §785, or Moses Khorenats'i, III, 27, 45).

3. *Goaded . . . fury:* an exact verbal parallel to 1 Macc. 2:24 of the zeal of Mattatthias.

4. *Decisive: kamakarut'eamb,* lit. "eagerly, spontaneously."

5. Hmayeak Mamikonean figures prominently in Lazar, but is mentioned only here by Ełishē. For *sparapet,* "general," see p. 7, n. 9.

6. *Uncompromising: yankhnay:* lit. "merciless"; cf. p. 126, n. 5.

7. *Heroically martyred:* as on p. 78, n. 4.

Nor did those who had fled for refuge to the forests of Ardzakh remain quiet[8] and peaceful, but they continually sent to the land of the Huns, urging and exhorting the Hun army and reminding them of the pact which they had made with Armenia and confirmed with a solemn oath.[9] Many of them were pleased to hear these words of flattery. But [the Armenians] also blamed them severely: "Why did you not come prepared for battle?" [*p. 128*] Although in the beginning they found no way to reach mutual agreement, later (the Huns) gathered a numerous force and attacked the borders of the Persian empire. They ravaged many provinces, took very many prisoners back to their own country, and clearly showed to the king their unity with the Armenian army.

When news of all this reached the Persian general he erupted in anger; in his great wrath he piled the blame on the impious Vasak as being the cause and author of all the calamities.[1] Then he set off and went to Persia, giving the court a full and accurate account in writing and throwing the blame on the apostate.

When the king heard of all the devastation of the country and had been accurately informed about the outcome of the great battle, he desisted from his arrogant boasting; he kept silent and refrained from his perpetual deceitful scheming. He inquired into the failure of that imprudent affair, and wishing to find out, said: "Who might there be who could inform me truthfully about these matters?" Now the person at court who knew about the impious venture was the *hazarapet*[2] Mihrnerseh; he came forward and said to the king: "I can tell you that, noble sovereign.[3] If you wish to hear the plain truth, have the leaders of the Christians in Armenia summoned. They will willingly come and explain everything to you accurately."

Then the king wrote to one of the greatest nobles, Atrormizd by name, whose principality touched on the land of Armenia and who had cooperated with the general in that war,

8. *Quiet: lĭeal:* cf. 1 Macc. 7:50, where Judaea was quiet (*lĭeats‘*) after the death of Nicanor.
9. Cf. pp. 78, 80.

1. *Author of all the calamities: aṙajnord amenayn ch‘areats‘*, as in 2 Macc. 4:1 of the slander against Onias.
2. *Hazarapet:* see p. 23, n. 4.
3. *Noble sovereign: ark‘ay k‘aj;* see p. 9, n. 2.

and he appointed him governor[4] of the land of Armenia. He despatched Mushkan Nisalavurt with all [*p. 129*] the surviving troops to the lands of the Aḷuankʻ and Lpʻinkʻ and Chiḷbkʻ and to Hechmatakkʻ and Tʻavasparkʻ and Khibiovan,[1] and to all the fortresses which the army of the Huns had destroyed because of their pact with the Armenians. The king was exceedingly chagrined, not only over the ravaging of the lands and the loss of troops, but even more at the destruction of the Pass:[2] only with difficulty over a long time had they been able to fortify it,[3] but then it had been taken easily and razed, and there was no likelihood of its being rebuilt. So he ordered Vasak, with the leading Christians, to be summoned to court.

The *marzpan* Atrormizd arrived in Armenia with goodwill and in peace. Following the king's orders he summoned Sahak, the saintly bishop of the Ṙshtunikʻ,[4] to learn from him details about the accusation.[5] And although the latter had destroyed a fire-temple[6] and had greatly harassed the fire-worshipers, he did not hesitate to come to the public tribunal.[7]

Furthermore, a pious priest from the house of the Artsrunikʻ, Mushē by name, who was a prelate in the land of the Artsrunikʻ,[8] had also destroyed a house of fire[9] and inflicted many sufferings on the magi by imprisonment and tortures; yet he did not hesitate either, but willingly came and presented himself to the *marzpan*.

4. *Governor: marzpan;* see p. 61, n. 7. Ḷazar, p. 73, calls him Atrormizd Arshakan. For this passage see Adontz/Garsoian, *Armenia,* p. 442, n. 21.

---

1. Is Tʻavasparkʻ the same as Tavasparan, p. 94, n. 16? Khibiovan is otherwise unattested to.

2. I.e., the Chor; see p. 94.

3. *Fortify: shinel,* lit. "construct"; the ref. seems to be to fortifications at the pass that were destroyed.

4. Sahak of Ṙshtunikʻ is first mentioned on p. 28 as a signatory of the letter to Mihrnerseh; he is one of the heroes of the last section of Eḷishē's *History.*

5. *Accusation: ambastanutʻiwn,* as on p. 81, n. 9.

6. *Fire-temple: atrushan,* for which term see p. 12, n. 4. This charge seems to refer to the episodes described on p. 69, though Sahak is not mentioned there; but see further p. 174 below.

7. *Public tribunal: atean hraparakin.* For *hraparak* see p. 42, n. 4. *Atean* is used on p. 56 of God's tribunal, on p. 84 of the shah's council, and frequently below of a tribunal of interrogation.

8. Mushē is explicitly called "bishop" on p. 28, as opposed to *aṙajnord* here. He is mentioned again on p. 179; see Ḷazar, p. 101, for his martyrdom.

9. *House of fire: krakatun,* see p. 70, n. 2.

Two other blessed priests, called Samuel and Abraham,[10] had destroyed the fire-temple in Artashat[11] and earlier [*p. 130*] had been imprisoned by the apostate Vasak; they also were added to the company of their virtuous companions.

They also brought to the same place the great Yovsēp and Ḷevond and Kʻajaj[1] and Arshēn. When the governor had gained information from them all, he wrote an accurate account of everything to the court, just as he had heard it from their mouths.

Now although Vasak had previously arrived at court and had narrated everything falsely, twisting the facts as he pleased, yet he had been unable to justify himself to the satisfaction of the king, who responded: "When the Christians also arrive, I shall hear you all together at the tribunal."

But since they were bringing the holy priests in bonds, it was two months and twenty days before they reached the winter palace.[2] When the great *hazarapet* heard that they had been brought into the city, he interviewed them himself. But although he was informed about everything by them, he was unable to lay hands on them or torture them because many of the Armenian nobles were still in control of the fortresses of the land and the governor was still fearful. Therefore he ordered the holy ones to be guarded carefully and he commanded the country to be subdued with goodwill. So [the governor] himself went around, assembled gatherings, and began restoration with firm promises.

He ordered the bishops to occupy each his own see,[3] to conduct worship openly according to former custom, and to come out freely in public.[4] He even allowed them to receive gifts and offerings as before.[5] Since the soldiers had occupied

---

10. Samuel and Abraham play important roles in ch. 7. On p. 179 Eḷishē notes that Samuel was from Arats in the province of Ayrarat, and that Abraham was a deacon from the same village; Ḷazar, p. 78, says that Abraham was Samuel's spiritual son.

11. Cf. p. 68, though Samuel and Abraham are not mentioned there.

---

1. On p. 179 Eḷishē says Kʻajaj was from Ṙshtunikʻ; according to Ḷazar, p. 79, he was a disciple of the bishop Sahak.

2. At Ctesiphon. For the length of journey cf. p. 53.

3. See: *ishkhanutʻiwn*, frequently used of nobles' domains; it also has the meaning of "authority" or "empire." For bishops each in his own *ishkhanutʻiwn* cf. *Kanonagirkʻ* I, 210 (the ninth canon of Antioch).

4. Cf. p. 83.

5. *Gifts and offerings: ĕntsaykʻ ew pataragkʻ;* for these traditional rights see *Kanonagirkʻ*, I, 384–385 (canon 32 of "Sahak").

and plundered many provinces, [*p. 131*] he ordered the taxes of
the country to be remitted and he even reduced the burden of
the royal cavalry for a time. And the monks, who had disappeared, he ordered to return and occupy each his own place.[1]

"Let [everyone]," he said, "perform all the rites of piety
now just as they did in former times in the days of their ancestors. And if any people have gone to a distant land," said the
governor, "I have authority from the court to allow them to return and recover their possessions, be they nobles, peasants, or
clergy[2]—whatever way of life they may have abandoned."

He sealed sworn oaths and sent [the message] to all parts.
Then many did return and repossess their lands.[3]

But what was most important of all, he sent out edicts
from the court that if anyone had been forced against his will
to accept magism, he could again embrace Christianity. And
the king proclaimed to those at the royal court: "As for those
who did not happily accept the Mazdaean religion,[4] the gods
are angered at such people,[5] nor am I pleased. But today I issue
the same edict to all, leaving each man to follow the decision of
his own mind; let him worship as he wishes to worship. They
are all my subjects."[6] So he spoke, and he put his order in writing for the whole country.

When they heard and saw this, many who were scattered
in distant places returned and reoccupied their possessions.[7]
And the nobles [*p. 132*] who were in the fortresses of the country or far away abroad,[1] when they saw the restoration of the
country and especially the re-establishment of the church, were
encouraged and emboldened to present themselves to the king.
Therefore they sent a message to the governor of the country,
asking him to present the nobles' petition at court. So he immediately had sent to them from the court by royal command an

1. Cf. pp. 22–23.
2. I.e., the three orders of traditional Armenian society. For the terms
azat and *shinakan* see p. 52, n. 6.
3. *Lands: kaluats*, lit. "holdings"; for the term see Adontz/Garsoïan,
Armenia, p. 362.
4. *Mazdaean religion: den mazdezn;* see p. 24, n. 5.
5. For the anger of the gods cf. p. 46.
6. *Subjects: tsaṙayk',* as on p. 67, n. 8.
7. *Possessions: araṙk';* for the term see Adontz/Garsoïan, *Armenia*, p. 362.

1. *Far away abroad: i heṙawor awtarut'ean,* as on p. 9, n. 7. The theme of
"abroad/foreign exile" (*awtarut'iwn*) is frequent; cf. pp. 49, 63, 98, 162, 164,
and 187, or Łazar, p. 57.

appeasing[2] letter and firm guarantee.[3] But although they knew the cruelty of the authorities and how they were false in everything, they still wished to share the saints' torments; for even if they had faced death they would not have hesitated from fear.

When the king heard this he ordered them to be summoned to his presence, not in bonds but with feet and hands untied. They immediately brought their wives and children and delivered to the governor their possessions;[4] then they went off in haste to the king's winter palace.

And while the king was still in his winter palace he ordered a tribunal to be held to question[5] them. The *hazarapet* presided in order to hear both sides. The proceedings[6] lasted many days, and the side of the apostates lost.

For they presented letters given out by Vasak and all his companions urging that [others] join with him in the pact to rebel: one letter to Georgia, one letter to Albania, likewise a letter to Aldznik', and a message to the Greek emperor, and a letter to the great general of Antioch.[7] All these letters had been authenticated[8] with Vasak's ring. Similarly, he had been implicated [*p. 133*] in the death of the magi in Zarehavan.[1] They also revealed letters and orders of his concerning the fortresses seized from the Persians, since he had been governor[2] at the time.

Furthermore, a noble called Atom from the Gnuni family,[3] whom he had sent on an embassy to the Greeks, came forward and accused him before the great tribunal with that very message which he had given him [sealed] with his own ring.

Mushkan Nisalavurt also brought forward an accusation

2. *Appeasing:* olok'anats'; see p. 126, n. 1.

3. *Firm guarantee:* ukht hastatut'ean.

4. *Possessions:* inch's, used of movable property, not real estate; cf. p. 131, nn. 3, 7.

5. *To question:* harts'ap'ordzi, as on p. 181; cf. also *Vkayk'*, p. 210.

6. *Proceedings:* ambastanut'iwn; as on p. 81, n. 9.

7. I.e., Anatolius, mentioned above, pp. 7, 23. For the term *sparapet* ("general") see p. 7, n. 9. On this episode cf. Łazar, pp. 63, 84.

8. *Authenticated:* vawerakan; for this term see Nyberg, *Manual* II, s.v. *vāparīkānēh.*

1. *Zarehavan:* in Bagrevand, see Hübschmann, *AON*, pp. 427–428. On the episode, cf. Łazar, p. 63.

2. For Vasak as *marzpan* cf. p. 63.

3. *Atom Gnuni:* first mentioned on p. 71.

against him, indicating with his companions in arms that even after the end of the war Vasak had caused much blood to be shed: how by false oaths he had tricked [Armenians] into coming down from their fortresses; some he killed, others he took captive as royal slaves and handmaidens.[4] In addition to all this mischief it turned out that he had stolen the tax[5] of the country which went to the royal Treasury.

There were also many of his apostate friends who revealed the crimes he had committed against Armenia. And the surviving magi and lifeguards,[6] who had been kept in prison and had later been brought to court, were questioned about him: "What do you know about his wrongdoing?" They replied: "That man was the cause and author of these calamities:[7] all the tortures which we endured, the great losses inflicted on the royal army, the ruin and captivity of Armenia, and the loss of the royal taxes."

[*p. 134*] While all these accusations against him were being repeated for so many days, his own relatives—who had also earlier denounced[1] him before the king—came forward. They began to expound and reveal in order how he had made friends with Heran the Hun[2] in concert with the king of Baḷas;[3] this was at the time that Heran had slaughtered the Persian troops in Albania and had raided the land of the Greeks, carrying off many prisoners and much plunder from the Greeks, Armenians, Georgians, and Albanians. [They also indicated] how the king himself had learned of his intentions and had slain the king of Baḷas. At that time Vasak was governor of Armenia and he had been found to be in collusion[4] with the king's enemies. These relatives also revealed how they had been privy to his wicked plans. All this they made public before the king, as well as many other deceits:[5] he behaved falsely not only to his

---

4. Cf. the exile of captives to work on royal estates; see p. 71, n. 2. *Royal slaves and handmaidens: ztsaṙays ew zaḷakhnays arkʻuni;* the two are very frequently associated in biblical texts.
5. *Tax: hark,* as on p. 22, n. 9.
6. *Lifeguards: pʻshtipan;* see p. 65, n. 1.
7. See p. 128, n. 1.

---

1. *Denounced: datakhaz,* which translates κατήγορος in Acts 25:16.
2. Heran is mentioned only here.
3. *Baḷas:* see p. 76, n. 8.
4. *In collusion: khorhrdakitsʻ;* cf. p. 49, n. 3.
5. *Deceits: khardakhutʻiwnkʻ;* only here in Elishē; cf. 2 Macc. 4:6, where it is used of Simon's folly.

friends but most of all toward the king himself, and from his youth he had never acquitted himself honestly.

Then the *hazarapet* gave the order: "Bring here some of the prisoners who are in gaol." They unbound and brought in Sahak, bishop of R̄shtunik', Saint Yovsēp, and the priest Łevond from among the blessed men.

When all the court proceedings had been explained to them, Bishop Sahak responded: "Those who have openly denied the True God do not realize what they are doing or what they are saying, for their minds are darkened.[6] They serve their lords for the wrong reasons and enter into a false covenant with their friends. They are Satan's snare,[7] because through them he carries out his cruel will—as [*p. 135*] is clear with this Vasak. For while he was nominally a Christian he thought he could outwardly[1] cover up and hide all his wickedness from your unwitting majesty; and he did conceal all his treachery with his Christianity. So you respected him and greatly honored him above his worth. You entrusted him with the land of Georgia. Ask that country if [its people] are satisfied with him. You gave him authority over Siunik'. Listen to what his kin say about him. You made him governor of Armenia. And the land which your forefathers had gained by great effort, he lost it all in a single year. Have you seen that when the honorable name of God, which he falsely bore, was removed from him all his villainy was laid bare? For if he has been shown to be false to his God, to whom among mortals will he be true?

"But had you not heard before all the charges against him which have now been uncovered? For whatever reason you concealed them, you yourself know best. It seems to me that he has diverted[2] you with false hopes. But neither you, nor he, nor anyone to come after you will be able to see that in us. So do as you wish; why ask us?"

The great *hazarapet*'s mind was astonished, and he carefully reflected on all the proceedings of the tribunal. Since he realized that the man had rightly been condemned for his un-

---

6. *Darkened: khawarayin,* as on p. 28 of Arhmn; cf. the theme of mental blindness on p. 14. See also n. 7 following.

7. *Snare: darank';* cf. the "gloomy lair" *khawarayin darank',* p. 51, of the magi. For the theme of Satan's snare see patristic references in Lampe, *Lexicon,* s.v. ἐνέδρα.

---

1. *Outwardly: i verin eress,* as on p. 11, n. 4.
2. *Diverted: khndats'oyts';* lit. "made happy."

worthy deeds, he entered the palace and expounded all the proceedings of the tribunal. When the king had been informed [*p. 136*] by the *hazarapet* of the man's guilt, he was exceedingly angry and deeply hurt.[1] But wishing to be patient in bringing ignominy on him, he kept silent for twelve days until the process[2] of the accusation had come to an end.

Then on one special day he ordered all the eminent nobles[3] to be invited to a banquet, including the apostate. According to previous royal customary usage he wore the robe of honor[4] that the king had given him; he also put on his headband and the golden tiara[5] on top. Round his waist he put the girdle[6] of pure hammered gold set with pearls and precious stones, earrings[7] in his ears, the necklace[8] round his neck, the sable cloak[9] on his back; dressed in all his marks of honor[10] he went to court, where he appeared to the assembly as more splendid[11] and distinguished than everyone else.

But the nobles who had willingly come from Armenia and had submitted to investigation and the saints who had arrived earlier were all held in bonds at the royal court. When they saw him coming to the palace dressed up in his finery with a numerous entourage, they began to mock him inwardly and say: "O senseless merchant,[12] you have sold the immortal and eternal honor and have bought the transitory—and even that in a few days you will lose."

1. *Deeply hurt: i khor khots'ets'aw*, as on p. 120[13] of Mushkan.
2. *Process: p'ursish;* see Nyberg, *Manual* II, s.v. *pursisn.*
3. *Eminent nobles: ereweli patuakank';* see p. 84, n. 3.
4. For the robes of honor in Iran see Christensen, *Iran,* pp. 403ff; and for Armenia, Toumanoff, *Studies,* pp. 134–135.
5. *Golden tiara: khoyr oskełēn;* see Hübschmann, *Grammatik,* p. 160, for further refs.
6. *Girdle: kamar:* see Nyberg, *Manual* II s.v. *kamār,* and Widengren, *Feudalismus,* p. 29.
7. *Earrings: gind;* cf. Moses Khorenats'i, II, 47.
8. *Necklace: gumartak;* see Nyberg, *Manual* II, s.v. *gumārtak,* and Armenian refs. in Hübschmann, *Grammatik,* p. 130.
9. *Sable cloak: samoyr;* cf. Faustos, V, 38, where it is mentioned as a gift from the shah to the *sparapet* Manuel. See further Hübschmann, *Grammatik,* p. 236.
10. *Marks of honor: awrēnk' patuoyn.*
11. *Splendid: shk'el;* cf. 1 Macc. 11:58 of Jonathan's splendid insignia as a friend of the King—a passage adapted by Moses Khorenats'i; see n. 7 above.
12. *Merchant: vacharakan:* cf. Matt. 13:14 and the preface to Agathangelos (esp. §9–10) on the spiritual interpretation of a merchant's endeavors, here turned around. For martyrs as eternal *vacharakank'* see *Vkayk',* p. 52.

On his arrival he sat in the inner gallery[13] which was the chamber[14] of the greatest nobles. [*p. 137*] Then the court chamberlain[1] entered and questioned him: "The king sent [me] to [ask] you from whom you acquired all these honors. Tell me straightway, for what just services?"[2] He reminded him of all the proceedings of the tribunal where he had been condemned. And even the things that had not been mentioned there, these too he indicated to him: that he did not legally[3] hold the lordship of the land of Siunik', but by treachery and intrigue he had had his uncle Valinak[4] killed and had taken the title for himself as a reward[5] at court. They had also condemned him on many other charges, to which all the upper nobility bore witness. He was entirely confounded[6] and no true word was found in his mouth.[7] When they had repeated twice and three times [the charges] and had reported within the palace, sentence of death was passed upon him.

Then the chief-executioner[8] entered, immediately stepped forward in front of all the magnates, stripped from him the honors bestowed on him by the court, and dressed him in the garb of a condemned man.[9] He was bound hand and foot, set like a woman on a mare,[10] led off, and delivered to the prison where all those condemned to death were kept.

But the Armenian nobles and holy bishops with the priests, although they were subject to great punishment,[11] did

---

13. *Gallery: dahlich;* see Meillet, "Sur les mots iraniens."
14. *Chamber: hraparak;* see p. 42, n. 4.

---

1. *Chamberlain: senekapan;* not used elsewhere in Elishē; Lazar, p. 64, calls Veh(den)shapuh the royal *senekapan.* Denshapuh figures prominently in Elishē and Lazar and is given various titles, including *hambarakapet* (Elishē, p. 143). For the office see Christensen, *Iran,* pp. 283, 390; Toumanoff, *Studies,* p. 168.
2. *Services: vastakk';* see p. 46, n. 2.
3. *Legally: ēst kargin,* κατὰ τάξιν, as in 1 Cor. 14:40.
4. *Valinak:* according to Koriun, pp. 21–22, Valinak of Siunik' was succeeded by Vasak; Koriun's picture of Vasak is very different from that of Elishē.
5. *Reward: k'rpikar;* see p. 46, n. 5.
6. As in Matt. 22:12 of the guest without a wedding garment.
7. Cf. 3 Kings 12:24.
8. *Chief-executioner: dahchapet;* see p. 48, n. 5.
9. Cf. the "dark (or mourning) garments" of the man condemned to death, p. 184.
10. Cf. the later Persian miniatures depicting women sitting behind a rider or facing backwards.
11. *Punishment: patuhas;* see Nyberg, *Manual* II, s.v. *pātifrās.*

not at all think of their afflictions which they had suffered or which they expected to come upon them, but rather they wondered at the great revelation effected by God. They consoled one another, saying: "We fought[12] bravely, let us endure[13] even more patiently.[14] We have learned from our holy fathers that the chief [*p. 138*] of all virtues is patience,[1] and perfect piety is heavenly wisdom.[2] But this no one can acquire without torments. Now when torments are drawn out, then the compensating reward will be that much the greater.[3] So if this is the case, let us beg God only that we may be able to endure all trials[4] and the Lord himself will provide the means for our salvation.

"We have heard of the sentence passed on the forty warriors of Christ who suffered many tortures. One of them hastened to the baths[5] and lost the crown,[6] but the thirty-nine patiently endured martyrdom and attained that promise for which they had longed. Now there is our colleague who separated from us at the beginning—behold, he becomes the accomplice of Satan.[7] While his soul is still in the body he has received the pledge[8] of the torments of hell, which provokes not only saints to lamentation, but even all brutal men."

So they spoke and shed many tears over the lost one. But then they began to sing spiritual hymns: "It is better to hope in the Lord than to hope in men. It is better to hope in the Lord than to hope in princes. All nations surrounded me, but

12. Cf. 2 Tim. 4:7.

13. Cf. Jude 3.

14. *Bravely, patiently: k'ajut'eamb, hamberut'eamb;* cf. 2 Macc. 15:17, Judas' exhortation to *hamberut'iwn* and *k'ajut'iwn.*

1. James 1:4; cf. 2 Pet. 1:6. But virtue, *aŕak'inut'iwn*, is a major theme in Ełishē. See the Introduction.

2. Cf. Prov. 1:7.

3. Cf. Heb. 10:35ff.

4. Cf. Heb. 10:32.

5. The ref. is to the forty martyrs of Sebastia who were left naked on the ice with baths of hot water at the edge of the pond to tempt them. One was tempted and apostatized. See Gray, *Two Armenian Passions,* p. 375, for another Armenian ref. to this popular story. For Armenian and other versions see *Bibliotheca Hagiographica Orientalis,* pp. 156–157.

6. For the crown of martyrdom, cf. p. 150, and see further refs. in Lampe, *Lexicon,* s.v. μαρτύριον, 4c and στέφανος.

7. *Accomplice: gortsakits',* here in contrast to 1 Cor. 3:9, where we are *gortsakits'* of God. On p. 6 the same epithet is applied to Yazkert.

8. *Pledge: aŕhawatch'eay,* which throughout the N.T. refers to heaven, not hell.

through the name of the Lord I conquered them."[9] They encouraged each other, saying: "Since we know this, brethren, let us not fear the godless nation of the heathen, who in their frenzy are more vicious than bees,[10] for their fury will also turn to their own destruction. But we shall call on the name of the Lord and rout[11] them all."

The apostate Vasak looked on the unity of the saintly prisoners, who accepted their torments with great joy and appeared just as cheerful and serene[12] as they had been previously at court. He looked and yearned, [*p. 139*] but no one [allowed] him to join them, as they kept him apart in his own bonds. Day after day he was brought and thrown like carrion[1] into the great square; he was mocked[2] and ridiculed and made the laughingstock[3] of the whole army. They robbed[4] him, taking away everything he possessed; and they so derided him in his poverty that his servants had to beg for bread[5] to bring him. So heavy were the land dues[6] imposed on his house that he had to resort to the possessions of his parents and grandparents as well as his own, and even to the women's jewelry to pay the fine—and still he was unable to pay off the debts to the court. They even went so far as to ask him: "Is there any treasure in the tombs of our ancestors?" If he found any he was to dig it out and give it as forfeit[7] for himself and his family, as many people had been included in the fine.

After he had been maltreated from all sides in this fashion, he succumbed to painful diseases there in prison. His entrails

9. Cf. Ps. 117:8–10.
10. Cf. Ps. 117:12.
11. Cf. Ps. 117:11.
12. *Serene: paytsaṙ,* lit. "shining," as of the stars on p. 70.

---

1. *Carrion: gēsh,* as on p. 8 of Yazkert or p. 77 of the magi.
2. *Mocked: dzaḷēin;* the only biblical parallel is Matt. 27:31, 41, of the mocking of Christ.
3. *Laughingstock: tesil,* as in 1 Cor. 4:9.
4. *Robbed: koḷoptetsʿin,* as in Ezek. 26:12.
5. *Beg for bread:* here the contrast with Vasak's splendor (*shkʿeḷ,* p. 136, n. 11) is emphasized; for Prov. 12:9 indicates that he who makes himself *shukʿ* will not lack bread. Cf. also Ps. 36:25: the seed of the righteous will not beg for bread.
6. *Dues: zparters harkatsʿ.* For *hark* see p. 22, n. 9; for *part* see Hübschmann, *Grammatik,* p. 228. The ending *-er* is itself a plural form, based on the collective ending in *-ear;* see Karst, *Grammatik,* pp. 177–179. Two lines below the usual acc. pl. *zparts* is used.
7. *Forfeit: tugankʿ;* for the term see Nyberg, *Manual* II, s.v. *tōxtan,* and Hübschmann, *Grammatik,* p. 253.

began to burn,[8] his chest hurt and was festered, his fat belly shrank. Worms crawled in his eyes and ran down from his nostrils; his ears were bunged up, and his lips were painfully pierced; the sinews of his arms decomposed,[9] and the heels of his feet were bent backwards. The stench of death emanated from him, and his domestic servants fled from him. Only his tongue remained alive in his mouth, but no confession was found on his lips. He tasted the death of suffocation[10] and descended to hell in hopeless misery. All his friends maligned[11] him, while his enemies were not satisfied with his unbearable afflictions.[12]

[*p. 140*] He who sinfully had wished to be king of Armenia had no known tomb, for he died like a dog and was thrown out as carrion.[1]

His name was not remembered among the saints; neither was his memory recalled before the holy altar in church. There was no crime he left uncommitted during his lifetime; nor was there any terrible evil which did not befall him on his death.

These recollections[2] have been written concerning him in order to reprove his sins,[3] so that everyone who hears and knows them may cast curses on him and not lust after his deeds.[4]

8. Cf. Ps. 38:4.
9. Cf. Job 30:17.
10. *Suffocation: heldzamldzuk;* cf. *Vkaykʻ,* p. 80, for such tortures.
11. Cf. Prov. 11:4 of the death of the impious.
12. The above description of Vasak's end is based on the death of Herod in Eusebius, *Historia Ecclesiastica* I, 7, and the death of Antiochus in 2 Macc. 9:9, as described in the Armenian versions:

Herod: diseases, burn, chest hurt, worms, painfully, stench
   of death emanated, suffocation, afflictions.
Antiochus: worms crawled in his eyes, stench of death.

Cf. also Eccles. 7:18: the revenge on the impious is fire and worm.

1. *As carrion: ibrew zgēsh;* cf. p. 139, n. 1. But some MSS, followed by Ter-Minasean, read *zēsh,* "(like) a donkey."
2. *Recollections: yishatakaran;* see p. 104, n. 9.
3. Cf. Ps. 38:12.
4. Cf. 1 Cor. 10:6.

Again Concerning the Same War and the Tortures of the Holy Priests

NOW in the sixteenth year of his reign[2] King [Yazkert] in great wrath again marched to the land of the Kushans to wage war.[3] Leaving Vrkan[4] and reaching the land of Apar,[5] he ordered that the nobles and priests be kept in the same fetters in the citadel[6] of Niwshapuh.[7] But two[8] of the blessed prisoners he made march with him. He struck fear into all the Christian communities through which he passed.

A certain Hun of royal descent from the land of the Khaylandurkʻ, Bēl by name,[9] was secretly inclined to the Christians and was eagerly being instructed in the truth by them. He had of his own will submitted to the king's authority, but when he

1. For the problem of numbering the chapters see p. 114, n. 6. The MSS note that this section is separate (artakʻoy) from the chapters that have gone before. But although the episodes described could be regarded as a supplement to the main theme of the revolt of 450/1, the basic themes in a literary and religious sense remain the same.

2. I.e., 453/4.

3. See pp. 9ff. for the first expedition against the Kushans.

4. Vrkan: Hyrcania; see Hübschmann, Grammatik, p. 86; Marquart, Erānšahr, pp. 72–74.

5. Apar: see p. 10, n. 1.

6. Citadel: dḷeak, which translates ἀκρά in 2 Macc. 4:27 and is translated by the Greek version of Agathangelos, §122 as λόφος.

7. I.e., Nishapur; see Marquart, Erānšahr, p. 74.

8. Two: i.e., Samuel and Abraham; see p. 143.

9. For the Khaylandurkʻ see p. 12, n. 2; there the MSS spell the name Khaylndurkʻ, Khaylĕndurkʻ, or Khaylĕnduk'. Bēl is otherwise unknown. For Christianity among the Huns see Maenchen-Helfen, Huns, esp. pp. 260–267.

saw the saints being tormented he became very embittered. But
since he was unable to help [them], he fled to the king of the
Kushans. [*p. 142*] He went and told him all the details of the
sufferings that the king had inflicted on Armenia. He also informed him about the breach in the Pass of the Huns[1] and
showed him the discord[2] in the army, whereby many nations
had defected from loyalty to the king. He also indicated to him
the muttering[3] of the land of the Aryans.

When the king of the Kushans heard this, he in no way
doubted or distrusted the man, nor did the suspicion he might
be a spy enter his heart. For he had learned a little earlier, and
Bēl as it were confirmed it, that [Yazkert] was marching on the
land of the Kushans; so he immediately made haste to assemble
his troops and organize an army to oppose him with force. For
although he was unable to face him in pitched battle, nonetheless, falling on his rear he inflicted many losses on the king's
army. And he pressed and assailed them so hard that, over-
coming them with a small number of troops, he turned them
back. In hot pursuit, he plundered many royal provinces, and
he himself returned safely to his own country.

When the king saw that he had returned from his campaign in disgrace and ignominy,[4] he moderated his pride a little and realized that all these calamities had occurred through
the disunity[5] of his army. But in the vexation of his heart he did
not know on whom to pour out the venom of his bitterness;[6]
while the great *hazarapet* was much afraid, for he himself was
the cause of all the disasters that had occurred.

He began to make suggestions to the chief-magus and
magi, who came [*p. 143*] before the king and said: "Noble king,
we know from our religion[1] that no man can withstand your
great power. But the gods have become angry with us[2] because

---

1. *Pass of the Huns:* i.e., the Chor, as on p. 78, n. 2. See p. 129 for the
destruction of the fortifications there.
2. *Discord: erkpaṙakut'iwn,* a term often used by Eḷishē of the disunity
among the Armenians; see p. 3, n. 4; p. 89, n. 1.
3. *Muttering: trtunj;* a term frequent in the O.T. for the Israelites. For
the situation here cf. 1 Macc. 11:39, which describes the disaffection of De-
metrius's troops with the same expression.
4. *Ignominy: vatt'arut'eamb,* as in 2 Macc. 11:13 of the defeat of Lysias.
5. Disunity: see n. 2 above.
6. Cf. p. 7.

---

1. *Religion: den;* see p. 9, n. 8.
2. For the anger of the gods cf. pp. 46, 131.

you have kept the Christians, who are opposed to our religion, alive until today." They further reminded him how "they cursed you in prison."[3] They uttered many other blasphemies concerning the saints and continuously disparaged them, driving the king to violent anger, until he made rapid haste to shed the blood of the innocent.

He gave a command with regard to the two who were there in the camp near him, Samuel and Abraham, that they should be secretly slain. As for those who were in the citadel distant from the camp about fifteen stages,[4] he ordered the intendant,[5] whose name was Denshapuh,[6] to precede him to the city where the holy priests of the Lord were, to bring them to justice, to interrogate them with terrible tortures, and to put them to death by the sword.

But the chief-magus to whom they had been entrusted had previously tortured them frequently, in excess of the king's command. For he was the governing religious authority[7] of the land of Apar and more enthusiastic in magism and more versed in the Zoroastrian religion[8] than most wise men. Furthermore—what they consider a great glory in their erring hierarchy—he had the title of *Hamakden;*[9] he also knew the *Ampartk'ash,* had learned the *Bozpayit,* [*p. 144*] and was versed in the *Pahlavik* and the *Parskaden.*[1] For these are the five doctrines[2] which comprise all the religion of magism. But beyond these is a further sixth, which they call *Petmog.*[3]

It seemed to him that he was perfect in all knowledge; he regarded the blessed ones as if they had strayed "from our great

3. This charge is not substantiated by any episode reported in Ełishē.

4. *Stages: awt',* equivalent to the Latin *mansio,* i.e., a day's journey.

5. *Intendant: hambarakapet,* cf. Łazar, p. 104[19]. For the etymology see Hübschmann, *Grammatik,* p. 178, and Nyberg, *Manual* II, s.v. *hanbārak.* For the office see Christensen, *Iran,* pp. 102, 283.

6. *Denshapuh:* see p. 22, n. 6.

7. *Religious authority: denpet,* otherwise unattested to; see Hübschmann, *Grammatik,* p. 139.

8. *Zoroastrian religion: zradashtakan awrēnk';* see p. 19, n. 1.

9. *Hamakden;* i.e., "fully (versed in Zoroastrian) religion"; see Hübschmann, *Grammatik,* p. 177.

10. *Ambartk'ash, Bozpayit:* see Hübschmann, *Grammatik,* pp. 96, 122.

1. *Pahlavik, Parskaden:* i.e., the Pahlevi code and Persian religion.

2. *Doctrines: kesht,* as on p. 61, n. 5, there translated "cult," but here rather in the sense of "code, dogma."

3. *Petmog:* i.e., the special code of the chief-magi. On this whole passage see Christensen, *Iran,* p. 117.

knowledge" through ignorance. He conceived the vain idea of torturing them unceasingly that perchance, through the inability of the body to endure afflictions, "I may hear from them some words of entreaty."[4] Therefore he separated the priests from the nobles, removed them far from them and cast them into a damp and gloomy dungeon.[5] He ordered that two barley [loaves] and a jar[6] and one-half of water [be given] to each six men at each [meal] time. And he allowed no one at all to approach the prison gates.

When he had tormented them in this way for forty days but had heard no word of vacillation[7] from them, he thought that one of his own servants had secretly received something from them and might have given them food on the sly. He went himself and sealed the skylight[8] and door of the prison, and had men he trusted take the allotted ration[9] to them. He did this for fifteen days.

Nonetheless, the blessed ones were in no way oppressed or troubled. Rather, with great patience they endured this austerity and with unceasing psalms performed the daily service.[10] At the completion of their prayers they would rest for a while in joyful gratitude, with the hard ground[11] as their bed.

[*p. 145*] But the guards in charge of the prisoners were greatly astonished at their sound health when they heard the ceaseless sound of their voices. Therefore they reported to the chief-magus and said: "These are not ordinary men without great power. For [even] if their bodies were of bronze they would have decayed from the humid dampness. It is a long time that the guarding of this prison has been entrusted to us, but we do not remember any prisoner living for a month in this dungeon. Now we say to you: If you have received a command for their death and you kill them, you know [what you are

4. *Entreaty: oḷokank';* see p. 126, n. 1.
5. *Dungeon: nerk'atun,* used of a cellar; in Gen. 6:16 of the lowest deck in the ark.
6. *Jar: dorak;* see Nyberg, *Manual* II, s.v. *dōrak.*
7. *Vacillation: t'ulut'iwn;* cf. p. 14, n. 1.
8. *Skylight: erd;* cf. the *erdik,* the hole in the roof of Armenian houses to let out smoke, on which see Khatchatrian, *L'architecture,* pp. 46 and 63ff. This is different from the *erd* of p. 199, n. 4.
9. *Ration: ṙochik;* see p. 64, n. 1.
10. *Daily service: hanapazord pashtawn,* which translates ἡ διακονία ἡ καθημερινή in Acts 6:1.
11. *Hard ground: getnakhshti,* i.e., from *getin* (ground, earth) and *khsteak* (bed, pallet).

doing]. But on the other hand, if you have been detailed to guard and not condemn them, then the prisoners are in terrible danger. Furthermore, we are awestruck and very fearful when we see such unbearable afflictions."

When the chief-magus heard this, he arose and went himself in the middle of the night to the dungeon skylight. Looking inside through the evening gloom, while they were resting from their worship, he saw each one of the prisoners shining like an inextinguishable lamp. Greatly terrified, he said to himself: "What is this great miracle? Our gods then have descended into this prison and their glory[1] has taken fire. If they are not close to them, it is impossible for a mere man to be clothed in such glorious light. I have so heard about this sect[2] that they are deranged in their great folly and take on false forms[3] in the eyes of ignorant men. Perhaps this was some such vision that appeared to me."

He was totally unable to understand the reality of the vision. And while he was thus reflecting, the saints again rose from each one's pallet [*p. 146*] for the customary worship. Then the chief-magus truly realized that what had appeared to him he had not seen in a confused way,[1] but the illumination was emanating from their very selves. Then for the second time he was terror-struck and said: "On which prisoner ever appeared such an apparition? I know of no one else nor have I heard from our ancestors." And because he was horribly shaken by the great miracle and his whole body was trembling,[2] he remained on the roof stupefied[3] and half-dead[4] until morning. When day dawned, like one ill for many days he arose and went to his lodging, but was quite unable to tell anyone at all what he had seen.

He summoned the guards and said to them: "Go and take

1. *Glory: p'aṙaworut'iwn;* cf. the *p'aṙk'* of the shah, p. 165, n. 5 below, and Agathangelos, §127. For the Iranian *farr* see Bailey, *Zoroastrian Problems,* chs. 1 and 2, and Christensen, *Iran,* p. 141. The theme of light around the martyr is common in hagiography; see Delehaye, *Passions,* p. 214. Cf. also 2 Macc. 15:13, for the figure of Jeremiah (*tserut'iwn p'aṙaworut'ean*) in the vision of Judas.
2. *Sect: kesht;* see p. 61, n. 5.
3. Cf. 2 Cor. 11:13–14 of Satan and false apostles.

1. *In a confused way: ayl ĕnd ayloy;* cf. p. 47, n. 1.
2. *Shaken, trembling:* see p. 14, n. 2.
3. *Stupefied:* see p. 91, n. 2.
4. *Half-dead: kisameṙ;* cf. 2 Macc. 3:29, the collapse of Heliodorus on seeing a vision; and cf. also p. 180, n. 3.

the prisoners to a really dry upper-room[5] and guard them there carefully, as you suggested." One of the executioners,[6] on hearing the chief-magus' orders, hastily ran and informed them as if it were great news: "He has ordered you," he said, "to move to a dry upper-room. Arise quickly, do not be slow, for even we pleaded [with him] about your misery."

But the saintly Joseph began to speak in a gentle way to the executioner, saying; "Go and say to your foolish leader: Have you not heard about the future coming of our Lord or about the wonderful mansions that are reserved for us in readiness from the beginning?[7] Therefore we easily endure this great tribulation for the love of that hope which we shall see. You did well to have pity for the great tribulation of [our] bodies. But we are not at all fatigued[8] like some godless person[9] who has no other hope in his mind [*p. 147*] than what is visible. But we, for love of our Christ, greatly rejoice at this, and we even consider it to be a perfect favor[1] so that we may inherit eternal blessings by these temporary tribulations.

"If we were to desire buildings, we have mansions in heaven made without human hands;[2] to them your royal palace offers no comparison. Likewise with garments and glory and untainted food:[3] if anyone were to wish to speak to you about them, your weak-mindedness would not bear to listen. For because of your inveterate blindness you do not see, or hear, or understand. Therefore you are mercilessly judging us, vainly and unjustly and without guilt [on our part]. But our King is liberal and beneficent,[4] and the door of his kingdom is open. If anyone were to wish to enter, let him enter boldly. He never begrudges anyone who turns to repentance.

"But as for the comforts which you have ordered to be provided us—we had the power back in our own country not to fall into the hands of your king, like the others who escaped

5. *Upper-room: vernatun,* in contrast to the *nerk'natun* of p. 144, n. 5.

6. *Executioner: dahich;* see p. 48, n. 5.

7. Cf. the picture of heaven on p. 103; here based on Matt. 25:34; John 14:2; 2 Cor. 5:1.

8. *Fatigued: dzandzrats'ealk',* as in 2 Cor. 4:16.

9. *Godless person: anastuats;* a frequent term for the Persians; cf. p. 73 of Anatolius and Florentius.

1. Cf. James 1:17.

2. Cf. 2 Cor. 15:1.

3. Cf. Matt. 6:25–29 and parallels.

4. Cf. p. 152, n. 3.

such troubles. But as we came willingly and readily, although we knew the perils of our danger and yet did not fear such hardships,[5] likewise we also wish that you bring even heavier afflictions upon us until your malice against us has been sated. For if our God, who is Creator of heaven and earth and of all things visible and invisible, in his benevolent love humbled himself to the race of mankind and put on a passible body,[6] accomplished the whole range[7] of virtue, fulfilled every act of Providence [*p. 148*] of his own will, was betrayed into the hands of his crucifiers, died and was placed in a tomb,[1] rose by his divine power and appeared to the disciples and to many others, ascended to his Father in heaven, sat at the right hand of the Father's throne, granted us heavenly power so that conformably with his immortality we too in our mortal bodies may be able to suffer with him and share in his immortal grandeur—and if he no longer considers our death as mortal but requites to us as immortals the rewards of our labors—then we count as insignificant these torments for love of the recompense[2] which he bestowed on the race of mankind."

When the chief-magus heard all that the chief-executioner had to say, he was disturbed and disconcerted in his mind; sleep departed from his eyes for many nights.[3] But one day in the evening watch[4] he arose and went to them, alone and noiselessly, without taking any of his servants with him. When he reached the door of the prison he looked in through a crack[5] and saw a vision similar to the previous one, except that they were in a peaceful sleep. Softly he called the bishop by name, for the latter knew Persian very well.[6] He came to the door and asked: "Who are you?" "It is I," he said, "I wish to enter and see you."

5. Cf. pp. 128–129.
6. For Ełishē on the Incarnation see pp. 39ff.
7. *Range: handēs;* cf. Rom. 3:25–26.

---

1. In the credal statement on p. 40 Ełishē simply says Christ was buried.
2. Cf. Rom. 11:35.
3. Cf. Gen. 31:40 of Jacob; or 1 Macc. 6:10 of Antiochus.
4. *Watch: pah;* see Hübschmann, *Grammatik*, p. 217.
5. *Crack: tsak,* the "eye" of the needle in the parable; cf. Matt. 19:24 and parallels.
6. Cf. p. 162, where Sahak interprets. According to Łazar, only the bishop Sahak among the captives knew Persian.

After he had come in among the saints, the sign was no longer visible to him, and he told them of the two appearances of the marvel. The priest Levond replied and said: "God who said light should shine in the darkness[7]—which indeed shone out and illuminated with wisdom the invisible creatures—has today made shine the same power in your darkened mind.[8] The blind eyes of your soul were opened [*p. 149*] and you saw the inextinguishable light of God's grace. Make haste, linger not, perchance you may again become blind and walk in darkness."

When he had said this, they all stood up, reciting from the forty-second psalm: " 'Send, Lord, your light and your truth, that they may lead and bring us to your holy mountain and your abode.'[1] Truly indeed, Lord, have you led and brought this wanderer to your unfailing joy and inalienable rest. Behold, this day is like [that] of your holy torments; just as you saved the condemned thief from the second death[2] and thereby opened the locked gate of Eden, so too have you found this man who was lost. He who was the cause of death for many, you have now made the cause of life for us and himself.[3] We thank you, God,[4] we thank [you] and join the holy prophet in saying: 'Not to us, Lord, not to us but to your name give glory for your mercy and truth, so that they may never say among the gentiles: Where is their God?'[5]—just as today your great power was revealed in this unbridled and darkness-enshrouded nation."

Then he who had freely found God-given grace began to speak by himself: " 'The Lord is my light and my life; of whom shall I be afraid? The Lord is the refuge of my life; by whom shall I be shaken?'[6] For I truly know that henceforth my enemies will be many, and they will wish to approach and consume my body. But you, Lord of all, came for the life of all,

---

7. Cf. Gen. 1:3.
8. Cf. 2 Cor. 3:14. But see p. 14 for the theme of light and darkness or blindness in Eḷishē.

---

1. Cf. Ps. 42:3.
2. Cf. Luke 23:43. For the idea of Christ taking the thief with him into paradise in place of Adam see also Grigoris Arsharuni, §29, par. 147; and cf. Hemmerdinger Iliadou, "Un sermon," esp. pp. 10ff.
3. An adaptation of Acts 13:28 and Heb. 5:9, which refer to Christ.
4. See p. 123, n. 3.
5. Cf. Ps. 78:10; 115:1–2; Joel 2:17.
6. Cf. Ps. 26:1–2.

that [*p. 150*] they might turn and live before your benevolence. Do not separate me from the holy lambs whom I have joined, lest as I leave your sheepfold[1] the evil beast fall on me again. Look not, Lord, on my impiety of many years, lest straying from the true life, I make disciples of many[2] to their destruction; but for those for whom I was the cause of death may I also become the cause of life. May Satan, who through me was scornfully arrogant among many who are lost, through me be humbled and shamed among his own disciples."

When they had thus spoken, they had him finish his prayers and they remained with him until the third watch.[3] Then they all slept peacefully until the morning-hour.

But he remained on his feet; he did not sleep but raised his hands up in prayer. While he was looking attentively to heaven through the skylight,[4] suddenly the building was filled with light. A luminous staircase appeared to him, which led from earth to heaven. Numerous groups of soldiers were climbing up; and the appearance of them all was extraordinary and handsome and awesome and wonderful, like the appearance of angels.[5] He retained in his mind the number in each of the groups he saw: one was a thousand, another thirty-six, another two hundred and thirteen.[6] They came so close that he even recognized three of them: Vardan and Artak and Khorēn. They held nine crowns[7] in their hands and were talking to each other, saying: "Behold, the time has come for these also to join our company. For we have been waiting for them and have brought them [these] tokens of honor as a pledge.[8] But one whom [*p. 151*] we did not expect has come, presented himself, joined [us] and become as one of Christ's soldiers."[1]

---

1. Although the theme is biblical, the word *p'arakh* (sheepfold) is not. But cf. Moses Khorenats'i, III, 68 (p. 359[2]), where it occurs in a passage adapted from the two Gregories of Nazianzen and Nyssa (see Thomson, *Moses Khorenats'i*, III, 68, n. 5.

2. Cf. Acts 14:20.

3. Cf. p. 148, n. 4.

4. As p. 144, n. 8.

5. This passage has close verbal parallels with Jacob's vision in Gen. 28: staircase, earth to heaven, climbing up, angels. For martyrs as a bridge to heaven cf. *Vkayk'*, p. 48.

6. For the numbers see pp. 120, 123.

7. The nine are those listed by name on pp. 119–120; for the theme of crowns see p. 138, n. 6.

8. Cf. p. 138, n. 8.

---

1. Cf. 2 Tim. 2:3.

Three times this wonderful vision appeared to the blessed man. He woke the saints from their sleep and told them the entire vision in order.

Then they rose up and prayed, saying: " 'Lord, our Lord, how marvelous is your name in the whole earth. Your great majesty has been raised higher than heaven. From the mouths of young suckling children you have confirmed blessing[2] that the enemy and opponent will be destroyed.'[3] Henceforth [we] shall no longer say: 'I shall see heaven, the work of your fingers,'[4] but: I shall see you, Lord of heaven and earth, even as you appeared today through your holy soldiers to this distant stranger, who had given up hope of life.

"Behold, Lord, in your mercy you have crowned your beloved ones, and in your compassion[5] you went out to seek this lost one;[6] you brought him back and joined him to the ranks of your saints. He not only saw heaven, the work of your fingers, but he saw heaven and its inhabitants; and while he was still on earth he joined the company of the myriads of your angels. He saw the souls of the just martyrs, he also saw the likeness of the glory of the invisible preparations,[7] and saw in their hands the sure token[8] which is kept ready by the Architect.[9] Blessed is he for this holy vision, and blessed are we for his approaching us, because through him we have learned for sure that he to whom such wonders are revealed has received a large portion of your inexhaustible[10] blessings. Your gifts, Lord, are inexhaustible, and without [*p. 152*] being asked you give with your abundant and generous liberality to whomever you please. And if you do not withhold from those who do not ask, open, Lord, the gate of your mercy to us who from our childhood have desired to share the blessedness of your saints. We make this newly found creature[1] of yours an intercessor for us; let not the ship of our

2. Cf. Matt. 21:16, which is based on Ps. 8:3. See next note.

3. Cf. Ps. 8:2–3.

4. Cf. Ps. 8:4.

5. *Mercy, crowned, compassion:* cf. Ps. 102:4.

6. Cf. Luke 15:4–6.

7. Cf. Rom. 9:23.

8. *Token: r̊bunay,* the Greek ἀρραβών, which in the Armenian N.T. is translated as *aṙhawatch'eay* (for which see p. 138, n. 8).

9. *Architect: chartarapet,* as in Heb. 11:10 of God; cf. p. 175 below. For patristic exegesis of this term see Lampe, *Lexicon,* s.v. τεχνίτης.

10. *Inexhaustible: anspaṙ,* as of the Lord's mercy, Lam. 3:22.

1. *Creature: dastakert,* which refers to an estate. It seems to be a calque on γεώργιον (which it translates in Prov. 24:5) in the sense of a field to be

faith sink in the billowing sea of sin."[2]

In such fashion they prayed for a long time, shedding abundant and intense tears for their own selves. They entreated the Benefactor[3] for mercy, that the voice of their supplications might be heard, that they might remain firm in their toils and afflictions lest they be deprived of the desirable crowns which the saints held in their hands—as they had been warned by the Holy Spirit that the time of their calling had approached; that they might go fearlessly, relieved of the uncertainty about the future which they had endured with much anguish; that through that small pledge they might attain the heavenly riches which they had long desired.

Since the chief-magus himself was the governor[4] of the land and the city prisoners had been entrusted to him, therefore in the morning he openly took the prisoners to his palace. He washed and cleansed them from the sores of the prison, then took the water in which the saints had washed and threw it over his own body. He set up a font in his own house and received Holy Baptism from them.[5] He communicated in the life-giving body and expiatory[6] blood of our Lord Jesus Christ. In a loud voice he cried out: "May this Baptism be for me a washing away of my sins and a new rebirth in the Holy Spirit,[7] and may the taste of this immortal Sacrament [bring me] to the inheritance of heavenly adoption."[8] He also placed [*p. 153*] before them a table of food for the body, offered them a cup of consolation, and joined them in [eating] the blessed bread.

But although he himself had attained heavenly blessings and was not afraid of human torments, nonetheless he was in

---

tilled, and hence of evangelizing; cf. 1 Cor. 3:9. See Lampe, *Lexicon*, s.v. γεώργιον and related words.

2. Cf. Agathangelos, §10, 16, for sailing through the stormy sea of sin. The theme of the church as a ship is very common; see Lampe, *Lexicon*, s.v. ναῦς.

3. *Benefactor: barerar,* a common term in the Bible and in Eḷishē.

4. *Governor: ishkhan.* See Christensen, *Iran,* p. 494, for this term, applied by Armenians to the *spāhbadh* who was governor of a province.

5. There are verbal parallels here with the story of the jailer in Acts 16 who was converted, washed the sores of Paul and Silas, and was baptized.

6. Cf. Rom. 3:25.

7. Cf. Titus 3:5.

8. Cf. Rom. 8:23.

great anxiety for his family lest they be betrayed as traitors to the royal cause.[1] Therefore he secretly summoned at night the nobles who were imprisoned in the same city, and lay on a great feast.[2] They all rejoiced greatly at the new wonder that had been revealed to them, and did not at all remember that any sufferings had been inflicted on them.

While they were at the table the saints recalled a priest who had been in holy bonds with them;[3] having lived among peasants he was more ignorant [than they] of the consolation of Scripture.[4] They ordered him to occupy the head of the table,[5] but the blessed one responded: "What is this you are doing? And why do you hide your secret intentions from me? I am more lowly than the least among you,[6] and more ignorant than the most insignificant of your pupils. How could I submit to this? It was already a great thing for me to share today your holy bonds. If you consider me worthy of your table, take each your own seat and allow me my own place." But the holy bishop with all the saints insisted, and they sat him above them all.

When the banquet[7] had come to an end and they had all joyfully participated in the food, Saint Joseph stood up and began to offer grace[8] in the following words:

[*p. 154*] "All rejoice in Christ,[1] for by this time tomorrow we shall have forgotten all the tribulations and torments we have endured. In return for our small travail we shall receive manifold relief; instead of this gloomy prison we shall enter the heavenly city of light,[2] the ruler[3] of which is Christ—he is the president[4] of the arena[5] where he first competed and won the

---

1. *Traitors to the royal cause: vnasakar yirs arkʿuni,* as in 2 Macc. 4:2; 14:26.
2. *Feast: tsakhs,* lit. "expense, extravagance."
3. I.e., Arshēn. But it is not clear if all refs. to "Arshēn" in Ełishē and Łazar are to the same man.
4. Cf. Rom. 15:4.
5. For ranking at the table, cf. p. 20, n. 4.
6. Cf. Mark 9:34; Luke 22:26.
7. *Banquet: akumb,* lit. "gathering."
8. *Grace: zurakhutʿean nuagn,* lit. "the hymn of joy."

---

1. Cf. Phil. 3:1.
2. Cf. Heb. 11:16; 12:22.
3. *Ruler: kʿałakʿapet,* the translation for πολιτάρχης in Acts 17:6, 8.
4. *President: handisapet.* For *handēs,* cf. p. 15, n. 15.
5. *Arena: asparēs,* the translation for στάδιον in 1 Cor. 9:24. For patristic exegesis of this theme see Lampe, *Lexicon,* s.v. στάδιον.

medal of victory.[6] Today it is the same Lord who accords us success[7] in receiving that same medal for the salvation of our souls and the glory of the illustrious holy church. Just as you see this brother at the head of our table, so he will be the first tomorrow to receive the crown through his martyrdom. For behold, the enemy of our lives who crowns the holy torments of Christ's servants has arrived and is close upon us."

When he had said this he received a corroborating reply from him [the chief-magus], whereby they were all greatly consoled.

He said: "May Christ so do to me by means of your holy prayers, and may he bring about my departure[8] from this world as you have said. Indeed, while you were speaking, my soul was inspired and I recalled the benevolence of Christ,[9] whose coming into this world took place because of our sins. May he have mercy on me as [he did] on the thief at the time of the crucifixion.[10] As through him he opened the closed gates of paradise so that he was the first to become a herald[11] to those who were to return there to joy, so may the Lord Jesus Christ also make me today a servant to your glorious company.

[*p. 155*] "Behold, for the sake of one sinner who returns to repentance the angels have unending joy in heaven, as they well know the desire of their Lord. Because he came to seek a single lost sheep, therefore they share in his joy over one returning to repentance.[1] Perhaps it was for my sake that the great Armenian general came with his numerous holy companions; he brought the crown for you but he gave the joyful news to everyone. They were especially amazed at me, as they did not know me while they were alive; now on their holy death they wish that I too receive a portion with the blessed ones.[2]

"I beg you, my lords and fathers, pray for my unworthi-

---

6. Cf. 1 Cor. 9:24–25, here adapted to the theme of martyrdom.

7. Cf. 2 Cor. 5:5.

8. *Departure: elkʻ vakhchani;* cf. the *elkʻ mahu* of Ps. 67:21.

9. Cf. Titus 3:4.

10. Cf. Luke 23:43 (though Ełishē uses *awazak* ["thief"], as in Matt. 27:38 and Mark 15:27, in place of Luke's *chʻaragorts* ["evil-doer"]).

11. *Herald: karapet,* the translation for πρόδρομος in Heb. 6:20. But there it is Christ who is the forerunner. For the theme of the thief as the first to enter paradise, see Lampe, *Lexicon,* s.v. λῃστής, 7d.

---

1. Cf. Luke 15:6–10.

2. Cf. Col. 1:12.

ness that I may become worthy to attain the great Gospel,[3] which has been proclaimed to my ears from your unlying mouths. Indeed I am anxious to see that day, and on the day the hour coming upon us.

"When will it be that I shall leave this burdensome and tiresome body? When will it be that I shall see you, Lord Jesus? When will it be that I shall be unafraid of death? When will it be that my ignorance will attain perfect knowledge? Help me, Lord, help me, and stretch out your almighty right hand to my succor, so that in accordance with the promise of my words deeds also may truly be accomplished with regard to me, and in me the name of our Lord Jesus Christ may be glorified among sinners."

When the blessed one had said this, they arose from table and gave thanks, saying: "Glory to you, Lord, glory to you, king, since you gave us food of joy. Fill us with the Holy Spirit, that we may be found pleasing before you and not be ashamed; for you compensate each according to his deeds."[4]

[*p. 156*] At the same time they held council as to how they might be able to save the chief-magus, lest when this news reached the court anger be stirred up like fire[1] against the survivors. But since they were unable to reach a decision in time, they unanimously turned to prayer, entrusting to God the life of the believer.

Then the nobles took their leave of the saints with flowing tears; in mournful joy they fell at their feet, begging them most earnestly to commend them to the Holy Spirit: "Lest any of us," they said, "weakening[2] and abandoning our common unity, become prey for the wicked beast."[3]

So the blessed ones in unison encouraged them, saying: "Be strong in the Lord, brethren,[4] and take consolation[5] in the benevolence of God, who will neither leave you orphaned[6] nor

---

3. Cf. Heb. 6:15; 11:33.
4. Cf. Rom. 2:6.

---

1. *Stirred up like fire: borbokʻestsʻi ibrew zhur;* a favorite simile of Ełishē's. Cf. p. 8, n. 3 (with refs.), pp. 13, 15, etc.
2. *Weakening: tʻulatsʻealkʻ;* a common theme in Ełishē; see p. 71, n. 3 for refs.
3. Cf. Jer. 16:4.
4. Cf. Eph. 6:10.
5. Cf. 2 Cor. 13:11.
6. Cf. John 14:18.

remove from us his mercy because of [our] faith in Christ. Through the many intercessors[7] we have with him, the flame of your lamps will not be extinguished[8] nor will the darkness-loving[9] enemy of your lives rejoice. But he is the same Lord who strengthened the first martyrs,[10] joining them to the company of his angels. Their holy souls and all the ranks of the just will come to aid and support you, so that with them you may become worthy of the same crowns."

So they spoke with them, and spent the whole night in [singing] psalms. At the hour of dawn they all said: "Make your mercy shine forth, Lord, on those who know you, and your righteousness on those straight of heart. Let not the foot of the haughty come upon us, or the hands of sinners make us tremble. May all those who work impiety fall there; they have been rejected, and will no longer be able to stand firm."[11]

[*p. 156*] Straightway the executioners arrived at the prison gate, entered inside and saw that he who previously was the chief-magus and who had been entrusted with guarding them was now sitting in their midst, listening to them, and even encouraging them not to fear death. When the executioners saw this amazing sight, they were most astonished at what had happened, but did not dare question him. However, they went and told Denshapuh, who had been charged with the tortures of the saints.

Now when he heard [the news] from the royal executioners, his mind was afflicted with great terror that perchance he himself might be involved because he was a very close friend of that man's. He ordered them all to be taken from the prison in bonds, and had them removed from the city to a distance of twelve Persian leagues.[1] Secretly he asked the chief-magus the reason for his being in bonds. The man responded, saying: "Do not talk to me secretly or listen to the counsels of light in darkness. For now my eyes have been opened since I have seen the

7. *Intercessors: barekhaws;* i.e., the saints. The term is also used of Christ and the Holy Spirit.
8. Cf. Matt. 25:8.
9. Cf. 1 Thess. 5:5.
10. *Martyrs: nahatak;* see p. 5, n. 2.
11. Cf. Ps. 35:11–13.

1. *Persian leagues: parsik hrasakh.* See Nyberg, *Manual* II, s.v. *frasang,* a varying measure of distance equivalent to 3¼–4 English miles; for further Armenian refs. see Hübschmann, *Grammatik,* pp. 183–184, and in general Mžik, *Erdmessung.*

heavenly light. If you wish to share in the counsels of life, question me openly in public and I shall tell you the wonderful deeds of God[2] that I have seen."

When he had heard all this from him and had verified his solidarity with the saints—that he could not be severed from agreement with them—he did not dare lay hands on him, although he had authority from the court. But he made haste to go and tell the king secretly everything just as he had heard it from him.

In response the king said to Denshapuh: "Let no one at all hear of this from you, especially concerning the great vision which appeared to him, [*p. 158*] lest ignorant men be confused and abandon our sure religion. Perhaps they will find people [saying that] while we were desiring to subject others, on them we were unable to have any effect, but teachers of our own religion were led astray after their errors.

"Furthermore, what is worst of all for us, it was not some insignificant person who was perverted to their religion, but a man who was *hamakden*,[1] famous in the whole Upper Land.[2] If we enter into a debate with him, as he is the most knowledgeable teacher of this land perhaps he will destroy our religion, shattering it from the foundations. But if we condemn him with other criminals, then the report of his Christianity will become well known and great dishonor will be brought on our religion. And if he is put to death by the sword,[3] there are many Christians in the army who will scatter his bones[4] throughout the whole world. It was only a minor disgrace for us in the eyes of all men when the bones of the Nazarenes[5] were honored and revered. But if they offer the same respect to magi and chief-magi, we ourselves will become the destroyers of our religion.

"But now I put you under oath to the immortal gods. First summon before you that embittered old man[6] to see if he can be persuaded by friendly means and repent and regret their

2. Cf. Acts 2:11.

1. *Hamakden:* see p. 143, n. 9.
2. *Upper land: Verin ashkharhk':* i.e., Apar; see p. 10, n. 1.
3. For the sword as the final instrument of a martyr's death see p. 40, n. 6.
4. The cult of bones is an important theme in this section, esp. p. 182; cf. also *Vkayk'*, p. 47.
5. *Nazarenes: natsrats'ik;* see p. 26, n. 5.
6. *Embittered old man: daṙnats'eal tser;* see p. 42, n. 6.

sorcery.[7] Treat him honorably in accordance with his former rank, and let no one know anything of his disgrace. Then if [*p. 159*] he is not persuaded and does not wish to obey your orders, bring many accusations against him from the country, so that he may be suspected of treachery in affairs of state.[1] Bring a public suit[2] against him and banish[3] him beyond Turan and Makuran.[4] There cast him into a dungeon[5] where he may suffer a miserable death. And bring a rapid end to life in this world for those of another religion[6] lest they overthrow the religion of our land. For if they have made a disciple of the learned chief-magus so quickly, how will ignorant men be able to resist their deceitful trickery?"[7]

Then Denshapuh went and sat in tribunal outside the camp, as we said, twelve leagues distant. He questioned the chief-magus, saying: "I have received authority in your case, not merely to question you verbally but also [to inflict] all forms of torments. But before I lay hands on you—receive honors, disdain ignominy, and spare your worthy white hairs. Abandon this Christianity, which you did not originally hold, and return to magism, as you were a teacher thereof for many."

The blessed one replied: "I beg you, my lord, who previously was considered in my eyes as a blood brother but today as a total enemy, do not pity me from your former affection but carry out against me the cruel will of your king. Just as you have received authority over me, [so] judge me."

When Denshapuh saw that he set the royal threats at

---

7. *Sorcery: kakhardut'iwn;* for this charge against Christians see p. 42, n. 5.

1. *Treachery . . . state:* as on p. 153, n. 1.
2. *Public suit: p'ursish;* see p. 136, n. 2.
3. *Banish: shkawt'ak;* as on p. 49, n. 6.
4. *Turan and Makuran:* in the region of Baluchistan; see Christensen, *Iran,* p. 84, and Marquart, *Ērānšahr,* pp. 31–33. All MSS of Eḷishē except *G K* and *X¹²* read Kuran for Turan (by confusion with Makuran?), a mistake repeated in some texts of the *Ashkharhats'oyts'* (e.g., 1865 ed., p. 613; but the text in Anania reads "Turan").
5. *Dungeon: virap;* not used elsewhere in Eḷishē, but reminiscent of the imprisonment of Gregory the Illuminator. See Agathangelos, §122 (*virap nerk'in*), Ḷazar, p. 3 (*khor virap*).
6. *Of another religion: ayladen,* as also on p. 179 (of Christians in the mouth of Persians). For *den* see p. 24, n. 5. The word is not attested to outside Eḷishē according to the *Nor Baṙgirk'.*
7. *Deceitful trickery: patir khabēut'iwn;* used on pp. 37[22], 47[3] of the demons, on p. 71[9] of the Armenians' deception by feigning apostasy.

naught, had no respect for persuasion, and wished the proceedings to be conducted more in public than in private, then he acted against him in accordance with the king's advice; secretly he was sent into distant exile.[8] As [Denshapuh] had been instructed by his master,[9] so he acted.

[*p. 160*] He [the king] also appointed two colleagues as assistants for Denshapuh from among the senior officials[1]—Jnikan, who was the royal *marzpet,*[2] and Movan, the chancellor[3]—under the *Movpetan movpet.*[4]

So these two with their retainers took the saints from that desert spot and that same night brought them as far away again to an even more terrible place. They made sure they were not observed by anyone in the army, not by Armenians or other Christians, nor by foreign pagans.[5] The attendants who had been in charge of the prisoners in the city were commanded to guard them carefully, so that no one might discover their tracks by which they would be led to the place of death, neither they nor any man whatever.

But there was a man from Khuzhastan[6] in the royal army who secretly observed Christianity. By chance[7] he had been appointed to the ranks of executioners and served in the day-guards with the instruments of torture. He came in the middle of the night and joined the groups of nobles. The first group supposed he was of the middle group, the middle that he was of the third, and all three considered him one of themselves. None

8. *Distant exile: heŕawor awtarut'iwn;* as on p. 9, n. 7 (further refs. p. 132, n. 1).

9. *Master: vardapet,* lit. "teacher," as on p. 51, n. 2.

1. *Senior officials: awag gortsakal;* for *awag* see p. 16, n. 9, and for *gortsakal,* p. 100, n. 3.

2. *Marzpet:* lit. "chief of the border"; not attested to elsewhere. For *marz* see p. 62, n. 6. However, several MSS here read *maypet* (or a corruption thereof), which is the reading on p. 179 and in Łazar, p. 88[12]. For *maypet* see Christensen, *Iran,* p. 390.

3. *Chancellor: handerdzapet;* see p. 62, n. 4.

4. *Movpetan movpet:* see p. 62, n. 3. "Under" is the translation for *i dzeŕanē* (as also Łazar, p. 88), which here has the meaning "under the authority of, second in command to."

5. The use of "pagans" (*het'anos*) for Persians is common in Ełishē, but *artak'in* (here translated as "foreign") is more difficult. It could mean "outside" (the church) and thus merely reinforce "pagan."

6. *Man from Khuzhastan: ayr mi khuzhik.* He is never named; for Khuzhastan see p. 48, n. 2.

7. *By chance: vichakeal,* with the sense of gaining some position by lot, as in Acts 1:26.

of them asked: "Who are you among us?"—neither from among the lords or the servants.

When they reached a deserted place which was completely barren of grass and was so terribly rocky[8] that they could not even find anywhere to sit, the three nobles went off to a distance and ordered the executioners to bind the saints' feet and hands. They put long cords on their feet, yoked them in couples, and dragged them along.[9] They [*p. 161*] pulled and tore them as they dragged them across the rocky places, so that not a bit of flesh remained on the saints' bodies.[1] Then they released them and brought them to a single spot.

It seemed to the nobles that "we have softened their obstinacy and have subdued their stubborn recalcitrance;[2] now whatever we say, they will obey our words, do the king's will, and be saved from insufferable torments." But they could not fully comprehend that they had inflamed them like valiant soldiers,[3] had drilled them in disciplined exercise, and had taught them to be like wild, bloodthirsty beasts. If the saints had any doubts earlier, on looking at the cruel wounds in their bodies they repudiated their former terror. Like insensible drunkards, they began to rival each other in their responses; and like thirsty men they rushed to the fountain,[4] to see who would be the first to shed his blood on the ground.

While the saints were engaged in these preparations, Denshapuh began to speak with them, saying: "The king sent me to you. All the desolation of Armenia, he says, and the losses of troops which have occurred—all these disasters were brought about by you; and it was because of your obstinacy[5] that many nobles are now tortured in bonds. However, if you wish to listen to me I shall tell you how today you may save your lives, just as you caused all the torments of death. The power is in your hands to free the nobles who are imprisoned. [*p. 162*] The

---

8. *Rocky: apaṙazh*, as in the parable of the sower, Matt. 13:20 and parallels.

9. For dragging (*k'arshel*) as a torture, cf. *Vkayk'*, p. 80, and Christensen, *Iran*, p. 306.

---

1. For this commonplace cf. Delehaye, *Passions*, p. 200.

2. *Recalcitrance: apstambut'iwn*, lit. "rebellion," as on p. 90, n. 3.

3. Cf. 2 Macc. 8:21, Judas' exhortation to battle (with verbal parallels).

4. Cf. John 6:14; 7:37. For exegesis of the fountain as referring to God and for spiritual thirst see Lampe, *Lexicon*, s.v. πηγή and διψάω.

5. *Obstinacy: yamaṙut'iwn*, a charge repeated on pp. 169, 186.

ruined country can be restored by your hands, and many who have been taken into captivity can return.

"Behold, you have seen with your own eyes how an illustrious man whom the king himself knew personally for his great knowledge of our rites, and who was perfectly versed in all our religion and beloved of all the magnates, and on whom almost all this land depended—because he despised the Mazdean religion[1] and was tricked into your foolish science, the king did not have regard for his great honor, but like a foreign[2] captive I banished him to such a distant exile that in his journey he will never reach the place of his punishment.

"Now if he did not spare his own foster brother[3] because of [our] honorable religion, how much less [will he have regard for] you foreigners who are guilty of treachery.[4] There is no other way to save your lives except by worshiping the sun[5] and fulfilling the king's desires, just as the great Zoroaster[6] taught us. If you do this, not only will you be released from your bonds and saved from death, but you will also be sent back to your country with munificent gifts."

The priest Levond stepped forward, and making Bishop Sahak interpret,[7] spoke: "How could we obey your equivocal[8] orders? Behold, first you rendered worship to the sun, then you attributed the carrying out of that worship to the wishes of the king. You honored the sun, loudly [*p. 163*] proclaiming his name; yet you honored the king more than the sun. You indicated that the sun serves creatures without so willing,[1] but that the king of his own free will divinizes whom he wishes and enslaves whom he wishes; yet he himself has not yet attained the truth. Do not talk to us as if we were children,[2] for we are grown up and not unversed in knowledge. I shall respond beginning from where you began.

1. *Mazdean religion: den mazdezn.* For this term and for *awrēnk'* (translated here as "rites") see p. 24, n. 5.
2. *Foreign: anashkharhik;* see p. 71, n. 2. However, on p. 179 Eḷishē says he was martyred.
3. *His own foster brother: bun dayekut'iwn;* for *dayeak* see p. 22, n. 5.
4. *Guilty of treachery: mahapart yirs ark'uni;* cf. p. 153, n. 1.
5. *Worshipping the sun:* see p. 17, n. 9.
6. *Zoroaster: Zradasht.* For Armenian traditions about Zoroaster see Eznik, §192, and esp. Moses Khorenats'i, I, 17, 18; cf. also p. 19, n. 1.
7. Cf. p. 148, n. 6.
8. *Equivocal: erkdimi,* lit. "two-faced"; cf. p. 10, n. 11.

1. For the sun as unconscious cf. p. 34.
2. Cf. p. 41, n. 1.

"Now you fixed on us the blame for the ruin of our country and the losses of the royal army. Our religion does not so teach us but enjoins us very strictly to honor earthly kings and to respect them with all our strength,[3] not as some insignificant man but to serve them as [we serve] the true God.[4] And if we suffer any wrong[5] from them, he has promised us the kingdom of heaven in return for this earthly one. Not only are we obliged to render them devoted service, but for love of the king we must go so far as to lay down our lives. Just as on earth we do not have the power to change him for another lord, so in heaven we have no power to change our true God for another,[6] as there is no other God save him.[7]

"But I shall speak to you [of matters] in which you are a little more knowledgeable. Which brave soldier would enter the battle last? If he were to do that he would not be called brave but very cowardly. Or which wise merchant[8] would exchange a valuable pearl for a worthless bead,[9] unless [*p. 164*] he were to become an ignorant fool like the leaders of your error?

"You have singled us out from among many noble colleagues, and you wish to destroy our firm convictions by stealth. We are not alone as you suppose. There is no empty place where our king, Christ, is not present.[1] Only those are deprived of him who have renounced him,[2] like you and your devilish[3] prince. For the soldiers of our country, who had become disciples of Christ through us, trampled underfoot the fearsome commands of your king and regarded as naught his magnificent gifts; they were despoiled of their ancestral dominions and regarded not their wives, children, or the material treasures of this mortal world.[4] Likewise, they did not spare

3. For Christian duty to kings cf. pp. 28–29, with reservations as expressed in Agathangelos, §52.
4. Cf. Rom. 13:1–7.
5. *Suffer wrong: zrkimk'*; lit. "be deprived." For this use cf. Matt. 20:13.
6. Cf. Rom. 1:25.
7. Cf. Deut. 32:39.
8. Cf. the taunt to Vasak, p. 136, n. 12.
9. Cf. Matt. 13:46. *T'rushay*, "bead," is a hapax.

---

1. Cf. p. 30.
2. *Who have renounced him: ork' urats'eal ek'* (2 pl) *i nmanē;* this is ambiguous, for the verb *uranal* can take *i* plus abl. of the person or thing renounced, or the phrase could be construed as a passive: "[you] who have been renounced by him."
3. *Devilish: ch'aradew;* cf. p. 44, n. 6, of Yazkert.
4. Cf. Matt. 19:29 and parallels.

their blood for love of Christ, but slew with harsh blows the worshipers of the sun who were your teachers, and inflicted terrible damage on your troops. Many of them fell in that battle, others were subjected to various trials; some endured distant exile, and still more were led into captivity. All of them preceded us to the kingdom of God, and have joined the supernal company of the angels. They have entered into the joy and felicity[5] prepared [for them], which the blessed man—of whom you said 'I have exiled'—has also attained. I call him blessed, and blessed the land through which he will pass and the place where he will die. [*p. 165*] He surpasses in honor not merely your royal court but even the luminaries of heaven that you worship."

Movan, the chancellor, said to them in response: "The gods are benevolent and deal patiently with men, so that they may recognize and learn their own insignificance and the [gods'] greatness, and may enjoy the gifts of the world which has been entrusted to the king's jurisdiction. From their mouths come edicts of death and life. You have no authority thus to oppose their will or to refuse to worship the sun, which illuminates the whole universe with its rays and provides nourishment for men and beasts by its warmth.[1] For its even-handed[2] liberality and impartial dispensation it has been named the god Mihr,[3] for it has no deceit or incomprehension. Therefore we are long-suffering with regard to your ignorance, because we do not hate men like bloodthirsty, carrion-eating beasts. Have regard for your selves and do not taint[4] us against our will with your blood. Abandon now your former transgressions, set straight your present course, so that for your sake others too may have mercy from the great king."

To this the bishop Sahak replied, saying: "Like a learned and well-instructed man you take excellent care of the country's prosperity and the king's glory.[5] But you impart very ignorant teaching by confessing many gods and not ascribing one will to them all. If the sublime beings[6] fight each other, how

5. Cf. Matt. 5:12; Luke 6:23.

1. Cf. p. 45 for the sun as a god who gives life.
2. *Even-handed: hasarakabashkh,* a hapax.
3. For Mihr see p. 32, n. 1.
4. *Taint: khaṙnekʿ,* lit. "mingle." Yuzbashyan translates as follows: "Do not make us participate in [the shedding of] your blood."
5. *Glory:* see p. 145, n. 1.
6. *The sublime beings: vehkʿn;* see p. 29, n. 5.

shall we—who are much humbler than they—[*p. 166*] be able to believe their words? Reconcile water and fire so that we may learn concord from them. Summon the sun to [your] home like fire; and if it cannot come lest the world remain in darkness, send the latter to it so it may learn from the former that it lacks nothing.

"But if the nature of your gods is one, let them be equal with each other and alike. Let fire not need nourishment, like the sun; let the royal servants not be encumbered with the expense of providing[1] for it. The one eats insatiably, yet dies continuously; while the other does not eat, yet without air the light of its rays diminishes. It grows cold in winter and freezes all the shoots of green grass;[2] in summer it becomes hot and burns all living creatures. That which itself is always in flux[3] cannot provide anyone with a stable life. I cannot blame you; he who has not seen the great King offers obeisance to his nobles.[4] But if any really wise man were to do that, he would be quickly condemned to death.

"Now as for the sun, if you wish to learn I shall tell you the truth. It is part of the created things of this world—one distinct part of many, half of which are above it, half below.[5] It is not holy in itself because of its pure light, but as God's command it spreads its rays through the air and by its fiery aspect warms all existing things[6] in the region below it. But the celestial beings have no share in its rays, since he [God] has placed the light in its globe as in some vessel,[7] and opening its mouth it pours it downward for the use and enjoyment of us below. Just as a ship, skimming over the immense waters of the sea, [*p. 167*] unconsciously follows its course guided by a wise and skillful captain, so too the sun effects the changes in its yearly cycle through its steersman.[1]

"And just as the other parts of this world have been estab-

---

1. *Providing: rochik*, as on p. 64, n. 1.
2. Cf. Job 38:27 (but there God brings rain to the green shoots).
3. *In flux: i pʻopʻokhman;* cf. James 1:17: in God there is no *pʻopʻokhumn.*
4. This image is taken from Philo, *In Gen.*, III, 34.
5. Cf. *Teaching*, §26off.: there are waters above and below the sun.
6. *Existing things: goyatsʻealkʻ;* see p. 34, n. 4.
7. As in Philo, *De Jona* pp. 597–598 (Lewy, §128). This is not the conception in *Teaching*, §267, where the luminaries are lit by God each day.

---

1. For the steersman (*kařavar*) see p. 14, n. 2, and for the yearly cycle see p. 34. This whole paragraph is indebted to Philo, *De Jona,* 597–598.

lished for the sake of our sustenance,[2] so [God] has given us this [sun] to provide light as one of the other parts, like the moon and stars or the ever-shifting winds and rain-bearing clouds,[3] and similarly among the parts of the earth, sea and rivers and fountains and all useful streams, and similarly the areas of dry land with all their uses. It is not right to call any one of these 'God.' If anyone were to dare to say so, he would destroy himself by his ignorance; and although he would honor them with the name of 'God,' they would have profited in no way. One kingdom does not have two kings.[4] And if you agree that man does not admit of this, how much further is such a confused state of affairs from the nature of God!

"So if you wish to learn the truth, soften the bitterness of your heart, open the eyes of your mind, and once awake do not walk blindly in the dark; you have fallen into an abyss[5] and wish to drag everyone down with you. If your own, who neither see nor understand,[6] follow your erroneous teaching, do not suppose that we shall do likewise; for the eyes of our minds are open and we see clearly.[7] With the eyes of the body we see Creation and understand that it was made by another and that all creatures are subject to corruption. On the other hand, the Creator of all is invisible to bodily eyes, but his power is comprehended by the mind.

[*p. 168*] "And because he saw us in great ignorance and pitied our despair—in which, like you, we once thought visible things were the Creator and we used to commit all sorts of dissolute acts[1]—therefore in his love he came and was incarnate from a human being, and taught us his invisible divinity. He even raised himself to a gibbet[2] in the form of the cross; and because men had gone astray after the luminaries, he stripped

2. *Sustinence: kenats‛,* lit. "life."
3. There are parallels here with Philo, *De Jona,* 597 (Lewy, §126).
4. Cf. p. 33.
5. *Blind, abyss:* cf. Matt. 15:14; Luke 6:39. But this paragraph repeats the basic theme of p. 14.
6. *Neither see nor understand:* a standard attack on idolatry, based on Ps. 115:1–8; 134:15–18. Cf. Agathangelos, §67.
7. *See clearly: sratesil,* a term frequent in the Armenian Philo, otherwise only attested to in Ełishē (according to the *Nor Baṙgirk‛*).

1. Cf. Wisd. of Sol. 14:23, where idolatry is discussed.
2. *Gibbet: kakhałan,* as in Agathangelos, §75, of Gregory; or Faustos, IV, 59. It is not used in the Armenian N.T. of Christ. This passage is reminiscent of the prayer of Gregory in Agathangelos, §8off.

the sun of the light of its rays,[3] so that the darkness might pay service to his humanity and those who were unworthy like you might not see the great ignominy of their lives. Just as today that same darkness clings to the soul and body of those who do not confess the crucified God, so you too are today in the same darkness and still torment us. We are ready to die following the example of our Lord. As and however you wish, fulfill your cruel desires."

When the impious Denshapuh had observed them and seen that they were all exceedingly joyful, he then realized that threats or cajoling words would have no effect on them. He ordered one of the youngest among them to be brought forward, a priest Arshēn by name, about whom the saints previously had had suspicions.[4] They bound his feet and hands and squeezed him[5] so tightly that all his sinews cracked from the pressure. For a long time he remained in these unbearable tortures.

The saint opened his mouth and said: "Behold, numerous dogs have surrounded me, and crowds of wicked men have beset me. They have pierced my feet and hands, [*p. 169*] and instead of my mouth all my bones have cried out.[1] Hear me, Lord, and listen to my voice;[2] and receive my spirit in the company of your holy warriors who appeared to your new creature.[3] Your merciful compassion has made me, who am the youngest, precede all the others."

After saying this he was no longer able to open his mouth from the insufferable tightening of the press. Then the executioners, immediately on receiving a command from the three nobles, cut off the blessed one's head with a sword and threw his body into a dry pit.[4]

At that very spot Denshapuh began to speak to the bishop, saying: "When I came to Armenia I had occasion to travel there for a year and six months. I do not at all remember hearing any word of complaint[5] from anyone about you, and even

3. Cf. Matt. 27:45; Luke 23:44.
4. But on p. 126 Eḷishē says that he was a "blessed" man.
5. For this torture cf. *Vkaykʻ*, p. 203, and Agathangelos, §102.

---

1. Cf. Ps. 21:17–18.
2. Cf. Ps. 26:7.
3. *Creature:* see p. 512, n. 1.
4. Ḷazar, p. 101, merely says that Arshēn was martyred by being beheaded; he has no details of tortures.
5. *Complaint: trtunj,* as on p. 142, n. 3.

less about Yoseph; for he was the leader[6] of all the Christians and faithful in all royal matters. Similarly, the governor[7] of the country who was there before my arrival was greatly satisfied with him; and I saw myself with my own eyes how he was positively considered as a father to the whole country,[8] and [how] he loved impartially the greatest and the least.

"It is now my turn to make a request of you: spare your honorable selves and do not surrender to a painful death in the fashion of that earlier one, whom you saw with your own eyes.[9] For if you are of the same obstinate mind, I have decided to cut your lives short with many tortures. I know that you have been seduced[10] by that man. But as he is sick of body and can find no healing through doctors, [*p. 170*] he is tired of a sickly life and prefers death to life."

To this Saint Yoseph replied, saying: "The praise that you gave first to this bishop and then to me your rightly paid, and you appropriately honored [us] for these white hairs. Such indeed is just. True servants of God must not turn against earthly princes[1] or lodge a complaint against any ordinary man for the sake of sordid material interests.[2] But humbly and modestly[3] they must teach God's commandments, act peaceably toward all without false[4] wisdom, and with impartial instruction lead everyone to the one Lord of Creation.

"As for this man's seduction of which you spoke, you did not lie but said the exact truth. But he does not seduce us like some stranger or lead us astray like some deceiving trickster;[5] rather he loves us greatly. Since our mother church[6] which bore us is one, and one our father the Holy Spirit who begat

---

6. *Leader: ishkhan;* cf. p. 27, n. 1, for Yoseph's position. On p. 152 (n. 4) the chief-magus is called *ishkhan.*

7. *Governor: marzpan;* see p. 61, n. 7.

8. Cf. 2 Macc. 14:37 of Razis.

9. These exhortations to save themselves are a common feature of hagiography; see Delehaye, *Passions,* pp. 186ff. Cf. also p. 17 above.

10. *Seduced: i hrapayrs.* Cf. Agathangelos, §156, where Diocletian describes Rhipsime as *hrapureal.*

---

1. Cf. Titus 3:1.

2. Cf. Titus 1:11; 1 Pet. 5:2. Ełishē has added "material" (*marmnawor*) to Paul's "filthy lucre."

3. Cf. Titus 3:2.

4. *False: khardakh;* cf. p. 134, n. 5, and 1 Tim. 6:5.

5. *Deceiving trickster: patroł khabebay;* see p. 159, n. 7.

6. For the church as mother see p. 67, n. 7.

us,[7] how could the children of the same father and one mother be at variance[8] and not united? What seems to you to be seduction has been our own same thought by day and night—that we might preserve the unity of our lives unbroken.[9] And if he is tired [and anxious] to leave this sickly body, even more so are we all. For there is no one at all born of woman who can preserve his body free of tormenting pains."

Denshapuh replied: "You do not realize how patient[10] I am being toward you. It is not at the king's command that I am continuing this debate[11] with you for so long, but I am tolerating you out of my own kindness. For I am not inhuman[12] like you, who hate yourselves and are enemies to others. Because I have eaten salt and bread[13] in your country, I have compassion and love for your land."

[*p. 171*] The priest Levond responded, saying: "Whoever has compassion and love for foreigners is fulfilling God's commandments.[1] But he must also look to his own soul; for we are not masters of ourselves, but there is [someone] who will seek accounting[2] from us both for foreigners and for our countrymen. Now as for your saying that I am listening to you of my own accord and not at the king's orders—if you are accustomed to transgress your king's commands, you do well, for he is a ravager of the land and a slayer of innocent people, a friend of Satan[3] and an enemy of God.[4] But we cannot transgress the command of our King, nor are we able to exchange our eternal life for the corruptible illusions[5] of this world.

7. For the Spirit as bestower of life see Lampe, *Lexicon*, s.v. πνεῦμα, G; in Syriac see Murray, *Symbols*, p. 81.

8. *At variance: erkpaṙak;* see p. 3, n. 4, for the importance of this term in Eḷishē.

9. *Unbroken: ankʻak;* see p. 62, n. 1, for the importance of this term.

10. *Patient:* cf. p. 165. It is a common theme in the mouth of the judge in hagiography; cf. *Vkaykʻ*, p. 226.

11. *Debate:* as on p. 32, n. 2.

12. *Inhuman: anagoroyn*, as in Rom. 1:31.

13. *Salt and bread.* The *Nor Baṙgirkʻ* notes several instances of this expression in the Armenian version of commentaries by John Chrysostom.

1. Cf. Col. 3:12, 14.

2. *Accounting: hamar;* cf. Luke 16:2; Rom. 14:12; and esp. Heb. 13:17. Cf. p. 26, n. 4, for the responsibility of the shah to give an accounting to the gods.

3. Cf. p. 138, n. 7 of Vasak, and p. 6, n. 9 of Yazkert.

4. Cf. James 4:4; and esp. Acts 13:10: "son of Satan, an enemy of all righteousness." Cf. also p. 175, n. 4; p. 185, n. 6.

5. *Illusions: patrankʻ;* used in Matt. 13:22; Mark 4:19 of riches.

"But as for your saying of me that he has not found healing from doctors and prefers death to life—these are not the words of those who see all the pains of the world. Come now, moderate a little your raging passion, attend to my true words, and look at the affairs of this world systematically. Whichever mortal will have a life without sadness? Are they not all full of ills, both internal and external? Cold and heat, hunger and thirst,[6] complete poverty and want. On the outside: injustice, rapine, foul lewdness with aggressive licentiousness; on the inside:[7] impiety, apostasy, ignorance, unrepentant error [derived] from willful independence.

"Now you scorned and despised doctors. But if I found no health from them, there is no cure because they are men. There are illnesses for which they find cures, and there are those which surpass their capacities. For we are all mortal, both he who heals and he who is healed. I wish that you resembled the medical art, [*p. 172*] since the reality of their healing is not insubstantial. For when they see someone ill, they do not delay to visit them, but quickly endeavor to offer them recovery. Notably, if any of the king's friends at court were to fall ill, when [the doctor] arrives at the great hall[1] and sees the multitude of notables and healthy fine young people, and even on entering the royal chambers and seeing there all the splendor and wonderful appearance of the courtiers, he would not be amazed at the marvelous sight. Likewise if it were on some jewel-bedecked couch entirely gilded on which the sick man were lying, he pays no attention to all that but orders the gold-braided covers to be removed, and putting his hand within he examines the whole body to see if its state is warm, if the heart is beating steadily in its place, if the liver is tender, and if the pulse of the veins is regular. And accordingly he will effect his cure, restoring him to health.[2]

6. Cf. *Vkayk'*, p. 80, for these as sufferings endured by martyrs.

7. *Outside, inside:* a common biblical theme; cf. Deut. 32:25; Ezek. 7:15; 2 Cor. 7:5.

1. *Hall: hraparak;* see p. 42, n. 4.

2. This whole passage from the top of p. 172 is based on Philo, *De Providentia*, II, 22 (pp. 59–60 of the Armenian). For medical knowledge at this time see Temkin, "Byzantine Medicine." Oganesyan, *Istorija Meditsini v Armeni*, does not exercise due caution in using this passage as direct evidence for Armenian practice, since he says nothing about its Philonic source. Instead of the state of the liver, Philo mentions the stomach and chest.

"Now if human medicine can thus set all at naught and advancing only its own art carries out its task, how much more is it right for you—who hold in your great power this whole land—first to take care to heal your souls of all diseased errors of this world, as everyone already has been subjected to you in a bodily sense. But now that you have become ignorant and have made your immortal souls mortal for the unquenchable fire of hell,[3] whether you wish it or not you are diseased in your bodies with an incurable disease. Yet you blame us for bodily pains which are not of our own free choosing [*p. 173*] but [have affected us] as happens to the bodily nature of every man.

"But Christ, the true living and quickening[1] God, of his own good will became a doctor[2] of souls and bodies. First by the pains of his own torments he healed all the races of mankind. And being even further moved to compassion, by his second birth[3] he begat us into health, painless and unwounded; he cured the old scars of the dragon[4] by his secret scourging; he rendered us unblemished and unspotted in soul and body that we might become companions of the angels and soldiers of our heavenly King.[5] Although you do not know this and have not enjoyed the heavenly gifts of God, you do not even wish to learn from us but you still desire to mislead us. That is impossible, it will never happen, and you cannot bring it about.

"But I shall tell you briefly about my diseased body. I rejoice and am happy when I see my body tormented. I know that the health of my soul is being strengthened within me, especially because I have as pledge the great teacher of the gentiles,[6] who consoled himself in the pains of his body and gloried in Satan's buffeting of his flesh,[7] saying: 'If we became participants in the likeness of his death, how much more will we participate in his Resurrection.'[8] But do you, who have

3. Cf. Matt. 3:12 and parallels.

---

1. *Quickening: kendanarar,* as in 1 Cor. 15:45, with reference to the second Adam.
2. For Christ as doctor see *Teaching.* §452, 565.
3. For the two births of Christ see *Teaching,* §388.
4. *Dragon: vishap,* as on p. 88, n. 6. For the devil as a dragon see Lampe, *Lexicon,* s.v. δράκων, 2a.
5. Cf. *Teaching,* §364, 414, and 640. The term *banakakits'* (companions) means "fellow [soldier] in the army" (*banak*); cf. 2 Tim. 2:3, for the heavenly soldiers. See further Lampe, *Lexicon,* s.v. στρατιώτης, 1b.
6. I.e., Paul; cf. 1 Tim. 2:7.
7. Cf. 2 Cor. 12:7.
8. Cf. Rom. 6:5.

power over us, judge us in accordance with your evil will. We are not at all fearful of your awesome and frightening threats, nor do we fear the cruel death which you are about to inflict on us."

Then he [Denshapuh] separated the blessed ones from one another a little [*p. 174*] and spoke only to the holy bishop: "The praise which I bestowed on you earlier you did not recognize as respect for your person. I shall remind you of the crimes you committed, so that you may yourself have yourself condemned to death.[1] Did you indeed destroy the fire-temple[2] in Ṙshtunik‘, and did you kill the fire?[3] As I have heard and confirmed, you also tortured the magi and removed the vessels of the cult.[4] Now tell me if you really did those things."

The saint replied: "Do you then wish to learn this from me, if you knew it before?"

Denshapuh said: "Rumor is one thing, truth another."

The bishop said: "As you suppose, tell me."

Denshapuh said: "I have heard that it was you who caused all the damage in Ṙshtunik‘."

The bishop said: "And since you have so learned for sure, why do you question me a second time?"

Denshapuh said: "I wish to learn the truth from you."

The bishop said: "You do not wish to learn from me what is advantageous to your own well-being, but your real desire is for my blood."

Denshapuh said: "I am not a bloodthirsty beast, but I seek vengeance for the gods' dishonor."

The bishop said: "You call the dumb elements gods,[5] and yet you wish to slay men who are in your own image. You will have to suffer vengeance with your king at the incorruptible[6] tribunal of God.[7] What in your evil desires you wish to hear from me I shall tell you. I did indeed destroy the [fire-] temple

1. It was Sahak who destroyed the fire-temple in Ṙshtunik‘; see p. 129. Sahak, also, was the only bishop who spoke Persian; see p. 162.
2. *Fire-temple: atrushan,* see p. 12, n. 4.
3. Cf. p. 46, n. 4.
4. The torturing of magi is mentioned on p. 129; the removal of the vessels (*spas,* see p. 54, n. 7) on p. 69.
5. Cf. p. 37 above and Agathangelos, §58ff.
6. *Incorruptible: ankashaṙ,* not a biblical expression. See p. 64, n. 4, for *kashaṙ,* "bribe."
7. Cf. Rom. 14:10; 2 Cor. 5:10.

and inflict the bastinado[8] on the magi, and the impure utensils[9] that were in the temple I threw into the lake.[10] But who can kill the fire? For the all-wise Creator of Creation took care at the beginning and rendered the nature of the four elements imperishable.[11] [*p. 175*] So then, kill the air, if you can; or destroy the earth so that it not bring forth grass; cut the throat of the river so that it dies. If you can do these three things, then you can kill fire.

"Now if our Architect[1] united the indissolubility of the four elements[2]—so the nature of fire is found in stones and in iron and in all tangible elements—why do you falsely slander me [by saying], 'You killed the fire?' Then kill the warmth of the sun, for it has a portion of fire; or give a command that fire not be struck from iron. That which breathes, moves, travels, eats, and drinks, [also] dies. When did you see fire traveling, or speaking, or knowing?[3] Do you then admit that what you have not seen living has died? How much more unpardonable is your impiety than that of all the heathen, who are more knowledgeable than you. For although they have strayed from the true God, they do not confess dumb elements to be God. So if you ignorantly say the nature of fire is destructible, these created things do not agree with you, because it is mingled in them all."

Denshapuh said: "I shall in no way enter into a debate and critique with you concerning the nature of created things. But admit to me: did you extinguish the fire, or not?"

The blessed one replied, saying: "Since you did not wish to become a disciple of the truth, I shall expound the will of your

8. *Bastinado: gan;* see p. 124, n. 1. It is not used on p. 129 describing Sahak's activity in Řshtunik'.

9. *Impure utensils: kah płtsut'ean;* cf. p. 69.

10. I.e., Lake Van, Řshtunik' being on its southern shore. The story in Łazar, pp. 62–63, of soldiers casting fire into the water refers to a different place.

11. *Imperishable: anmah.* See p. 32 for creation from nothing, and *Teaching,* §272, for an ambiguous statement implying preexisting matter from which the world was created. But here the implication is that the elements cannot die; see the next paragraph.

1. *Architect:* see p. 151, n. 9.

2. Cf. p. 33.

3. Cf. the sarcasm of an oath sworn to by sun, fire, and water, in *Vkayk',* p. 168.

father Satan.[4] I myself entered your fire-temple[5] and saw standing there the impious ministers of your vain religion and the fire-holder[6] blazing in front of them full of fire. I questioned them with words and not the rod: 'What in your own minds do you think of the fire of this cult?' They replied: 'We do not know. But this much we understand, that it is the custom of [our] ancestors and the strict command of the king.'

[*p. 176*] "Again I spoke to them: 'And what do you understand the nature of your fire [to be]? Do you suppose it to be a creator or created?' They all said in unison: 'We do not recognize it as a creator, nor as one that gives rest to those who have labored. Our hands have become calloused from the axe and our backs worn from carrying wood. Our eyes are bleary with tears from the acridity of its smoke, and our faces are sooty from the heavy dampness of its fumes. Even if we give it much nourishment, it is greatly hungry; and if we give none at all, it goes out completely. If we approach and worship, it burns us; but if we do not come near at all, it turns to ashes.[1] Such is the extent of our comprehension of its nature.'

"Again I said to them: 'Have you then heard who taught you such error?' They replied, saying: 'Why do you question us [merely] for the sake of hearing? Look at the facts before you: our legislators[2] are only blind in their minds; but our king is blind in one bodily eye, while his spirit has no eyes at all.'[3]

"So when I heard this from the magi I greatly pitied them, for in their ignorance they spoke the truth. I beat them a little with the rod, made them throw the fire into the water, and said: 'May the gods who did not create heaven and earth perish beneath heaven.'[4] And then I threw out the magi."

When Denshapuh had heard all this from the mouth of

4. Cf. p. 171, n. 4.

5. *Fire-temple: krakatun,* "house of fire"; see p. 12, n. 4 for the various terms used for fire-temples in Ełishē.

6. *Fire-holder: krakaran;* also used by Łazar, p. 63[1]. For the suffix -*aran* see Meillet, *Elementarbuch,* and §34b, and "La composition."

1. This paragraph has parallels in the *Teaching,* §523, which refer to the foul smoke and soot of sacrifices to idols and the useless labor spent on them. Cf. also p. 55 above for ashes, dust, blackened smoke, and impure filth. The final ref. here to ashes recalls the "ash-worship" found in Armenian hagiographical texts; see p. 12, n. 4.

2. *Legislators: awrēnsdir;* see p. 71, n. 1.

3. Cf. p. 14 for this theme.

4. Cf. Jer. 10:11.

the holy bishop, he was extremely terrified at the insults to the king and the disrespect [*p. 177*] for his religion. Therefore he was afraid to inflict torments on him lest perchance he might cause him to say even more insulting things about the king in the tribunal, and suspicion be thrown upon himself for those insults because he had disputed patiently[1] with them.

And since he was sitting in the tribunal girt with a sword to instill awe into the saints, roaring like an enraged lion[2] he drew the sword and wildly set upon the blessed ones; he struck the bishop behind the right shoulder and cut off his hand. The bishop fell to the ground on his left side; then raising himself again he picked up his right hand and loudly cried: "Receive, Lord, this willing sacrifice[3] whereby I have offered myself totally to you, and enroll me in the ranks of your holy soldiers."[4]

Furthermore, he encouraged his companions, saying: "Now my virtuous ones, the hour of our martyrdom has arrived. Shut the eyes of the body for a moment and you will see straightway our hope, Christ."[5] Then rolling in his own blood he said: "I shall bless the Lord at all times; his praise will be continuously in my mouth. My soul will boast in the Lord; the meek will hear and be glad."[6] This psalm he recited as far as this place: "The just have many tribulations; but the Lord preserves them from everything and protects all their bones."[7]

While there still remained a little strength in his body, even with his own eyes he saw companies of numerous angels coming from heaven and six crowns[8] in the hand of the archangel. He also heard a voice from above, saying: "Take courage,[9] my friends; for behold you have forgotten your lives of suffering [*p. 178*] and have attained your blessed crowns, which you fashioned through your own skill.[1] Take them, and place them

1. *Disputed patiently: payk'arets'aw erkaynmtut'eamb.* The verb is rare; for the noun *payk'ar* see p. 32, n. 2. For the theme of "patience" in these debates see p. 170, n. 10.
2. Cf. 1 Pet. 5:8 of the devil.
3. *Receive . . . sacrifice:* a liturgical expression; cf. Gat'rchean, *Pataragamatoyts'k'*, p. 150.
4. Cf. p. 173, n. 5.
5. Cf. 1 Thess. 2:19; 1 Tim. 1:1.
6. Cf. Ps. 33:2–3.
7. Cf. Ps. 33:20–21.
8. See pp. 178–179 for the list of six martyrs. For martyrs seeing their own crowns see Delehaye, *Passions*, p. 213.
9. Cf. Acts 27:25; Paul refers to his vision.

1. *Skill: chartarut'iwn*, "craft," as in Acts 19:24, 38.

on each one's head. For the material has been prepared and shaped by you, but the art of your labor has been fashioned by the all-holy hands of Christ. Receiving them now from his servants, you are crowned with Stephen."[2] He also saw distinctly that the sword was still glinting over the necks of the blessed ones.

When Saint Łevond saw that they no longer intended to question and condemn them one by one but that a general order for their death had been given, he said to the blessed Yoseph: "Approach, confront the sword, for you are superior in rank to [us] all."[3] After he had said this, they arranged themselves in order, and the executioners made great haste to cut off the blessed ones' heads all at once and throw them before the holy bishop. And he, giving up the spirit, cried out: "Lord Jesus, receive all our souls[4] and join us to the company of your dear ones." So they were all martyred at the same time in the same place.

If you wish to reckon among their number also the chief-magus who believed in Christ, they were seven, not including the two martyred in Vardēs[5] and another bishop called Taʿtʿik in Asorestan.[6] But the names of the six who all [died] in that spot are as follows:

Bishop Sahak from Ṙshtunikʿ
Saint Yoseph from Vayotsʿ Dzor, from the village of Hołotsʿimkʿ[7]
[*p. 179*] The priest Łevond from Vanand, from the village of Ijavankʿ[1]
The priest Mushē from Ałbak[2]

---

2. Cf. Acts 7:56 for Stephen's vision at his martyrdom.

3. For Yoseph was Catholicos; see p. 27, n. 1.

4. Cf. Acts. 7:59, as Stephen at his martyrdom.

5. I.e., Samuel and Abraham; see p. 143, where it is implied that Vardēs is near Niwshapuh. The MSS spell the name of the district very differently: Vatgēs, Vatget, Vrdēs, Vardgēs (as in Łazar, p. 87), Vardes, Vardēn. See Marquart, *Ērānšahr*, pp. 64–78.

6. The same Tʿatʿik mentioned on p. 28 as bishop of Basean, as Łazar makes clear, p. 88. Asorestan is Mesopotamia in Sasanian times; see Honigmann and Maricq, pp. 42–63.

7. *Vayotsʿ Dzor:* south of Lake Sevan; see Hübschmann, *AON*, pp. 348, 469. For Hołotsʿimkʿ cf. Łazar, p. 38[23], there called Kholotsʿimkʿ.

---

1. *Ijavankʿ:* not otherwise attested to.

2. For Mushē see p. 129, n. 8. Ałbak is between lakes Van and Urmia; see Hübschmann, *AON*, pp. 335–336.

The priest Arshēn from Bagrevand, from the village of Ełegeak[3]

The deacon Kʻajaj from [the same origin as] the bishop of Ṙshtunikʻ

Also the blessed chief-magus from the city of Niwshapuh[4]

The priest Samuel from Ayrarat, from the village of Arats

The deacon Abraham from the same village[5]

For these six saints martyred there in the desert, Denshapuh and the chief-magus and Jnikan the *maypet*[6] selected guards from their entourages and ordered them to watch over the bodies of the saints[7] in that very spot for ten days or more until the royal army should have moved on. To prevent, they said, any infidels[8] from coming and removing their bones, and distributing them throughout the whole land—at which people would be even more encouraged to go astray after the sect of the Nazarenes.[9]

But the man from Khuzhastan whom we mentioned above[10] remained there with the guards as one of them. He was a man full of wisdom [*p. 180*] and perfect in divine knowledge.[1] He was waiting on the lookout[2] for some way in which he could steal the bones from them.

Three days passed during which great terror fell on them all; like numbed and half-dead[3] men, they lay unable to rise. Then on the fourth day two of the guards were cruelly afflicted by a demon.[4] For the whole night awful voices cried out and thunderous crashings [were heard] from below like the rumbling of an earthquake. The ground shuddered beneath them,[5] and flashing swords cast lightning around them. They saw all

3. Ełegeak is in Bagrevand; see Hübschmann, *AON*, p. 423.
4. On pp. 159, 162 it is implied that he was exiled but would not reach his place of exile.
5. For the martyrdom of Samuel and Abraham see p. 143.
6. *Maypet*: see p. 160, n. 2.
7. For guarding the bones of martyrs, cf. *Vkaykʻ*, p. 34.
8. *Infidel: ayladen:* see p. 159, n. 6.
9. *Sect: ałand*, as on p. 9, n. 9. For Nazarenes (*natsaratsʻikʻ*) see p. 26, n. 5.
10. Cf. p. 160.

1. Cf. Rom. 11:33; Eph. 1:8; Phil. 1:9.
2. *Lookout: dētakn;* cf. p. 77, n. 2.
3. *Numbed, half-dead:* as the chief-magus on p. 146.
4. Cf. Mark 9:25.
5. Cf. Ps. 17:8; 76:19.

the dead bodies rise up and echo awesomely in their ears the very words of the tribunal, so that they were mutually terrified and even began to kill one another. They were so distraught and crazed that one did not know where the other had fled. In a great turmoil they went and told of all the torments they had endured.[6]

The three nobles took council and in astonishment began to say to one another: "What are we to do? How shall we deal with the inexplicable[7] sect of the Christians? For while they are alive, their lives are wonderful; they scorn possessions as if they had no need of them, they are pure as if disembodied, they are impartial like equitable judges, they are fearless like immortals. Even if we say all that of them as ignorant or brash[8] men, still what are we to do, since all the sick in the army have been cured by them?[9] And what is more significant than all this—whatever man's corpse ever stood up and appeared alive, or whoever heard spoken words from it?

[*p. 181*] "For our servants are not liars; we have been assured of their veracity ourselves. And if they had wished to inject any personal avarice, they would have made some hints to the Christians in the army and would have received the weight of each body in gold. Furthermore, the men who were tormented by a demon we know were not ill at any other time. It is clear that a great miracle has occurred today. If we keep silent there will be suspicion on us and our persons. But if we bring them before the king, when he hears about all these tremendous wonders from them there may occur some ruin[1] for our religion."

---

6. In addition to the parallels noted in nn. 4 and 5, and the imagery of crashings, flashing, and lightning (which have parallels in battle descriptions in Eḷishē and the Maccabees), this paragraph is closely patterned on the miracles described in *Vkaykʻ*, p. 234, which disturbed the guards set over the bodies of martyrs: three days passed, on the fourth day, earthquake, shuddered. There are verbal parallels also with the Armenian of Wisd. of Sol. 18:17-19: terror, half-dead, crazed. The earthquakes here are literary topoi, but the area has frequently been affected by real ones; see C. Melville, "Earthquakes in the History of Nishapur," *Iran*, 18 (1980): 103-120.

7. *Inexplicable: ankʻnin*, lit. "inscrutable," as in Job 5:9 of God, Eph. 3:8 of Christ.

8. *Brash: yandgneal;* cf. 1 Cor. 13:5 of love.

9. Cf. p. 16.

---

1. *Disintegration: kʻaktumn,* cf. Matt. 24:2 and parallels.

The chief-magus responded, saying to them: "Did they not make me *ostikan*[2] over the two of you? Why are you so troubled and distressed in your souls? You fulfill your duty and carry out the royal order. Now if this report becomes known and there is an interrogation[3] before the king, that investigation will be for us magi. Do not worry;[4] do not even think about it. If you are at all frightened in your souls, come to the temple[5] very early in the morning. For tomorrow the high *Movpetan movpet*[6] will offer sacrifice[7] there, and he will satisfy and convince your minds."

Now when the man from Khuzhastan heard all this and realized that they would thenceforth pay no further attention to the murdered saints, he immediately took ten men the fervor of whose Christianity he knew, and hastening to the spot found all [the bodies] in good condition.[8] Since they were all apprehensive of the executioners, they moved the saints elsewhere [*p. 182*] about two leagues[1] away. When they felt secure, they cleaned and set out the bones of the blessed ones; they brought them to the camp and kept them hidden. Gradually they showed them, first to the Armenian soldiers, and then to the many Christians who were in the army. The first fruits[2] they presented to the imprisoned nobles; these were suddenly released from their bonds, the threat of death passing them by—for edicts of amnesty[3] had been sent to Armenia.

This blessed Khuzhik, who was rendered worthy to serve the saints in secret, repeated to us whatever has been said about their death up to here, their condemnation and everything in order: their cruel dragging, the questioning and interrogation

2. See p. 84, n. 1.
3. As on p. 132, n. 5.
4. Cf. Matt. 28:14.
5. *The temple: dari t'ir* (with variant spellings in the MSS), which makes no sense in Armenian. Portugal Pasha (*Bazmavēp*, 1895, pp. 6–7) suggested the emendation *dar-i-Mihr* (Gate of Mithra), which was accepted by Acharian, *Armatakan Bararan*, s.v. *darit'iwr*, and Yuzbashyan, *Egishe*, p. 186, n. 15.
6. For the *Movpetan movpet* see p. 62, n. 3; for *rat* (high) see Nyberg, *Manual* II, s.v. *rat*.
7. *Sacrifice: yazē*; cf. p. 64, n. 12.
8. For the theme of preservation of martyrs' bodies see Agathangelos, §223, and Thomson, *Agathangelos*, §223, n. 1.

1. *Leagues: hrasakh*, see p. 157, n. 1.
2. Cf. 1 Cor. 15:20 of the resurrected Christ.
3. *Edicts of amnesty: hrovartakk' t'olut'ean*, as on p. 85, n. 7.

of the judges, the responses of each of the saints, their execution, the awful terror which fell on the guards, the despairing query of the three nobles, the collecting of their holy bones into one place to avoid scattering.[4] He placed these separately into six caskets,[5] he found out their various names and indicated them on the caskets. And the iron chains he placed with each one's bones, for the executioners had thrown them away, and he likewise indicated each one's clothing on the casket.

These six died a holy and desirable martyr's death on the twenty-fifth day of the month Hrotits',[6] in the great desert of the land of Apar, in the neighborhood of the city of Niwshapuh.

FURTHER, CONCERNING THEIR DISCIPLES THE CONFESSORS

Now the disciples of the blessed ones remained inside the city in bonds.[1] A royal chief-executioner[2] came and brought them outside the city.

He also removed from the city five Christians from Asorestan, for they too were in bonds for the name of Christ. He interrogated them, but they did not agree to worship the sun.[3] He tortured them with the bastinado, but they persisted in the same intention even more strongly. He cut off their noses and ears,[4] and had them taken to Asorestan to be set to labor on the royal estates.[5] They went very readily as if they had received great gifts from the king.

Then the same chief-executioner came again to the disciples of the holy martyrs. Choosing two of them who were the

---

4. *Scattering: khaṙn i khuṙn;* cf. p. 30, n. 7, for the phrase, and *Vkayk'*, p. 46, for a similar situation.

5. *Caskets: tapan,* as for the martyrs in Agathangelos, §760. *Tapan* also means "ark."

6. *Hrotits':* the twelfth month of the Armenian year. The twenty-fifth day of Hrotits' in the year 454 (see p. 141, n. 2) would fall on 26 August.

---

1. Cf. p. 141.

2. *Chief-executioner: dahchapet;* see p. 48, n. 5.

3. Cf. p. 17, n. 9.

4. Cf. the "nine" tortures, Christensen, *Iran,* p. 305, whereby the limbs were cut off one by one.

5. *Labor on the royal estates: mshakut'iwn ark'uni.* The stem *mshak* refers primarily to agricultural labor. The meaning here is clear from Łazar, p. 105. Cf. above, p. 71, n. 2, and below p. 187, n. 1.

most modest, he took them aside from the others and said: "What are your names?"

One of them replied: "By my parents I was named Khorēn, and he Abraham.[6] But in our spiritual rank we are servants of Christ[7] and disciples of the blessed ones whom you killed."

The chief-executioner responded, saying to them: "What then is your business, and who brought you here?"

[*p. 184*] To this Abraham replied: "That you should have learned from our teachers, because they were not insignificant[1] persons but had ancestral possessions of worthy sufficiency, and likewise servants; some were like us and others of superior station. We came with those who nourished and instructed us. For we have a command from our divinely-given religion to love them like holy fathers and to serve them like spiritual lords."[2]

The chief-executioner was angry and said: "You speak like undisciplined and defiant rebels.[3] While you were at peace and in your own country, all was well. But when they became criminally involved[4] in royal affairs and were condemned to death for their deeds, you should not at all have gone near them. Do you not see in the great camp that when some honorable person[5] is arrested[6] by royal [orders], he is clothed in dark garments,[7] is set apart in solitary confinement,[8] and no one at all is allowed to go near him? Yet you speak thus, boasting as if you were a disciple of an innocent man."

To this Khorēn replied, saying: "Your position is not unjust, nor ours false. The guilty noble should so serve him from whom he received honor that he may receive from him even greater presents above his rank. But in return for not doing

6. According to Łazar, p. 94, Khorēn was from Orkovi in Ayrarat, and Abraham from Zenakkʿ in Taykʿ.

7. Cf. Col. 4:7.

1. *Not insignificant: ochʿ duznakʿeay;* as on p. 158 of the chief-magus, or p. 163 of kings.

2. Cf. Eph. 6:1–7, for loving and serving. Note the emphasis on the secular holdings and position of the ecclesiastical leaders.

3. *Rebels: stambak;* see p. 84, n. 8.

4. *Criminally involved: gruah,* a hapax.

5. *Honorable person: patuawor,* cf. p. 84, n. 3.

6. *Arrested: dipah,* as in Gen. 42:16. For the etymology see Nyberg, *Manual* II, s.v. *dēpahr,* "custody."

7. For the garb of a condemned man cf. p. 137, n. 9.

8. As was Vasak, p. 139.

230

that, untoward[9] consequences befell him. If our teachers had been guilty toward God or had sinned against the king in some way, we would have acted in similar fashion toward them; we would not have gone near them at home, nor would we have followed them abroad. However, because [*p. 185*] they behaved justly in both respects yet you killed them for no reason and unjustly,[1] so we shall revere even more their holy bones."

The chief-executioner said to him: "I said earlier that you are a very rebellious person. It has now become quite clear that you are involved in all their crimes."

Abraham said: "In what crime?"

The chief-executioner said: "First in the death of the magi, and then in all the other things."

Abraham said: "That is not only our responsibility but [occurred] in regular order and in accordance with your laws. The kings give you an order and you carry it out through your servants."

The chief-executioner said: "I swear by the god Mihr,[2] you speak more stubbornly than your teachers. It is clear that you are even more criminal.[3] So it is not right for you to escape death unless you worship the sun and perform what our religion demands."

Khorēn said: "Up to now you were uttering slanders like a man, but now you are uselessly barking like a dog.[4] If the sun had ears you would be insulting it. But by nature it is without sensation, and you in your cruelty are more unfeeling than it. In what respect did you regard us as inferior to our fathers? Do you not wish to test us by words? But make a review[5] of your wickedness and our goodness, and your father Satan[6] will be put to shame—not only by us who are the more perfect but also by him who seems to you the least, and the latter will inflict severe wounds on your soul and body."[7]

When the chief-executioner heard this he was greatly enraged against them. [*p. 186*] He had them dragged about

---

9. *Untoward: dzakholaki,* "sinister," cf. p. 8, n. 2.

1. *For no reason and unjustly:* as on p. 81, n. 11.
2. For Mihr see p. 32, n. 1.
3. *Criminal: vnasakar;* see p. 153, n. 1.
4. For the theme of insults to the judge see Delehaye, *Passions,* pp. 191–192.
5. *Review:* as on p. 15, n. 5.
6. Cf. p. 171, n. 3.
7. Cf. p. 16, n. 6.

more cruelly than the previous [martyrs]. And so severely did they pull them around that many supposed they had died.

But after three hours had passed, the two of them began to speak again, saying: "This indignity we regard as minor, and the pains of the body as nothing compared to the great love of God in which our spiritual fathers were martyred. Come now, do not hesitate or linger; but what you did to them, carry out the same on us.[1] If their deeds seem very wicked to you, reckon ours doubly so; for they gave orders in words, but we brought them to fruition by deeds." Then he was even more enraged against them and ordered them to be bastinadoed to death. For each of them six of the executioners took turns. And while they were lying half-dead on the ground, he ordered the ears of them both to be cut off close; and they hacked them off[2] as if they had never been there.

Recovering from these severe torments as if from sleep, they began to offer supplications, saying: "We beg you, valiant soldier of the king, either put us to death like our fathers, or inflict your punishments following the example of these most recent [martyrs]. For behold our ears have received a heavenly healing and our noses are still in place during these tortures. Do not deprive us of half that heavenly blessing. Sanctify our bodies by dragging them and our ears by cutting them off; sanctify also our noses by removing them. For as much as you render us ugly in an earthly fashion, the more beautiful you make us in a heavenly fashion."

The chief-executioner replied mildly: "If I remain any longer beside you I think that you will teach me your obstinacy. So now I shall reveal to you the king's intentions. Only thus far was it ordered to punish you; as further punishment [*p. 187*] you are to go to Asorestan to be slaves on the royal [estates],[1] lest anyone on seeing you may persist in the same obstinate opposition to the king's orders."

The blessed ones said to him: "You have left our land half-tilled.[2] We will not cultivate[3] the royal land with half our bodies."

1. For the eagerness of martyrs cf. Agathangelos, §100. Compare the chagrin of those who fail to be martyred, as on pp. 187, 195.
2. *Hacked off: brets'in,* as in Judg. 16:21 of Samson's eyes being put out.

1. *Slaves . . . estates: mshak yark'unis,* see p. 183, n. 5.
2. *Half-tilled: kisagorts;* for the agricultural sense of *gortsel* cf. Gen. 2:5; for a different sense see p. 33, n. 2.
3. *Cultivate: vastakel;* for this sense cf. John 4:38. The noun *vastak* is

When the executioner heard this, he called the soldiers who were leading them and said: "Merely take them away from here. When you reach Asorestan let them go wherever they wish."

These were the eminent Armenian confessors, who had joyfully accepted mutilation[4] and tortures. But because they had been deprived of a holy death they went their long journey in mourning and sadness. The chains on their feet and hands did not seem as heavy to them as the question of why they had not been worthy to equal the brave martyrs.

After they had been brought to Babylonia, to a province called Shahuḷ,[5] although they were the object of royal punishment, nonetheless both openly and secretly they were greatly honored by the inhabitants of the country. However, the blessed ones at this too were greatly saddened as if supposing "we have labored little and are taking much ease." And they continually felt the same regrets.

There they endeavored to see the holy bonds of the nobles and to serve their bodily needs. This they indicated to the magnates of the land who belonged to the same holy covenant of Christianity. All agreed, the greatest and the least, to inform the whole land that all who so desired could share[6] with the holy prisoners in distant exile[7] by [caring for] their bodily needs.

Thus they gathered year by year according to each person's ability, one a little, another much, what people had ready to hand, be it dirhems or dahekans;[8] [these] they collected and gave to the blessed ones [*p. 188*] to take to them. And in this fashion they ministered until ten years of service were completed.

Because they were strictly guarded in that torrid country

---

often used by Eḷishē in the sense of military and other (nonlaboring) services performed by the Armenians for the shah; e.g., pp. 11, 42.

4. *Mutilation: kheḷutʿiwn;* as in Lev. 22:25 and 24:20 of blemished offerings and damage to a man.

5. *Shahuḷ:* Shapukh in *B* and Shahoḷ in *Ē; Shapʿul* or *Shabul* in Ḷazar, p. 106[8]. Identified by Ter-Minasean with "Shapur" (Bishapur in the province of Fars?).

6. *Share: ktsʿord,* reminiscent of Rom. 8:17, sharing in Christ's sufferings; or 2 Cor. 1:7, in Paul's sufferings.

7. *In distant exile: i heṙawor awtarutʿean;* see p. 132, n. 1.

8. *Dirhems, dahekans: dram, dahekan.* For *dahekan* see p. 23, n. 8. The *dram* was equivalent to 4.25 grams of silver; see Nyberg, *Manual* II, s.v. *drahm.* So Eḷishē picks up "little, much" by referring to silver and then to gold coins.

and were continually on the move through that same Shahuḷ, and through Meshov and Kashkar[1] and all Asorestan and Khuzhastan, afflicted by the great heat, Saint Khorēn died from the scorching [wind][2] and was buried by the inhabitants of the land with the holy martyrs.

But the blessed Abraham ceaselessly continued the same life of virtue. He went around collecting all the gifts of the faithful, brought them to far distant parts, and distributed them himself according to individual needs. This he continued doing until the twelfth year[3] of their condemnation[4] with the result that all unanimously begged him to agree to go to Armenia, so that when he came among [the Armenians] they might see in him the brave champions[4] who had been martyred by the sword, and they might see in him also the holy chains of their tortures.

When the martyrs and confessors and prisoners were seen in him, through him the whole country was blessed. Through him their children were blessed as they grew up; through him their youths were rendered discreet[5] and pure; through him their old men became modest and wise; through him their princes learned benevolence; through him mercy fell from God into the heart of the king to make the whole land prosperous and peaceful.[6] In him the churches gloried as in a brave and perfect warrior,[7] by him the martyrs' shrines were adorned, and in him the martyrs delighted and rejoiced.[8] Through him the plain of Avarayr[9] was gloriously bedecked with flowers[10]—not by the rain-bringing clouds, but by the holy [*p. 189*] martyrs who had shed their blood and scattered their white, sacred bones. When the confessor's much-enduring feet walked over

1. Meshov is Meshan in southern Mesopotamia; see Marquart, *Erānšahr,* pp. 40–42. Kashkar is the modern Wāsit; ibid., pp. 21, 142.

2. *Scorching: khorshak,* which in the Bible is generally associated with a burning wind.

3. *Twelfth year:* lit. "twelfth year of the condemned ones" (*patzhaworats'n*). The length of their imprisonment was nine years and six months (p. 194), plus further delays (p. 199) lasting until the fifth year of Peroz: i.e., 463/4, which makes twelve years from the defeat in 451.

4. *Champions: nahatak,* see p. 5, n. 2.

5. Cf. Rom. 13:13; 1 Pet. 4:7.

6. *Prosperous and peaceful: shinel ew khaḷaḷut'iwn aṙnel;* cf. p. 124, n. 2.

7. Cf. 2 Tim. 2:3.

8. Cf. 1 Pet. 4:13.

9. This is the only ref. in Eḷishē to the precise site of the battle. On p. 100, n. 4 he merely refers to the plain of Artaz.

10. As on p. 119, n. 1.

the extensive site of the battle, although the ground remained in its natural state, yet when the living martyr walked across it the living came to the living and the whole land came to life once more.[1]

"We know," they said, "that when all the monks[2] of Armenia see him, through him they will recall the spiritual ranks of warriors[3] who gave themselves to death for our sake and spilled their blood as a propitiatory sacrifice[4] to God. Through him they will remember the holy priests who were slain in foreign lands and appeased the wrathful anger of the king.[5] Through him perhaps they will also remember our bonds, and in their prayers will ask God that we may return from captivity[6] to our native land.

"For we are extremely anxious, not merely for our bodily wants, but more especially to see[7] our holy churches and pious ministers that we have established there. And if God will favor us once more to go and fulfill the needs of the survivors, we know that God will also open for us the door of his mercy, that [we] may follow the same path previously trodden by the feet of this saint."

With these thoughts in mind, the inspired nobles, after much entreating, brought the confessor to agreement. Since he had never had the habit of opposing the good, on this occasion too he hastened to fulfill immediately the command of those unanimously [*p. 190*] agreed on divine virtue. So he came to the land of Greater Armenia.

Straightway there made haste to meet him men and women, the greatest and the least, all the multitude of nobles and peasants.[1] Falling down before the saint they embraced his

1. This paragraph, with its repetition of "through him" (*novaw*) and the numerous blessings, is modeled on *Vkayk'*, pp. 142–143, a eulogy after the death of Saint Shmavon.

2. *Monks: miaynakeats'*, which could also mean "hermits"; see p. 22, n. 12.

3. *Warriors: paterazmol;* see p. 70, n. 4.

4. *Propitiatory sacrifice: i hashtut'iwn patarag*, reminiscent of numerous passages in Paul's epistles; cf. also p. 177, n. 3.

5. *Appeased ... anger: ts'atsoyts zsrtmtut'iwn;* cf. Num. 25:11 of Pinehas who turned away God's anger. For Pinehas, see p. 108 above.

6. *Return from captivity: geradardz.* Although the theme is common, this particular word is reminiscent of 2 Macc. 10:1 of Maccabeus recovering Jerusalem.

7. *Extremely anxious, to see: yoyzh andzkats'eal, tesanel;* as in Phil. 2:26.

1. See p. 52, n. 6.

feet and hands, saying: "Blessed be the Lord God on high who has sent us this angel from heaven to bring us the news of the Resurrection, so that we may become heirs of the kingdom.[2] For behold we see figured in you all those who have departed in hope of the Resurrection and those imprisoned in the expectation of release. In you we see the restoration of our land in peace; in you our churches take delight and joy; and through you our holy martyrs will be ceaselessly interceding before God. Bless us, our holy father. You are the mouth of the dead; speak with us in open blessing that we may hear secretly in our souls the blessings of the saints.

"You have opened the path[3] for those who are longing to return to their land. Beg God that they may quickly follow your holy lead. And just as you opened the road closed on earth, open also in heaven the gate for our prayers, so that the supplications of us sinners may enter before God in intercession for those same prisoners. And while we are in this impermanent body, as we have seen your blessed sanctity, so may we—who have long been oppressed and beset in our souls and bodies— also see our dear loved ones.[4] We believe with infallible hope that just as we finally were granted the sight of your holy love, so also we may soon be able to see the true martyrs of Christ, as we are continuously desirous[5] to behold their heavenly beauty."

[*p. 191*] But although the blessed confessor was received by the whole country in such a loving fashion, he did not wish to approach anyone at all for any bodily need; but he chose for himself a place away from all the press of the crowd, and with three virtuous brethren lived out his life in great austerity.

If anyone wished to set out coherently his life of virtue, only with difficulty could he describe it. For if you were to mention his vigils: he spent all his nights like an unextinguished lamp. If [you mention] the frugality of his diet, consider that he resembled the angels, who eat no food. If you wished to describe his mildness and humility, you would not be able to find any living person to compare with him. And if you wished to speak of his indifference to possessions, again just as a

2. Cf. 1 Cor. 6:9.
3. Cf. Isa. 57:14.
4. *Dear loved ones: sireli andzkalisn*, cf. Phil. 4:1.
5. *Desirous: khandakat'*, as in Song of Sol. 2:5 of desiring (spiritual) beauty.

dead man is not seduced by wealth, the same you must truly understand of that blessed one.

With tireless voice he was assiduous at worship; with unceasing prayers he was always conversing with God on high. He was salt for the insipid[1] and a spurring goad for the sluggish. Avarice was condemned by him, and drunken gluttony[2] severely reprimanded. He was a source of healing for Armenia, and many [who were] hurt secretly found health through him. He was a perfect instructor for his teachers, and a holy advising father for his fathers. At the report of his fame the ignorant became wise, and at the close sight of him the licentious became chaste. In the flesh he lived in a narrow cell,[3] and awe of his sanctity fell on those far and near. Demons were terrified and fled from him; angels descended and dwelt around him.

The Greeks blessed Armenia for his sake, and many barbarians [*p. 192*] hastened to see him in the flesh. He was dear to God's beloved, and many enemies of the truth[1] he brought to accept [God's] holy love. Right from his youthful years he had made a beginning of his virtuous life, and in the same virtue he ended his days. Just as he had not participated in the earthly institution of holy matrimony, so he did not become involved in any corruptible matters of this world for bodily needs. If it is necessary to speak plainly—just as he exchanged the needs of the body for necessary spiritual things, so he was transferred from earth to heaven.

THE NAMES OF THE PRINCES WHO FOR THE LOVE OF CHRIST GAVE THEMSELVES WITH READY WILLINGNESS TO IMPRISONMENT BY THE KING

From the house of Siunik': the two brothers Babgēn and Bakur[1]

1. Cf. Matt. 5:13 and parallels.
2. *Drunken gluttony: shuaytut'iwn orkoramolut'ean*, a conflate of Luke 11:34 and Prov. 28:7.
3. *Cell: khts'ik*, as of Daniel in Faustos, III, 14.
4. Cf. Matt. 4:11, after the temptation of Jesus.

---

1. Cf. p. 56, n. 7.

---

1. The following list is based on Lazar, p. 86, with the following variations: Lazar has *N*ershapuh (Artsruni); Eḷishē adds Nerseh and Ashot (Kamsarakan), Zuarēn (Andzevats'i); Eḷishē has Ṙap'sonean (with numer-

From the house of the Artsrunik': Mershapuh, Shavasp, Shngin, Mehruzhan, Pargev, and Tachat

From the house of the Mamikonean: Hamazaspean, Hamazasp, Artavazd, and Mushel

From the house of the Kamsarakan: Arshavir, T'at', Vardz, Nerseh, and Ashot

From the house of the Amatunik': Vahan, Arandzar, and Arnak

From the house of the Gnunik': Atom

From the house of the Dimak'sean: T'at'ul and Satoy, with two other companions

From the house of the Andzevatsik': Shmavon, Zuarēn, and Dat

From the family of the Artsrunik': Aprsam

From the family of the Mandakunik': Sahak and P'arsman

From the house of the Tashrats'ik': Vrēn

[*p. 194*] From the family of the Rap'sonean: Babik and Yohan

Of these thirty-five men, some were from the upper nobility and some from the lesser;[1] but they were all princes by birth and all citizens of heaven by spiritual virtue. And there were many other nobles, some from the royal house, others from these same princely houses, fellow warriors[2] and companions-in-arms[3] of the valiant champions. All of these willingly gave themselves up to holy bonds and torture.

Now we are not merely astonished at the fact that they willingly went to be tested, but we are more especially amazed that genteel[4] men like them, raised to dwell at liberty in snowy mountains, became inhabitants of torrid[5] plains. Those who like free deer used to roam flowering mountains were cast into the blazing land of the East, bound hand and foot. [Their food was] the bread of affliction, [their drink] the water of want;[6] they were locked in the dark by day and deprived of light by

---

ous variants in the MSS) for the more usual Rop'sean in Lazar. For this family see Toumanoff, *Studies,* p. 213, and for the Araveleank', ibid., p. 199. The other families have all been mentioned earlier in Elishē's *History.*

1. *Upper, lesser: awag, krseragoyn;* see p. 16, n. 9.
2. *Fellow warriors: nizakakits';* see p. 101, n. 6.
3. *Companions-in-arms: martakits',* cf. Josh. 1:14.
4. *Genteel: p'ap'uk;* see p. 67, n. 9 and p. 124, n. 9.
5. *Torrid: khorshak;* as on p. 188, n. 2.
6. Cf. Isa. 30:20.

night; without covers or beds they slept like animals on the ground[7] for nine years and six months.[8] Yet they endured tribulations so joyfully that no one ever heard a murmur[9] of blasphemy from their mouths but only continuous thanksgiving[10] like that of happy men worshiping God.

While they were in such dire straits, the thought came to the king's mind that in their great affliction they would have become weary of their bitter existence. So he sent the great *hazarapet*[11] to them, saying: "At least from now on come to your senses and do not persist in that same obstinacy. [*p. 195*] Worship the sun and you will be freed from your cruel bonds and each of you will again possess your ancestral properties."[1]

The blessed ones replied: "Have you come to question us in order to test us, or did the king really send you?" The *hazarapet* swore, saying: "There is not a word more here or a word less than what came from his mouth." Then they said to him: "Those who have once learned the truth will never deviate from it, but will remain true to themselves. Surely we did not persist then out of ignorance, and today you made us realize our afflictions. Not at all. But this is the regret in our minds—why did we not end our lives with the previous [martyrs]?[2] So now we beg you, and through you your king, do not question us any more about these matters, but carry out whatever you have decided in our case."

When the great *hazarapet* heard this, in his mind he very much praised the firmness of their conviction. From then on he began to form an affection for them as with ones loved by God. With wordy supplications he tried to persuade the king to release them from their bonds. For although he had been removed from the office of royal *hazarapet* and was found guilty of treachery on many counts[3]—he bore responsibility for the ruin of Armenia, for which he was dismissed to his home in great dishonor—nonetheless, he never wished to speak ill of the prisoners to the very last day of his life.

7. *Slept on the ground: getnakhshtirkʿ;* see p. 144, n. 11.
8. For the period of imprisonment see p. 188, n. 3.
9. *Murmur: trtunj,* as p. 142, n. 3.
10. Cf. Col. 3:16.
11. I.e., Mihrnerseh.

1. *Properties: keankʿ;* see p. 95, n. 4.
2. Cf. p. 187.
3. *Guilty of treachery on many counts: i bazum irs vnasakar;* see p. 153, n. 1, for this phrase.

Among the blessed ones, many who were very young had learned the schooling[4] of their native land; this was for them spiritual food[5] with which they encouraged themselves and consoled their companions. They were so enraptured in their minds and souls that even the eldest among them became young again like tender children. For although they had passed the age of study, [*p. 196*] yet with many psalms in their mouths they joined in the spiritual songs of the multitude of young men.

They so exalted their holy worship that some of the cruel executioners were greatly affected by the sweet sound, and as much as was in their power they offered them relief[1] beyond the king's order; they took loving care of them all and often fulfilled their material needs—especially because many miracles of healing were performed by God through them,[2] so that many afflicted by demons[3] were cleansed in that same city where the prisoners were kept. Since there was no priest among them [the citizens], the sick, and afflicted[4] of the city were brought to them and received from them healing of each one's malady.[5]

Likewise the great prince of the country, Harevshḷom Shapuh[6] by name, to whom all the condemned prisoners had been entrusted, showed great kindness and compassion[7] to them all. He treated the elder among them as fathers and cherished the younger among them as beloved sons. He frequently indicated in writing to the court the prisoners' sufferings and affliction and indicated the noble conduct of each one of them. He troubled the leading magnates and tried by all manner of devices, until through many intercessors the king was brought to agreement. He [the king] ordered their bonds to be loosed and the ordeal of their punishment to be ended; he

---

4. *Schooling: dprut'iwn*, i.e., reading and writing; cf. Koriun, p. 9 of Mashtots'. For a different meaning see above p. 31, n. 2.
5. 1 Cor. 10:3.

---

1. *Relief: diwrut'iwn*, as in Exod. 8:15 of respite from the plague of frogs.
2. Cf. pp. 16, 180.
3. *Afflicted by demons: diwahar*, common in the Gospels.
4. Cf. Luke 9:2.
5. *Malady: ts'awk'*, cf. esp. Matt. 4:24.
6. Łazar, p. 108, calls him a Jew and spells the name Hrewshnomshapuh. Cf. Faustos, IV, 37, for an earlier Persian general called Hrewshoḷum.
7. *Kindness and compassion: gut' siroy*; as in 2 Macc. 13:23 of the king receiving the Jews.

also ordered that they should put on robes of their princely rank. He established allowances[8] for them and ordered arms[9] to be provided from the treasury. He wrote to the great *sparapet,*[10] enjoining that they march to war with the royal army.

When this had been so arranged and the king's new command had been established, in the many places where they were sent they acquitted themselves so valiantly that testimonials[11] praising them were received at court. As a result [*p. 197*] the king's mind was soothed, and he ordered them all to appear before him. They arrived and presented themselves to Yazkert, king of kings. He was delighted to see them, spoke affably with them, and promised to restore to them each one's principality in accordance with his hereditary rank[1] and to send them back to their country practicing the Christian religion[2] for which they had been greatly tormented.

While they were in attendance at the royal court, at that same time the king's life came to its close in the nineteenth year of his reign.[3] His two sons opposed each other and fought for power; for two years bitter warfare raged.[4]

While they were occupied with this struggle, the king of Albania revolted. He was their nephew,[5] and following his ancestral faith had previously been a Christian; but Yazkert, king of kings, had forced him to become a magus.[6] So finding the occasion favorable, he was constrained to risk death; he reckoned it better to die in war than to rule his kingdom as an apostate.[7] This was the cause of all the delay in their [the Armenian nobles'] release and return to their country.

---

8. *Allowances: rochik,* as on p. 64, n. 1.

9. *Arms: sparazinut'iwn,* which implies full arms and armor.

10. *Saparapet:* see p. 7, n. 9.

11. *Testimonials: hrovartakk'* (letters, edicts; see p. 9, n. 10) *govut'ean* (of praise).

---

1. *Hereditary rank: hayreni patiw,* as in 2 Macc. 4:15. But there the Hellenizing Jews rejected their hereditary dignities.

2. *Practicing . . . religion:* lit. "with the religion (*awrēnk'* [see the Introduction]) of Christianity."

3. I.e., in 457.

4. During the reign of Hormizd III (457–459).

5. Moses Daskhurants'i, I, 10, following Ełishē's account of these events, adds that the king was called Vachē. He had married the daughter of Yazkert's sister, the latter being his mother; see p. 198.

6. *Magus: mog,* perhaps here merely "Zoroastrian"; cf. p. 198, where *mog* and *Christian* are contrasted.

7. For this theme cf. p. 72, n. 8.

Now the tutor of Yazkert's younger son, Ṙaham by name from the family of Mihran,[8] although he saw that the army of the Aryans was divided into two, nonetheless with one half he ferociously attacked the king's elder son. He defeated and massacred his army, and capturing the king's son ordered him to be put to death on the spot. The surviving troops he brought into submission, unifying the whole army of the Aryans. Then he crowned his own protégé,[9] who was named Peroz.[10]

Although profound peace had been brought to the land of the Aryans, [*p. 198*] the king of Albania did not wish to submit, but breached the Pass of Chor and brought through to this side the troops of the Massagetae.[1] Uniting with the eleven kings of the mountains,[2] he waged war against the Aryan army and inflicted much damage on the royal forces. Although they sent letters of entreaty two and three times, they were unable to bring him to terms. But in writing and by messages he blamed them for the pointless devastation of Armenia. He reminded them of the death of the nobles and the sufferings of the prisoners: "In return for so much devotion and service," he said, "instead of granting their lives you killed[3] them. It would be better for me to endure their tortures than to abandon Christianity."

When they saw that they had not been able to bring him to terms either by force or by kind treatment, they had much treasure taken to the land of the Khaylandurkʻ; they opened the Pass of the Alans,[4] brought through a numerous force of Huns, and warred for a year with the Albanian king. Although his troops were dispersed and scattered away from him,[5] not only were they unable to subject him but terrible afflictions befell them, some through the war and others by painful disease. So long did the blockade last that the greater part of the coun-

8. For Ṙaham see Nöldeke, *Sassaniden*, p. 139.

9. *Protégé: san;* see p. 22, n. 5, for the relationship of tutor (*dayeak*), as of Ṙaham, and protégé.

10. *Peroz:* reigned 459–484.

1. *Massagetae: Maskʻutʻkʻ;* for this identification see Toumanoff, *Studies*, p. 459, n. 98, and for the Massagetae see Marquart, *Erānšahr*, pp. 155–157.

2. See p. 94 for the eleven kingdoms.

3. *Killed: arew hatēkʻ*, lit. "cut off the sun"; cf. Faustos, V, 38: *arew shnorhel* ("to spare life") or Eznik §198, 229: *yarewē arkanel* ("to kill").

4. The Dar-i-alan.

5. *Dispersed, from him: tʻawtʻapʻetsʻan i nmanē*, as in 1 Macc. 9:7 of Judas seeing his army melting away.

try was ravaged, yet no one vacillated or deserted him.

The Persian king sent another message to him: "Have my sister and my niece sent out, for they were originally magi and you made them Christians.[6] Then your country will be yours." Now this wonderful man was not fighting for power but for piety. He sent off his mother and wife, [*p. 199*] completely renounced the world, took the Gospel,[1] and wished to leave his country.[2]

When the king heard this, he was greatly afflicted with remorse and regret and placed the blame for all the harm on his father. He sealed a solemn oath[3] and had it brought to him, to this effect: "Only do not leave your country and I shall do what you say." He requested the property of his youth, for when he was young his father had granted him a thousand houses.[4] This he received from the king, and there he settled with the monks. In such fashion he spent all his time in divine worship, never recalling that he had previously been a king.

All these prolonged troubles, which lasted until the fifth year of Peroz,[5] king of kings, were the reason for the Armenian nobles not being released. But he greatly increased their allowances and their attendance at court[6] above the custom of [previous] years.

In that same fifth year he restored to many of them their properties and held out the hope to others that in the sixth year they would all be finally released [in possession of] their property and rank.

But I must return to that another time.[7]

As for the wives of the blessed heroes and prisoners and of

---

6. See above, p. 197, nn. 5, 6.

1. *The Gospel:* see Lampe, *Lexicon*, s.v. εὐαγγέλιον, D9 for the "Gospel" as a way of life—not necessarily monastic.

2. *His country:* the use of *ashkharh* is ambiguous, as it can refer to one's land or this earthly life (as opposed to heaven or hell). It seems fairly clear that "renounced the world" (*ashkharhn*) refers to the second, "to leave the country" refers to the first; see the following paragraph.

3. See p. 41, n. 3.

4. *Houses: erd,* as in Exod. 12:3: οἰκία. For the term cf. Agathangelos, §837, where it refers to land, and Faustos, IV, 55, for the expression *tun erd,* referring to the nine thousand Jewish families. For a different meaning of *erd* see p. 144, n. 8.

5. I.e., 463/4.

6. *Attendance at court: i tachar mtanel,* lit. "entrance to the palace."

7. Is this statement rhetorical? Cf. the unfulfilled promises of a similar nature in Moses Khorenats'i, I, 4, n. 9; I, 12, n. 21; III, 67, n. 7.

those who fell in the war, I could not fully number them throughout the land of Armenia, for there are many more whom I do not know than those whom I do.[8] [*p. 200*] I am personally[1] acquainted with five hundred, not only older [women] but many of the younger generation.[2]

All of them without exception exhibited a heavenly zeal,[3] appearing no different from those who have not experienced the world. For if some were older and some younger, yet they were clothed with a single virtuous faith.[4] They did not at all recall the memory of the comfort[5] of their matronly[6] nobility, but like laboring men used to peasant[7] tasks they endured the toils of country life, and even more than their husbands accepted and sustained such labors.

Not only in the spirit were they consoled by the invisible power of the hope of eternity,[8] but in the tribulations of the body they bore even more [easily] their heavy load.[9] For although they each had their domestic[10] servants, none could be distinguished among them as being mistress or maid.[11] All wore the same clothing and both alike slept on the ground.[12] No one made another's bed,[13] for they did not distinguish one's straw

8. *I do: gitits'em;* the subjunctive may have the force of "I *could* know."

1. *Personally:* as on p. 42, n. 11.
2. *Older, younger: awagagoynk', krseragoynk';* used of age or rank, see p. 16, n. 9. In what follows Eḷishē sometimes emphasizes age, sometimes rank.
3. The theme of heavenly zeal and the equality of old and young is paralleled in Philo, *De Vita Contemplativa,* pp. 25–26 of the Armenian text of the 1892 ed., and Conybeare, pp. 174–175. Ter-Minasean's ed. reads *erkrawor* (earthly) for *erknawor* (heavenly), which must be a printer's error.
4. Cf. 1 Thess, 5:8.
5. *Comfort: p'ap'kut'iwn,* see p. 124, n. 9.
6. *Matronly: mayreni,* with an emphasis on their ancestry, *mayreni* being the female equivalent of *hayreni,* a frequent expression in Eḷishē generally translated as "ancestral." Cf. the *hayreni awrēnk'* discussed in the Introduction.
7. *Peasant: shinakan,* in direct contrast to their *azatut'iwn* (nobility); see p. 52, n. 6.
8. Cf. Titus 1:2; 3:7.
9. Cf. Ps. 37:5.
10. *Domestic: dzeṙnasun,* as of Vasak's servants, p. 139; used in Agathangelos, §131, of clients of the Arsacid family.
11. *Mistress or maid: tikin, nazhisht;* a frequent contrast in the books of Esther and Judith.
12. *On the ground: getnakhshtik',* see p. 144, n. 11.
13. *Make a bed: ankoḷnark,* lit. "bed-thrower," hence the ref. to straw; cf. 1 Kings 9:25.

from another's. Their mats[14] were the same shade of gray; their pillows[15] the same shade of black.

They had no confectioners[16] for individual delicacies nor separate bakers to serve them in accordance with their noble rank, but they shared all they had. The Friday evening [fast][17] they observed like solitaries[18] who dwell in the deserts. [*p. 201*] No one poured water over another's hands; the younger did not offer the older towels. The delicate women did not use soap, nor were they offered oil for merry feasting. Immaculate dishes were not set before them, nor plates[1] for jollity. No butler[2] stood at their door, and no illustrious men were invited to their homes. Nor did they have any recollection of who was one of their domestic nurses[3] and who one of their dear relations.

The hangings and bed curtains of the newly married brides became dusty and sooty;[4] spiders' webs were spun in their nuptial chambers. The chairs of honor in their houses were destroyed; the vessels for their banquets were broken. Their palaces crumbled and fell; the fortresses of their refuge were demolished and razed. Their flower gardens dried up and turned to sand; the wine-bearing stocks of their vineyards were uprooted.[5]

With their own eyes they saw the ravaging of their property; with their own ears they heard the torments and sufferings of their dear ones. Their treasures were confiscated by the court, and there remained no ornaments at all for their faces.[6]

---

14. *Mats: p'siray*, derived from ψίαθος, a rush mat.

15. *Pillows: snark' bardzits'; snar* is the head of the bed, cf. John 20:12; *bardz* is a cushion or pillow, cf. Mark 4:38.

16. *Confectioners: khakhamok'* (*khahamok'* in *A*), elsewhere attested to only in Philo (according to the *Nor Bargirk'*). For the root see Hübschmann, *Grammatik*, p. 160.

17. *Friday evening (fast): shabat'amut.*

18. *Solitaries: miaynakeats';* see p. 22, n. 12.

---

1. *Plates: bazhanakal*, "which holds a portion," a hapax.

2. *Butler: nuirak*, the translation of ῥαβδοῦχος in Acts 16:35, 38. Cf. Faustos, IV, 35, for the *nuirakapet* named Zig.

3. *Domestic nurses: bnakasun* (cf. *dzeṙnasun*, p. 200, n. 10) *dayeak*, here in the feminine sense; see p. 22, n. 5.

4. This is based on the lament in 1 Macc. 1:25–28 after Antiochus robs the temple (bed-curtains, brides). For the hangings and bed-curtains (*srahak, srskapan*) cf. Faustos, IV, 20, of the booty abandoned by Arshak.

5. *Uprooted: tashtakhil*, a hapax.

6. Cf. Isa. 3:20.

The delicate women of Armenia, who had been cossetted and pampered[7] in their litters[8] and sedan-chairs,[9] regularly attended the houses of prayer without shoes and on foot,[10] begging with tireless entreaties that they might be able to endure their great tribulation. Those who from their childhood had been raised on the marrow[11] of steers and the dainty parts of game, most joyfully ate grass, living like wild animals[12] and not at all mindful of their accustomed luxury. The skin of their bodies turned black[13] in color, for by day they were burned by the sun, and the whole night they lay on the ground.

[*p. 202*] Psalms were perpetually murmured on their lips; and readings from the prophets were their supreme consolation.[1] They were joined in couples like willing and equal yoked pairs, plowing straight the furrow[2] of the kingdom so that they might arrive at the haven[3] of peace without losing their way.

They forgot their feminine weakness and became men heroic at spiritual warfare. Waging war with the gravest sins, they struck away and cut out their deadly roots. By sincerity they overcame deceit;[4] and by holy love they cleansed the livid stains of jealousy.[5] They extirpated the roots of avarice; and the mortal fruits of its branches dried up.[6] By humility they smote pride;[7] and by the same humility they attained the heights of heaven. By their prayers they opened the closed gates of heaven;[8] and by their pious supplications brought down angels for salvation. From afar they heard the good news; and they glorified God on high.

7. Cf. Lam. 4:5.

8. *Litters: bastem*, from the Greek βαστέρνιον.

9. *Sedan-chairs: gahaworak*, the translation of φορεῖον in Song of Sol. 3:9.

10. *Without shoes and on foot:* see p. 81, n. 3.

11. *Marrow: ułeł*, also used of "brains."

12. *Grass, animals:* as on p. 124, n. 13, with parallels in 2 Macc. 5:27.

13. Cf. Job 30:30, from heat. The same epithet is applied to Gregory on his emergence from the pit, Agathangelos, §217.

1. Cf. p. 125, n. 1.

2. For this imagery see Lampe, *Lexicon,* s.v. αὖλαξ, and Murray, *Symbols,* pp. 195ff.

3. Cf. Agathangelos, §1, 3, and Hambye, "Symbol of Coming to Harbour."

4. Cf. 2 Cor. 11:3.

5. Cf. 1 Pet. 2:1.

6. Cf. Hos. 9:16.

7. Cf. 2 Cor. 12:20.

8. Cf. p. 154.

The widows among them became second brides of virtue,[9] removing from themselves the opprorium of widowhood. The wives of the prisoners willingly chained the desires of the flesh and shared the torments[10] of the holy prisoners; in their lifetimes they resembled the valiant martyrs in their death, and from afar became consoling teachers for the imprisoned. With their own fingers they toiled[11] and sustained themselves; the stipend allotted them from the treasury they made their yearly allowance[12] and had it brought to them for consolation. They resembled bloodless grasshoppers who exist without food by the sweetness of their song and live by merely breathing the air, exhibiting the likeness of the incorporeal beings.[13]

The ice of many winters melted; spring arrived and the [*p. 203*] returning swallows came again.[1] Life-loving mortals saw this and rejoiced, but they were never able to see their desired ones. Spring flowers recalled their faithful[2] husbands; their eyes longed to behold the dear beauty of their faces. Hunting dogs[3] were no more, and the chase of the hunters was silenced. They were recalled only by commemoration,[4] and no yearly festival brought them back from afar. They looked at their places at the table and wept; in every hall[5] they remembered their names. Many columns[6] were set up in their memory, and the names of each one were inscribed thereon.

9. For brides of Christ see Lampe, *Lexicon*, s.v. νύμφη, B.

10. Cf. Rom. 8:17; 2 Cor. 1:7.

11. *Toiled: vastakets'in;* see p. 187, n. 3 and n. 2 above for this agricultural imagery.

12. *Allowances: t'oshak;* see p. 21, n. 1. Eḷishē implies that the women sent their own allowances to their imprisoned husbands.

13. This image of grasshoppers (*chpuŕn*) is from Philo, *De Vita Contemplativa*, p. 15 of the 1892 ed., Conybeare, p. 165.

1. For this theme cf. *Teaching*, §655–656.

2. *Faithful: psakasēr,* lit. "crown-loving." This combines the ideas of martyrdom and of the bridal crown; for both themes see Lampe, *Lexicon*, s.v. στέφανος. For bridal crowns cf. *Kanonagirk' I*, 170.

3. *Hunting-dogs: barak;* see Zekiyan, "Barak." Cf. also Agathangelos, §211.

4. *Recalled by commemoration: bnagrawk' yishatakets'an;* for this use of *bnagir* as a liturgical commemoration see Gat'rchean, *Pataragamatoyts'k'*, p. 102, n. 3, and for *yishatak* cf. p. 140[4].

5. *Hall: atean,* which can also mean the space in church in front of the bema.

6. *Columns: ardzan;* see Khatchatrian, "Monuments funéraires," for these significant features of Armenian architecture.

Although their minds were thus agitated[7] from every side, they did not lose heart or slacken in heavenly virtue.[8] To strangers they appeared as mourning and suffering widows, but in their souls they were adorned and consoled with heavenly love.[9]

No more were they accustomed to ask a visitor from afar: "When shall we be able to see our dear ones?" But the desire of their prayers to God was that, as they had begun, so they might be able valiantly to complete [their course] full of heavenly love.

And may we and they together inherit the city of blessings and attain the promises made to those who love God in Christ Jesus our Lord.[10]

7. *Agitated: alēkots;* storm imagery is dear to Ełishē; for this word cf. pp. 44, 152.

8. Ełishē returns to his basic theme; see p. 14.

9. Cf. Matt. 5:4.

10. A conflate of Rom. 1:7; 1 Cor. 2:9; and Heb. 11:16.

Appendix
Bibliography
Indexes
Map

Appendix

The Armenian War According to Lazar P'arpets'i

ONE other early Armenian historian also describes in some detail the revolt against the Sasanian shah led by Vardan, the Armenian defeat in 451, and the subsequent fate of the nobles and clergy imprisoned in Iran. These events take up about one third of the *History* of Lazar P'arpets'i, written around A.D. 500. Lazar's main interest is in the decades that followed these disasters, when his patron Vahan Mamikonean (Vardan's nephew) rose to preeminence and was eventually appointed governor of Armenia by the shah Valarsh in 484. Since Lazar's *History* has never been translated into English, it seemed worthwhile to offer here a rendering of the section relevant to Vardan, for Lazar's interpretation of the war is often at variance with Eḷishē's. The differences have been discussed in the Introduction to this book.

A full study of Lazar's *History* lies outside the scope of this work. But it is important to note that the Armenian text as it has come down to us (and as translated here) does not accurately represent the original version; fragments earlier than the surviving manuscripts have recently been discovered. (See Dowsett and Sanspeur in the Bibliography.) These fragments do not betray any clear motivation for the rewriting of Lazar's *History,* which took place between the twelfth and fifteenth centuries, though the later version is more verbose. I have not attempted to annotate my translation of Lazar, but offer it in the hope that it will make various comments in my Introduction more easily verifiable by those who do not read classical Armenian.

SECTION II

20. The *hazarapet* of King Yazkert was a certain Mihrnerseh by name, a malicious and evil-minded man, who for many years had meditated on impious plans for the destruction and ruin of weak souls. He had as a wicked and insidious ally in his impious, poisonous and long-standing scheme a man from the family of Siunik', called Varazvaḷan. Just as Satan in paradise by means of the serpent deceived the companion of the first-created, likewise through him [Varazvaḷan] he endeavored to accomplish the pleasure of his own cruel will. This Varazvaḷan was the son-in-law of the prince of Siunik', Vasak. According to some people's report there existed great hatred between Varazvaḷan and the daughter of the prince of Siunik', for which reason the girl's father regarded his son-in-law with great resentment and attempted to venge the insult to his daughter by murder. Eventually he expelled him from Armenia.

The malevolent Varazvaḷan, knowing of Vasak's relentless anger and being unable to endure his father-in-law's severe tyranny because of the mighty haughtiness he displayed during his rule as prince, fled to Persia and took refuge with Mihrnerseh, *hazarapet* of the Aryans. Immediately he conceived a diabolical plan, becoming the author of our country's destruction, for he knew the willing interest of Mihrnerseh in that wicked plan. The impious project involved an alliance with the devil; he denied the truth and worshiped the elements established by the Creator for the service of mankind—the sun and moon. With willing alacrity he separated himself from the holy and righteous preaching of life—which the martyr and apostle to Armenia Gregory, enduring many strenuous labors, by indefatigable prayers and perpetual supplications night and day, had taught and implanted in every soul; [this] the impious Varazvaḷan despised and rejected. Entering the house of ashes, [*p. 40*] he declared the fire to be god, denied the indivisible and consubstantial Holy Trinity, and with the impious Mihrnerseh became an apothecary of death and cupbearer of destruction for the souls of all weak-minded persons. Thereafter the merciless prince Mihrnerseh became the teacher of the impure young noble of Siunik', Varazvaḷan, instructing him tirelessly day and night: "Look with your mind's eye and see such a kingdom [as this] which is more fearsome than, and superior to, all [other] kingdoms. Look at the power of its cavalry and discipline and its military equipment, which intimidate and overawe all who see and hear of them, both subjects and those not subject. Look likewise at the distinction, infallibility, and splendor of the religion that is clearly worthy of this great kingdom. For who in the whole world does not see the glory of the sun by whose rays are illuminated all creatures rational and irrational, or the usefulness of fire, which gives nourishment and enjoyment to all men? Thereby the elements and the blowing of the temperate breezes cause plants and seeds to ripen and be brought to maturity, thus offering to mankind a good livelihood and joy. Now, although those [Armenians] are not subject to us, they see all this and do not understand, for they do not possess such great comprehension as do we or such wise intelligence. And because they have been unable to recognize the deities of such [as us] or the advantages which are distributed by each of the gods to mankind, it is truly clear that the gods, angered, did not desire to make these fools aware of the distinctive blessings which are bestowed on the world by each one. But those nations that are subject to our great power and governed by such a fearsome and strong hand are destroyed forever while we, blamed by the gods, will be punished."

When the insane pupil Varazvaḷan heard this senseless teaching of his deceitful teacher Mihrnerseh, he was unable to recover from the folly of his possessed and perplexed mind or reply to his irrational teacher: "How could a god who is lacking and incomplete in himself grant to another a request for such perfection? For someone can give to a suppliant his possessions; while someone who possesses nothing of his own but has, as it were, a part of more parts that he has received from another, can give from that part whatever he has. But what he does not possess himself it is clear he cannot bestow on another. For if someone, burnt by heat, needs coolness and yet when offered it seeks it still from heat, he does not obtain his request; such a seeker is recognized by everyone to be very foolish and ridiculous. For that same seeker knows very well what his desire needs, [*p. 41*] but the one from whom he wishes to ask it does not possess it nor is he able to give it. If he ask such a one with many entreaties and long importuning, he is foolish and full of regret; as if one were to seek dryness from water, or one were to look for humidity from fire, or one were to beg the sun for cool-

253

ing, or one were to demand light from the night. But they keep the portions allotted them by God, keeping that limit and providing according to each one's portion; they are forced increasingly to administer to the world, not of each one's own will, but in accordance with the command of their Creator, who is the true God, Creator of all being—of time and matter, warmth and cold, dryness and humidity, light and darkness, who holds in himself everything completely. To those who request of him in a worthy manner he gives, fulfilling everything according to each one's needs and desires."

All this the impious Varazvalan had learned from his youth and knew well. But plunged into base rancor against his father-in-law, the renegade reflected in his mind—prompted by the colluding demon who was present in his heart: "This plan, effort, and undertaking of mine will render me two benefits. On the one hand, if Armenia agrees to apostatize I shall be blest with great gifts and honors from the Aryans as a trustworthy instigator and assistant in such an important and serious matter. On the other hand, if the [Armenians] do not accept but oppose it, they cannot resist such a great force and will perish completely with their families and property. Perhaps my own enemy will also perish in this affair. And even if I attain no other benefit, nonetheless the news and sight of my enemy's destruction will be more satisfying for me than all the lucre and wealth in the world."

Divine Providence was not unaware of all these wicked thoughts that the lawless noble of Siunik' and his son had pondered in their hearts and brought to a head. They first received from the just Judge, God, recompense commensurate with their deeds here below, for he became an object of derision to his own family and the people of the province. By his fellow conspirator, his demon, he was tormented for many years in front of all with daily ridicule; rolling on the ground he foamed uncontrollably, unable to say: "I have sinned." So the demon, having found that man entirely void of human mercy, then tormented him with severe and terrible ignominies for a long time, and strangled him. He left to his offspring the remnants of his fetid and decaying victuals, according to the saying in the sixteenth psalm: "They were sated with food—which another translator calls pork—and left the remnants to their children." Thus, having received here the punishment for his sins, he was preserved [*p. 42*] for the unquenchable fire in Tartarus, to enter the eternal and unceasing furnace. Thereby there began gradually to become clear the earlier prophetic vision of the holy martyr Gregory that was revealed to him by God: the fountain of life in which the flocks of black goats washed and turned into the color of white fleeced sheep and appeared shining like the sun. Half of those who were washed turned back on their heels, passed through the water, and changing from the likeness of white lambs took on the black color of wolves; they attacked the lambs and butchered them. Just as these in the earlier vision of the saint turned from lambs to wolves, so did this man from the family of Siunik' become the cause for the destruction of many and the ruin of Armenia.

21. When the impious Mihrnerseh heard all this he was overjoyed, for he had found a venomous assistant and promulgator for his perverted and wicked plans, the devilish Varazvaḷan. Joyfully entering the presence of King Yazkert, he began to speak with him separately, saying: "Not only for profitable advantages—how it is proper for lords to benefit from their servants—not only for this must lords concern themselves, but they must also consider the salvation of souls, so that the servants' souls do not perish. For just as you are busied with your profits and taxes to benefit therefrom, so too the gods value even more enthusiastically and desire to see the salvation of souls. And to do the gods justice, no one can describe the gifts and honors which are heaped on such a man by the gods—and especially if someone saves many souls from error, brings them to the [right] path, and deflects maledictions from the just. The glory and splendor which are consigned to such souls from the gods, no one can indicate, describe, or set down. So how many countries are there over which you rule like a god? Those you wish to destroy or those you wish to save, you are able to do so. And foremost of all, how needful and valuable is the great land of Armenia, and likewise Georgia and Albania? Merely look at the advantages which you receive from those lands. But what is most significant and important, for the salvation of so many lost souls you pay no attention nor do you concern yourself with it. You do not realize that you will have to give a reckoning to the gods for such a great number of persons. For if you care about the salvation of so many souls, know that their welfare and prosperity would bring more profit and advantage than all the prosperity of the realm you control. And I see further profit and very great and significant advantages in this matter for the land of the Aryans. Indeed you yourself know, as do all the Aryans, [*p. 43*] how great and valuable is

Armenia; it is a close neighbor of the [Roman] Empire and has the same religion and cult, for the emperor controls their realm. Now if you were to render them familiar with our religion and they were to accept it and be able to recognize that up to then they had been in error but now were on the right road, then indeed they would love you and the land of the Aryans and would reject and draw away from the emperor and his religion and empire. Henceforth their land would be in close friendship and unity with ours. And when the Armenians are intimate with us, then the Georgians and Albanians will be ours too. Although I had been concerned earlier with this important matter and had been planning to indicate it to you, I have been even more convinced by that man from the family of Siunik', who was sensible enough to abandon the false religion he professed until now and to choose our true and infallible religion, which he willingly and eagerly accepted. By him I have been made much more aware and convinced of the spiritual and material advantage which would accrue from this enterprise to your realm and indeed to the land of the Aryans in general. Since this man has applied himself with sincere love and has chosen the good, he is worthy of more eminent glory and greater honor than all his companions and kinsmen, so that his family and all the Armenian nobility may see the tremendous benefits and éclat which you have bestowed on him and they too, being stirred to zeal for such a life and reward, may happily accept your command and emulating one another may hasten to fulfil your wishes. And if this so happens, the Aryan realm will remain for ever in peace and surety. But if this does not so turn out, I have doubts about the future, lest they may desire to serve those to whose religion they are true and there be no small dilemma for the land of the Aryans from this matter."

When Yazkert, the Persian king, heard all this argument from his malevolent and perverse *hazarapet*, Mihrnerseh, he was pleased and applauded its reasoning; he revealed to the magi and other Aryan nobility all of Mihrnerseh's words. The Aryans were all astonished and praised the advice, so he immediately summoned the magi, and setting down the tenets of the Mazdaean religion he had it brought to Armenia. He also composed edicts addressed to all the Armenian nobility in the following terms:

22. "I do not know whether it was because of other great preoccupations or because they did not consider such weighty

and significant matters that the earlier kings who were my predecessors before me and occupied this royal throne paid no heed to this business. But I have considered and have been informed by the magi and other wise and great men of this Aryan land, that as we enjoy the profits [*p. 44*] and subjection of those who are under our authority, so we must even more care for and ensure the salvation and safety of all their souls. And if we are unexpectedly discovered to be remiss in such a great responsibility, we have been informed by our religion that we will suffer severe punishment from the gods. Now if we were punished for not warning any one of you, you should be even more fearful that if you are slothful with regard to each one's spiritual welfare you will be punished by us and the gods. Therefore we have written down our infallible and just religion and had it brought to you. And we wish, that as you are a useful country and dear to us, you should study and accept our just and balanced religion and not serve that religion which—it is clear to all of us—is false and profitless. So when you hear these commands of ours to you, accept them willingly and happily and do not put your minds to anything else at all. We also had a further wish, so we order you to send us in writing that supposed religion of yours [explaining] how you were lost until today. And when you become familiar like us with our true religion, the Georgians and Albanians will not be able to resist our and your will."

23. When all the Armenian nobility had received this edict and had read all its contents, they realized he was sending them in writing their impious religion, and they recognized the secret arrows of the enemy, which he deceitfully shoots at Christ's unsullied flock. The right-minded congregation of Christ's holy flock were saddened and confounded as to why such bitter things full of poison had been conceived and uttered by them. "May they not grow," they said, "among the weak-minded and vainglorious souls of incredulous people, setting down precious roots, so that many are destroyed, straying from the true and just faith of Christ."

Consequently, at the command of the Armenian magnates the holy bishops of the various provinces of Armenia and the honorable priests and monks convened. These were: Joseph, who although he was by ordination [only] a priest, yet at the time held the throne of the Catholicosate of Armenia; lord Anania, bishop of Siunikʻ; lord Mushē, bishop of the Artsrunikʻ; lord Sahak, bishop of Tarawn; Saint Sahak, bishop of the

257

Ṙshtunikʻ; lord Melitē, bishop of Manazkert; lord Eznik, bishop of Bagrevand; lord Surmak, bishop of Bznunikʻ; lord Taʻtʻik, bishop of Basean; lord Eremia, bishop of Mardastan; lord Gad, bishop of Vanand; lord Basil, bishop of Mokkʻ; lord Eḷbayr, bishop of the Andzevatsikʻ; lord Tachat, bishop of Taykʻ; lord Kʻasun, bishop of Tarberun; lord Zavēn, [*p. 45*] bishop of Mananaḷi; lord Eḷishē, bishop of the Amatunikʻ; lord Eremia, bishop of the Apahunikʻ. These were all bishops. From among the honorable priests [were]: the holy Ḷevond, Khorēn from Mren, David and other honorable priests, and many senior monks including the wonderful and angelic lord Aḷan, who was from the family of the Artsrunikʻ. And those assembled from among the nobles were: the lord of Siunikʻ, Vasak; the lord of the Artsrunikʻ, Nershapuh; Vriv Maḷkhaz; the lord of the Mamikoneans and *sparapet* of Armenia, Vardan; the lord of the Vahevunikʻ, Giwt; the lord of Mokkʻ, Artak; the lord of the Andzevatsikʻ, Shmavon; the lord of Arsharunikʻ, Arshavir; the lord of the Apahunikʻ, Manēch; the lord of Vanand, Aṙawan; the lord of Arsharunikʻ, Arshavir; the lord of the Amatunikʻ, Vahan; the lord of the Gnunikʻ, Atom; the lord of the Palunikʻ, Varazshapuh; the lord of Ashotsʻ, Hrahat; the lord of the Dimaksean, Hmayeak; the lord of the Abeḷeankʻ, Gazrik; the lord of the Aṙaveleank, Pʻapʻag; Vrēn Dziunakan. All these great magnates, with the lesser nobility and the pious bishops and the senior priests and monks, wrote a reply to the edict [addressed] to King Yazkert and all the nobility of the court in the following terms:

24. "In our illuminating and true religion, which seems vanity and babbling to you, it is written: 'Servants, be obedient to your bodily masters as to God.' And according to our best ability we revere first the command of our religion, and then your great empire. We have decided not merely to serve you with the fear of men, ostentatiously and following the example of wicked servants, but with true willingness and readiness to fulfill in everything your desire and command; and not only to serve you with the tribute of money but also to shed on your behalf our own blood and that of our sons. But as for the salvation or destruction of our souls, let that concern not trouble you at all. And as for the gifts or punishments you fear from your gods on account of our souls, as you explained, may that advantage or punishment fall from God upon our own selves and souls. But do you only keep silent about these matters and excuse us. For as it is impossible for human nature to change the

Providence of heaven to a different view, so it is impossible for us who from the beginning have been instructed and confirmed in this religion to obey and accept such a command as yours—which we cannot even bear to hear mentioned, for we wish to have nothing to do with it.

"But as for your religion, which you put in writing and had brought to us, we shall never obey you. While we were at court and among the magi who are called your 'teachers of the law,' we mocked and despised them [*p. 46*]—let alone that you should induce us to read and listen to your letter, which is quite superfluous and pointless to us. Rather, for the greater honoring of your rule we did not wish even or open to see your letter. For the religion which we know to be false and the babbling of witless men, which we have often heard from your false so-called teachers and of which we are as knowledgeable as you, should be neither read nor heard. Because at its reading we are forced to laugh, so that the religion, its founders, and those who worship such chicanery are together insulted. Therefore we did not consider it appropriate or convenient to set our religion in writing and have it brought to you according to your order. For if we did not think your false and ridiculous religion worthy of being read and introduced among us lest we insult you by mocking your religion—which in your great wisdom you should have considered in writing it down and having it brought to us—how could we send in writing such a divine and true religion to your ignorant majesty to be mocked and insulted? But let this much of our faith at least be clear to you: we do not serve, like you, the elements, sun and moon, wind and fire; we do not render worship to the many gods that you name on earth and in heaven. For we know and firmly serve the one only true God, who made heaven and earth and everything in them. And he only of those called god by you is God and Creator, King of Kings and Lord of Lords; to him only is it right for all rational [creatures] to offer worship and service."

25. The holy priests wrote all this down in a letter and in concert with all the nobles of Armenia had it sent to the king of the Aryans, Yazkert. Ordering the magi and all the magnates of the court to be summoned, he had the letter the Armenians had sent opened and read before everyone. When the king, with the magi and all the court nobility, had heard the contents of the letter, stirred indignantly to anger he asked the magi and all the Aryan nobility: "How does it seem to you for subjects to write to their lord with such fearless presumption?"

Then the rows of magi and of all the magnates of the court, standing up, said: "They have communicated to you the destruction of themselves and their land. But how you must indicate to them your sovereignty and their subjection, that is in your power." They aroused the wrath of the king and of all the nobility even more by saying: "Unless they had from somewhere else the hope of support, they would have been unable even to contemplate such words, let alone send them in a letter to your majesty." This the malicious Mihrnerseh said.

[*p. 47*] When King Yazkert heard all this from the magi and all the court nobility, roused to anger he immediately ordered edicts to be sent to Armenia, Georgia, and Albania. He ordered it to be written in the text of the edict that all the magnates and senior members of the lesser nobility of the three countries should come promptly without delay to court; "and whoever is slow and lingers," he said, "will suffer the death penalty without any pardon." After this edict had arrived in the three countries and had been read before the Armenians, Georgians, and Albanians, on hearing such an urgent summons to them all they immediately realized the motive for this, that the urgency of this summons boded nothing peaceful but was for the destruction of their souls. Saddened and troubled, they took refuge and protection in God's help.

Then the three countries exchanged messages and formed a mutual covenant, confirmed with many oaths on the Gospel. They considered that not to go would give the impression of rebellion, yet they were disturbed and anxious about going. They reckoned that to go was best, and they invoked God's help for the outcome. However, they indissolubly and fearlessly confirmed one another's minds, words, and thoughts through the Holy Gospel, saying: "We shall go, yes, but we shall not agree to deny the Creator of heaven and earth. And this will accrue to us from God when we show ourselves to be one body and one spirit in Christ, remembering the Holy Apostles, the preachers of the holy church, who were one heart and one spirit. By their intercession our Savior and Lord Jesus Christ will direct our reply before the fearful king and save us from the onslaught of the evil beast who is bearing down on us; for God has never abandoned from his care those who have united in a good purpose. But if anyone removes and separates himself from this covenant of unity, the Son of man, as he himself indeed says, will deny man and cast him from his face before the Father and the angels of heaven."

United thus by covenants and oaths, the three nations, Armenians, Georgians, and Albanians, went to the court.

Those of the greatest Armenian nobility who set out directly at that time were the following: from the family of Siunik', Vasak, lord of Siunik'—who at that time was governor of Armenia; from the Artsruni family, Nershapuh; from the Ṙshtuni family, Artak; from the Khoṙkhoṙuni family, Gadisho; from the Mamikonean family, Vardan, *sparapet* of Armenia and lord of the Mamikonean; from the Mok family, Artak; from the the Apahuni family, Manēch; from the Amatuni family, Vahan; from the Vahevuni family, Giut; from the Andzevats'i family, Shmavon. And from Georgia, the *bdeashkh* Ashushay and other magnates of that country.

[*p. 48*] *26.* When they had all arrived at court they presented themselves, first before the magnates of the royal court and then before King Yazkert. The Persian king, Yazkert, gave a command that in the morning all the great nobility of the court with the [most] eminent magi should come before him in his pavilion. And the king's orders were carried out the next morning.

Then he commanded those Armenians, Georgians, and Albanians who had made the journey to be led before him. First of all he asked the Armenian magnates and nobles: "First and foremost I wish to hear from you how I am considered by you and how you consider yourselves to be one." They replied in unison: "The plan and purpose of your command are clear to all Aryans and non-Aryans without hearing any response from us." Then the king repeated: "[They are] clear and obvious to all who are under my rule and unable in any way to oppose my command. But I wish to hear from you and to know your understanding as to what you think of me. Speak to me." They replied: "We recognize you as king—as do all, so do we even more. You have authority similar to God's over us and every man in your realm, to kill or save his life."

When King Yazkert and all the court nobility had heard the answer in these terms from them, King Yazkert said to them: "Your replies in the letter which you had brought to me are very divergent and different. For in the letter it was made clear that 'there are matters in which we serve you and agree not to oppose your will and command; and there is something which you must not ask of us and in which we are unable to obey you and accept.' Now, that is the principal and most important and necessary demand made of you by my majesty and

261

all the Aryans; thereby is made known our authority and solicitude for you and your honest subjection and obedience to us. For we are pleased with the duty and service that up to today you have shown to us kings and to the land of the Aryans; and now I wish to send you back to your own country with honor and great glory. Merely accomplish this further desire of mine, our concern for the salvation of your souls, and turn from the path of destruction in which you have been wandering until now like a blind man in the dark. But if you intend otherwise and really continue obstinately in the same mind and false religion in which you Armenians, Georgians, and Albanians have lived until now, I shall consider as nothing these many services and duties of yours, but shall annihilate you with your wives, children, and nation."

[*p. 49*] When the nobles of the three lands heard all these words—of honor, promises, and threats of death—from King Yazkert they were all silent for a while except Vardan, lord of the Mamikonean and *sparapet* of Armenia. Steping forward with a fearless and courageous heart, he replied to King Yazkert in front of the whole assembly, saying: "There are many among the nobility of these three lands who are superior to me in rank and age, and there are many who are inferior. As for service and duty which servants must pay their lords and kings, you who are lord of all and also all the Aryans know well how I and each one of these men have rendered them up to the present; and there is no need for me or any of these men to explain to you his service and offices. Henceforth I have made this my prime intention, that if there is any way to turn my single self into many, my strength and ready willingness, my life and possessions, whatever is in my house, I shall make yours even more than ever, and I have decided to wear myself out on behalf of the lord of the Aryans and the land of the Aryans. But the religion which I have learnt from God from my childhood it is impossible to abandon and exchange for fear of a man. For if I had received from a man the righteous teaching which I have confirmed in my mind, and knowing it to be true I denied it, I would consider myself pitiable. How much the more [pitiable] to exchange that religion which I have received and learned from the mouth of God for the fear of man and for vain glory. Far be it. That is my answer, for which I prefer to die than live in apostasy without God. As for the others who all stand before you, those who are Christians are able each one to give answer for himself."

When the nobles from the three countries of Armenia, Georgia, and Albania heard the fearless reply of Vardan, the *sparapet* of Armenia, and [saw] the exceedingly angry face of the king, they replied, saying: "May the king grant us a few days to consider among ourselves and to give you reply in solid unity; for the question asked of us concerns the choice of the soul on which depends eternal salvation or destruction. It is not right to return to you an answer to such a momentous question in haste and without scrutiny; for you request our detachment from our ancient and customary ancestral tradition, and you exact the acceptance of a religion which neither we nor our fathers accepted or loved." The king with all the nobility agreed to this proposition, and granting their request for a delay, they dismissed the assembly.

[*p. 50*] *27.* Then all the nobles from the three countries of Armenia, Georgia, and Albania gathered in one spot; disturbed, they took council to discover by what means and plan they could find a way out. After vacillating and being undecided for a few days, they came to this common conclusion and agreed: "We have no other way of escaping this trap which the wicked hunter Satan has set around us save to give an apparent acceptance of their orders for a while. Then, going to each one's country, we can either live subject to the true faith of Christ into which we were born by the renewal of the font through the all-holy teaching of the martyr Gregory and his descendants; or, abandoning our country, we can each go abroad with wife and children, taking refuge and security in the saying of the life-giving Savior, who says: 'When they will pursue you from this city, flee to the other.' But if, merely considering our own salvation, we oppose the impious commands of the prince, we shall be the cause of eternal destruction to a numberless multitude of men and women, old men and youths, whom they will bring hither and subject to their impious cults from generation to generation."

Now although each one individually had come to such a decision and they were all in unison after conferring day and night with one another for a few days, yet they could not reveal their unanimous intention to the Armenian general, Vardan, lord of the Mamikonean, knowing in their minds that he would be unable to accept or agree to such a plan, since he had fixed the faith of his soul on the firm rock of Christ. On the other hand, they were unable to endure not revealing and telling him all this, for they knew that without him all their plans and pretexts and actions would be incomplete and ineffective. Although they thought they would be able by means of their planned excuse to escape by deceit and to frustrate the intention of the king and the edict of all the Aryans and to return to each one's land, yet they realized that their proposed plan of action would be imperfect and incomplete because they had all seen and fully realized from written accounts that from the beginning all such actions had been brought to completion [only] through the Mamikonean family and with their cooperation.

When all the nobles who had gathered at the court, both greater and lesser, had decided on this, they went in concert to the lord of the Mamikonean and the general of Armenia, Vardan, and revealed their plan to him. Explaining all their intentions and what they had decided to do, they all added their entreaties and supplications: "Regard [*p. 51*] us with steadfast mind; regard also the present situation of a host of thousands of men plunged into terrible afflictions. Remember the lamentations of mothers, consider the orphaning of children, the forced exiling of old men and women, and all other similar unendurable and evil misfortunes. Even if it were merely the body's fate to endure all this with travail and death, it would still be hard and bitter and lamentable—how much the more when it involves the general stumbling and destruction of soul and body. The scope of the danger that has befallen us is not a merely transitory one, but the darkness of impiety has fenced in and will tenaciously envelop our holy churches and congregations, our women and children, forever. And if you, agreeing with our plan, can persuade your mind to acquiesce for a while, we know that our numerous company will obtain mercy, and that the churches of the three countries will not be given over to general destruction, nor all the populace of those lands led into captivity. For the holy faith cannot be toppled from its foundations; but if for a while some shaking occurs, the right hand of the Almighty will set it up again as firm as ever. That this will so happen is definite if you are able to weaken a while for our sake, so that the all-merciful healer, the word of God, may cure both us and yourself."

When the Armenian general, Vardan, lord of the Mamikonean, heard this speech from the Armenian, Georgian, and Albanian nobles, he completely refused to accept or agree to such a proposal or to participate in such a plan in any way. But, greatly troubled, he cried out loudly to them all: "Far be it from me to be false to my Creator, either speciously or in truth, or to deny before a lawless and pernicious nation him who will deny his deniers before the Father and the holy angels. Far be it from me, that considering the troubles and suffering of my wife, children, and family, I forget him who said: 'Who loves his wife and children more than me, is not worthy of me.' But you magnates and nobles who have now come [here] from the three countries, by the grace and mercy of Christ you are filled with all valor and excellence; for in accordance with a noble training you excel in all discipline, and among all armies and nations you are the most renowned in battle and all martial exploits. You have also learned the true and righteous faith from God through the apostolic shepherd and martyr Gregory and his descendants. You are each able to answer for yourself, and as you plan so will you be able to act. But let none of you say to me what I cannot endure to hear in words, let alone carry out in fact."

[*p. 52*] When all the nobles from the three countries heard this speech from Vardan, the Armenian general and lord of the Mamikonean, although they were plunged into unbearable sadness and distress yet they were in no way weakened in their decision but thought of other means of entreaty in view of the pressing danger. Assembling in one spot, they summoned to themselves Artak, the prince of Mokk'. They strongly urged him to have a private talk with their *sparapet,* the prince of the Mamikonean family, and to press him with the most indefatigable entreaties. He himself was a modest man, thoughtful and valiant; and Vardan, prince of the Mamikonean, loved Artak with especial honor. The latter agreed to the Armenian nobles' command and promptly undertook the attempt to supplicate him assiduously. Artak, prince of Mokk', acted in accordance with his commission, sometimes alone and sometimes in concert with the Armenian nobility, who did not cease day and night to urge on him [Vardan] the same arguments and entreaties for many days. They were all also pressed urgently and unceasingly to the same purpose by the *bdeashkh* of Georgia, Ashushay, who was a wise and prudent man and had as wife an Artsruni, the sister-in-law of the great *sepuh* of the Mamikoneans, Vardan's brother. The aforementioned Ashushay was exhorting even more assiduously all the Armenian nobility and the lord of Mokk', Artak, to urge these arguments on the Armenian general, Vardan without delay. He himself did not cease to reason with him with tireless protestations, urgently making him see how great the loss to the three countries was through his refusal, and how great would be the safety for many and the prospect of repentance for himself if he agreed and accepted.

When the greater and lesser nobles of the three countries saw how inflexible and unresponsive to their importuning and beseeching was the will of Vardan, the *sparapet* of Armenia, those among them who were most familiar with the church's Holy Scriptures then pressed upon him opportune proverbs from the Holy Bible in terms appropriate to the time. They reminded him, as a learned man versed [in Scripture]—for he was very erudite and familiar with the teaching of Scripture, having been instructed and educated by the holy patriarch Sahak, his grandfather—of what Saint Paul wrote about the Creator: "He made him who did not know sin into sin for our sake"; and also of Paul's own condescension and desire to make himself anathema for the salvation of his kin, as he wrote in the letter to the Romans: "With prayers I sought to be anathematized by Christ for the sake of my brothers and children and relatives in the flesh, who are Israelites, whose are the adoption [*p. 53*] and the glory and the covenants and the Law and the cult and the Gospel." "Agree," they said, "to become yourself an example and cursed for our sake. You are not greater and superior in righteous faith to the Holy Apostle of Christ, Paul; but the peoples of Armenia, Georgia, and Albania are much more numerous and more virtuous than the people of the crucifying Jews."

When the great magnates and lesser nobles of the three countries had pressed such extensive arguments and earnest entreaties on the Armenian general, Vardan, they then brought the Holy Gospel. They all together placed their hands on it and swore: "If you can feign acceptance, only for a while, of the king's proposals and free us from the assaults of the ensnaring enemy, we shall obey you and do everything you say, sacrificing ourselves for the Holy Covenant and shedding our blood for the salvation of the whole country. And if we must abandon our land and all our possessions and flee abroad we shall so choose with our wives and children and willingly accept poverty and beggary, provided only that we escape this wrath. And whoever reneges on these words and is false to this Covenant, deceitfully abandoning the oath on the Holy Gospel and the unanimity of this company, shall himself be abandoned and estranged like Judas, who fell away and left the band of the Holy Apostles. Such a one will share his fate without [a chance of] repentance or remission; he will be delivered to the unquenchable furnace which God has prepared for Satan and his satellites. And for whatever harm, captivity, or trouble may befall the three countries, from such a one and his companions the Revenger will seek [retribution] for eternity. But the benevolent and favorable protection which the Savior Christ will provide and bestow on many souls in the three countries if you agree with us for a while, will remain as an eternal legacy for the salvation of your own soul and of your nation."

When the Armenian general, Vardan, lord of the Mamikonean, heard this speech from the nobility of the three lands and saw the Covenant to which they had sworn and sealed with a fearsome oath on the Holy Gospel, bursting into tears he agreed to feign weakness for a while for the sake of the three countries and their numerous population of men and women.

28. Thus united, they all agreed to fulfill the king's command deceptively. Going to the *house of ashes,* some of them, though not all, affected to bend their heads to the vain cult, in appearance but not in reality. And some, although they knew their fall to be irreparable, yet desiring [*p. 54*] the glory of this world gave up the glory of the uncreated God for the material and transitory life of this world.

When the Persian king and all the court magnates and magi saw this, in great joy they offered various oblations to their gods. On that day they celebrated a great and joyous festival, reckoning that day to mark the unshakable establishment of their kingdom and [reckoning] that from then on they would live in peace, no longer frightened of their enemies. They dressed and adorned in royal garments the magnates and lesser nobility of the three countries, Armenia, Georgia, and Albania, and showered on them all numerous and varied gifts and honors, villages, and estates according to each one's need; then they dismissed them and sent them back in haste to each one's country. They dispatched with them a host of false teachers, whom they call magi, exhorting them to learn their ridiculous breathings and mimicking, murmuring speech—like that of snake charmers and ventriloquists. They commanded that in the three lands schools of deceit be established and that everyone equally, men and women, be instructed in the teaching of the magi.

They willingly agreed to take the host of magi with them. Then they took leave of King Yazkert and the court magnates, offering the king and all the Aryan nobility, especially the most pernicious Mihrnerseh, false praise and feigned thanks, each one dissembling for a while according to the ability of his intelligence. And this was the simulated form of thanks they all expressed: "All the kings who were before you on your throne, your ancestors, loved us, caring for our prosperity and material advantage. But you have shown your love for us to be even greater, since you decided to make known to us and bestow on us our eternal life. And if we served your ancestors with all ready willingness in every duty which they imposed on us, yet to you every person must offer service not as a single individual but [he must] make his one person many and give indefatigable devotion to your majesty, serving your interest day and night. For you have given anxious attention to the salvation of our lost souls."

Each one of them according to his ability spoke similar or even more elaborate words of praise, then kept silence. But the Armenian *sparapet*, Vardan, lord of the Mamikonean, setting forth his future actions in the form of a straightforward speech without deceit as if composed for the praise of the king and all the host of the Aryan nobility, spoke thus: "You all know well the service and duty [*p. 55*] paid to this court and to your majesty by my ancestors from the time we became subject to you, so it is not necessary for me to inform you in detail of these matters of which you are more accurately informed than I. But although I am far inferior to my ancestors, nonetheless to the best of my ability I have resolved to satisfy you with dutiful service. When I was set to a task at your command, your generals and my companions could see my task and duty loyally performed according to my strength. So now henceforth this is my wish and to this shall I strive: if up to now I have done anything unworthy of repute or praise, henceforth I shall attempt with all my power and strength, with God's help, to perform such actions that their fame will be repeated not merely before you Aryans, but also at the emperor's court and among other nations forever."

This was the speech made as if by God's grace by the Armenian *sparapet*, Vardan, lord of the Mamikonean, whose heroic martyrdom for God would render him famous for eternity. When the Persian king and all the court nobility heard this speech, though surprised they profusely praised and thanked him. For God had concealed the promises which the Armenian *sparapet*, Vardan, had said he would accomplish for the sake of the great repute which God had granted him—the fame of martyrdom among nations forever.

Then the [nobles of the] three countries, Armenians, Georgians, and Albanians, bade leave to them all; and taking with them the groups of numerous magi returned to their own lands, frequently reconfirming even on the journey the Covenant sworn on the Holy Gospel. Taking leave of one another, they went to their lands to remind each other at the [appropriate] time, with God's permission, of the tasks they had planned to fulfill. But the Persian king, Yazkert, did not let the *bdeashkh* of Georgia, Ashushay, and the two sons of Vasak, prince of Siunik', Babik and Amirnerseh, go with the other Armenian nobles; considering the uncertainty of future events, in suspicion he retained them.

29. When the Armenian magnates and the lesser nobles in their company reached Armenia, half-alive and half-dead, they did not seem in such health as on their earlier splendid return from that distant journey. Groups of Christ's ministers came to meet them, bearing with them the sign of the life-giving cross and the relics of the holy, apostle-like martyr, Gregory, and singing psalms which the prophet David had composed by the grace of the Holy Spirit—[psalms] [*p. 56*] in singing which [the nobles] themselves too had once joined, chanting these canticles with even greater heavenly joy and delight than the ministers. But now one could hear the sound of weeping and the sound of lamentation, the cry of mourning and the noise of wailing. Anxious children fled from their fathers' bosoms in consternation, thinking them transformed; and not seeing the familiar figures they were terrified. Looking steadfastly at the faces of their mothers they saw them to be continually wailing and shedding torrents of tears. So the children too burst out weeping; no one was able to quiet them, neither nurse nor tutor. When those who had deceitfully and not in truth apostatized saw this they immediately wished to arise and thrust a sword into themselves; they preferred not to live a moment longer than to see and endure such misery. They ate the food of joy, according to the psalmist's saying, as if they were eating ashes, and they mingled tears with their drink. For no one agreed to share their table, neither wife nor child, not freeman, serf, or servant.

Then one could see them all divided from one another and rent asunder; to them applied the sweet and pleasant saying of the Savior Christ: "There are also other sheep, who are not of that fold; they too must be brought hither so that they may become one flock of one shepherd." This is the true [flock] whom God united, fulfilling his sayings, when the enemy, unexpectedly kicking, scattered them high and low and made them like a flock that has no shepherd. Because of all this, the wives of the great nobles broke into mournful laments, as did the widows in public squares and the young married women and the maidens in locked chambers and the brides in boudoirs. The holy bishops, with the honorable priests and ecclesiastical clergy, old men and youths and the whole multitude of the congregations raised a cry and wept in the house of God. And one could see the faces of all the orthodox populace covered with streams of blood.

Nonetheless the groups of magi zealously forced the introduction of fires into the Lord's holy temple, and the building of fire-temples in other notable and beautiful sites. And they had porters organized to carry wood for the upkeep of the fire of the insatiable false deity, who in his insensible consumption returns no thanks to his worshipers, but wears out these sooty-faced, obscene ministers as they remove the redundant waste of the ashes.

30. So when the lord of the Mamikonean and *sparapet* of Armenia, Vardan, saw all these troubles, he summoned to himself all his family, his brothers, freemen, serfs, and all [*p. 57*] his retainers, and he began to speak with them, saying: "I did not deny my Creator and the Lord Jesus Christ willingly or from fear. Far from it. Nor did I reject the teaching and faith of the Holy Gospel which my grandfather, lord Sahak, taught me and confirmed in me. But for a while [only] until this moment, I weakened in dissimulation, for the salvation of you all, to repent and be saved when I found myself among you. For I know and recall the preaching of the holy prophets: 'I do not desire the death of a sinner, but his return and salvation.' And elsewhere the Holy Spirit says: 'When you turn and lament, then you will live.' Now, as I abandoned him in appearance for a while for your sake, I wish in return to abandon truly and utterly all the things of this mortal life. And I have decided and choose to go into exile for the name of Christ with such of you as are able to share my intentions despising all the vain life of this world."

When he had so spoken to the members of his household, his blessed brother Hmayeak replied: "Hasten to fulfill your plan and do not delay. For no one can be a guarantor for himself even for an hour. If by [the grace of] God we survive and reach the day of death without remorse, we are quite unable sooner or later to escape death. Be it in penury or in exile, by him alone we live and in his name we boast continuously. Let us merely cast from us the repute of apostasy, and joining Christ's flock, let us willingly undertake all the sufferings that may befall us—famine, or sword, or penury and death in exile."

Thus in unity they despised and scorned all the vain pomp of this worldly life. With their retainers and family who agreed with them, they decided to set out immediately for the Greek Empire where they would be able to take refuge, either together or scattered here and there. Arriving at a village called Aramanay in the province of Bagrevand, near the borders of Basean and Tuartsatap', they wished to rest for a few days; then they made rapid preparations to press on with their journey.

News of this plan and of the departure from Armenia of the great Armenian *sparapet*, Vardan, lord of the Mamikonean, in the company of his brothers, household, and followers, quickly reached Vasak, prince of Siunik', who was the *marzpan* of Armenia at that time, [*p. 58*] and also all the magnates and lesser nobility of Armenia. They were brokenhearted and terrified; in their search for salvation for themselves they all realized that "now we know that we are completely lost and we have no way of escaping this disaster at all." For they all well knew that without the leadership of that family no Armenian affairs or undertakings were brought to completion. The prince of Siunik', Vasak, took counsel with all the Armenian magnates and senior nobility and converted them all to his own wishes, saying: "We must quickly send select priests and senior members from among the Armenian magnates after the Armenian general, Vardan Mamikonean, to bring him back here by means of their entreaties. For without them all these desires and plans of ours will come to naught.

Vasak, prince of Siunik', wrote a letter and sealed it with his own ring and ordered all the other great Armenian magnates to write letters; when they had each sealed the letters with their rings, he had the sealed Gospel of the Covenant brought. Then, naming honorable men from among the clergy—the blessed priest Levond, and the blessed priest Jeremiah from Nor K'alak', and the blessed priest Khorēn from Mren; and also senior members from among the Armenian magnates: Arshavir, prince of the Arsharunik'; Hmayeak, prince of the Dimak'sean; and Gazrik, prince of the Abeḷeank'—Vasak, prince of Siunik', gave them all the letters and the Gospel of the oath and despatched them as messengers after him (Vardan). They caught up with him and his company in the village of Aramanay mentioned above.

After giving notice, they came before him and explained to Vardan, lord of the Mamikonean and *sparapet* of Armenia, in the presence of his brothers Hmayeak and Hamazasp, the reasons for their rapid pursuit after them. [They also told them about] the council and the speeches sealed with an oath by all the Armenians in unison with Vasak, prince of Siunik'. They brought forward the Gospel of the oath and presented it to the blessed Vardan and his brothers. They also put into their hands the letters of Vasak, lord of Siunik', and of the other Armenian nobles, bishops, and princes and giving a summary of everyone's words they said to the blessed [Vardan]: "Here you are with your brothers and like-minded family, concerned only with saving your own selves and escaping. But we shall all suffer eternal destruction, for without you neither we nor our children could ever be able to gain salvation and survive. But as you have been concerned to take thought for yourselves, so likewise do not allow so very many souls to perish, for there are many of us here who are of your kin and blood. Be crowned with us too by Christ, just as you desired and tried to be crowned on your own."

When the saintly *sparapet* of Armenia Vardan, lord of the Mamikonean, with all his blessed brothers heard this speech from the priests and nobles who had come as messengers, [*p. 59*] and when he had seen the Holy Gospel of the Covenant and had read the letters of the prince of Siunik', Vasak, the *marzpan* of Armenia, and of each one of his other companions, he replied on behalf of them all: "I and my brothers and family have determined that the most important thing to be preferred over everything else in the world is to seek and find the salvation of one's soul. And we have absorbed that firm and unshakable saying, in which we believe irrevocably: 'What does it profit a man if he gain the whole world and lose his own soul? Or what payment will a man give for his soul? But we seek not merely the profit of our [own] souls, we also rejoice at the salvation of others. Let no one think of us that we have fled from fear of the sword, of which no one in our family was ever frightened—never! And that this family always was more concerned about a friend's well-being than its own—that all you Armenians know indubitably from written history and by listening to your elders. But it was because we recalled all the deceitful trickery which you continually practiced against our ancestors that we set off in flight. You have constricted us as in a fence, and since you hold yourselves apart from us our family has found itself alone in great and mortal tribulations. But no one from our family has opposed the holy and heavenly envoy of yours, the Gospel; nor do we now, God forbid! You alone knew whether you act sincerely or falsely, you and this Holy Gospel which knows everything and judges according to each one's deeds."

31. When the saintly Vardan, lord of the Mamikonean and *sparapet* of Armenia, had said this, he and his blessed brothers and friends returned to their companions in the Armenian camp. After they had all come together, the immediate thought of the holy Armenian *sparapet,* Vardan, was not merely to celebrate divine service in his lodging with the priests and numerous other ministers of his entourage—which they zealously conducted day and night without fail—but he also desired to go to church accompanied by all the Armenians. But although he was distressed at not going, yet, being prevented, he willingly waited for a brief time, concerned about the needs of his companions as well as about his own household and himself. He was especially concerned about Ashushay, the *bdeashkh* of Georgia, and about the sons of the prince of Siunik', Vasak, whom the Persian king, Yazkert, had kept behind at court. The saintly Vardan pondered these matters, not because he had need of help in the task before him—for he was not planning to seek any fame in victory; rather he longed to be able to shed his blood for the benefit of the covenant [*p. 60*] of the church—but he was worried as a benevolent man lest some trouble befall these men from the king and they come to harm.

However, Vahan, prince of the Amatunik', did not permit the Armenian general, Vardan, any rest or delay; sometimes in person and sometimes through others, he pressed him to proclaim a revolt immediately, urging him to be concerned only with the salvation of his soul. But in fact he was not so much concerned with that, as in his speeches he incited [Vardan] to declare [a revolt], but rather he was motivated by the earlier grudge which Vasak, prince of Siunik', and Vahan, lord of the Amatunik', bore each other. He realized with his perceptive understanding that Vasak, prince of Siunik', would either not

273

agree to revolt and would be put to an unworthy death by his own companions, or if he agreed to revolt because of the peril, his two sons imprisoned at court and threatened with maltreatment would be put to death or be held for a long time in strict confinement and prison and be tortured unmercifully. However, the holy man of God, Vardan, lord of the Mamikonean and general of Armenia, did not pay attention to anyone's arguments but was concerned about his companions and ardently hastened to martyrdom. Thus he was compelled to stretch out the days of spring until the days of the approaching hot weather. When the months of broiling heat arrived, the entire Armenian host set out for cooler places. They came to the province called Tsaḷkotn, near to the strong fortress called Angḷ. In that area the men camped to pass the hot season.

32. But the magi, whom the Armenian nobles had brought with them from the court as teachers, saw that they themselves and their religion were despised in the [Armenians'] eyes—for the nobles' wives, whom the magi had expected to instruct, abhorred even setting eyes on them and firmly commanded tutors never to let their sons or daughters come near them; while the men, who pretended to pass themselves off as apostates, did not even permit the false teachers to eat bread in their presence, so [the latter] went about miserably half-dying from hunger. The magi were unable to leave and flee, yet to remain with the Armenians would mean death and destruction for themselves. So all the while they made every effort to write to the court secretly about the rebellion.

When Vardan, the Armenian *sparapet,* realized that the fact of the rebellion had become very well known and that by extended inaction great harm would result, he held a council for many days and assembled the honorable bishops, the illustrious priests, and the outstanding lesser nobility. Since they still did not at that moment wish to reveal their plans to Vasak, the *marzpan* of Armenia, knowing that his delay in turning to salvation was not merely on account of his sons, and recognizing the more powerful motivation of his vainglorious and God-detesting thoughts, [*p. 61*] consequently the blessed Vardan said clearly to them all: "For how long will we endure to hide the truth and perish? This news had spread out and filled every spot. But let us go forth in open light as in the daytime and summon the sons of light."

Someone from the royal house whose name was Zandaḷan, of baneful origin, a son of iniquity who had committed many impenitent evils during his lifetime, heard of the Armenians' plans from some people and went immediately to inform his counterpart Vasak. When the greater Armenian nobles heard report of his deceitful deeds, they seized him in a village called Artsak and brought him to yet another village called Berkunkʻ in the same province of Bagrevand, where they imprisoned him. A few days later they stoned him to death in just retribution for his impious crimes.

Then in unison all the Armenian greater and lesser nobility, with the bishops and the whole host of priests and common people, gathered openly in the presence of the blessed *sparapet* of Armenia, Vardan, lord of the Mamikonean. In his company they all went directly, as Scripture bids, to the prince of Siunikʻ, Vasak, *marzpan* of Armenia, and revealed to him their unanimous plan. Although he tried to delay, on the one hand because of his sons who were at the court, and on the other because his character was always inclined to nurture evil, yet they did not allow his mind to waver this way or that. Although he was unwilling, nonetheless he was constrained to agree to join them. The Armenian nobles then ordered the holy bishops and priests to bring the Gospel of the Holy Covenant; the whole host of the army, nobles and commoners with the prince of Siunikʻ, Vasak, and all the greater and lesser nobles, swore and confirmed their oath. And those who had not yet sealed the Gospel with their ring, sealed. Raising in unison their hands to heaven, the whole multitude spoke as follows, men and women in joyful harmony:

"You, Holy Father, Maker of heaven and earth, and your only begotten Son, our Lord Jesus Christ, and the Holy vivifying Spirit, the indivisible and inseparable unity of the Trinity, we confess to be Creator of heaven and earth, of things visible and invisible. You alone are God, and there is none other besides you. In your benevolence, for the salvation of the world, at the end of days, you, one of the Holy Trinity, were born of the Holy Virgin Mary; you endured all afflictions in the body which you took from the Holy Virgin, Mother of God; you were taken and nailed to the wooden cross, on which, shedding your holy blood, you freed [*p. 62*] this world from slavery to the curse of sin; you were buried and rose and ascended to heaven; you gave the good news of your promise, to draw to yourself all who confess you, true God, King of Kings and Lord of Lords. And we testify and confess you to be God of Gods and Lord of Lords, God the expiator of our sins—we who have denied [you]

275

and repented, who have transgressed and taken refuge in your mercy, who have fallen and been raised up. Receive us as the apostate Son, we who have squandered and soiled the robe of Holy Baptism, whom you had adorned with the washing of the font; in dissolute impiety we have wallowed in the mire of apostasy like a herd of pigs.

"So now again we beseech you, true heavenly Father, saying: We have sinned against heaven and before you. Grant us through the intercession of the illuminating Apostles and through the labors of the holy martyr Gregory, their equal and coworker, forgiveness for our sins. Clothe us in our former garment and clean our feet of the impediments of evil whereby the enemy pierced and lamed us. Put on our feet the shoes of protection, of the Holy Gospel. Set on the finger of our right hand the ring, the design of your cross; when we have sealed all our limbs with it, the slanderer will take fright and flee from us. As you shed your holy blood on behalf of sinners, grant that we too may shed our blood for this confession and for the forgiveness of each one's sins. And whoever, drawing away from the Covenant of these oaths, will violate the pact and reject our union, let him go out with Judas, who was expelled from the company of the Holy Apostles, and standing on the left-hand side without any forgiveness, let him hear from you the fearful words which you will speak on the day of retribution: 'Go from me, cursed ones, to the everlasting fire that has been prepared for Satan and his satellites.' "

As the entire host of men and women uttered this unanimous confession of blessing and curses in a loud voice, the whole earth resounded at the clamor of the army. When all the words of the Covenant of faith had been set in writing, the first to seal it with his ring was Vasak, prince of Siunik', and then with their rings all the Armenian magnates and greater nobility; placing it on the Gospel of the oath, they gave it to the honorable bishops and to the senior priests who were there. When all this had been so completed, with great joy and spiritual songs they made for the house of the Lord; and worshiping the one and only true God, full of ardor they made their prayers with protracted and indefatigable genuflections.

On finishing their prayers, the multitude of common soldiers made for the *house of ashes* without waiting for the order of their superiors. Seizing [*p. 63*] the brazier, they threw the fire into the water as into its brother's bosom—according to the saying of the false Persian teachers. But when the water embraced it, like an enemy rather than a brother it extinguished it. They ordered the host of magi to be guarded carefully for that day; and the next morning at dawn they slew a good number of them with the sword in the village called Zarehawan.

33. Having accomplished all these deeds in the order I have described, they remained in that spot for the days of the hot season. Then they hastened to descend to the plain of Ayrarat, for they heard that Mihrnerseh, *hazarapet* of the Aryans, had come to the city of P'aytakaran, was gathering an army, and was aiming at attack on Armenia through Albania. The Albanian nobles, who were allied with the Armenians, anxiously urged them to join them in Albania in order to attack [the Persians].

When [the Armenians] had arrived in the province of Ayrarat and had heard this news from the regions of Albania, Vasak, the prince of Siunik', pressed the blessed Armenian general, Vardan, lord of the Mamikonean, to go and oppose them with an army; he would remain where he was with the specious excuse: "I shall make my preparations here; perhaps," he said, "the malicious Mihrnerseh may think up some other evil to inflict on us." But Vasak was weaving a path of treachery in his heart, having as accomplices other apostates among the Armenian nobility. But the blessed Armenian general, Vardan, lord of the Mamikonean, said to Vasak, prince of Siunik': "As we have decided, we must first send messengers to the emperor, and then I shall do without delay whatever you command me." And he, in order to accomplish more rapidly his own plan, agreed to do what the blessed general, Vardan, said.

Immediately they wrote letters to the emperor and to all the nobles of the Greek court, and also to other princes and prefects: to the *bdeashkh* of Aḷdznik', to the prince of *Angeḷ-tun,* to Tsop'k' and Hashteank' and Ekeḷeats', and to the other princes of every region, and to the great general of Antioch. They sealed all these letters, first the prince of Siunik', Vasak himself, with his own ring, and then all the Armenian magnates. They equipped for the journey to Greece the prince of the house of the Amatunik', Vahan, as being a thoughtful and prudent man; and the saintly young noble Hmayeak, brother of the blessed Armenian general, Vardan, from the family of the Mamikonean; and the blessed Mehrujan, brother of the saintly Aḷan, from the family of the Artsrunik'. Entrusting the letters to them, Vasak, prince of Siunik‘, and all the nobles of Armenia despatched them to the emperor and to all the other Armenian princes mentioned above.

[*p. 64*] *34.* The Armenian general, blessed Vardan, lord of the Mamikonean, took with him those of the Armenian magnates who with an ardent love were anxious to meet the moment of martyrdom; they were the following: Khorēn Khorkhoṙuni, Arshavir Kamsarakan, T‘at‘ul Dimak‘sean, Artak Paluni, Giut Vahevuni, Hmayeak Dimak‘sean, other magnates and nobles, and also many of the Armenian troops who with willing enthusiasm were desirous to avenge the Covenant of the holy church and give themselves to death for the holy and true faith of Christ. And there were other troops from the cavalry of the *Mardpet,* anxious to exhibit valor in war. The malicious prince of Siunik‘, Vasak, knew these not to be in agreement with his own wicked intention, so he sent them off in combat readiness with Vardan. But those of the Armenian nobility, both the most eminent and those of the common multitude whom he knew to be inclined toward the cause of evil and not loyally intent on keeping the covenant—these he kept behind with himself.

The blessed Armenian general, Vardan, lord of the Mamikonean, with his companions and the other troops in his entourage took leave of the prince of Siunik‘, Vasak, and of the other nobles who remained with him, and with truehearted intentions marched off to war. They entered the house of the Lord—that is, the holy church—in order to worship the Lord God omnipotent; picking up the Holy Gospel and the crucifix of the life-giving cross, [Vardan] kissed them and placed them ardently on the pupils of his eyes and his forehead. All those with him did the same with fervent adoration; then they all set out, spurred on by zeal. Scarcely had they left, and while Vardan, the blessed Armenian general, was only a few days' journey away from Ayrarat, when the prince of Siunik‘, Vasak, immediately sent messengers to Mihrnerseh, the *hazarapet* of the Aryans, and revealed to him by letter his deceitful plan. Likewise he sent letters to Nikharakan Sebukht and the other nobles whom Mihrnerseh had set over Armenia. The latter had made his confidant Vehshapuh governor, who was at the time chamberlain of the court and then later chancellor of the Aryans. To him also the deceitful prince of Siunik‘, Vasak, wrote, indicating his treacherous wishes: "Do not worry," he said, "about those who have come with Vardan against you, and do not be at all afraid. For they are many whom I have kept here with me, and numerous others I have scattered here and there. So he has very few and not many [soldiers]." But the impious one did not remember that the hearts of princes [*p. 65*] are in the hands of God. For as much as the evil-minded one thought he was doing them a favor, all the more did the power of God change it into violent wrath and thereby incite them against him. Which came about in due time and was piled upon his head as an example.

35. When the blessed Armenian general, Vardan, lord of the Mamikonean, reached Albania, the Persian generals were informed of the Armenians' arrival. On hearing this news, they made haste to cross the great river called the Kura and precede them to the village called Khaḷkhaḷ in the land of the Albanians. When the holy Armenian *sparapet*, Vardan, saw the numberless host of the Persian army, and on looking at his own forces saw they were so very few, he began to harangue the Armenian army, recalling the saying of the Holy Spirit which the mother of the prophet Samuel, joyfully emboldened in Christ, sang as follows: "Let the strong not boast in his strength, nor the great boast in his grandeur. But let him who will boast, boast in God. For victory and defeat do not lie with the few or the many but with the command of God's Providence." Speaking thus, the blessed Armenian general, Vardan, lord of the Mamikonean, saw the will of his companions and of all the troops with them—how they were strengthened and encouraged with zealous love; and with jubilant mind he praised the Savior of all, the Lord Jesus Christ.

Arriving at the moment for battle they saw the Persian forces drawn up in order. The blessed Armenian general, Vardan, also drew up his own army with his complement of cavalry opposite them. Dividing it into three divisions he entrusted each to its own general. On the right wing he appointed as general the prince of the Arsharunik', Arshavir Kamsarakan, who was the son-in-law of the Armenian general, the saintly Vardan, lord of the Mamikonean, having married his daughter; as adjutant he gave him the noble Mush from the family of the Dimak'sean. The left wing he entrusted to Khorēn Khoṙkhoṙuni; and in support he appointed Hmayeak Dimak'sean. The saintly Armenian general, Vardan, set himself in the center of the field of action. Having thus arranged their battleline and taking refuge in God's mercy, they attacked the enemy.

The first on the field of battle were the Kamsarakan Arshavir and Mush, the noble Dimak'sean. From ignorance of the terrain they ran into deep and thick bogs. Through the excessive rush of their horses Arshavir Kamsarakan and Mush fell into the mud and were stuck with their horses. There the blessed noble Mush Dimak'sean was killed and martyred by Nikharakan. But Arshavir Kamsarakan, dismounting from his horse, [*p. 66*] on foot slew Vurk, brother of the king of the Lp'ink'. While he was dragging his horse out from the thick deep bog, one of his boots came off his foot and remained buried in the mud. On one foot, covered in mire, despite all his armor, the Kamsarakan pulled his horse out onto dry ground; then with intrepid bravery, like a bird, he attacked on horseback, terrifying the enemy wing on his side and putting them to flight. He saw that the blessed Armenian *sparapet*, Vardan, lord of the Mamikonean, with his companions and all the Armenian forces had also put [their opponents] to flight; so they drove the Persian host before them. Some of them they struck as corpses to the ground with their swords; others they cast into the river and drowned them; while the rest they scattered over the plains and thick forests.

But some of the Persian nobles, boarding boats, hastily fled to the other side of the great river. So the blessed Armenian general, Vardan, quickly urged Arshavir Kamsarakan, prince of the Arsharunik', to shoot arrows after the fleeing boats, trusting in that man's prowess in drawing the bow and his unerring aim. Then Arshavir Kamsarakan, as he was always prompt to accomplish the saintly general's words, immediately obeyed his command and shot at the sailors and fleeing [Persians]. Hitting the sailors and many others on the boats, he seriously wounded them; with the collapse of the wounded the ships sank, and many of the sailors and Persian leaders fell into the river and perished. Help from on high having thus granted them the victory, they returned to their camp, thanking and blessing God.

After staying in that spot for that day, on the morrow they set forth, crossed the great river called the Kura, and reached the pass in the barrier between the principality of Albania and the Huns. Finding there the guards of the pass and many other Persian soldiers, they put them to the sword. They entrusted the pass to an Albanian of the royal line called Vahan, and sent him as ambassador to the Huns and to other garrisons of the region, so that he might persuade them to join forces with them. Willingly and readily they agreed to help and confirmed it with an oath.

36. While all this was being accomplished through God's favor in accordance with their wishes, suddenly a messenger reached the blessed Armenian general, Vardan, and all the troops with him; he gave them grievously sad news: "The impious Vasak has been false to God's Covenant and has deceitfully violated the oath on the Gospel. He has abandoned and rebelled against the true union. [*p. 67*] Similarly those Armenian nobles who remained there with him have also rejected it and rebelled with him; turning their faces away from the path of justice they have strayed after Satan. They sent a messenger to the Persians and through letters made a compact with them. They removed the garrisons of the Armenian fortresses and installed their own troops to guard them. Transferring from their various tutors the sons of the Mamikonean and Kamsarakan families and of the other Armenian magnates, he had them brought to the fortified castles of the principality of Siunikʻ, and he ordered those castles to be guarded securely. Then the treacherous Vasak had the children taken to the Persian king. Those who were led astray after Satan with the apostate Vasak are the following: the prince of the Bagratunikʻ, Tirotsʻ; the prince of the Khoṙkhoṙunikʻ, Gadishoy; the prince of the Apahunikʻ, Manēch; the prince of the Vahevunikʻ, Giut; the prince of the Palunikʻ, Varazshapuh; the prince of the Abeḷeankʻ, Artēn; the prince of Urts, Nerseh; and others from the royal line and some nobles from each family."

When they heard of these calamitous evils done by the treacherous prince of Siunikʻ, Vasak, and by the other nobles in his entourage, the blessed Armenian *sparapet,* Vardan, lord of the Mamikonean, and the nobles and the army with him were unable not to be distressed. They entrusted themselves and the imprisoned children to the custody of the all-powerful Right Hand in these words: "Behold, Christ the Savior of all has taken a winnowing-fan into his hand to clean out his threshing-floor and to separate the grains of wheat, to gather into the barns of heaven and to deliver the straw as fuel for the unquenchable furnace without mercy. Let us be the purified grains of wheat, let us await with desire the day of our martyrdom, on which if we are worthy to share the lot of the saints our virtuous death will crown us. He [Christ] will protect and nourish the children in each one's place and restore them to their principalities; and putting the satellites of Satan to shame with great contrition, he will confound them here and in the world to come."

When the blessed one had said this, they all together marched from Albania to Armenia, to the province of Ayrarat. Staying there according to their custom for the bitter days of winter weather, they all were anxiously desirous to see the days of the month of spring and the arrival of the day for the crown of their own martyrdom. For no one any longer thought of victory or defeat, but like thirsty men they were longing for the cup of salvation and were waiting to meet and accept their end.

The treacherous prince of Siunik', Vasak, did not cease writing letters to the princes and ,peasants and priests of Armenia; he showed false covenants and vain testimonies supposedly brought from the court to this effect: "The king of kings has permitted Christianity in [our] [*p. 68*] land and does not seek reparation for the death of the magi. Concerning the revolt he says: 'I shall not remember it at all provided that you abandon the counsel and suggestions of Vardan and do not perish with him.' " Concerning himself the apostate Vasak wrote: "I am the mediator in all this, and I will ensure that Armenia is unharmed." The treacherous Vasak delivered these letters to false priests; and the names of these nonpriests are: a certain Zangak, Sahak Dzaynol, and a certain Peter Erkat'i; Sahak and Peter were from the province of Siunik'. To them, unbeknown to the blessed general Vardan, the treacherous Vasak entrusted his letters for them to circulate in Armenia. When those who were feeble in faith and without hope read these [letters], they trusted in the words of the traitor—to their perdition. But when those who were firm and desirous of martyrdom heard all these fantasies, they were strengthened and confirmed all the more, and awaited with hope the day of their promised salvation.

37. All those faithful to the covenant passed the days of winter's cold blasts and reached the great feast of Easter. Then there was joy to the whole world, to angels and mankind, for there were reconciliations of peace among themselves through the good news of the Resurrection of the Life-giver, which they celebrated with great rejoicing.

After a few days had passed, they heard that a large army had arrived in the province of Her and Zaravand. The blessed Armenian *sparapet,* the lord of the Mamikonean, Vardan, advised the faithful, who had gone to their homes for the days of the festival in order to celebrate the festival of Easter with their families: "A numerous force has arrived, bringing heavenly crowns for those who love God. So let whoever wishes to receive one make haste lest he let it slip to his regret. And if anyone has different intentions—like those others who erringly followed Satan—let him linger and stay wherever seems good to him. For no one is crowned with his companions unless he is tortured. But each person lays up treasure for himself, earthly or eternal."

On hearing this, the lovers of the truth and of immortality were stirred up, vying with each other like flocks who at the sound of the flute hasten after the shepherds. It seems to me that Abraham did not run so fast to bring the calf to the angels who promised to give him his son, as the Armenian army hastened to follow the blessed Vardan, *sparapet* of Armenia, in order to go to Christ's banquet and to eat the bread of angels.

Since they were all thus of one mind and one spirit like the Holy Apostles, the blessed *sparapet* of Armenia, [*p. 69*] Vardan, in unison with the nobility around him sent a prince of the Amatuni family whose name was Aṙandzar, with about three hundred cavalry, to go and spy out the host of the Persian forces. He was to challenge them should it be possible, said [Vardan], with a view to their bringing us rapidly the crowns of the kingdom which, through them, will be granted us by the Savior Christ, the Giver of eternal blessings. When Aṙandzar and the troops with him had set off, it was so granted them by God that they saw the Persian camp. Falling on the powerful rear guard with a united rush, they struck many with the sword and turned the others in flight back upon the Persian army. They themselves joyfully returned safe and sound to the Armenian forces and told them of God's power with which the Savior had favored them.

When the blessed *sparapet*, Vardan, and all the army heard this, they gave thanks and blessed omnipotent God. They also informed them that the generals were Mushkan Niusalavurt and Dolvech, and let them also know of their rapid advance to the center of the country. Hearing this, the blessed *sparapet* of Armenia and those around him were even more anxious to march against them: First, so that they might quickly reach the hour of martyrdom—for they were zealously praying continuously, day and night, to become worthy of such a heavenly fate; and second, they said, perhaps the outcome of the war would be decided there in the province of Her and Zaravand, and there was no one to prevent the Persian army from advancing into Armenia to assail and ravage by murder and captivity. But although the Armenians, with such intentions in mind, wished to make haste, nonetheless the Persian army with greater rapidity advanced into the province of Artaz, near the village called Avarayr, a spot surrounded by the plain of Tḷmut. They had chosen this place for fear of the Armenian army, regarding it as a convenient and safe refuge for themselves. Throwing up entrenchments in the center [of the plain], they encamped.

38. On the Friday of the great feast of Pentecost, the Armenian forces arrived near that spot and found the Persian army quite unprepared. Had they wished they could have caused especial damage to the loose ranks of those lazy [soldiers]; but they let them be and held off for that day. For those who had set their desires on martyrdom from then on had not considered victory in order to see the perpetual destruction of the damned, but they were always and continuously anxious to reach the goal of the call and of the desired martyrdom.

So gathering together they encamped near the Persian army until the day should have run its appointed course. When evening came and they had completed the office of the hour of prayer according to custom, [*p. 70*] they happily enjoyed a frugal meal. When all was finished, they received a command from the holy priests to spend that night in prayer and vigilant supplication. During the whole night groups of priests, both with sections of the psalter and with words of instruction, encouraged the host of the army to be valiant for a while and inherit unfailing blessings. The holy priest Yoseph, who occupied the throne of the Catholicosate of Armenia, ordered the blessed man of God Ḷevond to counsel the congregation and exhort them. The whole night the holy priest Ḷevond indefatigably strengthened and instructed them all with apostolic teaching, with bountiful wisdom, the explanation of parables, and inspired preaching. His words flowed from the mouth of the just one like sweet honey, and he was the delight of his hearers. By divine influence there was happily revealed the shining radiance in his inner man and the angelic appearance of his countenance. Similarly, on a previous occasion, while the saint was asleep, his teacher Mashtots‘, the man of God, with his other disciples, the blessed Koriun and Ardzan, had seen in a vigil a bright light radiating around him. Immediately these blessed men had realized through the Holy Spirit the saint's fate, that he would die a martyr's death. Although they had not revealed this miraculous vision to him, yet through their extensive journeys news of this vision had become well known and spread abroad. In his extensive spiritual teaching he recalled to everyone the lives and fortitude of those who had gone before, first of all the ineffable suffering of Saint Gregory, then that of all the others. "Knowing that the end of this life [comes] sooner or later," he said, "they chose to gain eternal life. Some by torture and death, some by fasts and sleeping on the ground, others by caring for the poor and strangers, they unknowingly became worthy to receive the angels. Others again, made famous by good government and just judgment, became God's elect. For a martyr's fate does not befall everyone, but on appropriate occasions [one attains it], as Divine Providence bestows. Those who acquire it are obliged to purchase at a just price what passes not away in exchange for this transitory [world], and eternal blessings for this corruptible [world]. Now you have been preserved for this great and honorable cup, hasten to become worthy of attaining in [heavenly] light the portion of the inheritance of the saints, whose excellence the psalmist sings: 'Excellent before the Lord is the death of his saints.' Behold, the ascetic Gregory, your teacher, summons you to the heavenly city of Jerusalem, to the delightful and sweet banquet of Christ, from which are banished pain and sadness and lamentation."

[*p. 71*] The saintly Łevond encouraged each one of the high-ranking Armenian nobles by many other spiritual words and grace-filled teaching assisted by the blessed Yoseph, who although he had been ordained [only] to the priesthood, yet worthily had been appointed to the throne of the Catholicosate. As they advised and animated them with spiritual exhortation the whole night long, every man in the willing audience became armed with the armor of the Holy Spirit, as with fearless strength. They considered the regular hours of that night to be longer than those of other nights and longed to see the morning of their salvation, so that they might attain and drink the cup of the kingdom of heaven.

The blessed Vardan, lord of the Mamikonean, listening with attention to the inspired words and the teaching that prompted to martyrdom of the angelic lord Yoseph and Łevond, replied: "The honor of ordination of the holy priests of the church does not come from men, but is granted in succession by the Holy Spirit. Likewise the words of these [priests] turn all the salubrious thoughts of their audience to heaven;

just as now for the whole night with unresting voice they have been urging everyone to the heavenly banquet by reminding us of the torments of Saint Gregory. Many of us standing here are not merely disciples of his but participators by kinship in those torments. Let us make haste to reach the marriage of Christ and his inviting messengers, the band of Holy Apostles, and the banquet of Christ, who, opening the gate of the kingdom, waits to receive all and make them joyful. Its happiness is eternal, unfading, and unending. Let us hasten without delay, and let no one be found like Judas, who was rejected from the apostolic band—as tonight you have seen [some] cowards who ran after Satan. But I receive with eagerness the cup which I have desired since long ago; and in accordance with the saying I cry: 'I shall receive the cup of salvation and call upon the name of the Lord.' "

When the saintly general had so spoken, at the hour of the cockcrow the holy Yoseph and Levond with all the priests ordered the Liturgy to be celebrated. Sustained thereby and armed with the Spirit, they set forth for the paradise of delight planted by God. When the Armenian army had participated in the honorable Mystery of the body and blood, they hastened to the heavenly task before them.

39. For by then the time of dawn was drawing near and the Persian army was arming and preparing to draw up the line of battle. The saintly Vardan, lord of the Mamikonean, divided his forces into three divisions: as commanders of the center he appointed the lord of the Artsrunik' and the *mardpet*, Mihrshapuh, with the prince of the Arsharunik', Arshavir, [*p. 72*] and the blessed man Artak, prince of Mokk', and other senior princes. On the right he put in command the blessed Makhaz Khorēn with the blessed T'at'ul, prince of Vanand, and the holy man Nersēh K'ajberuni and other senior nobles. On the left he disposed himself with his own troops and the prince of the Aṙaveleank', P'ap'ag, and other leading princes of Armenia. For on that side appeared more clearly the camp of the forces of Siunik' and the standards of other warriors. He left his own brother Hamazaspean as rear guard and commanded him to bring force to bear on no one, but to encourage [them] merely by words with a view to their salvation.

When the saintly Vardan had thus divided the Armenian army into three sections and they had been blessed from the mouths of the holy priests, blessing God the two sides rushed upon each other, Armenians and Persians. Then, vying with each other, the men desirous of the martyr's crown advanced and at first turned the Persian army to flight. But another large part of the Armenian troops who [were fighting] under pressure and not of their own will and who were discouraging and turning back the others who were desirous of heavenly blessings, then turned in flight and suffered eternal damnation. When the Persian army saw the Armenian troops too weak and fatigued to destroy their own forces, and when they noticed furthermore that the Armenian troops were deserting in flight, they surrounded them and immolated them. And there the latter, attaining their desired goal, were slaughtered. Then the Persian troops pressed hard after the Armenian fugitives; catching up with them, some they killed, others they stopped and held in some stronghold. But some of these, striking down the armed night guards and killing many of them, escaped safe and sound. In the morning they brought those of the Armenian fugitives they had captured to the camp and slew them by the sword; many others they killed by throwing them under elephants. The survivors of those who fled were scattered to various places in Armenia.

Now those who in the hour of that blessed and heavenly summons became worthy to be martyred with Saint Vardan are the following:

> From the family of the Khoṙkhoṙunik', the blessed Khorēn
> From the family of the Palunik', the blessed noble Artak
> From the family of the Gndunik', the blessed Tachat
> From the family of the Dimak'seank', the blessed Hmayeak
> From the family of the K'ajberuink', the blessed Nerseh
> From the family of the Gnunik', the blessed Vahan
> From the family of the Ēntsayink', the blessed Arsēn
> From the family of the Srvandzitk', the blessed Garegin

After inquiring with extensive searching and many investigations, we learned that the number of the martyrs who were crowned on the battlefield with the great nobles was [*p. 73*] 276. And those who were brought out of the strongholds and killed by the sword or trampled by elephants were 760. Altogether there were 1,036. Each one's name Christ the Recompenser keeps recorded in the book of life. But from the Persian army those who fell in the battle on that day, as has been accurately reckoned and told to us, confirmed by the Persian generals, were 3,544.

40. After the battle had thus come to an end and the benevolent God had called his dear ones to himself, Mushkan Niusalavurt sent a report to the king of the Aryans, Yazkert, informing him of the outcome of the battle; he wrote the good news of the victory and specified by name the number of the fallen from both sides in the battle. When King Yazkert heard of the slaughter of fine soldiers from among the Persian army and of the death of Vardan, he was plunged into terrible distress, recalling his bravery and virtue, which he had frequently shown to his enemies on behalf of the land of the Aryans. He ordered a reply made to the report and summoned Mushkan Niusalavurt with his army to court. And he ordered a certain Atrormizd, from Armenia, to be left as *marzpan;* he instructed him by letter not to disturb the Armenian populace but to subdue them peacefully and to allow everyone to practice Christianity freely. When Mushkan saw King Yazkert's letter and had heard the orders it contained, he appointed Atrormizd Arshakan *marzpan* in Armenia and entrusted to him all matters according to the instructions in the king's letter. Then Mushkan with the nobility and all the other troops returned to Persia. Atrormizd remained as *marzpan* of Armenia, and he sent many conciliatory letters to different parts of Armenia to this effect: "Come, settle down without fear, and do not be alarmed." He wrote and sealed these words of good news, that everyone would be allowed to practice Christianity in the fashion that each person desired. At this news all [the Armenians] in Persia and Siunik' joyfully gathered together.

41. He also formed an army of many picked men from Persia and Siunik' to attack those who had gathered around the blessed Hmayeak in the fortresses of Tayk'. Dividing this army into two, he appointed as its generals Arten Gabełean and Varazshapuh Paluni. For a great number of the Armenian refugees, greater and lesser nobles, men of the city and common people, had gone to Tayk' and gathered around Hmayeak, brother of the saintly general Vardan. Hmayeak had stayed in Greek territory to seek troops from the emperor—as was narrated previously in its place. They had gone and met the emperor [*p. 74*] Theodosius. When he heard the reason for their coming he heard them kindly and agreed to help them with an army. But while he was preparing to carry out his promise, the saintly [emperor] reached the end of his life and died. In his stead Marcian became emperor; when he had been informed of the state of affairs in Armenia he asked the court nobles: "What sort of reply does it seem to you should be made to these men who have come to us from Armenia?" Anatolius, who was at the time *asparapet* of Antioch, and a certain Florentius, Syrian by race, who was a court noble, replied and said: "It does not seem good to us to despise the covenant and treaty which long since the previous emperors made and sealed, and to disturb by war affairs peacefully settled, and to remove a country from subjection to its king. It is furthermore necessary to consider the uncertain outcome of this business, as no one can know how—whether easily or with severe trouble—that war will end." Speaking thus, they deflected the king's intentions; so the Armenians' expectations were thwarted and failed. And while news of the reply was thus delayed, the war between the Armenians and Persians took place.

When the Armenian magnates and princes who had gone to the land of the Greeks saw that they had received no help for their trouble, they turned back in haste, so that at least they might not miss the hope of salvation, but be rendered worthy to drink the cup of martyrdom with their companions. But not arriving in time for the battle, they stopped for a while by the mountain called Parkhar near the borders of Khaḷtikʿ, where they found a very strong site, to see how they might prepare for the tasks ahead. Meanwhile, [the Persians] with knowledgeable guides came up during the night, and at dawn with drawn weapons fell upon the companions of Hmayeak Mamikonean at the village called Orjnhaḷ in the province of Taykʿ, for at that point they had come down from their fortified places on Mount Parkhar. The refugees each rapidly mounted his horse; some unarmed, some armed, they were attacked by the Persian troops. But turning them back, they put them to flight; many were struck to the ground right in the village, and others in the vineyard. There too the blessed noble Hmayeak received the crown of perfection which he had desired and so earnestly sought in order to follow his saintly brother. He was soon heard, for God looked at his desire, fulfilled his request, and crowned the saint.

Now when the army of faithful who had gathered around the saintly Hmayeak [*p. 75*] saw what had happened, they were plunged into deep mourning and downcast; they had no hope at all of consolation, but each one saw settled for himself the fate of a dishonorable death and cruel destruction. Discouraged, they went back up Mount Parkhar casting about for some means of assuaging the disaster and the great and fearful cause for mourning that had befallen them. When Atrormizd, *marzpan* of Armenia, heard of the loss of so many good men from the army of Persia and Siunik', although he was profoundly upset and disturbed, nonetheless on hearing of the death of the rebels, Saint Vardan and Hmayeak, he consoled himself and greatly rejoiced on learning of the complete extermination of these brave generals.

42. He then held a council to decide how they might find a way to hunt down the fugitives without involving the Aryans in a struggle, and how to submit Armenia to their will and impose tribute. They came to the firm conclusion that to avoid a struggle they would be able to win over the populace only by a false oath and a vain promise. The *marzpan,* Atrormizd, sent word to them [the princes] following King Yazkert's letter, falsely swearing to them that "we shall put none of you to death, nor deprive anyone of his title or honor." Having thus subjected these men in a deceitful way, he arrested them all and had them marched to the Aryan court: the great prince of the Artsrunik', Nershapuh; the prince of the house of the Amatunik'; the prince of the house of Vanand; the prince of the house of the Arsharunik', Arshavir; the prince of the house of the Andzevatsik', Shmavon; Vahan, the prince of the house of the Amatunik'; the prince of the Gnt'unik'; the prince of Ashots'; P'ap'ak', prince of the Aṙaveḷeank'; Vrēn, the prince of Tashir; Aprsam, prince of the Artsrunik'; and other magnates and great nobles they despatched to the court of King Yazkert. The treacherous prince of Siunik', Vasak, also wished to make the journey to the court, but he had the others sent in advance of himself.

[He also sent] some of the holy Armenian priests whom he had earlier arrested and held in various parts of Siunik' in strong castles: the holy priest Yoseph, who held the throne of the Catholicosate at the time, and lord Ḷevond, and the priests of Arats, lord Samuel and lord Abraham. With these they also arrested and sent the holy bishop of the Ṙshtunik', lord Sahak; and the domestic chaplain of Nershapuh, prince of the Artsrunik', lord Mushē; and the holy priest Arshēn and the holy deacon K'ajaj. But the holy bishop of Basean, lord T'at'ik, had been sent previously to Khujastan by the Persian generals at the denunciation of the prince of Siunik', and was held there in strict captivity. He also had sent away the children that he had seized from the families of the Mamikonean and Kamsarakan [*p. 76*] and from other noble Armenian families, supposing he would render great service to King Yazkert and to the whole land of the Aryans and that he would receive royal status and honors. But this was turned by God into even greater ridicule for him on the day of his humiliation when Yazkert and all the nobility of the court covered him with derision and disgrace, in accordance with the invisible workings of the power of God, the equitable Judge.

When the traitor Vasak had sent all these [prisoners] ahead of himself to Persia in the thirteenth year of Yazkert, king of Persia, he himself set out with a substantial retinue and a powerful escort in order to approach the Persian king and, after demonstrating to the king and the Aryan nobility his so-called and deceitful loyalty, to receive as reward in his raving mind the crown of Armenia. "But if I fall at all short in this," he said, "I shall still obtain all the rest—honor and dignity—without any doubt or hesitation; indeed they are [already] mine." But he did not ask the Lord God, who speaks through the prophet: "They became kings, but not through me; and they made pacts, but not in accordance with my will." So, at the moment when the traitor, as he supposed, was to obtain such great honor, the Word of God, who seeks what is just, forestalled him, stripped off and scattered the mask of his treacherous plans, and upset all his bitter intentions, like the baneful counsel of Achitobel.

While he was on the [same] road along which they were taking the holy priests of God as prisoners, seated on mules, the host of travelers accompanying the impious Vasak came across the champions of Christ. When the latter asked: "Whose is this host?" they were told by some people: "It is the lord of Siunik"'s." And they said: "Here he is, coming up close to us." Ceasing their questions, the saints continued on their way. The holy Yoseph asked that man of God, Levond: "I know that Vasak has caught up with us and in his shameless impudence is likely to greet us. Consider and tell us how we should act, and we shall so do." The saintly Levond replied, sayng: "Do not seek to learn the Savior's teaching from a man: 'Into whatever city or village you enter give greetings; and where someone is found to greet you, your greeting will remain on him. But if there will be no one worthy, your greeting will return upon yourself.' " When they had finished their mutual questioning, the traitor Vasak, lord of Siunik', came up to them. Having discovered from them [who they were], he immediately dismounted from his horse and greeted [*p. 77*] the saints. They

291

suspected no enmity at all in him, and addressed him with joyful affection. And especially the holy Levond, whose visage was always happy and smiling, spoke for a long time with Vasak, prince of Siunik', in a gay and vivacious manner. When the latter heard the blessed one's sweet and graceful words, rendered insane by the devil, he supposed that "they do not know the evils I have wrought against them." Therefore being even more reassured by the words of that man of God, Levond, he accompanied them for a long way.

After they had finished their conversation the lord of Siunik' wished to entertain them; he invited the holy ones to dine with him that day in the inn. When the traitor Vasak had got a little in front of them, the holy Levond shouted out after him, loudly calling him by his noble title: "Lord of Siunik', lord of Siunik'." He quickly replied: "My lords, what say you?" And the holy one said: "While we were having all this conversation with you we forgot to ask the most necessary and important question: Where are you going?" When the traitor Vasak heard this he was plunged into great distress, and said angrily: "I am going to my lord, to receive from him great compensation appropriate to my great services." The holy Levond replied: "The devil who has tricked and seduced you into being false to the pact of the Holy Gospel makes you suppose that only by the throne of Armenia can the Aryans compensate you worthily for your great services. But there is nothing they can give you as reward; if indeed you bring back your head on your shoulders alive to Armenia, then the Lord God has not spoken with me." When the treacherous prince Vasak heard this he was downcast and paralyzed in his vain hope. He immediately realized his personal destruction, which ever sooner was to overwhelm him. For the holy one's word did not miss the mark and everything came to pass.

43. When the treacherous prince of Siunik' reached the court, he first saw the nobility of the royal court and then had an audience with King Yazkert. The king and all the royal magnates received him for a while with honor and pomp. For although they knew his fault and the oath and pact which he had deceitfully made with the saintly Vardan and all the princes of Armenia in order to destroy them and show his own fidelity, nonetheless they gave no indication to him that they knew but kept silent as if they were ignorant. They honored him as a faithful man devoted to their interests, until there arrived at court the holy priests of God and the senior Armenian magnates and nobles who had rebelled, accompanied by the children of the Mamikonean and Kamsarakan and other [*p. 78*] rebel families; these the traitor first of all brought before the *hazarapet*, Mihrnerseh, and the other nobles of the court.

The impious *hazarapet* of the Aryans ordered that first the priests should be brought before him. He asked the holy priest of Arats', Samuel, and his spiritual son, the holy deacon Abraham, who had extinguished the fire of Artashat: "With what presumption and by whose command did you dare to do such an act worthy of death? Did you not consider the awe of kings and the fear of princes; did you dare to lay your hands on such a great fire? For if such insolence had been paid to a man, the deed would have been worthy of immediate death—let alone if it were done to the gods." When the two holy ones, lords Samuel and Abraham, heard this they replied in unison, both truthfully and contemptuously, showing their fearless audacity and mocking at their hearers' stupid questioning. They said: "To fear with a right and just fear kings and princes, our own religion commands; but to exchange the fear of God for the fear of man, we do not accept. Now as for that fire which you told us that we killed, we have harmed it neither by the bastinado nor by cruel beatings. But we saw that the times were troubled and observed the neglect of its ministers, who set at naught the fear of their gods, but abandoned it with contempt as worthless and went off; and we saw the fire abandoned, no one to tend the ashes and left thus for many days without anyone caring for it, so we took the ashes and threw them out. For we used to see that being done continuously by its own ministers as they regularly carried away the ashes and spread them on the ground. But as our detractors have made you understand about us that we took the fire and threw it into water—for that it is not at all worthy of your just majesty to be angry at us and hold us to be guilty of death, but rather you should render us praise and honor. For if indeed, as you claim, you are repeating what you have heard from your teachers and that testimony is true that water is a brother to fire, not only did we not extinguish or damage the fire, but we honored it and did it a good turn. So, if anyone is worthy of death, it is those who abandoned and scorned the fire and went away—not we, who took it and gave it to its brother for him to cherish lovingly and with great respect, and in time to restore."

44. In similar fashion they threatened and interrogated the other holy priests of God, the saintly Yoseph, and worthy

Catholicos of Armenia; and the holy bishop of the Ṙshtunikʻ, lord Sahak; and the all-holy priest, lord Ḷevond; and the other holy priests who were with them in the interrogation, the holy Mushē Aḷbakatsʻi, who was the domestic chaplain of Nershapuh, prince of the Artsrunikʻ; and the holy priest Arshēn, who was from the province of Bagrevand from the village called Eḷegeak; and the holy deacon [*p. 79*] Kʻajaj, who was also from the province of Ṙshtunikʻ, a pupil of the holy bishop Sahak. "By what reckless audacity have you personally piled up on your own miserable selves so many [actions] deserving of death? You have destroyed the fire-temples, you have killed so many noble fires, which the gods bestowed on the Aryans' land to preserve it from evil and harmful events which might be loosed upon us and all regions by our enemies; [from such] these fires have kept us and [still] preserve us unharmed. You have killed the magi, you have destroyed by your sorcery Vardan, such a noble man, for he was a support to the lord of the Aryans and the memory of his great feats [is preserved] in the land of the Aryans. He is remembered by many generals and other Aryans with whom he fought, and even the godlike king himself with his own eyes noticed his valor at Marviṙot. There are few men in the land of the Aryans who could render him and his deeds due praise. Yet you through your useless and harmful teaching have miserably destroyed such a man. In such a country [as yours] has been poured out the limitless blood of Aryans and non-Aryans. So can you not then of your own accord find for yourselves a way to die and be delivered from the beneficent light which, unworthily and unjustifiably, you see today rather than suffer a cruel death from the many tortures you [must] endure in just compensation for your deeds?"

On hearing all this threatening speech and the reproachful words of the venomous *hazarapet* of the Aryans, Mihrnerseh, and of all the court nobility, the man of God, Ḷevond, stepped forward and responded: "All those who stand in this inquiry before your lordship, and with whom you have been speaking at length, have the distinction of the honor of priesthood in accordance with our religion and the divine authority of the church." And indicating the saints one by one, he introduced each one to them, [saying] who this one was or what another's name was, and with what rank in the Christian clergy they were honored. For although they had heard by repute the names of the saints and each one's role that he played in Armenia, nonetheless the names of the saints were unknown to them and they were ignorant of each one's rank in the Christian hierarchy. Of the holy Yoseph he said: "This one whom you see here, although you will notice that he is younger than I in years, yet in honor he is worthily set higher and is the head of the priesthood of all Armenia." And indicating the holy Sahak, he said: "This one holds the supreme order of consecration according to the true and rightly divine ordination of our religion, while the others and I are merely in the order of priesthood. But if any lesser individual [*p. 80*] joins now [with us] in the quest for perfection and is found worthy, such a one is even greater in the kingdom of God, where envy has no part. This is not my own remark, but he who is our Creator and teacher said: 'Whoever readily serves everyone will be called the greatest in the kingdom of God.' Now, you have ordered us to make some reply to your many words and threats against us. For not as ignorant men did we accomplish thoughtlessly such a great and fearful deed, and now repent; nor, as some now suppose, are we standing before your majesty in fear and not in joy—rather we rejoice and are glad at what we did. But we shall endure all sorts of torments, and we await death with the longing that we may be rendered worthy [of it].

"As for what you said about destroying fire-temples or killing fire, it is said in our Scripture: 'Let gods, who did not create heaven and earth, perish under the earth.' For fire is composed of many elements; sometimes it is extinguished by these same elements of which it is composed, and sometimes it is increased by them and burns. Now, fire is born from iron and stone and water and wood. There is also the white pearl from which fire is born. Fire is derived from clay mixed with silver when someone exposes it to the sun's rays. And the fire that is born from iron, if you pile iron on top of it, is extinguished. And that [fire] which derives from stone, if you hide it with stones, goes out. The same happens with that which is derived from water and from any other element. But the fire that is derived from wood, burns up and is strengthened by wood. Now neither the fire nor the wood is worthy to be called god—who both begets and vivifies. So would it not be the ultimate wicked error to call mutual enemies "brothers," and men's creations "God"? He who reduces to nothing his own brother or parent like enemies, how can he know how to honor or injure those who injure or worship himself. And again they consume mercilessly that from which they are born. Fire is not absent from any element; so then all elements of the earth are gods. But if you so believe, why with blinded mind do you call part of them gods and insult the other part by putting it to impure use? For example, with bricks and stones you use some for building palaces, and some for building privies and latrines; with silver, part you form into cups and part into chamber pots. With fire you roast and cook oxen and sheep for the gods; with water you wash away sewage and slops and filth, yet part of it, by itself or mixed with wine, you drink without being frightened or horrified. But why should we be obliged to mention in detail or enumerate your folly? The vigilant and brave hero Vardan and those of his ilk, unable [*p. 81*] to serve such stupidity, protested to you continually that your cults were false and your teachings irrational; but you paid no attention, for frenzy does not allow reason to be recognized, as is the case now. Therefore, unable to endure it, they gave themselves to death and were crowned; and we encouraged them and were their true teachers."

After the holy man of God, Levond, had said all this, as with one mouth the holy priests praised it loudly and rejoiced greatly. Hearing the saints' loud praises and seeing the joy on their faces, the impious Mihrnerseh and the other Aryan nobles who were sitting in his presence erupted in great anger. He said to them: "Our religion bids us be angry at no one before we have heard something from his mouth. Now, we have seen you rejoicing at the speech of this pernicious man, and we have been well informed about all his deeds and bewitching teaching whereby he destroyed that excellent man, the valiant Vardan, and his companions. Therefore cruel retribution and death have worthily been prepared for him. But do you let us know whether what you have to say is the same as what this criminal with fearless audacity was presumptuous enough to say before us."

Saint Yoseph and Saint Sahak replied: "For a long time we have frequently all reflected together on these words and the response which lord Levond addressed to you in a manner befitting his holy rank, encouraged by God's support. And today, with the knowledge granted him by God, he has beautifully expounded our thoughts before you. We are all of the same mind and of the same intention, and we seek to become worthy to die therein. But in your bitter passion and anger you have insulted him. Blessed are those who with the eyes of the mind are clear-sighted and righteous. But [even] the greatest when seized by bodily disease become weak—as do also the lesser. So do not insult anyone when angered with such passion, for you yourself are worthy of much blame."

Furious at the saints because of these insults, as if they had turned their derision toward the king, the impious prince commanded the executioners to strike the mouths of the blessed ones violently with chains, until their mouths were full of blood, which flowed out. This done, he dismissed the tribunal. But the saints, after the manner of the Holy Apostles, left the tribunal rejoicing that they had been worthy of insults and blows in defense of the name of Christ.

45. As for the other prisoners among the magnates and senior nobles who were in the same tribunal, Mihrnerseh commanded the executioners [*p. 82*] to take them away and keep them in strict confinement until the king himself, he said, should interrogate them and hear whatever they had to say. The next morning the impious Mihrnerseh came before King Yazkert to inform him about all his own questioning and the Armenian priests' replies. The king was enraged and ordered that on the morrow a great tribunal should be held in his presence and that every man, Aryan or non-Aryan, and whoever held any royal rank should present himself prepared before him, and that all the prisoners should be brought into his presence. But the youths and children of the Mamikonean, Kamsarakan, and other families he ordered the impious Mihrnerseh to assign to whomever he might wish.

When all the soldiers who had any royal rank heard this, they came early to the tribunal. But the apostate prince of Siunik', Vasak, robing himself in all the dignities he had from the king, entered the royal chambers in great pomp. For apart from the rank of kingship which he lacked, there was no other royal honor which he did not possess. And he supposed that he was then to receive the throne of the great country of Armenia. But the wretched one did not know that the Lord had withdrawn from him, that the evil demon was strangling him, and that the saying of the holy man of God, Levond, was then being fulfilled against the wretch. When the whole chamber was full of Aryans and non-Aryans, the king ordered the Armenian rebels to be brought in bonds into his presence.

They were brought and set before the king. He questioned them, saying: "By what audacity, or with what intention, or by what deceit, or with what source of support in mind, did you engage in such a terrible business, in which you should have

297

seen the ruin of yourselves and your country, as indeed happened and you can see?" When the Armenian nobles heard this they were silent for a while and gave no answer. The king repeated his words in the terms of his first question, and demanded from them an immediate reply. They responded and said: "May your benevolent majesty be pleased to hear one man, whom we shall designate from among us, who will explain the entire progression of our affairs—what we planned and did. For it is not right for us all to speak before you as a disordered mob."

The king and all the nobles willingly agreed, and he so ordered. Then [the Armenians] put forward the Kamsarakan, Arshavir, and asked them to hear from him the entire explanation. Arshavir Kamsarakan, strengthened by the Holy Spirit, stepped forward and fearlessly began to speak before the king and all the nobles as follows:

"From the beginning the causes of these affairs have been known to us even when they were born in the minds of your kings. You put your plans [*p. 83*] into effect, you ordered us to submit to them, and you forced us to accept a religion which neither we nor our ancestors' ancestors recognized or had served. Many times we protested that it was impossible for us to accept and serve a religion which our ancestors had not served, which seems to our minds obnoxious and an outrage. And to such complaints on our part your veracious court can bear witness. Although we did not wish to obey, through the violence of your wishes we were forced to accept that cult. From fear we falsely honored it with our lips, wishing to avoid for a while your terror by false pretenses. But in our hearts we considered that an abominable act and we hated it; so we decided to escape by some means, return to our country, and then leave our country and go with wives and children to perish in a foreign land. The first to act according to these plans was the most famous of the country's princes, your servant Vardan. Persians from the greatest families who are now alive and present here with you know this and can attest to my words. Taking only his wife and family, he set out and fled from your tyranny to the land of the Greeks.

"When the lord of Siunik', Vasak, became aware of this, he quickly sent after him the greatest magnates and nobles and holy priests as messengers, and sealing with his own ring the Holy Scriptures of our religion—on which they had taken an oath—he had it brought to him. With them he also sent me. He wrote in the letter to him as follows: 'Why have you fled, and what is the terror that makes you afraid and which you have not at all made clear? So do not flee and do not be afraid of anyone. For if you are terrified of the lord of the Aryans and of his might, fear not. Return, and we shall send a letter to the emperor and give ourselves over to his service. And he, believing that we give over such a great country to his service of our own desire, will joyfully accept it and give us an army. Then they and we united will give continual trouble to the lord of the Aryans and to the Aryans. But if the emperor has other plans and does not accord [us] his assistance—while I was *marzpan* of Georgia and controlled the Alan Pass, many Hunnish generals became friends with me by pacts and oaths, and today under the same pact visit me frequently. The tribute of all Armenia is under my control and all the agents are in my hand. And there is much more money, taken from the Persian agents who were in Armenia, that is in my treasury. If I have part of this sent to the Huns, I shall bring over such a vast number of them that the land of Persia would not suffice them for booty.'

"Having written all this [and confirmed it] by an oath, Vasak, the lord of Siunik', forced Vardan to return; the latter was near the territory of foreign princes [*p. 84*] who are not subject to your rule. The letter which this lord of Siunik' wrote to Vardan survives and the seal is here in our possession. Order it to be seen. And concerning his own sons, he writes as follows: 'Those Persians in Armenia I shall all put into secure fortresses in bonds, until the king is obliged to release my sons.' He did arrest a few Persians and held them for a while. And when he had deceitfully brought to conclusion the plan he had adopted for our destruction, then he released them. He wrote letters to the emperor and other court nobles and to the general of Antioch, and he sent Vahan Amatuni and others from each of the noble families to the Greeks. He brought Vardan and us with an army to Albania in order to wage war, and tricking us without our realizing it, he pushed us into this disaster. He killed that so excellent servant of yours and was the cause of the slaughter of such a large number of Persians and Armenians and of the ruin of the country. And now, behold him in full regalia sitting like a benefactor in your midst, quite unconcerned. But command to be seen all those letters which he wrote and sealed to the emperor and to the whole land of the Romans and to many others. As you Aryans wish, so command and accomplish against us. For where letters and seals are produced, as your justice demands, there is no need of superfluous words and much speech."

When the Persian king and all the court nobility heard this systematic account from Arshavir Kamsarakan and when they saw the letters written to Vardan by the lord of Siunik' and had realized [the truth], King Yazkert was greatly amazed and all the court nobles were astonished.

46. Then the king called forward the prince of Siunik', Vasak, and with an extremely angry heart began to upbraid him: "We have heard of all your treacherous acts and deeds. But now, tell me: with what plan or with what intention did you presume to undertake and carry out such pernicious acts, for you were the prince and head of Armenia? First, in exhorting men [to rebellion], as we have been accurately informed from the letters written by you which we have had read. Although you made our meritorious and excellent servant, the valiant Vardan, and his companions swear an oath, you deceived them by letters to the emperor and his general. It was treachery to make such valiant and notable subjects of mine as Vardan and other companions take such an oath. Furthermore, by sending him with an army to Albania you emboldened him to attack the Persian forces. You treacherously betrayed and ruined the land of the Aryans, and you were the cause of the loss of so many of my servants, both Aryans and non-Aryans. For [*p. 85*] if the emperor or the king of the Huns had wished to win over from me by force such a servant of mine as Vardan, I would have battled with all the might of the Aryans and would not have rested until I had won him back to myself. But now you, with your own hand, have slain such a valuable servant and have ruined a great and excellent country, yet you have insolently dared to come and visit us as if we were ignorant of your treachery. But know this, that henceforth you are no longer lord of Siunik'; all the crimes which you planned and carried out will be piled upon your own evil head. And the taxes of my land of Armenia and of the Persians whom you killed, and the great amount of money which you extorted, we have ordered to be compensated from your household and from your sons until all is paid."

Although the pitiable renegade Vasak wished to speak and make some response, no one at all heeded his words or was well disposed toward him. For his violation of the oath on the Holy Gospel and the curse of the blessed man of God, Levond, rebounded on him; they beset, surrounded, and fenced him in.

Although he had performed services for the Persians, which he tried to indicate at that time, yet it was of no avail; they rather provided even more grounds for accusation and harmed him. The saying of the psalmist was fulfilled for him: "He shall emerge condemned from his own tribunal and his prayers will be turned into sin." King Yazkert commanded him to be deprived there in his presence with opprobrium of every honor he possessed; the guards scourged him, and stripped him of all the insignia of his princely rank and expelled him from the royal chamber with ignominy. On that same day they appointed his enemy, the junior noble of Siunik', the apostate Varazvaḷan, as lord of the land of Siunik'. As long as he held the principality of Siunik' he committed many injustices and built many fire-temples there, a scandal to his house; for a long time he was tormented by the devil, as described above, and perished cruelly with a bitter death.

The traitor Vasak remained at court for a few years in great affliction and much distress. He spent his days sighing and languishing every day and hour, even spreading the palms of his hands in hostile derision and beating his own face, saying: "Behold, accept these insults brought upon you by your violation of the oath on the Holy Gospel and the blood of the martyrs, Saint Vardan Mamikonean and his other dear companions, who have inherited eternal life and earned good repute on earth that will last for all the generations of their families. But you, said he, sinful one, you live in misery and anguish the short days of your life, and are reserved for eternal and unending hell." Such were his sighings and weeping [*p. 86*] until the day of his death, told us by veracious servants of the same prince Vasak. His end came there in Persia, according to the saying of the holy man of God, Ḷevond.

47. King Yazkert ordered [the following priests and nobles] to be held in strict confinement in Vrkan until the sixteenth year of his reign: the holy priests of God, lord Yoseph the Catholicos, lord Sahak bishop of the Ṙshtunik', the blessed priest lord Ḷevond, lord Musheḷ, domestic chaplain of Nershapuh, prince of the Artsrunik', lord Samuel priest of Arats, lord Abraham the deacon, lord Arshēn, priest of Eḷegeak, lord K'ajaj the deacon—these eight priests, and the Christian Armenian nobles held prisoner, whose names were: two brothers from the family of Siunik', Babken and Bakur; from the family of the Artsrunik', Nershapuh and Shavasp and Shngin and Pargev and Tachat; from the family of the Mamikonean, Ha-

mazaspean and Hamazasp and Artavazd and Mushel; from
the family of the Kamsarakan, Arshavir and T'at' and Vard-
zay; from the family of the Amatunik', Vahan and Ařandzar
and Ařnak; from the family of the Gnunik', Atom; from the
family of the Dimak'sean, T'at'ul and Satoy, with two other
family members from the family of the Andzevats'ik', Shmavon
and Ařavan; from the family of the first Ařaveleank', P'ap'ak
and Varazden and Dat; from the family of the Artsrunik', Aprsam; from the family of the Mandakunik', Sahak and P'arsman; from the family of the Tashrats'ik', Vrēn; from the family
of the Řop'seank', Babik and Yohan—in all thirty-one men
from the Armenian nobility.

48. In the sixteenth year of his reign King Yazkert set out
with his whole host and marched to war against the Kushans.
He ordered the Armenian prisoners, priests and nobles, also to
join his march from Vrkan. On reaching the land of Apar and
coming to the capital called Niwshapuh, he commanded the
Armenian prisoners, priests and nobles, to be kept there in the
fortress of Niwshapuh. But the two blessed priests, lords Samuel and Abraham, he ordered to march on with him. He had
them continually afflicted with cruel treatment and strong
chains and beatings, in order to put fear and trembling into the
Christians who were with him in his army. When they arrived
at the enemies' borders, not even partially were the king's ob-
jectives realized; but completely vanquished, he returned covered in shame, having lost the most elite and eminent men of
his army as well as other common soldiers in the cavalry. For
the enemy did not fight the Persian army in opposing battle-
lines, but unexpectedly [*p. 87*] falling upon each wing, they put
many to the sword, then themselves disappeared again unharmed. Using these tactics for many days, they exhausted the
Persian army by their savage attacks.

When King Yazkert saw his ignominious humiliation, he
was plunged into deep gloom and depression; dejected, he
sought to find out why such grave ignominy had befallen him.
Being in doubt, he attributed the cause sometimes to the disunity of his army and sometimes to the laziness of his magi,
saying: "So they were unable by offerings and worthy sacrifices
to gratify the gods, who in their anger were unwilling to assist
us. Since they withdrew their support, the enemies' side has
been strengthened, while we have been defeated and have returned covered in shame." The magi, realizing the king's grief,
took counsel on the advice of the impious *hazarapet,* Mihrner-

seh, and began to speak with the king as follows: "Noblest of the Aryans, let your mind linger on no other reasons for the disasters which the enemy have inflicted on us other than the anger of the gods, who have been deeply angered at us on account of the deicide Armenian priests. They were worthy of death long ago, but since you took no measures they have remained alive until today. For if they had merely been murderers and you had kept them for so long without inflicting death, that would have been a very grievous action and worthy of blame—let alone that they dared lay hands on the gods to kill them. Yet they live and see the sun. Justly do we find ourselves punished by the gods."

On hearing this from the magi, the king supposed their false reasons to be true ones. Aroused to great wrath against the captive priests, he reckoned that it was really because of them that so many of his soldiers had been killed. He immediately commanded that the priests in his company, the holy priest Samuel and the holy deacon Abraham, should be taken to some obscure place, very far from the army, and there beheaded, so that none of the Christians could find their bones and honor them. But before they were killed, he ordered the right hand of Saint Samuel to be cut off and placed in the hand of lord Abraham; and similarly, he ordered that Saint Abraham's right hand be cut off and placed in lord Samuel's hand: "In return," he said, "for having dared to lay their hands on the honorable fire and killing it." Then their heads were to be cut off with the sword. In this way the saints were martyred in the month of Hrotits', on the seventh day of the month, in the province called Vardgēs.

49. Then King Yazkert ordered messengers to be sent immediately and in great haste with regard to the blessed bishop [*p. 88*] of Basean, T'at'ik, who was in prison in Asorestan and had been tormented for a long time with cruel tortures. He ordered him to be killed there and his body to be concealed, so that none of the Christians could find and honor his bones. When the messenger[s] arrived there, the magi carried out the order and were filled with joy. But before the death of the saint, for many days they cruelly flayed the saint's body from the bones; then in accordance with the king's order they cut off his head with the sword and killed him.

50. He gave similar commands with regard to the other holy priests whom they had left imprisoned in the fortress of Niwshapuh. He ordered Vehdenshapuh, the chief-steward, to take with him two other assistants from the nobility, Jnikan, the royal *maypet,* and Movan, the chamberlain delegated by the chief-*mobed,* and to go directly to bring from prison the holy priests who were held there, and the Armenian nobles; to take them far from the city to a remote and desert spot, and there with cruel tortures, as might seem best to him, to deprive them of life. But the king cautioned Vehdenshapuh with strict orders not to let anyone know of their removal from the city, of the road along which they would be taken, or of the place where they were to be put to death. "For we have heard with accuracy," he said, "that those who belong to the erring sect of the Christians especially rejoice in death for this reason. They say about the bones of those who die for their god, that if anyone has in his house even a small fragment of them no harm or evil machination touches him, or his house, or his dear ones. Furthermore," he said, "they claim that in judicial proceedings [the relics] give success, wisdom, bravery, and security. They attempt by personal efforts and money, even at the cost of their lives, to obtain at least a tooth or nail of such persons and to take it to their homes. In addition, this too we have learned from trustworthy men who belonged to their erring sect and later accepted our luminous and just religion, that their wives, sons, and daughters, when brought by anyone ornaments of gold, silver, or pearls, if the smallest piece of these dead men's bones is given them think this to be the most estimable and precious. Why should I say more? The wives of these Christians think nothing of taking off and giving away the ornaments of their fathers and mothers made with great labor in their memory, necklaces or strings of very valuable pearls, in order to buy fragments of such people's bones. So be careful and let their execution be in a place where the executed and those who hope for their bones will be cheated of such expectations and veneration."

When the chamberlain Vehdenshapuh heard all these instructions from the king [*p. 89*] in the land of Apar, he entered the fortress of the capital Niwshapuh and spoke false words, deceitfully giving good news: "The king of kings has commanded me to release to their own country the Armenian priests who are here in prison. And as for the other nobles from Armenia he gave a pledge that 'when I come I shall release them from prison.'" When the populace in the capital heard this, they supposed that what Vehdenshapuh had said was right. But when the holy priests heard it, they immediately realized by the inspiration of the Holy Spirit that the noble hour of hope for their martyrdom had arrived. They began to speak with the Armenian nobles with whom they were imprisoned, saying: "Although Vehdenshapuh really wished to hide his true intention he was unable. For the two of us are to accomplish our fate just as everyone has heard from us. You, by the mercy of Christ, are to be released from your bonds; but we, completing by the power of the Holy Spirit the troublesome days of this pilgrimage of life, will go to our native land and eternity, where are the ranks of Apostles and the resting-places of the saints, to the camp of the Lord and Creator of all, Christ, who said: 'Where I am, there also will my servant be.' "

51. While they were still so speaking, one of the executioners, who had friendly relations with the imprisoned Armenian nobles and who had been accurately informed by the blessed Khujik, came and revealed to them the true plans. He let them know the truth, how the king had given orders for the execution of the priests. When the princes heard the true state of affairs, they wept bitterly—not indeed that they did not desire the holy ones' martyrdom, for which they themselves desired to become worthy, but because they would be inconsolably deprived of them.

But when the saints had heard confirmation of their good news from this man, they were strengthened and rejoiced greatly. Glorifying God, they immediately prepared for the evening service, for it was already much later than the hour of service on other days. Because the chamberlain had arrived in the capital rather late, he was therefore obliged to spend the night there. After the saints had celebrated the order of the evening service, they enjoyed their light and meager rations as if they were a sumptuous and delicious meal. They prolonged the joy of their happy and delicious dinner through the consolation and power of God, the Holy Spirit. Rising from dinner and glorifying and blessing God, they completed their prayers. The holy priests of God ordered the imprisoned nobles to pray and keep vigil in turn for that night, saying to them all: "If you were to send one of your company today to Armenia, would you not joyfully send to each one's [*p. 90*] dear ones letters of greeting and happy news? Also you would beg God that the one of you who was traveling might safely reach every one's family and carry out your charge to him. Now behold, we are journeying from you to God. Do you all beseech the Savior Christ and his Holy Spirit that we may all with fearless courage be worthy of the delightful path that leads to heaven, to bring for you greetings and recommendations to the most merciful Christ and to the holy company of Apostles and prophets and of all the saints. By their continual intercession may the tender compassion of the most merciful Creator Christ console and save you; may he deliver you from the visible bonds in which you stand, and put to shame your rivals and enemies. May he let you see Armenia and your families, and gathering there the bones of each one of you, may he place them beside the bones of your fathers. And delivering your souls from the invisible bonds of Satan, may he keep you unharmed until the day of our Lord Jesus Christ."

When all the nobles heard this charge from the holy priests of Christ, they replied and said: "Whom indeed would sleep overcome in the kingdom, where there is neither vigil nor oppressive tiredness? Or who indeed would grieve and be sad in that unfading delight, from which pain, sadness, and lamentation are banished? For us this day is harbinger and pledge of that day when the teachings of the holy priests of God will be openly preached among us. And why should sadness arise in the heart of any of us who have become worthy in our lifetime of seeing our own parents and spiritual teachers in the flesh like angels and at their death like angels? But we weep and are grieved, like the Savior of all Christ on seeing Jerusalem, or Lazarus, whom he raised from the dead: why has this immortal and pure creature of the Creator's, enslaved by the enemy's deceit, returned again to dust and fallen subject to pain and death?"

When the holy priests of God heard such words of spiritual comfort from the nobles, with great joy they all began to stretch their hands to heaven, to thank God, and say: "We thank you God, who by the grace of the preaching of the Holy Apostles have given birth to many [more] apostles, and by the grace of the ascetic martyrs have given birth to numberless heroes—like the apostle and confessor lord Gregory, the doer of the righteous deeds, and the teacher of pure and lively instruction. Instilling zealous fervor in everyone, he begat teachers and numberless heroes, many monks, infinite groups of nuns, and rendered every person a true temple for the indwelling of the Holy Trinity. [*p. 91*] We thank you, Savior, who through the pastor, Saint Gregory, made the sheep more rational than the shepherds, and rendered the pupils among the people more knowledgeable than the teachers. Behold, we have now been strengthened and encouraged by the grace-filled words of our spiritual offspring, [as have] fathers by sons, teachers by pupils, priests by congregations. And now in joy we depart from them; they have put us on the road and send us to you. Although they remain in the body, they are with you and beside you, and by you are strengthened. Protect them every day with your right hand; fortify them with the strength of your Holy Spirit; console them with the joy of your word; give them your peace and increase on them your grace."

Having thus blessed the prisoners and entrusted them to the mighty Omnipotent, they said: "He will keep you safe and by his Holy Spirit will console you continually. Be not sad, but rejoice gladly in him who said: 'I shall not leave you orphans. I am coming,' he said, 'to you.' He has indeed come and is in our midst; he will free you from the bonds in which you stand, and will preserve you in the hope of his support. He will let you say with frank boasting: 'For you we die daily. We have been reckoned as sheep for slaughter.' The Lord of all will crush Satan under your feet; he will show you to be eminent and glorious in the midst of this impious nation; and he will bring you back to your land. He will protect your homes, nourish your children, and cause your offspring to inherit the possessions of their fathers. To him be glory, now and for all eternity. Amen."

After Saint Levond had uttered these words of instruction and consolation at the behest of Saint Yoseph and Saint Sahak, they and he blessed the nobles and the others in their company; and entrusting them all to the Holy Trinity, they finished their prayers. Every one of the blessed captive nobles became like those who had gathered in the upper-room; and they communed with the Holy Apostles, filled with the Holy Spirit's grace, encouraged and trusting in the hope of heaven.

52. While the minds of all the audience were delighting in the spiritual teaching of the apostle-like teachers, as in sumptuous and delicious food, there suddenly arrived large numbers of executioners [sent] by the *ambarapet* with many brightly-lit torches. For in accordance with the fixed and immutable crowing of the bird [ordained] by divine command, it was already the hour for the crowing of the cock. They had with them a host of smiths with the tools of their trade—anvils, hammers, chisels, and files—to file away, break, and remove the irons from the hands, feet, and necks of the saints. And when they were unable to break them [*p. 92*] with their files, they shattered the iron nails with hammers, placing them on anvils and

breaking them to remove them. For they were stronger and heavier than the kind of ordinary iron with which they chained other condemned prisoners. The magi had had them made expressly for them as for men who counseled evil, ruined the country, and slew the gods—and especially the chains of the holy Catholicos Yoseph, which were said to surpass even the strength of the other chains and to be extraordinary.

When the holy priests of God saw the executioners arriving with Vehdenshapuh and noticed the large number of smiths, they were all grieved and upset because they had desired [to answer] the heavenly summons with the same ornaments that for God's name they had become worthy of bearing willingly and joyfully on their bodies for such a long time. If they had worn them to the place of martyrdom where they would become worthy of eternal glory, then only would they have happily put behind them the chains and bonds of the earthly burdens of this world. For example, those men and women who long for vain glory insatiably immerse themselves in gold and precious stones and pearls, which they delight to fasten on their hands and feet and necks. And if any enemy or tyrannical prince were to fasten on them [iron chains] for punishment and have them kept in them without removing them, they would be exceedingly grieved and unable to bear them even for a while. But they fasten [jewels] on themselves, neither thinking them heavy nor feeling them; they even are jealous of such things when they see them on others, asking: "Why is that also not part of my adornment? But since it is on another, how shall I appear superior?" And if anyone were to pile up on such a person the entire amount of this world's precious goods until they were suffocated and choked, he would not say it was too much. But those who embellish themselves with transitory adornments did not appear to all those who saw them so beautiful and splendid and honorable as the happy and angelic sons of their father, the martyr Gregory, in their desirable chains that they wore with pride and joy on their holy hands and necks. The smiths came up to them and for a long time tried with files and by various other means, yet were unable to break the solid nails. Then, putting them on anvils and striking them with hammers, they were scarcely able to pry away the irons from the saints' bodies, cruelly lacerating and wounding their flesh. However, they counted the fearful pains of their suffering as nothing; but while the task dragged out until the third hour of the day, with the imprisoned Armenian nobles in prayer they blessed and glorified Christ who soothes pain.

[*p. 93*] *53.* Then Vehdenshapuh and his assistants ordered the most illustrious men of the capital and some of the most eminent magi to be summoned secretly at night; and following the king's command he bade them: "Consider each one his own safety and that of his family, and bear in mind the dread of kings, who like the gods can take away or restore life, can bring honor or dishonor. From this day until the whole royal army arrives in Vrkan, let no Armenian, from wherever he be— either from among the young imprisoned Armenian nobles who are in the capital, or the young imprisoned priests whom we are today leading forth, or any Armenian at all who unexpectedly may have from elsewhere come to live here—let none of them outside the city gates. Otherwise you will find no forgiveness, but with your families will be punished by the king and die a bitter death; but we shall be guiltless of such evils which will befall you. So take care with fear and attention that both we and you together are rewarded with grateful thanks." For, in accordance with the king's command, they were afraid lest any of the young imprisoned nobles, secretly disguising himself, might ferret out the road of their departure. But the Savior Christ had indeed sent with them the man who would indicate and reveal to the world that great treasure; while they, like the Jews, were ordering Pilate's army to guard the tomb which God the Word had opened through the angels, and he was revealing himself to those who believed in his name. As he had said, and by fulfilling [the same] shows his words to be eternally true: "Who believes in me will also do the work that I do, and will do even more."

When the executioners had completed their task according to Vehdenshapuh's order, they then made haste to march the saints away from the capital. When the Armenian nobles who were to remain in the prison of the capital in bonds saw this, they were encouraged and had confidence in the hope of heaven. With fearless audacity, in front of the whole host of the Persian concourse, falling at the feet of the holy priests of God they joyfully and with happy hearts kissed their feet in an extended greeting, beseeching them and saying: "Remember us in your unfailing joy and in the kingdom." Likewise the holy priests of God with joyful hearts and happy faces embraced them all to their bosoms and said: "May the God of hosts bless you, and give you lasting patience for the glory of his name; and may he strengthen you before the nations of the heathen. Having released your bodies from the visible bonds in which you stand, may he lead you to the land of your birth and lay your bones to rest in the graves of your fathers; [*p. 94*] and having released your souls from the invisible bonds of Satan, may be bring you to the land where you are sending us. And may he settle you with us in the eternal dwellings where Christ is on the right hand of God the Father."

When the impious [Persians] saw that the mutual parting of the holy priests and Armenian nobles was so joyful, they mocked in their hearts and laughed at them, reckoning them to be ignorant of the king's order. In secret they said to one another: "If these priests knew the death which has been prepared for them, they would indeed have much cause for weeping over themselves and they would not be able to laugh like this and rejoice." But the impious ones did not realize that that in fact was their joy and the reason for their happiness and for that they were rejoicing with unquenchable exultation, both those who were departing and those who remained. When the holy priests and Armenian nobles had greeted each other, they went their way, summoned to martyrdom. As the holy priests of God set forth, they were quickly joined by other young men from among the servants of the blessed ones, who had left Armenia with them in ready willingness to attend and serve them in captivity; these too desired to become worthy of the lot of the good portion—most of all the priest Khorēn, who was from the province of Ayrarat, from the village called Orkovi, and the blessed priest Abraham, who was from the province of Tayk', from the village called Zenakk'. Vehdenshapuh and his companions brought them forward and asked them: "Where are you planning (to go)?" They were told: "Where you are leading our spiritual masters and teachers, with them we are prepared to go, either to life or death." Vehdenshapuh was angered; he ordered them to be forcibly arrested and held in the capital. He commanded in accordance with his previous orders that they should be watched with a strict guard until the time that the whole royal army should reach the city: "Only then," he said, "may a servant of the imprisoned Armenian nobles leave the capital for any domestic needs, wherever their lords may send them." When the blessed priests Khorēn and Abraham saw that the executioners were forcibly restraining them in the capital, they were greatly troubled and distressed, reckoning themselves unworthy of a heavenly crown like that which their holy teachers, sons of the martyr Gregory, were to receive.

54. Then the *ambarapet*, Vehdenshapuh, set out from Niwshapuh with the priests, at the sixth hour of the day, along the road that leads to Vrkan. This news reached the ears of a certain merchant, a native of Khuzastan, who in the practice of his trade had often traveled to Armenia and who knew the Armenian language very well. From his youth he had lived a virtuous life, being the son of Christian and believing parents, and [*p. 95*] he was closely acquainted with the blessed priests of God and the Armenian nobles who were in prison. On their behalf he had spent much of his possessions and had rendered them many services while they were in Vrkan, endeavoring daily to see how he might become worthy [to acquire] a portion of the saints' relics at their death. When he heard of the king's orders, in haste and without delay, heeding no one, he left his horses and his goods to his servants and friends; taking his sturdiest and strongest horses, and posing as a member of the army he set out along the road that leads to the land of Apar. He traveled in the company of the *ambarakapet*, Vehdenshapuh, indicating to him with great diligence inns along the route where they might rest. Vehdenshapuh was pleased with all the Khujik's attentions, liked him greatly, and greeted him solicitously, for it was God who prospered the matter.

Since the Khujik was on terms of frank intimacy with the great prince the *ambarapet*, to make polite conversation the latter asked him about his village and parents, what sort of people they were and from which religion. The Khujik in subterfuge gave him enigmatic responses and false and circumstantial reasons for his present undertaking: "I am the son," he said, "of religious parents who following their ancestors were faithful servants of fire and sun, to which they dedicated me from my childhood. By their protection I have survived until today and live recognizing clearly the gods' support for my person." The blessed Khujik recalled the excuses of Paul, the teacher of the gentiles, who now would be a Pharisee by faith and on another occasion a Roman, but who was more fittingly neither of them but was by faith a preacher and teacher of the Gospel. He was from the province of Cilicia, from the city of Tarsus, but more especially a member of the holy and spiritual celestial army. However, he would mislead for a while the minds of his audience in order to propagate and confirm the truth. In like fashion the Khujik too satisfied for the moment with false words the mind of Vehdenshapuh, so that fulfilling the purpose of his journey he might attain his desire.

The *ambarapet,* Vehdenshapuh, regarded his encounter with the Khujik as [a gift] from the gods, seeing that he was an expert in everything, and he valued him even more as trustworthy and suitable for the business on which he was traveling. Therefore he did not allow him for a single hour to leave him, but day and night kept him beside him with much honor and affection. And he confided to him the king's purpose and the importance of the business on which he was traveling. For, as said above, it was God who was directing events according to his own will, for the destruction and shame of the company of the impious and for the profit [*p. 96*] and glory of his holy church. So was fulfilled the saying of the Holy Spirit who said: "They laid plans but not through me; they made pacts but not at my behest." And the psalmist says: "They laid a plan which they were unable to carry through."

Then the blessed Khujik adduced business he had to attend to elsewhere and sought leave from Vehdenshapuh, diverting the *ambarapet*'s thoughts from all acts and suspicion of self-interest and rather showing himself as even more loyal to him. For he knew by the inspiration of the Holy Spirit that God would not allow him [Vehdenshapuh] to let him go. So Vehdenshapuh did not at all agree to honor the Khujik's request, but secretly said to him: "You who have been raised religiously and live for the glory of fire, will you not readily stay with me and see the destruction of the impious murderers of fire who have been condemned to death, and rejoice thereat?" When the blessed Khujik heard this suggestion from the *ambarapet,* with a deep obeisance he thanked Vehdenshapuh for his kindness; but in his own heart he glorified and blessed the omnipotent God who orders all things, for letting him speak with the *ambarapet* and having him request the one who would reveal the saints' relics to go with them to the place of God's martyrs—he who was to scatter and bring to naught the king's command, and to indicate and distribute the great heavenly treasure of the saints.

So the blessed Khujik raised his heartfelt prayers to the Lord God, begging the Almighty to grant him intelligence and breadth of heart, so that he might become worthy to write faithfully on the tablets of his mind, as in an inscription, all the questions of the tyrants and the responses and prayers that each one of the saints offered to God in the hour of his death, with a view to being able to describe them truthfully and co-herently as a record for all faithful hearers in succeeding generations forever. From the willing Giver he received through this intercession the object of his request, continuously to bring the message with joyful heart to all orthodox congregations in every place, for their wonder and to the glory of Christ's name.

55. But Vehdenshapuh did not think it right to tell the Khujik at the beginning what he was going to do with the holy priests, but merely said: "We are taking them to Vrkan and there we shall release them." That day they entered a village called Ṙevan, some six or more leagues distant from Niwshapuh according to the Persian measure of reckoning, and stayed there until the morning watch. At the morning watch they arose quickly in secret, without informing any of the villagers or those in their own party, and in the company of only the blessed Khujik and the impious executioners by whom they were going to execute the saints according to the king's order, they silently left the village. The executioners took the saints [*p. 97*] and traveled for the whole remaining part of the night through the untrodden desert, for a Persian league or more from the village. At dawn they reached a rocky place, rough and sandy, where no herdsman or traveler ever passed by, since there was never any road there.

The three princes took chairs and sat down: the *ambarapet,* Vehdenshapuh, the royal *maypet,* Jnikan, and the chamberlain, Movan. But the blessed Khujik turned his attention to the Creator of all.

When the holy martyrs had been brought before the tribunal, Vehdenshapuh said to them: "You have committed innumerable evil deeds and are responsible for much damage to the Aryans. For if you had been the cause of the death of merely two or three persons, that would still be a serious matter and you would not be worthy of living—let alone [your destroying] such a great country as is Armenia, and [causing] so much blood to be shed there. Of all this you are guilty, and it was all accomplished by your actions and advice. Yet despite these many crimes of yours and your guilt, the king of kings showed great kindness to you, for he commanded you, saying: 'If they agree to worship the sun and fire and undertake to observe our religion, I shall forgive their guilt and shall let their nobles who are in prison return to Armenia; and I shall give each one property and rank and honor.' So do you remember that and consider your own selves and the many captive souls who are in prison; willingly and readily accept the king of king's command; and as you were the cause of much blood, so now be the cause of life for many. But if you do not agree and still persist in that willful stupidity, you will die and he will order them to be killed. And all the blood which has been shed previously and which will now be shed will be claimed from your souls by the gods." Such was the speech of Vehdenshapuh and his companions to the saints.

They commanded the blessed bishop Sahak to translate for Saint Yoseph and Saint Levond and their other companions; for the holy bishop alone knew Persian and no one else among the saints was familiar with it. The holy bishop Sahak then replied, saying to Denshapuh and to the others who were sitting with him: "Do not make me," he said, "repeat to them words which are unworthy of their attention. For why should I retail to them a speech which seems to me odious and ridiculous; for I know, when they hear it, they will mock you and your message alike. Do what you will, but do not continue to address futile words and vain speeches to us."

Denshapuh and the others were angered and said to the saint: "You are obliged to speak to them; let us know their reply and wishes." So the holy bishop related in brief to his saintly companions the king's words and messages. [*p. 98*] When the saints heard them they loudly mocked at the speech; and when the impious princes realized that, they became even more furious. But the holy Catholicos replied, saying: "This question was posed in a tribunal at court before Mihrnerseh, *hazarapet* of the Aryans, and he heard from us our response and wishes—which he made known to the king. The wishes and response of us all are the same; we do not change our words— now being rash like thoughtless people, and now repenting and regretting like guilty people. This thought and quest alone grows daily in our hearts: why should not our acts of virtue and good deeds be revealed in ourselves today more than yesterday and the day before in the faith which we hold: to think of it, live by it, and to die together? But as for the worship of the sun which you mention, if the king ordered: 'If you agree and accept, you and the captive nobles will live; and if you foolishly do not wish to accept, you will die and we shall order them to be killed'—far be it from us to deny the truth and serve gods falsely so-called, who are not gods at all. And by our denial let none of the believing prisoners be released only to fall into eternal and indissoluble bonds. They now, even more than we, seek from God our death for God rather than our life in apostasy. But if it were possible for you to know now by foresight how senseless and pernicious seems to us that message which you have brought us at the king's command, you and he who sent you would reckon yourselves and the king the most pitiable of all miserable men. But whatever you wish do quickly, or when you desire."

When the holy Catholicos Yoseph had said this, Vehdenshapuh and his confidants became exceedingly angry; he ordered Saint Sahak to say to him: "Although these insults whereby you have slandered us as irrational and wrong seem to us serious, yet in comparison with the arrogant audacity with which you dared to address unworthy remarks to the god-like king, your insults against our persons seem to us as nothing and insignificant. But know this: you yourself have sought your own destruction, and you have received it. For you to live hereafter is impossible. Nonetheless, we must find out the will and choice of each of the others, for our religion so decrees."

56. He ordered Saint Sahak to say to them: "Do not heed this man's foolish words. Hold yourselves apart from such absurd advice, and like [rational] men choose life rather than death. As for this one who has now dared to speak such words deserving of death, since [*p. 99*] he is very guilty and unworthy of life, his own evil deeds will not permit him to live. But as for you, although you are somewhat guilty, if you merely do the king's will and worship the sun, he has ordered your guilt to be forgiven you and you to be sent with honor safe and sound to your homes."

Vehdenshapuh and his other confidants further commanded Saint Sahak to say to the blessed man of God, Levond: "We have heard about you, that there is no one so knowledgeable about the Christian religion as you, and that it was especially on the basis of your advice that Armenia was ruined. Now a mind so great and wise must recognize the benevolence of the king of kings in forgiving such great guilt and acquainting you with the true god. But, as you were adviser and many died from your actions, be now an adviser for life and let these and numberless other persons live. Tell them to worship the sun and they will live; and you will be famous in your own land and among all nations." The holy bishop Sahak took the time patiently and mockingly to translate all the *ambarakapet*'s words and those of his impious colleagues, so that he could inform these impious ones through the saints' replies about the will and desire and unshakable conviction in the faith of each of the blessed ones.

The holy man of God, Ḷevond, began to speak alone with Saint Sahak, saying: "We should respond to these men in the same way as the Savior replied to Pilate in the tribunal. But in order that we may make them understand the intrepid search of our desire, say to them: Behold you have repeated whatever you have heard about me—that I am versed in our religion and am the teacher of a large number of congregations. This indicates to you the approach of my life to its end. Now should I today forget, alter, or lose, for fear of a mortal and foolish man, the choice of my good wisdom, to which you yourselves bear witness and which I have learned from God and not from man? Far be it! I shall hear and be reproved by the saying: 'You taught many; yourself you did not teach.' As for the honor and glory that you promise to give—may we never receive honor from an earthly and mortal man, which the worm and caterpillar corrupt and the thief digs out and removes, we who are clothed in glory and honor from the heavenly and immortal right hand of the One on High, [glory and honor] which neither heaven, nor earth, nor the precious things therein can equal in value. We are but one thing short for our blessed glorification—the cup of death, which we are as anxious to drink as men fainting of thirst. Give us drink quickly; let us joyfully free ourselves from the agitated [*p. 100*] troubles of this life. Drag out no longer the foolish and pernicious instructions of your raving king."

When the holy man of God, Ḷevond, had finished his reply, the blessed priests Mushē and Arshēn and the blessed deacon Kʻajaj implored the holy bishop Sahak to say to the impious prince on their behalf: "Whatever our holy teachers and spiritual fathers, the lords Yoseph and Ḷevond, have said is also our own wish and desire. Complete immediately what you have come [here] for, and do not delay. We beg God to grant us and to make us worthy of eternal honor and the kingdom of heaven."

When Vehdenshapuh and his impious colleagues heard this, they were stirred to great anger. They had wished to make further seductive speeches and vain remarks to the holy martyrs, thinking that perhaps they might be able to separate one of them from the indissolubly united band—which was impossible. They began to insist further that the holy bishop Sahak translate for them whatever else they might wish to say to the saints. But the holy bishop Sahak replied to Vehdenshapuh and his other accomplices: "Up to now I have willingly explained for you and have translated to the saints what you said, although I certainly did not wish to serve you or the obscene instructions of your king. For indeed what need has a man, who has his wits and is sane of mind, to listen to such nonsensical words as yours—let alone repeat them into the ears of such wise and thoughtful men. This much alone [is enough] so that the ridiculousness of your folly may be made clear, and the firmness of our true and divinely-inspired preaching may be strengthened and confirmed in us."

57. The three impious princes were angered and were no longer able to endure any more [the remarks] of the saints. As if to vindicate the king of the great insults they had inflicted on him, Vehdenshapuh himself stood up in front of his colleagues and struck the holy bishop Sahak's ear with his sword, extending the wound down nearly to his girdle. Staggering from the blow, the holy bishop did not collapse and fall to the ground but supported himself on a rock, and on behalf of all the saints began to speak as follows: "We thank you, Christ, life-giving Lamb, who often as an undying sacrifice have been administered without being consumed and distributed by our hands. As we lovingly make this sacrifice receive us all as worthy victims in a sweet odor." As the holy bishop so spoke, although torrents of blood flowed from the saint's wound, yet he was strengthened by the grace of the Almighty as if he had not been wounded at all.

Then they ordered the holy Catholicos Yoseph to be beheaded [*p. 101*] by the sword. As the executioners stripped the holy one, he said three times: "My body, return to dust and to your rest, for the Lord has justified you." And thus he received his death by the sword.

As for Saint Ḷevond, the impious princes ordered the executioners to strip the saint and to drag him forcibly over the sharp rocks and stony ground of the mountain. In this fashion they dragged him around for a long time until they had torn and pulled the skin from all the saint's flesh on his shoulders and back, so that his bones were bared of skin. For all the Persians said that the holy man of God, Ḷevond, in particular had been the instigator and cause of all the acts of Vardan and of all that had occurred at that time in Armenia. While some of the executioners were dragging the blessed Ḷevond about, others beheaded with the sword the blessed priests Mushē and

Arshēn and the holy deacon K'ajaj, who at the moment of their death exclaimed: "Lord Jesus, receive our souls."

When the executioners who were dragging around Saint Levond were weary, they brought him back, barely alive, to the spot where the other saints had been martyred. There they struck off the saint's head with the sword. At the moment of his death he said in a joyful voice: "I thank you, Christ, who in your great mercy have assisted and preserved me from my childhood, have brought me to this hour, and have made me worthy of the portion of your saints. Into your hands, Savior, I commend my soul." The holy bishop Sahak had still a little breath, but after the death of all the others they beheaded him with the sword. Offering prayers in a weak voice and saying "Amen," he gave up the ghost.

Thus in the sixteenth year of the reign of Yazkert, on the twenty-seventh of the month Hrotits', the six saints were crowned in the land of Apar, near the village of the magi called Ṙevan: the holy Catholicos Yoseph from Vayots' Dzot; the holy bishop Sahak from Ṙshtunik'; the holy priest Arshēn from Bagrevand; the holy man of God, the priest Levond from Vanand; the holy priest Mushē from Aḷbak; the holy deacon K'ajaj from Ṙshtunik'. Arshavir Kamsarakan ardently and thoroughly questioned the blessed Khujik; and just as he heard from him so he repeated to us the words and death of each of the saints. Thus we have written a trustworthy account.

When Vehdenshapuh and the other princes with him left that spot, they chose nine men and left them there as a guard. Among these, the first that Vehdenshapuh chose by God's providence was the Khujik, whom he begged to remain as a very close confidant receptive to his own commands. They ordered [*p. 102*] the guards as follows: "For ten days or more, until the royal army has departed, watch these corpses carefully so that when they are devoured by birds the bones may fall in various places—onto the top of mountains or to the bottom of deep ravines. Perhaps, he said, some Christian may come, informed by somebody; and finding their bones he may take them and disperse them among all the Christians. Then we would be guilty before the king."

The guards remained there according to the command of Denshapuh and Movan the chamberlain and Jnikan the *maypet*. During those days the blessed Khujik considered by what means God might indicate a way whereby he would be made worthy of stealing the saints' relics from the other guards.

While the blessed man was engaged in such reflections, unexpectedly on the evening of that same day there was a severe
earthquake in that spot. Great noises and fearful voices resounded from the depths; masses of gathered clouds covered
the earth; thunderings and lightning shook the mountains. A
column of light descended like a rainbow from heaven, surrounding and enveloping the bodies of the martyrs. The guards
were struck to the ground, half-dead, no one knowing at all
where his neighbor was; they rolled on the ground, unable to
stand steadily, for the shaking of the severe earthquake threw
them up and down from the ground. Tottering thus on their
feet and silenced in speech, they all were dumbfounded. But
the right hand of the Almighty kept the blessed Khujik unconcerned. With joyful mind he praised God, realizing then that
the quest of his long-standing desires now was being fulfilled.
In like manner these fearful events continued the whole night
and all day and a second night until the hour of dawn; only
then did the voices resounding from the depths fall silent, the
thundering of the clouds dissipate and subside, the earth cease
from shaking, and the lightning flashes fade away. This occurred only around the spot [of the martyrs' bodies] for about
two *asparēs* [furlongs]. When the guards had recovered a little
from their dazed and numb terror, they looked around in order
to flee from the place. But their hearts so trembled from fear
that they were unable to rise from the ground. They merely
looked at one another, unable to speak.

Around the ninth hour of the second day the blessed
Khujik arose; pretending to be limping and looking behind
him he fled from the place in order to encourage them [the
guards] to get up and follow him away from the area. When
they saw the blessed Khujik going off with a hobbling gait,
they recovered at the thought of their peril and rushed away
from the place after him. In their fear they dared not turn to
look at the spot, but hastened to press after Vehdenshapuh and
his colleagues. However, the blessed Khujik parted from them
along a different road. When the guards reached [*p. 103*] the
princes on the sixth day they told them about all the disasters
that had befallen them during one day and two nights. On seeing the color of their faces and hearing one by one of the fearful
happenings, Vehdenshapuh and his companions were terrified,
and for many hours were stupefied in amazement. Taking
council they were unable to find any way out except merely to
attempt to silence the guards, so that they would reveal to no

one at all nor repeat to anyone the death of the priests or the appearance of such miracles. But they themselves were privately plunged into numbness through anxiety and astonishment. Vehdenshapuh and Jnikan said to each other: "The affairs of Christians are not something frivolous and light; but the power of their religion and faith is certainly great. Harmed through ignorance we are lost and are insensible of it."

When the blessed Khujik was sure that God had removed all suspicion on every side and he had also heard the replies of the princes to the guards, he realized that no one was watching over the saints' relics. Taking with him ten or more companions whose Christian faith he knew to be very strong, and some horses and four-sided boxes for each of the saints, he set out silently at night on his errand. On approaching the spot they strayed from the place where the saints' bodies lay because the night was exceedingly dark. After struggling around for a while they became depressed, supposing themselves unworthy of finding the heavenly treasure. But while they anxiously wandered about the area, suddenly in luminous form an eagle swooped down from heaven and settled on the body of the holy man of God, Levond. The place was made brighter than day, and the body of each of the saints was clearly revealed. With joyful hearts they gratefully worshiped the Lord God. Setting to work they gathered each one into a separate box, for they were individually pointed out to the blessed Khujik as if in writing. A sweet odor emanated from the saints' bodies, filling with joy the sense of them all.

Quickly putting them on the horses, they transferred them to another spot in the desert, about three Persian leagues from that place. They waited for seven days for all suspicion of what had happened to disappear. Then they cleaned off from the saints' bones their sweet-smelling flesh, which they wrapped in linen-cloth in a worthy manner and carefully buried with honor in the desert. Taking the bones they brought them to the capital and kept them in secret for many days. Then quietly they began to give them to some of the virtuous Christians who were in the army. Those who received them counted it a token of salvation for their souls and bodies. Speedily they had them sent to each one's homeland to profit the spiritual health [*p. 104*] of their families and the province. But the first fruits of this great divine treasure the blessed Khujik brought first of all to offer to the imprisoned Armenian nobles. Having become worthy to receive such a token of their salvation, they then knew that God in his Providence was watching over them and that there would come a time for their deliverance from prison by the intercession of the saints, in accordance with the remark of the holy man of God, Levond. In his exhortation on that night [before he departed] he had announced what would befall them by God's grace: that they would see their [native] land. Those words of the saint were to be accomplished in due time.

Then the blessed man of God, the Khujik, began to describe [these events] to the imprisoned Armenian nobles one by one. But it grieves me to call him the Khujik from now on, though no one has bothered to tell us the name of that wonderful man. However, the Omniscient preserves it inscribed until the day of his great visitation, and liberally will reward his labors being well pleased at his name. He told without reserve of the Almighty's great attention and power bestowed on him, and how in Vardgēs Christ had revealed and made known to him the king's intention and had sent and guided him in hope. "He made me appear honored and trustworthy," he said, "to the *hambarapet*, Denshapuh, so that the impious one begged me and forcibly led me through God the Almighty's guidance to the desirable place of the saints' martyrdom. For his will everything is possible. I was rendered worthy of seeing everything that I did not expect to see and to hear in detail what I did not reckon myself worthy of hearing—I saw in order and heard the interrogation of the tyrants and individual responses of the saints, the prayers and death of each one. Now of this great fortune the grace of the Holy Trinity made my unworthiness worthy through your untiring intercession, so that I was able to act for you as bearer of the heavenly treasure of the saints' relics. He [God] put to flight in shame the alarmed guards and terrified the hearts of the unbelieving sentinels; he scattered the plans of the witless king and exalted the name of his holy church." Such glorious and joyful words did the tireless and blessed merchant impart to all the believers in Christ. He had once been a merchant of earthly treasure, but suddenly through his good works he became a merchant of the great heavenly treasure of the martyrs' relics.

This was the principal topic of conversation and consolation for the imprisoned Armenian nobles in their goings and comings, their sitting and rising in prison, their festivals and first days of the months. Repeating the story with insatiable joy they encouraged and renewed the weakened spirits of all their hearers and confirmed them in the right faith. Especially the lord of the Arsharunik', Arshavir Kamsarakan, drew his spiritual food and sweet reflection every hour of the day and night from the teaching of the saints, notably the words and spiritual advice of Saint Levond, each one's replies to the murderers' interrogation, and the prayers uttered by each one at the moment of death. [*p. 105*] These he repeated, introducing them into the canons of the psalms; continually and tirelessly he rehearsed them. These we heard in their entirety from that admirable Kamsarakan and promptly wrote them down with care. Although in our weakness we were not able to remember everything in the right order, yet we have not been in the slightest negligent, nor through laziness did we procrastinate and forget something.

58. After King Yazkert at the appointed time had entered his capital in Vrkan with the whole host of nobles and troops who were with him, the inhabitants of the capital who were in Niwshapuh in accordance with Denshapuh's command then permitted the Armenian princes who were imprisoned in the fortress to send out their servants and any one else in their company wherever they wished on errands. When the blessed priests Khorēn and Abraham heard of this, they immediately hastened to Vrkan. Publicly falling before the *ambarapet,* Denshapuh, they protested: "When you took away from Niwshapuh our spiritual lords and teachers, whom we also wished to accompany, you strictly ordered us to be held under heavy guard up to now. If you have taken them away to some foreign land of no return, do us the kindness of informing us [so that] we too may go and be in exile with them. We are ready to live or to die if we only see them, of which we desire to be worthy. And if you have killed them, be willing to give the same order for us. We reckon such a death to be more honorable and estimable then any glory or grandeur of this world."

On hearing such words from them Vehdenshapuh and the whole assembly were astonished at their fearless outspokenness. He replied to the blessed ones: "No one will show you the path of your teachers. But on your behalf we shall ask the king of kings. He [only] has the authority to give any orders concerning you." Entering inside, Denshapuh told King Yazkert everything that the blessed priests had said and requested. The king gave an order: "If no one brings to light any charge against them and no plaintiff is pursuing them, let them worship the sun and agree to honor the fire. Then they will receive great gifts from us and will be sent back to their own country. But if they do not agree to obey our command they will be punished by maiming. They will be sent to Asorestan to labor with the royal slaves, and they will be enslaved until their death." Denshapuh came and informed the blessed priests Khorēn and Abraham of the king's order. When the honorable priests heard it they replied as with a single mouth: "We are ready not only for maiming for the sake of Christ's name, but also for [the torture of] scraping and death. But as for [*p. 106*] worshiping the sun, as you say, we are saddened and distressed at the folly of your error and we beseech God to guide you away from the stupor of your ignorance—let alone that we should imitate you. God forbid that we should abandon the Creator and worship creation."

When the princes heard such fearless replies from the mouths of the blessed priests, they carried out the king's orders. Cutting off the priests' ears, they had the men sent to Asorestan, to the province called Shap'ul, where they were to be enslaved and set to royal labor. When the faithful in Asorestan heard of the coming there of the blessed ones, they went out joyfully to meet them and honored them like relics of holy martyrs. And they were indeed worthy of such respect. Also each person brought whatever wealth he possessed and laid it at the feet of the blessed ones for them to take and distribute for spiritual purposes, to the salvation of their own selves and their families. The blessed priests took a suitable part of the offerings of the faithful and had it sent to the land of Apar, to the imprisoned Armenian nobles. Each one joyfully and very eagerly begged the blessed ones to make him worthy of such a spiritual journey. So it happened that the blessed priest Abraham, receiving the offerings of the southern regions of Asorestan, took them and distributed them among the imprisoned Armenian heroes according to each one's needs. Many times in succession the Christians of the land acted thus; and the blessed priest Abraham himself for many years was the intrepid bearer of provisions from the Christian donors of that land, until the release of the imprisoned nobles to Armenia. The blessed priest Khorēn lived for several more years and died there in Asorestan.

But the blessed priest Abraham returned to Armenia on the surety of the faithful of that land [Asorestan]. They inscribed at court their houses and possessions as security for his service until his death, and they diligently carried out the duties imposed on him, thereby gaining the release of the blessed man. Without any doubt his appearance to all who saw the man was as the form of an angel. Being consecrated to the rank of bishop of the land of the Bznunik', he enlightened the populace of that land with many reforms, and died in that same position at a ripe old age. Of which [fate] may we also become worthy in Christ Jesus our Lord, to whom be glory for ever. Amen.

Section III

59. So, returning to the first book [§19], let us continue the story in [chronological] order. In the seventeenth year of King Yazkert, Ashusha, the prince of Georgia, approached the nobles of the royal court, buying each one of them with large and munificent sums of money, and most especially the impious *hazarapet*, Mihrnerseh. With great effort and hard work he persuaded him to have King Yazkert asked to grant him [Ashusha] the sons of the blessed martyr Hmayeak of the Mamikonean family. These the treacherous prince of Siunik', Vasak, had taken from their tutors as the sons of condemned men and had brought to the court so they might be put to death. They were very young. And benevolent God, through the intercession of the holy blood of their fathers, convinced the king's mind; to everyone's disbelief he granted Ashusha, as a very dear and well-deserving man, his momentous request.

When Ashusha saw this and had received from the king this great favor, he stood up in the [audience] chamber in front of everyone; and falling to the ground he rolled this way and that, and then struck his head on the ground. In this fashion he performed his prostration. When the king and all those in the chamber saw this, they were greatly astonished at what the man was doing. The king asked him: *"Bdeashkh* of Georgia, what is this new performance that you have shown us today?" Ashusha replied: "Benevolent monarch, you have granted me an unprecedented favor, which no other subject among my companions had ever gained from you. So it is right for me to do obeisance to you with a new form of prostration, such obeisance as you have never seen from any other subject." When the king and the whole multitude of nobles heard such words from Ashusha, they greatly praised him, and were greatly astonished.

[*p. 108*] *60*. Yazkert, king of Persia, lived out the span of his life and died in Fars. His two sons succeeded him, but they were mutually antagonistic and made war on each other. The younger gained the victory, and having slain the elder became king. His name was Peroz. In that same [first] year of his reign he sent his foster brother Yĕzatvshnasp, whom he loved very dearly, with orders to release the Armenian nobles from prison and to provide them with allowances at Hrev. "Let them stay there," he said, "with their cavalry and carry out whatever task Ashtat, father of Yĕzatvshnasp, may set them to." When Yĕzatvshnasp arrived, he gave them the good news, saying: "The king of kings has reprieved your death sentence; he has ordered you to be released from prison, and has arranged allowances for you at Hrev and for your wives in their own land. He has ordered you to perform royal duties and to obey and carry out everything that my father Ashtat commands you." When the Armenian nobles heard all Yĕzatvshnasp's words, they glorified God their protector and benefactor, from whom they confidently and patiently expected other blessings through the intercession of the saints' relics.

As Yĕzatvshnasp frequented the Armenian nobles he gradually became familiar with them. It happened, as if by Divine Providence, that he patronized Arshavir Kamsarakan, and came to love him with the love of Jonathan for David. He also took care of the other Armenian nobles with perpetual intercession. They then took the Armenian nobles to Hrev, and arranging allowances for each one, entrusted them to Ashtat for him to use in military service. God magnified and honored them in the eyes of the general of the army, by rendering their valor successful and renowned, while before all the citizens of Hrev and the province the right hand of the All-Highest granted to the sick many and various cures through the saints' relics, which the priests among them kept secretly among themselves. Therefore they were praised and celebrated by the general and all the province as valiant and admirable men. The prince of Hrev, Hrev-Shnomshapuh, was very friendly to Armenian prisoners; their valor, good repute, and ability he frequently made known in writing to the magnates at the palace and to his friends at court.

61. But many tried to ferret out some bodily weakness in the blessed prisoners, and even dared to question them on that topic, forgetting the beam in their own eye, according to the saying of the Savior, yet with presumptuous conceit searching for the straw in the eyes of others. When I hear this I quiver and am appalled. For I look at their willing acceptance of various tortures for the hope of eternity and I see [*p. 109*] their patient endurance: they despised magnificence, considered as naught authority; they rejected possessions, fearlessly gave themselves to death, endured bonds for a lengthy time, bore prison and insults, suffered ignominy rather than honor; they were tormented by hunger, exhausted by thirst; they hated overabundance of possessions, delighted in the lot of poverty, despised comfort, loved austerity—and as for all the other innumerable and significant kinds of deprivation that these men happily endured in their bodies, I am unable to record any aspect of weakness in such persons. Observing the many virtues of the blessed prophets and Holy Apostles, we are unworthy to notice any mortal aspect in them—we who are filled with a myriad of iniquities which we could never recall or think of without repenting. One alone is just and holy, he who said: "I alone have conquered the world."

Now some of those imprisoned nobles whom we have seen with our own eyes were truly heavenly beings on earth and seemed [to be] angels in the flesh. They had personally established schools for themselves and studied the church's testaments; through their spiritual conduct they typified in themselves the life of eremitical virtue; they zealously performed the canons of the psalms and the readings of the Scriptures. Day and night they continued in them unceasingly, in public and at home; sometimes openly and sometimes on occasion in secret they did not hesitate to increase [their practices]. On taking up arms they worshiped in their minds; on attacking the enemy they prayed in their hearts. From every battle, by the help of the Almighty, they returned safely, victorious and renowned. Those who by reason of old age or poverty of intellect, in accordance with the nature of the flesh, were not strong enough to study kept sleepless vigils with ever greater readiness, praying at length and standing tirelessly. One could see them all as sons of light and children of the kingdom.

Likewise the women whose husbands had been martyred, and other women whose husbands were imprisoned in Hrev, surpassed each other in purity and virtue, dying every day to their bodily passions. In accordance with the prophet's saying they were living martyrs. In regard to them no word can describe precisely the severe austerities of their lives, which surpassed those of many men. Rendering the natural weakness of women's bodies stronger than men's, they were gloriously victorious. Delicate women, daughters of princes and wives of nobles, would eat millet instead of fine wheat flour, would drink water in moderation instead of pure wine, would wear rough wool instead of silken garments embroidered with gold, [*p. 110*] would lie on the ground on brushwood instead of in elaborate beds. Those who formerly slept late became sleepless like celestial beings. They did not anoint themselves with perfume, they did not arrange the hair of their heads with combs. And what is impossible for women to overcome—speaking too much and frequently turning the eyes this way and that from under a veil—they curbed, and they moderated their tongues from excessive speech.

The all-merciful God looked down on the prayers and labors of these men and women together; recalling the heroism of Saint Vardan and of all those united with him and the intercession of the martyred priests of God, he gracefully permitted the prisoners to return to Armenia. They came to each one's home in the sixth year of the reign of Peroz. And living, each the [span] allotted by the Lord, they died and were peacefully buried in their fathers' graves, at God's pleasure, all having been blessed by the mouth of the holy Catholicos, Giut.

Bibliography

The Manuscripts

Full details of the manuscripts used for the critical edition and cited in the commentary to this book will be found in the bibliography of the critical edition of Ełishē by Ter-Minasean, listed under Armenian Texts.

Abbreviations

AB	*Analecta Bollandiana*
BF	*Byzantinische Forschungen*
BM	*Banber Matenadarani*
BSOAS	*Bulletin of the School of Oriental and African Studies*
CSCO	*Corpus Scriptorum Christianorum Orientalium*
DOP	*Dumbarton Oaks Papers*
GCS	*Die Griechischen Christlichen Schriftsteller der erstern drei Jahrhunderte*
HA	*Handes Amsorya*
JTS	*Journal of Theological Studies*
MSL	*Mélanges de la Société de Linguistique*
OCA	*Orientalia Christiana Analecta*
OS	*Ostkirchliche Studien*
PBH	*Patma-banasirakan Handes*
PO	*Patrologia Orientalis*, ed R. Graffin and F. Nau, 1903–
PW	A. Paully, G. Wissowa, and W. Kroll, *Real-Encyclopädie der klassischen Altertumswissenschaft*, 1893–
REA	*Revue des études armeniénnes*
RHL	*Revue de l'histoire des religions*
RSL	*Revue des sciences religieuses*
VDI	*Vestnik drevnej Istorii*

329

Armenian Texts

Agathangelos. *Agat'angełay Patmut'iwn Hayots'*, ed. G. Tēr-Mkrtch'ean and St. Kanayeants'. Tiflis, 1909. Reprinted with Introduction by R. W. Thomson (Delmar, N.Y.: Caravan Books, 1980). Translation, commentary, and details of the non-Armenian versions in R. W. Thomson, *Agathangelos, History of the Armenians* (Albany, 1976).

Alishan, Ł. *Nuagk'*, vol. 3. Venice, 1867.

Anania Shirakats'i. *"Yałags Erkri."* In *Matenagrut'yunĕ*, ed. A. G. Abrahamyan. Erevan, 1944.

Ashkharhats'oyts'. Short recension in Anania Shirakats'i, *Matenagrut'yunĕ*. Long recension, ed. A. Soukry, *Géographie de Moise de Corene*. Venice, 1881.

Bible. Astuatsashunch', ed. Y. Zōhrapean. Venice, 1805.

Canons of Shahapivan. In *Kanonagirk'*, I.

Cyril of Jerusalem. *Catecheses* = *Koch'umn Ĕntsayut'ean*. Venice, 1832.

David. *Dawt'i Anyałt' P'ilosop'ayi Matenagrut'iwnk'*. Venice, 1932.

Ełishē. *Ełishēi vasn Vardanants' ew Hayots' Paterazmin*, ed. E. Tēr-Minasean. Erevan, 1957. For translations see this edition; those quoted in this commentary are: E. Ter-Minasean, *Ełishēi Vardanants' Patmut'yunĕ* (Erevan, 1946; in modern Armenian), and K. N. Yuzbashyan, *Egishe* (Erevan, 1971; in Russian).

——— *Life* [of Ełishē]: *Patmut'iwn srboyn Ełishēi vardapeti, Sop'erk' Haykakank'*, no. 11. Venice, 1854.

Ephrem. *Commentaire de l'evangile concordant: version arménienne*, ed. L. Leloir, *CSCO*, 137, 145. Louvain, 1953, 1954.

Eusebius. *Historia ecclesiastica* = *Patmut'iwn Ekełets'woy*. Venice, 1877.

Eznik. *De Deo*, ed. L. Mariès and C. Mercier, *PO*, 28. Paris, 1959.

Faustos Buzand = P'awstos Buzandats'i. *Patmut'iwn Hayots'*. Venice, 1933.

Girk' T'łt'ots. Tiflis, 1901.

Gregory of Narek. *Matenagrut'iwnk'*, Venice, 1840.

Grigoris Arsharuni. *Meknut'iwn Ĕnt'erts'uatsots'*. Venice, 1964.

Hermes. "Hermeay Eŕametsi aŕ Asklepios Sahmank'," ed. H. Manandyan. *BM*, 3 (1956): 287–314.

John Catholicos. *Patmut'iwn Hayots'*. Tiflis, 1912. Reprinted with introduction by K. Maksoudian, (Delmar, N.Y.: Caravan Books, 1980).

John Chrysostom. *Commentary on Matthew* = *Yawetaranagirn Matt'ēos*, 2 vols. Venice, 1826.

Juanshēr. *Hamaŕōt Patmut'iwn Vrats'*. Venice, 1884.

Kanonagirk' Hayots' ed. V. Hakobyan, 2 vols. Erevan, 1964, 1971.

Kirakos Gandzakets'i. *Patmut'iwn Hayots'*, ed. K. A. Melik'-Ōhanjanyan. Erevan, 1961.

Koriun. *Patmut'iwn varuts' ew mahuan srboyn Mesropay vardapeti*. Tiflis, 1913.

Łazar P'arpets'i. *Patmut'iwn Hayots'*, ed. G. Tēr-Mkrtch'ean and St. Malkhasean. Tiflis, 1904. The "Letter" is printed on pp. 184–204 of this edition.

Mkhit'ar of Ani. *Patmut'iwn*, ed. K. Patkanean. St. Petersburg, 1879.

Mkit'ar of Ayrivank'. Armenian text, ed. K. Patkanean. In *Trudi vostochnago otdelenija imperatorskago russkago arkheologicheskago obshchestva,* pt. 14. St. Petersburg, 1869. Translation by M. Brosset, "Histoire chronologique par Mkhithar d'Airivank, XIIIe s." *Memoires de l'Academie imperiale des sciences de St. Pétersbourg,* 7th ser. 13. no. 5 (1869).

Mkhit'ar Gosh. *Girk' Datastani,* ed. Kh. T'orosyan. Erevan, 1975.

Moses Daskhurants'i. *Patmut'iwn Aḷuanits' Ashkharhi,* ed. J. Emin. Moscow, 1860.

Moses Khorenats'i. *Patmut'iwn Hayots',* ed. M. Abeḷean and S. Yarut'iwnean. Tiflis, 1913. Reprinted with Introduction by R. W. Thomson (Delmar, New York: Caravan Books, 1981). Translation and commentary by R. W. Thomson, *Moses Khorenats'i, History of the Armenians.* Cambridge, Mass., 1978.

——— "Geography." See *Ashkharhats'oyts'.*

——— Collected works in *Matenagrut'iwnk'.* Venice, 1865.

Nerses Shnorhali. *Yaḷags erkni ew zarduts' nora, Hanelukner, Oḷb Edesioy.* Erevan, 1968.

Philo. (P'ilon Ebrayets'i). *Bank' Erek'.* Venice, 1882.

——— *Chaŕk'.* Venice, 1892.

——— *De Jona.* H. Lewy, *The Pseudo-Philonic De Jona, Part I,* Studies and Documents 7, London, 1936. Text also in *Mnats'ordk.* See below.

——— *De Providentia.* Text in *Bank' Erek'.* See above.

——— *De Vita Contemplativa.* F. C. Conybeare, *Philo about the Contemplative Life.* Oxford, 1895. Text also in *Chaŕk'.* See above.

——— *In Exodum.* Text in *Mnats'ordk'.* See below.

——— *In Genesim.* Text in *Mnats'ordk'.* See below.

——— *Mnats'ordk'.* Venice, 1826.

Primary History. Printed as Introduction to Sebēos. For a translation see Thomson, *Moses Khorenats'i,* Appendix.

Proclus. *Tome.* Armenian text in *Girk' T'ḷt'ots'.*

Ps.-Callisthenes. *Alexander Romance* = *Patmut'iwn Aḷek'sandri Makedonats'woy.* Venice, 1842.

Samuel of Ani. *Hawak'munk' i grots' Patmagrats'.* Vaḷarshapat, 1893. Longer recension trans. in M. F. Brosset, *Collection d'historiens arméniens,* II, 340–483. St. Petersburg, 1876.

Sebēos. *Patmut'iwn Sebēosi,* ed. G. V. Abgaryan. Erevan, 1979.

Simeon Aparanets'i. *Banasteḷtsut'yunner.* Erevan, 1976.

Step'anos Ṙōshk'ay. *Zhamanakagrut'iwn kam Tarekank' ekeḷets'akank'.* Vienna, 1964.

Stephen Orbelean. *Patmut'iwn Tann Sisakan.* Tiflis, 1911.

Stepehn of Taron (Asoḷik). *Patmut'iwn Tiezerakan.* St. Petersburg, 1885.

Teaching of Saint Gregory. Armenian text in Agathangelos. Translation and commentary in R. W. Thomson, *The Teaching of Saint Gregory: An Early Armenian Catechism.* Cambridge, Mass., 1970.

Ter Israel. *Le synaxaire arménien,* ed. G. Bayan, *PO* 5, 6, 15, 16, 18, 19, 21. Paris, 1909–1930.

Thomas Artsruni. *Patmut'iwn Tann Artsruneats'.* Tiflis, 1917.

Vardan Vardapet. *Hawak'umn Patmut'ean.* Venice, 1862.

Vark' ew Vkayabanut'iwnk' Srbots', 2 vols. Venice, 1874.

Vkayk' Arevelits'. Abraham Khostovano£i Vkayk' Arewelits', ed. G. Tēr-Mkrtch'ean. Ejmiatsin, 1921.

Wisdom of Ahikar. *Patmut'iwn ew Khratk' Khikaray Imastnoy*, ed. A. A. Martirosyan, 2 vols. Erevan, 1969, 1972.

——— *The Story of Ahikar from the Aramaic, Syriac, Arabic, Armenian, Ethiopic, Old Turkish, Greek and Slavonic Versions*, by F. C. Conybeare, J. R. Harris, and A. S. Lewis, 2nd. ed. Cambridge, 1913.

Georgian, Greek, and Syriac Texts

Apocalypse of Moses. In C. Tischendorf, *Apocalypses Apocryphae.* Leipzig, 1866.

Athanasius. *Contra Gentes and De Incarnatione*, ed. R. W. Thomson. Oxford, 1971.

Ephrem. *Commentaire de l'évangile concordant: texte syriaque*, ed. L. Leloir. Chester Beatty Monographs 8. Dublin, 1963.

Epiphanius. *Adversus Haereses*, ed. K. Holl, *GCS*, 25, 31, 37. Leipzig, 1915, 1922, 1933.

Eusebius, *Historia ecclesiastica*, ed. E. Schwartz, *GCS*, 9. Leipzig, 1913.

Hippolytus. *Die Chronik*, ed. A. Bauer and R. Helm, *GCS*, 46. Berlin, 1955.

John of Ephesus. *Historiae Ecclesiasticae Pars Tertia*, ed. E. W. Brooks, *CSCO*, 105, 106. Paris/Louvain, 1935–1936.

K'art'lis Tskhovreba, ed. S. G. Kaukhchisvili, vol. 1. Tiflis, 1955.

Narratio de Rebus Armeniae, ed. G. Garitte, *CSCO*, Subsidia 4. Louvain, 1952.

Origen. *Contra Celsum*, ed. P. Koetschau, *GCS*, 2, 3. Leipzig, 1899.

Philo. *De Vita Mosis.* Loeb Classical Library.

Plato. *Gorgias.* Loeb Classical Library.

Procopius. *Wars.* Loeb Classical Library.

Secondary Literature

Abgaryan, G. V. *Sebeosi Patmut'yunĕ ev Ananuni aṙeltsvatsĕ.* Erevan, 1965.

Acharean, H. *Hayerēn Armatakan Baṙaran*, 7 vols. Erevan, 1926–1935. Rev. ed., 4 vols. Erevan, 1971–.

Adontz, N. *Armenia in the Period of Justinian*, trans. and rev. N. G. Garsoian. Lisbon, 1970.

Akinean, N. *Eḷishē vardapet ew iwr Patmut'iwn Hayots' Paterazmi*, 3 vols. Vienna, 1932, 1936, 1960.

Alishan, Ḷ. *Hayapatum.* Venice, 1901.

Asmussen, J. P. "Einige Bemerkungen zur sasanidischen Handarz-Literatur." In *Persia nel Medioevo* (see below), pp. 269–276.

Avdalbegyan, T. "Has, sak u baž," reprinted in his *Hayagitakan Hetazotut'yunner*, pp. 362–413. Erevan, 1969.

Avdall, J. *History of Armenia by Father Michael Chamich*, 2 vols. Calcutta, 1827.

Bailey, H. W. *Zoroastrian Problems in the Ninth-Century Books,* 2nd. ed. Oxford, 1971.

Bedirian, P. S. "Système des alternances vocaliques en pré-arménien," *Rendiconti, Istituto Lombardo, Classe di lettere e scienze morali e storiche* (Milan), 109 (1975): 451-459.

Benveniste, E. "Elements parthes en arménien," *REA,* n.s. 1 (1964): 1-39.

——— "Le terme iranien *mazdayasna,*" *BSOAS,* 33 (1970): 5-9.

Bianchi, U. "Alcuni aspetti abnormi del dualismo persiano." In *Persia nel Medioevo* (see below), pp. 149-164.

Bibliotheca Hagiographica Orientalis, ed. P. Peeters. Subsidia Hagiographica 10. Brussels, 1910.

Boyce, M. *The Letter of Tansar.* Serie Orientale Roma 38. Rome, 1968.

——— *Zoroastrians: Their Religious Beliefs and Practices.* London, 1979.

Brock, S. P. "A Martyr at the Sasanid Court under Vahram II: Candida," *AB,* 96 (1978): 167-181.

——— "Some Aspects of Greek Words in Syriac," *Abhandlungen der Akademie der Wissenschaften zu Göttingen,* 96 (1975): 91-95.

Brosset, M. F. *Collection d'historiens arméniens,* 2 vols. St. Petersburg, 1874, 1876.

Ch'amch'eants', M. *Patmut'iwn Hayots',* 3 vols. Venice, 1784-1786.

Chanashean, M. V. *Patmut'iwn ardi Hay Grakanut'ean.* Venice, 1953.

Christensen, A. *L'Iran sous les Sassanides.* Annales du Musée Guimet 48. Paris, 1936.

de Durand, M.-G. "Un traité hermétique conservé en arménien," *RHL,* 190 (1976): 55-72.

Delehaye, H. *Les passions des martyrs et les genres littéraires,* 2nd. ed. Subsidia Hagiographica 13B. Brussels, 1966.

Der Nersessian, S. *Armenian Art.* Printed for the Calouste Gulbenkian Foundation, n. d.

——— *Etudes byzantines et arméniennes,* 2 vols. Louvain, 1973.

——— "Miniatures de la bataille des Vardaniens," in *Etudes byzantines et arméniennes,* I, 701-704. Louvain, 1973. Reprinted from the Armenian version in *Sion,* 1952, pp. 62-65.

——— "Le réliquaire de Skévra et l'orfèverie cilicienne aux XIIIe et XIVe siècles," *REA,* n.s. 1 (1964): 127-147; reprinted in *Etudes byzantines et arméniennes,* Louvain, 1973. I, 705-725.

Dowsett, C. J. F. "The Newly Discovered Fragment of Lazar of P'arp's History," *Le Muséon,* 89 (1976): 97-122.

Duchesne-Guillemin, J. *La religion de l'Iran ancien.* Paris, 1962.

Eremyan, S. T. *Hayastanĕ ĕst "Ashkharhats'oyts'"-i.* Erevan, 1963.

——— *Map* = Map at end of *"Hayastanĕ"* (see above).

Fiey, J.-M. "Āḏarbāyḡan chrétien," *Le Muséon,* 86 (1973): 397-435.

——— "Chrétientés syriaques du Horāsān et du Segestan," *Le Muséon,* 86 (1973): 75-104.

——— "Diocèses syriens orientaux du Golfe persique," *Memorial Mgr Gabriel Khouri-Sarkis.* Louvain, 1969. Pp. 177-219.

———— "L'Elam, la première des métropoles ecclésiastiques syriennes orientales," *Melto*, 5 (1969): 221-267.

———— "Médie chrétienne," *Parole de l'Orient*, 1 (1970): 123-153, 357-384.

———— "Les provinces sud-caspiennes des églises syriennes," *Parole de l'Orient*, 2 (1971): 329-343.

Garitte, G. *Documents pour l'étude du livre d'Agathange*. Studi e Testi, 127. Vatican, 1946.

———— *Narratio de rebus Armeniae*. See under Greek Texts.

Garsoian, N. G. "Le rôle de l'hiérarchie chrétienne dans les relations diplomatiques entre Byzance et les Sassanides," *REA*, n.s. 10 (1973/74): 119-138.

———— "Prolegomena to a Study of the Iranian Aspects in Arsacid Armenia," *HA*, 90 (1976): col. 177-234.

———— See also Adontz, N.

Gat'rchean, Y. V. *Srbazan Pataragamatoyts'k' Hayots'*. Vienna, 1897.

———— *Tiezerakan Patmut'iwn*, 2 vols. Vienna, 1849, 1852.

Gnoli, G. "Politica religiosa e concezione della regalità sotto i Sassanidi." In *Persia nel Medioveo* (see below), pp. 225-251.

Gray, L. H. "Two Armenian Passions of Saints in the Sasanian Period," *Mélanges Paul Peeters* I, *AB*, 67 (1949): 361-376.

Greppin, J. A. C. *Classical and Middle Armenian Bird Names*. New York, 1978.

Grumel, V. *La chronologie*. Bibliothèque byzantine: Traité des études byzantines 1. Paris, 1958.

Hambye, E. R. "The Symbol of the 'Coming to Harbour,'" *Symposium Syriacum 1972*, *OCA* (Rome) 197 (1974): 401-411.

Harmatta-Pékáry, M. "The Decipherment of the Pārsik Ostracon from Dura-Europos and the Problem of the Sāsānian City Organization." In *Persia nel Medioevo*, (see below), pp. 467-475.

Hasratian, M. "L'ensemble architectural d'Amarass," *REA*, n.s. 12 (1977): 243-259.

Hats'uni, V. *Hay Drōshnerĕ*, 2nd. ed. Venice, 1930.

Hemmerdinger Iliadou, D. "Un sermon de S. Ephrem sur le bon larron," *AB*, 85 (1967): 429-439.

Honigmann, E. and Maricq, A. "Recherches sur les *Res gestae divi Saporis*," *Mémoires de l'Académie royale de Belgique, Classe des lettres*, 47 (1953): fasc. 4.

Hübschmann, H. *Armenische Grammatik, Erster Teil: Armenische Etymologie*. Leipzig, 1897; reprinted Hildesheim, 1962.

———— *AON = Die altarmenischen Ortsnamen*. Strassburg, 1904; reprinted Amsterdam, 1969.

Inglisian, V. "Die armenische Literatur," Handbuch der Orientalistik, I, 7. Leiden/Cologne, 1963.

K'alant'aryan, A. A. "Sasanyan Knk'adroshmneri ev drants' kiraṙakan orosh koḷmeri masin, *PBH*, 1977, no. 3: 195-205.

Khatchatrian, A. *L'Architecture arménienne du IVe au VIe siècle*, Bibliothèque des Cahiers archéologiques, 7. Paris, 1971.

———— "Les monuments funéraires arméniens des IV-VII siècles et leurs analogues syriennes," *BF*, 1 (1966): 179-192.

Kiwlēsērean, B. *Eḷishē, k'nnakan usumnasirut'iwn.* Vienna, 1909.

Lafontaine, G. "La tradition manuscrite de la version arménienne des discours de Grégoire de Nazianze: Prolégomènes á l'édition," *Le Muséon,* 90 (1977): 281–340.

Lambton, A. K. S. "Islamic Mirrors for Princes." In *Persia nel Medioevo* (see below), pp. 419–442.

Lampe, G. W. H. *A Patristic Greek Lexicon,* 5 pts. Oxford, 1961–1968.

Letter of Tansar. See Boyce, M.

MacKenzie, D. N. *A Concise Pahlavi Dictionary.* London, 1971.

Maenchen-Helfen, O. J. *The World of the Huns.* Berkeley, 1973.

Mahé, J. "Les définitions d'Hermès Trismégiste à Asculépius," *RSL,* 50 (1976): 193–214.

Manandian, H. "Les poids et les mesures dans les plus anciennes sources arméniennes," *REA,* n.s. 3 (1966): 315–345.

———— *The Trade and Cities of Armenia in Relation to Ancient World Trade,* trans. N. G. Garsoian. Lisbon, 1965.

———— *Yunaban dprots'ē ew nra zargats'man shrjannerĕ.* Vienna, 1928.

———— See also Hermes under Armenian Texts.

Mariès, L. "Le *De Deo* d'Eznik," *REA,* 4 (1924): 1–213.

———— "Etude sur quelques noms et verbes d'existence chez Eznik," *REA,* 8 (1928): 79–210.

Marquart, J. *Eranšahr nach der Geographie des Ps.-Moses Xorenac'i.* Abhandlungen der Akademie der Wissenschaften zu Göttingen, Phil.-Hist. Klasse, N.F. 3. Berlin, 1901; reprinted Wiesbaden, 1970.

Meillet, A. *Altarmenisches Elementarbuch.* Heidelberg, 1913.

———— "De la composition en arménien," *MSL,* 18 (1913): 245–270; reprinted in *Etudes de linguistique,* I, 159–184.

———— "De quelques mots parthes en arménien," *REA,* 2 (1922): 1–6; reprinted in *Etudes de linguistique,* II, 197–202.

———— *Esquisse d'une grammaire comparée de l'arménien classique,* 2nd. ed. Vienna, 1936.

———— *Etudes de linguistique et de philologie arméniennes,* 2 vols. Lisbon, 1962; Louvain, 1977.

———— "Etymologies arméniennes," *MSL,* 11 (1900): 390–401; reprinted in *Etudes de linguistique* II, 57–68.

———— "Sur les mots iraniens empruntés par l'arménien," *MSL,* 17 (1911): 242–250; reprinted in *Etudes de linguistique,* II, 142–150.

———— "Sur les termes religieux iraniens en arménien," *REA,* 1 (1921): 233–236; reprinted in *Etudes de linguistique* II, 193–196.

Muradyan, A. N. *Hunaban dprots'ē ev nra derĕ hayereni k'erakanakan terminabanut'yan steḷtsman gortsum.* Erevan, 1971.

Murray, R. *Symbols of Church and Kingdom: A Study in Early Syriac Tradition.* Cambridge, 1975.

Mžik, H. *Erdmessung, Grad, Meile und Stadion nach den altarmenischen Quellen.* Vienna, 1933.

Nalbandyan, V. S. *Vardanants' Paterazmĕ ev D. Demirchyani "Vardanank'ĕ".* Erevan, 1955.

Nöldeke, T. *Geschichte der Perser und Araber zur Zeit der Sasaniden,* 1879; reprinted Leiden, 1973.

Nor Baṙgirkʿ Haykazean Lezui, ed. G. Awetikʿean, Kh. Siwrmēlean, and M. Awgerean, 2 vols. Venice, 1836, 1837.

Nyberg, H. S. *A Manual of Pahlavi, Part II: Glossary.* Wiesbaden, 1974.

Oganesyan, L. A. *Istorija Meditsini v Armenii.* Erevan, 1946.

Ormanean, M. *Azgapatum,* 3 vols. Constantinople, 1912; reprinted Beirut, 1959.

Patkanian, M. K. "Essai d'une histoire de la dynastie des Sassanides d'après les renseignements fournis par les historiens arméniens," trans. from the Russian by E. Prud'homme, *Journal Asiatique,* 6th ser. 7 (1866): 101–238.

Patkanyan, Ṙ. *Erkeri Zhoḷovatsu,* 7 vols. Erevan, 1963–1973.

Perikhanian, A. G. "K voprosy o rabovladenii i zemlevladenii v Irane parfjanskogo vremeni," *VDI,* 1952, no. 4: 13–27.

———— "Notes sur le lexique iranien," *REA,* n.s. 5 (1968): 5–30.

———— *Sasanidskii sudebnik, Kniga tysiachi sudebnykh reshenii.* Erevan, 1973.

La Persia nel Medioevo. Atti del Convegno Internazionale, Accademia Nazionale dei Lincei, Quaderno no. 160. Rome, 1971.

Pharr, C. *The Theodosian Code.* Princeton, 1952.

Portugal Pasha. "Kʿani mi parskerēn baṙer or gortsatsuats en i Patmutʿean Eḷishēi," *Bazmavēp,* 53 (1895): 5–7.

Renoux, A. *Le Codex arménien Jérusalem 121, PO,* 163, 168. Turnhout, 1969, 1971.

Sanspeur, C. "Le fragment de l'histoire de Lazare de Pʿarpi retrouvé dans le Ms. 1 de Jérusalem," *REA,* n.s. 10 (1973/74): 83–109.

Sarkissian, G. H. "Les deux significations du terme *dastakert* dans les anciennes sources arméniennes," *REA,* n.s. 5 (1968): 43–50.

Tallon, M. *Livre des lettres, 1er groupe.* Mélanges de l'université Saint Joseph, 32, fasc. 1. Beirut, 1955.

Temkin, O. "Byzantine Medicine: Tradition and Empiricism," *DOP,* 16 (1962): 97–115.

Ter-Minasean. See *Eḷishē* under Armenian Texts.

Ter-Petrosyan, L. H. *Abrahamu Khostovanoḷi "Vkaykʿ Arewelitsʿē".* Erevan, 1976.

Thomson, R. W. *Agathangelos. See Armenian Texts.*

———— "The Maccabees in Early Armenian Historiography," *JTS,* n.s. 26 (1975): 329–341.

———— *Moses Khorenatsʿi. See Armenian Texts*

———— *Teaching. See Armenian Texts.*

———— "*Vardapet* in the Early Armenian Church," *Le Muséon,* 75 (1962): 367–384.

Toumanoff, C. "On the Date of the Pseudo-Moses of Chorene," *HA,* 75 (1961): cols. 467–476.

———— *Studies in Christian Caucasian History.* Washington, D.C., 1963.

———— "The Third-Century Armenian Arsacids: A Chronological and Genealogical Commentary," *REA,* n.s. 6 (1969): 233–281.

Trever, K. V. "Kushani," *Sovetskaya Arkeologija,* 21 (1954): 131–147.

———— *Ocherki po istorii i kultury Kavkazskoi Albanii,* Moscow/Leningrad, 1959.

Widengren, G. *Der Feudalismus im alten Iran.* Cologne, 1969.

———— *Die Religionen Irans.* Stuttgart, 1965.

van Esbroeck, M. "Abraham le Confesseur (Ve s.) traducteur des passions des martyrs perses," *AB,* 95 (1977): 169–179.

———— and Zanetti, U. "Le manuscrit Erévan 993: Inventaire des pièces," *REA,* n.s. 12 (1977): 123–167.

Winkler, G. "Zur frühchristlichen Tauftradition in Syrien und Armenien unter Einbezug der Taufe Jesu," *OS,* 27 (1978): 281–306.

Yuzbashyan, K. N. See *Ełishē* under Armenian Texts.

Zekiyan, L. B. "*Barak* nell'armeno classico." In *Studi Iranici,* pp. 217–221. Rome, 1977.

Index of Scriptural Quotations and Allusions

This index lists the verbal parallels between the Armenian text of Ełišē and the Armenian version of the Bible. The numbering of books is therefore that of the Armenian version, not that of the English Bible. References are to the pages of this book, not to the pages of the Armenian text of Ełišē.

Genesis
    1.3: 199
    1.26: 143
    3.7: 79
    4.24: 107
    6.16: 195
    22.9: 100
    26.13: 172
    28: 200
    28.12: 163
    31.40: 198
    42.16: 230
    43.30: 171

Exodus
    2.11: 159
    2.12: 159
    2.14: 159
    3: 88
    3.14: 162
    4.2–4: 159
    8.10: 107
    8.15: 240
    12.3: 243

(Exodus, cont'd)
    14.21: 161
    20.5: 107
    24.12: 84
    32.27–28: 160
    32.32: 85
    32.33: 85

Leviticus
    22.25: 233
    24.20: 233

Numbers
    25.6–8: 160
    25.11: 235
    25.13: 160

Deuteronomy
    4.26: 73
    5.9: 107
    31.28: 73
    32.25: 219
    32.39: 212

Joshua
  1.14: 238
  3.16: 161
  6.5: 120
  6.20: 120, 162
  10.13: 161

Judges
  ch. 6–7: 161
  6.3: 57
  7.3: 95
  7.12: 57
  9.35: 17, 102
  16.21: 232

1 Kings (1 Samuel)
  9.25: 244
  10: 161
  17: 161
  17.54: 116
  25.11: 104

2 Kings (2 Samuel)
  2.30: 172
  5.4: 161
  17.29: 104

3 Kings (1 Kings)
  12.24: 188
  18.4: 160
  18.13: 160
  18.19: 160

4 Kings (2 Kings)
  2.11: 160
  3.26: 174

1 Chronicles
  12.28: 172
  26.9: 172

Ezra
  7.14: 100

Esther
  1.14: 96
  6.3: 137

Job
  3.20–22: 163
  5.9: 227
  16.23: 100
  30.17: 191
  30.30: 246
  38.27: 214
  39.16: 146

Psalms
  8.2–3: 201
  8.4: 201
  17.8: 226
  21.17–18: 216
  26.1–2: 199
  26.7: 216
  32.10: 70
  33.2–3: 224
  33.20–21: 224
  35.11–13: 206
  36.25: 190
  37.5: 107, 244
  38.4: 191
  38.12: 191
  42.3: 199
  43.14: 100
  57.8: 153
  67.21: 204
  76.19: 226
  78.2: 129, 176
  78.10: 199
  102.4: 201
  102.26–28: 162
  105.1: 131
  106.1: 131
  106.32: 176
  115.1–2: 199
  115.1–8: 215
  117.8–10: 190
  117.11: 190
  117.12: 190
  134.15–18: 215
  135: 16
  135.1: 131
  135.17–18: 131
  138.16: 101

Proverbs
1.7: 189
5.4: 98
11.4: 191
12.9: 190
17.20: 136
24.5: 201
26.22: 133
28.7: 237
28.15: 16, 62
28.23: 133

Song of Songs
2.3: 79
2.5: 236
3.9: 246

Isaiah
3.20: 245
5.25: 111
6.10: 106
9.2: 164
9.20: 62
11.15: 98
13.21: 106
26.17: 171
27.1: 101
27.9: 170
30.20: 238
38.14: 171
42.8: 162
43.17: 160
44.6: 107
48.11–12: 162
51.17: 149
51.22: 149
57.14: 236
59.7: 61
59.10: 62, 115
59.10–11: 16
59.11: 62
62.7: 108

Jeremiah
4.28: 107
13.23: 155
16.4: 176, 205
19.4: 139

(*Jeremiah, cont'd*)
31.15: 171
51.30: 173
51.34: 17

Lamentations
3.22: 201
4.5: 245

Ezechiel
7.8: 66
7.15: 219
21.7: 171
24.10: 62
26.12: 190

Daniel
3: 62
3.22: 67
11.18–30: 11
13.31: 176

Hosea
9.16: 246

Joel
2.16: 176
2.17: 199

Amos
6.4: 176

Nahum
3.3: 171
3.10: 17, 132

Zephaniah
3.19–20: 108

Malachi
4.2: 101

Judith
6.3–4: 171

Wisdom of Solomon
3.11: 153
6.15: 58
9.14: 71
14.12: 71
14.23: 215
15.4: 71

Ecclesiasticus (Sirach)
7.18: 191
22.30: 99
ch. 44–45: 14, 161

1 Maccabees
1.15–16: 11
1.25–28: 245
1.50: 115
1.67: 158
2: 14, 158, 161
2.24: 16, 116, 179
2.37: 133
2.48: 117
3.17: 126
3.18: 125
3.19: 13
3.22: 126
3.24: 169
3.28–30: 147
3.29: 57
3.41: 121
3.43: 95
3.56: 95
4.15: 241
4.17: 129
4.23ff: 131
4.27: 173, 192
4.35: 162
5.4: 129
5.14: 108
5.34: 169
5.53: 131
6.10: 198
6.37: 170
6.39: 164
6.42: 169
6.43: 128
6.49: 175
7.41: 127
7.42: 169
7.50: 180

(*1 Maccabees, cont'd*)
8.30: 93
9.7: 242
9.8: 157
9.10: 73
9.12: 168
10.49: 169
11.39: 193
11.49: 178
11.58: 187
12.10: 93
12.34: 135
12.50: 118
12.52: 136
13.48: 16, 129

2 Maccabees
1.7: 57
1.16: 110
1.22: 169
1.32: 169
3.16: 105
3.21: 169
3.28: 102
3.29: 196
4.1: 180
4.2: 203
4.6: 185
4.38: 62
5.6: 179
5.7: 106
5.27: 177, 246
6.9: 169
6.19: 110
6.25: 156
7.2: 16, 98, 125
7.5: 106
7.14: 177
7.16: 153
7.24: 71
7.36: 13
8.21: 210
8.23: 168
9.1: 15, 134
9.9: 15, 191
9.26: 93
9.28: 15, 75, 123
10.1: 235
10.28: 169
11.8: 169
11.12: 134
11.13: 193

(*2 Maccabees, cont'd*)
  11.14: 136
  12.15: 127, 169
  12.22: 171
  13.8: 106
  13.15: 168
  13.17: 157
  13.23: 240
  14.22: 126
  14.26: 203
  14.37: 217
  14.44: 170
  15.13: 196
  15.17: 120, 189
  15.18: 95, 110

3 Maccabees
  1.12: 12
  1.14: 110
  2.1: 102
  4.4: 169
  4.6: 105
  4.7: 171
  5.2: 133
  5.22: 136
  5.28: 101
  6.11: 71
  6.19: 122
  6.25: 141
  7.5: 121

Matthew
  3.11: 106
  3.12: 220
  4.11: 237
  4.24: 240
  5.4: 248
  5.12: 213
  5.13: 237
  6.25–29: 197
  7.13: 142
  7.25: 98, 155
  8.12: 107
  9.36: 98
  10.23: 106
  12.25: 63, 87
  13.14: 187
  13.15: 106
  13.20: 210
  13.22: 218
  13.46: 212

(*Matthew, cont'd*)
  14.31: 16, 100
  15.14: 107, 215
  16.18: 98, 155
  19.24: 198
  19.29: 212
  20.13: 212
  21.9: 161
  21.16: 201
  22.12: 188
  22.42: 161
  23.37: 165
  24.2: 227
  25.8: 206
  25.34: 197
  26.31: 98
  27.31: 190
  27.38: 204
  27.41: 190
  27.45: 216
  28.14: 228

Mark
  3.24: 87
  3.24–25: 63
  4.19: 218
  4.38: 245
  9.25: 226
  9.34: 203
  9.42: 107
  9.47: 107
  12.13: 71
  12.32: 107
  14.27: 98
  15.27: 204

Luke
  1.36: 91
  2.1: 75
  3.16: 106
  3.23: 91
  6.23: 213
  6.39: 107, 215
  6.48: 98
  9.2: 240
  11.17: 63, 87
  11.34: 237
  11.34–36: 62
  11.54: 71
  12.9: 106
  12.48: 89, 175
  13.34: 165

(*Luke, cont'd*)
15.4–6: 201
15.6–10: 204
16.2: 218
22.26: 203
23.43: 199, 204
23.44: 216

John
1.4–9: 164
3.5: 117
4.38: 232
5.34: 116
6.14: 210
6.51: 143
6.53ff: 106
7.37: 210
7.42: 161
14.2: 197
14.18: 205
16.20: 163
20.12: 245

Acts
1.24: 116
1.26: 209
2.11: 207
4.35: 165
5.17: 63
6.1: 195
7.56: 225
7.58: 165, 225
8.23: 98
13.10: 143, 218
13.28: 199
14.20: 200
15.29: 73
16: 202
16.35: 245
16.38: 245
17.6: 203
17.8: 203
19.24: 224
19.38: 224
25.11: 175
25.16: 185
27.25: 224

Romans
1.7: 248
1.25: 212

(*Romans, cont'd*)
1.31: 218
2.1: 117
2.6: 118, 205
3.25: 202
3.25–26: 198
5.20: 155
6.5: 220
7.22: 75
8.14: 161
8.17: 161, 233, 247
8.21: 107
8.23: 202
8.38–39: 150
9.23: 201
11.28: 164
11.33: 226
11.35: 198
12.1: 177
12.8: 76
12.19: 117
13.1–7: 212
13.12: 107
13.13: 234
13.14: 106
14.9: 153
14.10: 221
14.12: 108, 218
15.4: 203
16.2: 76

1 Corinthians
ch. 1–3: 98
2.9: 74, 248
3.8: 155
3.9: 189, 202
4.9: 190
5.5: 204
6.9: 236
6.19: 106, 111
8: 73
9.24: 203
9.24–25: 204
10.3: 240
10.6: 191
10.25–28: 73
13.5: 227
14.40: 188
15.20: 228
15.22: 159
15.45: 220

2 Corinthians
1.7: 233, 247
1.23: 138
3.14: 199
4.16: 197
5.1: 155, 197
5.10: 108, 164, 221
7.5: 219
8.11–12: 155
10.17: 153
11.3: 246
11.13–14: 196
12.7: 220
12.20: 246
13.11: 205
15.1: 197

Galatians
2.12: 17, 142
3.27: 106

Ephesians
1.8: 226
3.8: 227
4.1: 175
4.12: 155
4.18: 142
6.1–7: 230
6.5: 65
6.7: 65
6.10: 205
6.11ff: 150
6.14: 143, 164
6.16: 61, 143
6.17: 109

Philippians
1.9: 226
2.7–10: 162
2.15: 102
2.26: 235
3.1: 203
3.20: 68
3.21: 118
4.1: 236
4.3: 85, 172
4.18: 177

Colossians
1.5: 74
1.12: 204
2.7: 155
2.14: 143
3.12: 218
3.14: 218
3.16: 70, 239
3.18–22: 109
3.24: 65

1 Thessalonians
2.19: 177, 224
5.5: 206
5.8: 164, 244

2 Thessalonians
1.7: 160

1 Timothy
1.1: 224
2.7: 220
6.5: 217

2 Timothy
1.1: 138
1.8: 155
2.3: 143, 200, 220, 234
4.1: 153
4.7: 189

Titus
1.2: 244
1.11: 217
3.1: 217
3.2: 217
3.4: 204
3.5: 100, 143, 202
3.7: 244

Hebrews
1.12: 162
2.10: 164
2.14: 159
3.1: 164, 175

(*Hebrews, cont'd*)
5.9: 199
6.4: 160
6.15: 205
6.20: 204
8: 11
9: 11
9.11: 155
10.29: 143
10.30: 75
10.32: 189
10.35ff: 189
11: 14, 161
11.6: 155
11.10: 201
11.16: 164, 203, 248
11.26: 155
11.32ff: 161
11.33: 205
12.8: 161, 164
12.22: 203
13.1–7: 83
13.6: 116
13.8: 162
13.17: 80, 218

James
1.4: 189
1.17: 197, 214
2.5: 106

(*James, cont'd*)
3.6: 107
4.4: 218
5.11: 74

1 Peter
1.2: 84
1.3: 117
1.17: 153
1.19: 143
2.1: 246
2.13: 83
2.17: 83
4.7: 234
4.13: 234
5.2: 217
5.8: 224

2 Peter
1.6: 189

1 John
2.2: 164
3.16: 160

Jude
3: 189

Index

References are to the pages of this book, not to the pages of the Armenian texts. Minor variations in the spelling of Armenian names have not been noted. References to "Map" are to the map at the end of this book.

Abełean family, 258, 272, 281

Abimelech, 17

Abraham, bishop of the Mamikonean, 37

Abraham, confessor, 9, 19–23, 26,
35, 230–237, 310, 322, 323

Abraham, martyr, 182, 194, 226,
290, 293, 301–303

Abraham, patriarch, 11, 100, 159,
283

Achab, 160

Achitobel, 291

Agathangelos, 2, 17–21, 41

Ahikar, 21

Akē, 144 (Map D6)

Akēats'i family, 152

Akinean, N., 23, 24

Ałan Artsruni, 32, 36, 41, 258, 277

Alan Pass (Dar-i-Alan), 242, 299

Ałbak, 225, 318 (Map C6)

Albania , *see* Ałuank', Caucasian
Albania (Map B7)

Ałdznik', 32, 64, 103, 145, 184, 277
(Map D4)

Alexander Romance, see Ps.–Callisthenes

Alexandria, 41, 51

Alishan, L., 50, 51

Ałuank', 64, 72, 103, 114, 121,
125–129, 132, 145, 146, 181, 184,
185, 241, 242, 255–282, 299, 300
(Map B7)

Amatuni family, 82, 94, 144, 158,
238, 258, 261, 283, 290, 302. *See
also* Aṙandzar, Aṙnak, Manēn,
Vahan

Amirnerseh, 269

Anania, bishop of Siunik', 81,
257

Anania Shirakats'i, 47

Anatolius, 61, 124, 289

Andzevats'i family, Andzevats'ik',
82, 94, 238, 258, 261, 290,
302 (Map C5). *See also*
Aṙavan, Shmavon, Vahrich,
Zuarēn

Angeł-tun, 277 (Map C4)

Angł, 109, 274

Ani, 119

Antioch, 25, 157, 184, 277, 289,
299

Antiochus, 8, 11, 13, 15, 47

Apahuni family, 82, 94, 125, 144, 258, 261, 281. *See also* Manēch
Apar, 30, 34, 64, 192, 194, 229, 302, 304, 311, 317, 323
Aparhats'ik', 168
Aprsam Artsruni, 152, 238, 290, 302
Aragatsotn, 131 (Map B6)
Aramanay, 271, 272
Aṙandzar Amatuni, 158, 238, 283, 302
Arats, 226, 290, 293 (Map C6)
Aṙavan Andzevats'i, 302
Aṙaveḷean family, 258, 290, 302. *See also* Dat, P'apak, Varazdēn
Aṙawan of Vanand, 258
Ardzak Artsruni, 41
Ardzakh, *see* Arts'akh
Ardzan, 284
Arhmn, *see* Haraman
Arkhni, 119
Armavir, 130 (Map B6)
Armenia: Lower Armenia, 145; Soviet Armenia, 19, 53
Aṙnak Amatuni, 238, 302
Arp'aneal, 119
Arsacids, 38, 60
Arsēn Ēndzayats'i, 151, 172, 287
Arshak, 51, 60
Arsharunik', 258, 272, 290, 322 (Map B5)
Arshavir Arsharuni, 128, 151, 168, 258, 272, 286, 290
Arshavir Kamsarakan, 238, 278–280, 298, 300, 302, 318, 322, 325
Arshēn, 178, 182, 216, 226, 290, 294, 301, 316–318.
Artagerk', 119 (Map B5)
Artak Mokats'i, 94, 258, 261, 265, 286
Artak Paluni, 151, 172, 200, 278, 287
Artak Ṙshtuni, 94, 144, 261
Artashat, 33, 82, 119, 131, 151, 182, 293 (Map C6)
Artashēs (2nd cent. BC), 51
Artashēs (5th cent. AD), 60
Artashir (king of Armenia), 40
Artashir (Persian general), 170
Artavazd Mamikonean, 238, 302

Artaz, 31, 34, 40, 152, 283 (Map C6)
Artēn Galbeḷean, 144, 281, 288
Artsak, 275
Arts'akh, 146, 177, 180 (Map B6-7)
Artsruni family, 32, 36, 37, 81, 94, 168, 172, 181, 238, 257, 258, 261, 265, 286, 290, 301, 302. *See also* Aḷan, Aprsam, Ardzak, Goter, Gurgēn, Mehruzhan, Mershapuh, Nershapuh, Pargev, Shavasp, Shngin, Tachat, Thomas, Vahan, Vasak
Aruch, 131
Aryans, 64, 82, 134, 146, 169, 170, 174, 193, 242, 254, 255–264, 268, 277, 278, 288, 290–300, 303, 313, 314; non-Aryans, 64, 82, 261, 294, 297, 300
Arznarziwn, Arznarzn, 36, 65 (Map C4-5)
Ashnak, 131
Ashot Kamsarakan, 238
Ashots', 258, 290 (Map B5)
Ashtat, 325
Ashushay, 261, 265, 269, 273, 324
Asia, 123
Asorestan, 35, 225, 229, 232–234, 303, 323
Athens, 41, 48, 51
Atom Gnuni, 122, 151, 184, 238, 258, 302
Atrormizd, 8, 180, 181, 288, 290
Atrpatakan, 6, 120, 125, 131
Attila, 6
Avarayr, 7, 8, 12, 15, 19, 20, 32, 34, 40, 45, 46, 48, 49, 51, 234, 283 (Map C6)
Awshakan, 130 (Map B6)
Ayrarat, 80, 81, 132, 277, 278, 282, 310 (Map C6)
Ayruk Sḷkuni, 151

Babgēn Siuni, 237, 301
Babik Ṙap'sonean, 238, 302
Babik, son of Vasak, 269
Babylon, 67
Babylonia, 233
Bagratuni family, 125, 144, 281. *See also* Tirots

Bagrevand, 31, 81, 226, 258, 271, 275, 318 (Map C5)
Bak, 174
Bakur Siuni, 237, 301
Baḷas, 128, 185 (Map B7)
Banturak, 79, 90
Bardzraboḷ, 119
Barsauma, 35, 36, 47
Basean, 81, 258, 271, 290, 303 (Map B5)
Basil, 82, 258
Bēl, 9, 192, 193
Berkunk', 275
Blue Mountain, 178
Blur, 34
Byzantium, *see* Constantinople
Bznunik', 81, 258, 324 (Map C5

Caucasian Albania, 4, 6, 7, 46. *See also* Aḷuank' (Map B7)
Caucasus , 4, 13, 16, 46, 129
Chalcedon, 6, 36, 39, 48
Chaldaeans, 67
Chamchean, M., 50
Chiḷbk', 147, 181
Chor, 34, 66, 125, 127, 146, 242
Christ (*references of theological signifi-cance only*), 5, 67, 90–92, 117, 120, 123, 138–139, 142, 198, 202–204, 215, 220, 275; representations of, 49
Christopher, 35
Constantine, 31
Constantinople, 7, 8, 24, 28, 30, 36–38, 48, 51, 52
Ctesiphon, 62

Dasn, 65, 103 (Map D5)
Dat Andzevats'i, 238
Dat Aṙaveḷean, 302
David, king, 160, 269, 325
David Mamikon, 57
David the Invincible Philosopher, 41, 42
Denshapuh, 18, 75, 194, 206–210, 216, 218, 221–223, 226, 278, 303–323
Derjan, 35 (Map C4)
Dimak'sean family, 128, 172, 238, 258, 272, 287, 302. *See also* Gazrik, Hmayeak, Mush, Satoy, T'at'ul

Diocletian, 17
Dionysius the Areopagite, 45
Dolvech, 283
Draskhanakert, 130 (Map B6)
Dvin, 30–34, 38, 39 (Map B6)
Dzoḷakert, 130 (Map B5)

Eden, 199
Egyptians, 159
Ekeḷeats', 277 (Map C6)
Eḷbayr, 82, 258
Eleazar, 14
Eḷegeak, 226, 294
Elias, 160
Elisha, 82, 258
Elpharios, *see* Florentius
Ēnjuḷ, 144
Ēntsayin family, 172, 287. *See also* Arsēn
Ēntsayin K'ajberuni, 168
Eramunk', 130
Eraskh (Araxes R.), 33 (Map B5–C7)
Eremia, bishop of Apahunik', 82, 258
Eremia, bishop of Mardastan, 81, 258
Erkaynordk', 119
Eruand, 51
Euḷaḷ, 81
Euphrates, 32
Europe, 123
Eusebius, 8, 15, 41
Eustratius, 49
Eznik, 21, 41, 81, 258

Fars, 324
Faustos Buzand, 2, 15, 27, 47, 52, 53
Florentius, 124, 289

Gabeḷean family, 126, 144. *See also* Artēn, Khosrov
Gad, 82, 258
Gadara, 16
Gaderon, 123
Gadeshoy Khoṙkhoṙuni, 94, 144, 261, 281
Galfayean, Kh., 52
Garegin, 4, 67
Garegin Sruandzit, 172, 287
Gaṙni, 119, 130

Gat'rchean, Y., 50
Gav, 147
Gazrik Abeḷean, 258, 272
Gazrik Dimak'sean, 128, 151
Geḷk', 168
Georgia, Georgians, 4, 64, 72, 100, 103, 125, 127, 145, 146, 184–186, 256–269, 299, 324; Georgian Chronicles, 45
Gideon, 161
Giut, Catholicos, 34, 39, 327
Giut Vahevuni, 94, 144, 151, 258, 261, 278, 281
Gḷuar, 147 (Map B6)
Gnt'uni family, 172, 287, 290. *See also* Tachat
Gnuni family, 122, 172, 184, 238, 258, 287, 302. *See also* Atom, Vahan
God, *see* Christ, Spirit, Trinity for references of special theological interest
Gorgias, 16
Goter Artsruni, 36, 37
Gṙeal, 119
Greeks, 3, 11, 31, 36, 61–65, 123, 133, 145, 146, 184, 185, 237, 271, 289, 298, 299. *See also* Roman empire
Gregory the Illuminator, 1, 7, 12, 14, 19, 20, 35, 38, 41, 49, 252, 255, 263, 265, 269, 276, 285, 286, 306, 308; church of, 31, 34, 38
Gregory of Narek, 45
Gregory of Nazianzen, 47
Gurgēn Artsruni, 47

Hamazasp Mamikonena, 238, 272, 302
Hamazaspean Mamikonean, 168, 238, 286, 302
Haraman, 5, 78, 79, 85, 98
Harevshḷom Shapuh, 240
Hashteank', 277 (Map C4)
Hechmatak, 147, 181
Her, 126, 157, 282, 283 (Map C6)
Heṙan, 185
Hermetic treatise, 21, 22
Herod, 8, 15
Het'um II, 49
Hmayeak Dimak'sean, 151, 172, 258, 272, 278, 279, 287

Hmayeak Mamikonean, 8, 179, 270, 272, 277, 288–290, 324
Hoḷotsim, 40, 225
Hrahat, 258
Hrev, 325
Hrev-Shnomshapuh, 325
Huns, 7, 66, 93, 94, 121, 129, 130, 132, 146, 168, 180, 181, 193, 242, 280, 299, 300. *See also* Bēl, Heṙan

Ijavank', 225
Inchichean, L., 51
India, 111
Isaac, 100
Israel, 14, 161

James, 17
Jephthah, 161
Jeremiah, 271
Jerusalem, 285, 306
Jesus, *see* Christ
Jews, 11, 15, 25, 112, 266, 309
Jnikan, 209, 226, 304, 313, 318, 320
John the Baptist, 91
John II Catholicos, 30, 37
John V Catholicos (historian), 23, 38, 39, 47
John Chrysostom, 21, 22
John of Ephesus, 27–29
Jonathan, 325
Jordan, 91
Joseph, bishop of Ayrarat, *see* Yoseph
Joseph, husband of Mary, 79
Joshua, 161
Jṙayl, 33
Juanshēr, 45
Judas Iscariot, 266, 276, 286
Judas Maccabaeus, 16, 47
Justin/Justinian, 49

K'ajaj, 182, 226, 290, 294, 301, 316, 317
K'ajberuni family, 172, 287. *See also* Nerseh
Kamsarakan family, 238, 281, 290, 293, 297, 302. *See also* Arshavir, Ashot, Nerseh, T'at', Vardz
Kapoyt, 119
Karēn Sahaṙuni, 151
Karin, 31 (Map C4)

Karinean, Y., 52
K'ashkar, 234
K'asu, 81, 258
Katishk', 168
Kawat, 29, 31
Khalamikh, 31
Khalkhal, 127, 279 (Map B6)
Khaltik', 35, 146, 177, 179, 289
    (Map B4)
Khaylandurk', 66, 192, 242
Khibiovan, 181
Khoranist, 119
Khorēn Khořkhořuni, 151, 168,
    172, 200, 278, 279, 286, 287
Khorēn, martyr, 230, 231, 234,
    310, 322, 323
Khorēn, from Mren, 258, 271
Khořkhořuni family, 94, 125, 144,
    172, 261, 281, 287. *See also* Gade-
    shoy, Khorēn
Khosrov Anushirvan, 24, 27–31
Khosrov Gabelean, 151
Khosrov, king, 51
Khras, 147
Khurs Sruandzit, 152
Khuzhastan, 18, 19, 35, 99, 209,
    226, 228, 234, 290, 305, 311
Kirakos Gandzakets'i, 47, 48
Kiwlēsērean, B., 22, 23, 50
K'oleank', 152
Korduk', 64, 65, 103, 146
    (Map D5)
Koriun, 12, 42, 283
Kuash, 131
Kura R., 127, 279, 280
    (Map B5–7)
Kushans, 4, 34, 63, 64, 66, 72, 100,
    111, 192, 193, 302

Lazar P'arpets'i, 3–9, 13, 14,
    18–20, 23–30, 32, 36, 41, 45,
    48–50, 53, 251
Lazarus, 306
Leo I, 37
Levond, 7, 9, 14, 45, 48, 109, 152,
    158, 165, 175, 182, 186, 199, 211,
    218, 225, 258, 271, 283, 285, 286,
    290–301, 307, 314, 315–322; Le-
    vondeank', 39, 40, 46
Lop'nos R., 128 (Map B6)
Lp'Ink', 64, 103, 128, 147, 181,
    280

Maccabees, 7, 8, 11–18, 24, 25, 47,
    156
Makuran, 208
Mambrē, 41
Mamikonean family, 37, 41, 94,
    145, 171, 238, 258, 261, 264, 281,
    290, 293, 297, 301, 324. *See also*
    Artavazd, David, Hamazasp,
    Hamazaspean, Mushel, Vardan,
    Vasak
Mananali, 258 (May C4)
Manazkert, 81, 258 (Map C5)
Mandakuni family, 238, 302. *See
    also* P'arsman, Sahak
Manēch Apahuni, 94, 144, 258,
    261, 281
Manēn Amatuni, 144
Marcian, 6, 36, 37, 40, 124, 138,
    288
Mardastan, 81, 258 (Map C6)
Mardoyali, 81 (Map C4)
Marutha, 20
Marvirot, 294
Mary, 49, 79, 86, 90, 91, 138,
    275
Mashtots (*or* Mesrop), 2, 12, 19,
    40–42, 46, 48, 283
Massagetae, 242
Mattathias, 13, 14, 16, 47, 157
Mehruzhan Artsruni, 238, 277
Melet, 81
Melik' Yakobean, Y., 52
Melitē, 258
Melitene, 31
Mershapuh Artsruni, 36, 238
Meshov, 234
Mesrop Mashtots, *see* Mashtots
Mesrop of Vayotsdzor, 48
Metsamawr R., 33 (Map B6)
Mihr, 85, 88, 213, 231
Mihran, 242
Mihran Mihrevandak, 31
Mihrnerseh, 3, 4, 7, 21, 28, 45, 77,
    82, 140, 142, 148, 180, 252, 253,
    255, 256, 260, 268, 277, 278, 294,
    296, 297, 302, 314, 324
Mihrshapuh, 286
Mkhit'ar of Ayrivank', 48
Mkhit'ar Gosh, 44, 45
Mokk', 36, 43, 82, 94, 168, 258,
    261 (Map C5). *See also* Artak
Moses Daskhurants'i, 46

Moses Khorenats'i, 2, 15, 19, 21,
41, 42, 47, 48
Moses, prophet, 88, 159
Movan, 209, 213, 304, 313, 318
Mren, 258, 271
Mush Dimak'sean, 128, 279, 280
Mushē, bishop in Artsrunik', 81,
181, 257, 290
Mushē, companion of Ełishē, 41
Mushē, priest from Ałbak, 225,
294, 301, 316–318
Mushcḷ Mamikoncan, 238, 302
Mushel, priest, *see* Mushē
Mushi, 144
Mushkan Niusalavurt, 8, 34, 149,
170, 173–175, 181, 184, 283,
288

Nakhchavan, 34 (Map C6)
Narbey, pseudonym for Kh. Gal-
fayean
Nazarenes, 80, 207, 226
Nerseh K'ajberuni, 151, 168, 172,
286, 287
Nerseh Kamsarakan, 238
Nerseh, prince of Urts, 144, 281
Nersēs Shnorhali, 46, 47
Nershapuh Artsruni, 94, 151, 258,
261, 290, 294, 301
Nershapuh R̄mbosean, 122, 125
Nestorians, 35, 36
Nikharakan Sebukht, 278, 280. *See
also* Sebukht
Niwshapuh, 30, 192, 226, 229,
302–304, 311, 313, 322
Nisibis, 61 (Map D4)
Noah, 11, 159
Nor K'ałak', 271 (=Vałarshapat,
Map B6)

Ołakan, 119 (Map C4)
Olives Mt., 91
Orjnhał, 289
Orkovi, 310
Ormanian, M., 50
Ormizd, god, 5, 33, 34, 38, 78, 85
Ormizd, shah, 83
Orotn, 119 (Map C7)

Paluni family, 126, 144, 172, 258,
281, 287. *See also* Artak, Varazshapuh

P'andurak, see *Banturak*
P'apak Aŕaveḷean, 258, 286, 290,
302
P'aŕakhot, 130
Pargev Artsruni, 238, 301
Parkhar, 289 (Map B4)
P'arsman Mandakuni, 151, 238,
302
P'askh, 147
Patkanean, R., 51
Paul, 17, 49, 266, 311
P'aytakaran, 140, 147, 277
(Map C7)
Peroz, 33, 35, 39, 40, 242, 243, 325,
327
Peter, apostle, 16, 49
Peter, false priest, 144, 282
Philo, 21–23
Pilate, 91, 309, 316
Pinehas, 160
P'iwk'uan, 147
Plato, 22
P'oskh, 147
Ps.–Callisthenes, 21, 49

Raffi, pseudonym for Y. Melik'
Yakobean
Ṙaham, 242
Ṙap'sonean family, 238. *See also*
Babik, Ṙop'sean, Yohan
Ṙevan, 313, 318
Roman empire, 3, 4, 28, 53, 64, 79,
138, 299
Rome, 123
Ṙop'sean family, 302. *See also*
Ṙap'sonean family
Ṙshtunik', 36, 43, 44, 81, 94, 144,
181, 221, 225, 258, 261, 290, 318
(Map C5). *See also* Artak, Ta-
chat

Sagastan, 99
Sahak, bishop of Ṙshtunik', 9, 81,
181, 186, 211, 213, 225, 257, 290,
294–296, 301, 307, 314–317
Sahak, bishop of Tarawn, 81,
257
Sahak, Catholicos (the Great), 37,
38, 40–42, 46, 48, 266, 270
Sahak, false priest, 144, 282
Sahak Mandakuni, 238, 302
Samuel of Ani, 46

Samuel, martyr, 181, 194, 226, 290, 293, 301–303
Sardeank', 130
Sasan, 60
Satan, 43, 60, 73, 85, 103, 139, 143, 164, 186, 189, 200, 218, 223, 231, 263, 267, 281, 283, 286, 306, 307, 310
Satoy Dimak'sean, 238, 302
Sebaste, 18
Sebēos, 22, 28, 29, 31, 36, 39
Sebukht, 126. *See also* Nikharakan Sebukht
Sēir, 123
Seleucids, 15, 25
Set'ean, E., 51
Shahapivan, 40 (Map C5)
Shahuḷ, 233, 234. *See also* Shap'ul
Shapuh, 60, 97, 110
Shap'ul, 323. See also Shahuḷ
Shavasp Artsruni, 23, 32, 33, 38, 39, 238, 301
Shiroy, 34, 38
Shishmanean, Y., 52
Shmavon Andzevats'i, 94, 151, 238, 258, 261, 290, 302
Shmavon, saint, 21
Shngin Artsruni, 238, 301
Shushanik, 45, 52
Simeon Aparants'i, 48, 49
Simon, 16
Sinai, 88
Siunik', 46, 81, 94, 114, 115, 125, 132, 141, 151, 186, 188, 237, 252, 257, 258, 261, 281, 282, 286, 288, 290, 301, 324 (Map C6). *See also* Babgēn, Bakur, Vaḷinak, Vasak
Skevra, 49
Spirit (references of theological significance only), 143, 217
Sruandzit family, 172, 287. *See also* Garegin, Khurs
Step'anos Ṙōshkay, 48
Stephen, martyr, 18, 225
Stephen Orbelean, 46
Stephen of Taron, 27, 39, 41, 46–48
Surēn, 30, 31, 39, 49
Surmak, bishop, 81, 258
Surmak, Catholicos, 40

Tabriz, 49
Tachat Artsruni, 36, 37, 238, 301

Tachat, bishop of Tayk', 81, 258
Tachat Gnt'uni, 151, 168, 172, 287
Tachat Ṙshtuni, 33, 34
Tachiks, 47
Tachkastan, 64, 112
Tarawn, 81, 257 (Map C4)
Tarberun, 258. *See also* Turuberan (Map C4–5)
Tarsus, 311
Tartarus, 254
Tashir, 290 (Map B6)
Tashrats'i family, 238, 302. *See also* Vrēn
T'at' Kamsarakan, 238, 302
T'at'ik, 81, 225, 258, 290, 303
T'at'ul Dimak'sean, 151, 238, 278, 302
T'at'ul Vanandats'i, 168, 286
Taurus, 33
T'avasparan, 147
T'avaspark', 181
Tayk', 8, 81, 179, 258, 288, 289, 310 (Map B5)
T'eark'uni, 30
Ter Israel, 44
T'et'als, 72
Thaddaeus, 49
Theodosia, 52
Theodosius II, 6, 36, 61, 122, 124, 288
Thomas Artsruni, 20, 22, 23, 26, 32, 36–39, 42, 47
Tiflis, 52
Tigran, 51
Tiran, 60
Tiridates, *see* Trdat
Tirots' Bagratuni, 144, 281
Tḷmut R., 169, 283 (Map C6)
Tmorik', 36, 146, 177, 178 (Map D5)
Trdat (Tiridates), 1, 19, 20, 31, 34, 49, 51, 123
Trinity (references of theological significance only), 163
Trpatunik', 152
Tsakhanist, 119
Tsaḷkotn, 274
Tsawdēk', 64, 65, 103 (Map D4)
Tserents', pseudonym for Y. Shishmanean
Tsop'k', 277 (Map C3)
Tuartsatap', 271

Turan, 208
Turks, 49
Turuberan, 81 (Map C4-5). *See also* Tarberun

Urts, 126, 144, 281 (Map C6)

Vahan, from Aḷuankʻ, 129, 280
Vahan Amatuni, 94, 151, 238, 258, 261, 273, 277, 290, 299, 302
Vahan Artsruni, 34-36
Vahan Gnuni, 172, 287
Vahan Mamikonean, 5, 251
Vahevuni family, 94, 125, 144, 258, 261, 281. *See also* Giut
Vahrich Andzavatsʻi, 33, 34
Valarsh, 251
Vaḷinak Siwni, 188
Van, 119 (Map C5)
Vanand, 82, 225, 258, 290, 318 (Map B5)
Varazdēn Aṙaveḷean, 302
Varazshapuh Paluni, 144, 258, 281, 288
Varazvaḷan, 3, 4, 8, 252-255, 304
Vardan, historian, 45, 47
Vardan Mamikonean (I), passim
Vardan Mamikonean (II), 23, 24, 30, 31, 36, 37, 39
Vardanashat, 130
Vardēs, 225
Vardgēs, 303, 321
Vardz Kamsarakan, 238, 302
Varsken, 52
Vasak Artsruni, 33, 36, 37
Vasak Mamikonean, 145
Vasak Siuni, 3, 6-8, 11, 15, 17, 27, 35, 40, 46, 94, 115, 122, 125, 127, 130, 132, 133, 142, 145, 147, 149, 158, 166, 173-178, 180-191,

252, 258, 261, 269, 271-282, 291, 292, 297-301, 324
Vashakashat, 119
Vat, 147
Vayotsʻ Dzor, 40, 225, 318 (Map C6)
Vehdenshapuh, *see* Denshapuh
Vehshapuh, *see* Denshapuh
Venice, 50, 52
Vkaykʻ Arevelitsʻ, 18, 20, 21
Vndoy, 33, 38, 39
Vṙam, 60; fire of Vṙam, 121
Vṙamshapuh, 60
Vrēn Dziunakan, 258
Vrēn Tashratsʻi, 152, 238, 290, 302
Vriv Maḷkhaz, 258
Vrkan, 192, 301, 302, 309, 311, 322
Vurk, 128, 280

Yazkert I, 97
Yazkert II, passim
Yĕzatvshnap, 325
Yohan Ṙapʻsonean, 238, 302
Yoseph (Joseph, Yosēp, Yovsēp), 9, 18, 39, 40, 48, 81, 82, 95, 122, 152, 158, 175, 182, 186, 197, 203, 217, 225, 257, 283-286, 290-296, 301, 307, 308, 314-318

Zandaḷan, 274
Zandik, 112
Zangak, 144, 282
Zarehavan, 184, 277 (Map C5)
Zarevand, 126, 157, 282, 283 (Map C6)
Zavēn, 258
Zenakkʻ, 310
Zoroaster, 211
Zrvan, 5, 78
Zuarēn Andzevatsʻi, 238

Map: The Armenia of Ełishē

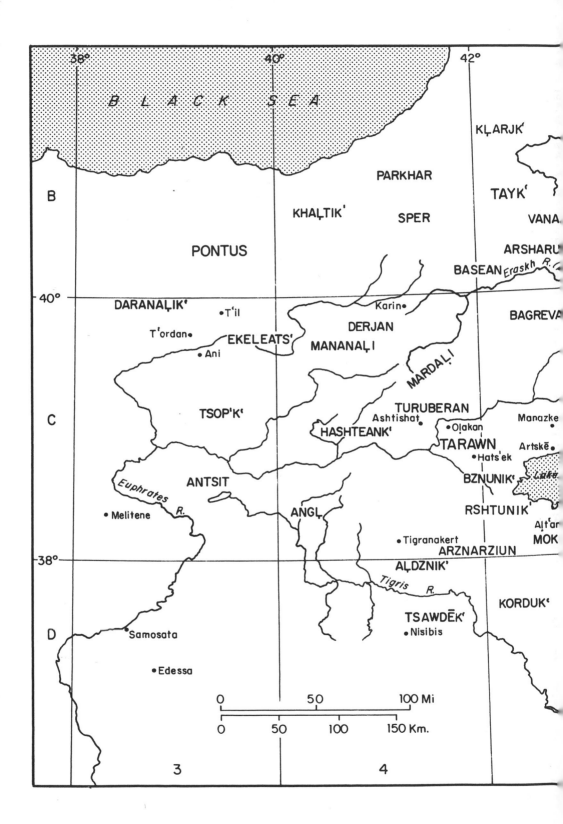

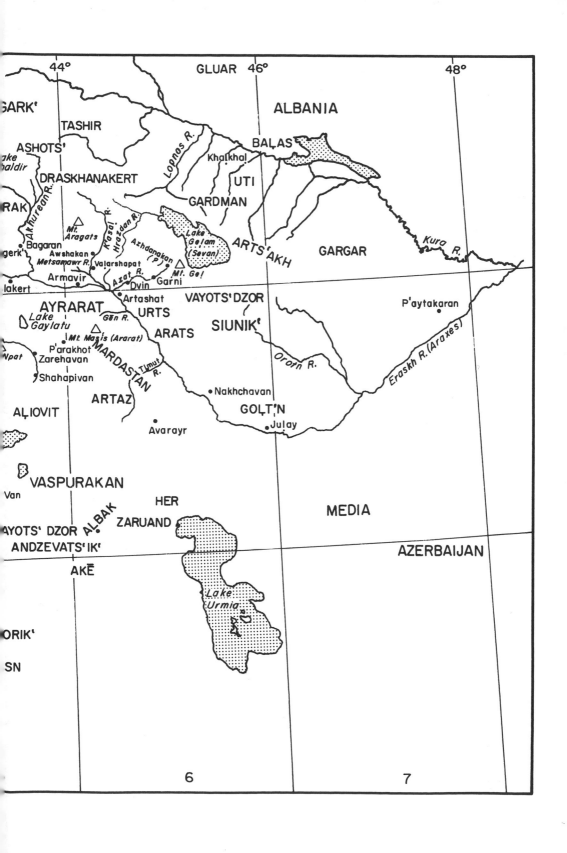

ŠARK'
TASHIR
ASHOTS'
Lake
haldir
DRASKHANAKERT
RAK
Akhurean R.
Mt.
Aragats
Bagaran
gerk'
Awshakan
Metsamawr R.
Valarshapat
Kosai R.
Hrazdan R.
Armavir
Azat R.
Dvin
Garni
lakert
Artashat
AYRARAT
Lake
Gaylatu
Gěn R.
Mt. Masis (Ararat)
URTS
ARATS
P'arakhot
Npat
Zarehavan
Shahapivan
MARDASTAN
Tlmut R.
ARTAZ
ALIOVIT
Avarayr

GLUAR 46°
ALBANIA
BALAS
Khalkhal
UTI
Lopnas R.
GARDMAN
Lake
Gelam
(Sevan)
ARTS'AKH
Azhdanakan
(P.)
Mt. Gel
VAYOTS'DZOR
SIUNIK'
GARGAR
Kura R.
P'aytakaran
Orotn R.
Eraskh R.(Araxes)
Nakhchavan
GOLT'N
Julay

48°

VASPURAKAN
Van
AYOTS' DZOR
ANDZEVATS'IK'
AKĒ
ALBAK
HER
ZARUAND

MEDIA
AZERBAIJAN

Lake
Urmia

ORIK'
SN

6   7